GERSHOM SCHOLEM

The Tauber Institute Series for the Study of European Jewry

The Tauber Institute Series is dedicated to publishing compelling and innovative approaches to the study of modern European Jewish history, thought, culture, and society. The series features scholarly works related to the Enlightenment, modern Judaism and the struggle for emancipation, the rise of nationalism and the spread of antisemitism, the Holocaust and its aftermath, as well as the contemporary Jewish experience. The series is published under the auspices of the Tauber Institute for the Study of European Jewry—established by a gift to Brandeis University from Dr. Laszlo N. Tauber—and is supported, in part, by the Tauber Foundation and the Valya and Robert Shapiro Endowment.

For the complete list of books that are available in this series, please see www.upne.com

Noam Zadoff
Gershom Scholem: From Berlin to Jerusalem and Back

*Monika Schwarz-Friesel and Jehuda Reinharz
Inside the Antisemitic Mind: The Language of Jew-Hatred in Contemporary Germany

Elana Shapira
Style and Seduction: Jewish Patrons, Architecture, and Design in Fin de Siècle Vienna

ChaeRan Y. Freeze, Sylvia Fuks Fried, and Eugene R. Sheppard, editors
The Individual in History: Essays in Honor of Jehuda Reinharz

Immanuel Etkes
Rabbi Shneur Zalman of Liady: The Origins of Chabad Hasidism

*Robert Nemes and Daniel Unowsky, editors
Sites of European Antisemitism in the Age of Mass Politics, 1880–1918

Sven-Erik Rose
Jewish Philosophical Politics in Germany, 1789–1848

ChaeRan Y. Freeze and Jay M. Harris, editors
Everyday Jewish Life in Imperial Russia: Select Documents, 1772–1914

David N. Myers and Alexander Kaye, editors
The Faith of Fallen Jews: Yosef Hayim Yerushalmi and the Writing of Jewish History

Federica K. Clementi
Holocaust Mothers and Daughters: Family, History, and Trauma

*A Sarnat Library Book

AN INTELLECTUAL BIOGRAPHY

GERSHOM SCHOLEM

From Berlin to Jerusalem and Back

NOAM ZADOFF

Translated by Jeffrey Green

BRANDEIS UNIVERSITY PRESS WALTHAM, MASSACHUSETTS

Brandeis University Press
An imprint of University Press of New England
www.upne.com

Manufactured in the United States of America
Designed by Eric M. Brooks
Typeset in Quadraat by Passumpsic Publishing

Library of Congress Cataloging-in-Publication Data
NAMES: Zadoff, Noam, author.
TITLE: Gershom Scholem: from Berlin to Jerusalem and back: an intellectual biography / Noam Zadoff; translated by Jeffrey Green.
OTHER TITLES: Von Berlin nach Jerusalem und Zuruck. English
DESCRIPTION: Waltham: Brandeis University Press, 2017. | Series: The Tauber series for the study of European Jewry | Includes bibliographical references and index.
IDENTIFIERS: LCCN 2017001006 (print) | LCCN 2017042725 (ebook) | ISBN 9781512601145 (epub, mobi & pdf) | ISBN 9781512601121 (cloth: alk. paper) | ISBN 9781512601138 (pbk.: alk. paper)
SUBJECTS: LCSH: Scholem, Gershom, 1897–1982. | Jewish scholars—Germany—Biography. | Jewish scholars—Israel—Biography. | Jews—Germany—Intellectual life. | Jews—Israel—Intellectual life.
CLASSIFICATION: LCC BM755.S295 (ebook) | LCC BM755.S295 Z3313 2017 (print) | DDC 296.092 [B]—dc23
LC record available at https://lccn.loc.gov/2017001006

5 4 3 2 1

TO
MIRJAM,
AMOS, AND
EMILIA

For the writer, language is a placenta. Language is not only a sweet and glorious conquest, but legitimization, a home.

NORMAN MANEA,
"NOMADIC LANGUAGE"

If authority be required, let us appeal to Plutarch, the prince of ancient biographers. . . . "Nor is it always in the most distinguished achievements that men's virtues or vices may be best discerned; but very often an action of small note, a short saying, or a jest, shall distinguish a person's real character more than the greatest sieges, or the most important battles." To this may be added the sentiments of the very man whose life I am about to exhibit.

JAMES BOSWELL,
THE LIFE OF SAMUEL JOHNSON

CONTENTS

ACKNOWLEDGMENTS

I wish to thank the teachers, friends, and colleagues who helped me in the different phases of writing this book. To Moshe Zimmermann, Michael Brenner, Itta Shedletzky, Matthias Schmidt, Ada Rapoport-Albert, Rachel Elior, Moshe Idel, David Ruderman, Dan Laor, Jacob Barnai, Richard Cohen, David Myers, John Efron, Jens Malte Fischer, Tilo Schabert, Shaul Magid, Malachi Hacohen, and Eric Jacobson, thank you for discussing different aspects of Gershom Scholem's life and work with me, and for helping me sharpen my observations on the complexities of his life.

I am grateful to the friends, colleagues, and students of Scholem who shared with me their memories and insights, especially Jürgen Habermas, Hartmut von Hentig, Mayer Abramowitz, and Avraham Shapira. My gratitude goes also to the archives that opened their doors to me and allowed me to search their collections: the Archives Department at the National Library of Israel, the Central Archives for the History of the Jewish People, the Hebrew University of Jerusalem archive and Oral History Division, and the archive of the Wissenschaftskolleg zu Berlin.

I would also like to thank Ernst Peter Wieckenberg for the friendly way he opened for me a window into the intellectual world in Germany after World War II. My parents, Diana and Efraim Zadoff, and my parents-in-law, Huberta and Richard Triendl, were always ready to help with matters concerning the book.

The English publication of the book was made possible thanks to generous support from the Israel Institute in Washington and the Borns Jewish Studies Program and the History Department at Indiana University. Special thanks go to Jeffrey Green for his accurate and attentive translation, which shows the strong personal interest he took in the book; to Jeanne Ferris for editing the book meticulously and patiently; and to Sylvia Fuks Fried and Eugene Sheppard at Brandeis University Press and Phyllis Deutsch and Ann Brash at University Press of New England for their advice and support.

Finally, my thanks to my dearest of all, Mirjam, Amos, and Emilia, whose support and patience made the writing of this book possible.

INTRODUCTION
THE METAPHYSICAL CLOWN

> "I call myself a metaphysical clown," Scholem says; "a clown hides himself in a theater." . . . How much of Professor Scholem is theater? Scholem: "Ask Mrs. Scholem." Mrs. Scholem: "One hundred percent."
>
> CYNTHIA OZICK, "THE FOURTH SPARROW"[1]

When the young Jew from Berlin, Gerhard Arthur Scholem—the fourth and youngest son of Arthur Scholem, the owner of a printing house, and his wife, Betty—decided to change his name to Gershom Shalom, he sought to express two great changes in his life. First, by omitting his middle name[2] (which was also his father's name), he was turning his back on the past and on the bourgeois German Jewish culture that his father represented. And second, by changing the remaining names to Hebrew ones, he was facing the future, both the rebirth of the Jewish people and that of Hebrew culture, first in Berlin and later in the Land of Israel. The first time the young man who would become one of the beacons of modern Jewish studies used the Hebrew name Gershom in his writings was in his signature at the end of a letter to his friend Harry Heymann in early 1917, beneath which he wrote: "P.S. Now everyone is changing their name, now I'm Gershom."[3] Taking the name Gershom connected the young Gerhard to the son of Moses in the Bible, who was born while his father was exiled in Midian. He was given that name because "I have been a sojourner [*ger* in Hebrew] in a foreign land" (Ex. 2:22). Evidently the adoption of that name, aside from the similarity in sound to his German name, expressed Scholem's feelings about the country of his birth. In choosing to take a Hebrew name, he was not alone. He belonged to a generation in which many young people were motivated by Zionism to emigrate to Palestine. Half a year later Scholem signed a letter to his friend Aharon Heller with his full Hebrew name: "Gershom Shalom."[4] (When his last name is transliterated into German or English, it retains the German spelling, Scholem.)

A few years ago I bought a used copy of the German volume of Scholem's correspondence with Walter Benjamin, a friend of his youth. This book was published in 1980, and the copy came from the estate of Hedi Strauss, who had immigrated to Palestine from Germany in 1938 and worked in Jerusalem as an editor in German and English.[5] On the first page of the book there is a short dedication in Scholem's handwriting: "For Hedi Strauss, with heartfelt thanks and good memories (Für Hedi Strauss, mit herzlichem Dank und zur guten Erinnerung)." The fact that in the 1980s, so many years after the turning point in Scholem's life, he wrote this dedication in German in a book that he gave to a woman from his homeland in the State of Israel made me think that perhaps the step he took was, after all, not as final and decisive as he had presented it.

In his old age, after having received international recognition as the founder of the academic field of study of Kabbalah, Scholem wrote his memoirs. *From Berlin to Jerusalem*—published first in German in 1977, around his eightieth birthday, and then in an expanded Hebrew edition in 1982, a few weeks after his death—describes in detail his understanding of his Zionist immigration. In the very title of the book we find the unidirectional movement that Scholem ascribed to his life between two poles: Berlin and Jerusalem. Scholem's life story creates a contrast for the reader between origin and destination, past and future. Hence, Scholem chose to end the book in 1925, when at the age of twenty-eight he was appointed a lecturer at the recently established Hebrew University of Jerusalem. The movement proclaimed in the title of the book and described throughout it is Scholem's personal narrative, the story of "the life of a young Jew whose path took him from Berlin of his childhood and youth to Jerusalem and Israel."[6] However, despite the eloquent writing, which describes a lost world with great literary power, the book leaves the reader with many questions: Why did Scholem choose to end the story when he had half a century of scholarly and public activity still to recall? Why did he choose to shed light on this chapter of his life in particular, and to leave the later chapters, which were no less fascinating, shrouded in darkness? Why did Scholem publish the book in German first? These questions were the point of departure for the present study. Between Scholem's account of his move from Berlin to Jerusalem in his book and his description of it on various public occasions yawns a great gap, indicating that the course of his life was far more complex than the way he presented it. The aim of this book is to explore the ambivalence that attended his emigration and his life in Israel, and to analyze that ambivalence in its historical context.

No one who reads the vast autobiographical material found in print and in his archives can avoid the impression that Scholem planned his posthumous legacy very carefully. Like many other men of his generation, as a young man he wrote hundreds of pages in multiple diaries. Together with numerous letters, he brought these diaries with him to Palestine and carefully preserved them throughout his life. Writing the diaries and keeping them safe for many years shows that he was highly cognizant of his role as a scholar and a writer and suggests that he kept the personal records as valuable legacy for generations to come.[7]

Working for many hours in Scholem's private archive at the National Library of Israel in Jerusalem often gave me the feeling of searching a pharaoh's tomb, filled with unknown invaluable treasures and hidden clues that can shed light on episodes in his life. Indeed, I often had the impression that Scholem designed biographical decoy chambers, in the same way that a pharaoh's tomb is structured. By sometimes providing complex and contradictory biographical information, Scholem apparently wished to distract the biographer seeking the historical person from grasping his true essence, by hiding behind an abundance of historical details.

Reading Scholem's published and unpublished writings in a historical context, looking carefully for hidden intentions, and comparing personal documents with the impressions he left on his contemporaries are key to the effort of drawing a new portrait of Scholem.

In the summer of 2006, at the beginning of my research, I interviewed Jürgen Habermas in Munich. I had been looking for friends and acquaintances of Scholem who could shed light on the way he was perceived in Germany, and I wrote a letter to the famous philosopher. Several weeks later the phone rang in my apartment, and to my astonishment Habermas was on the line, offering to meet me at the café of the famous Munich Literaturhaus. As a young Israeli who had grown up outside of the German context, I was at the time not fully aware of Habermas's position in the German intellectual world, so I was quite surprised that when I entered the café with Habermas, complete strangers at nearby tables smiled at me with recognition and appreciation. In what turned out to be a vivid and friendly conversation, Habermas told me about his first meeting with Scholem, how he and Scholem had become close friends, and about their friendship over the years. That same afternoon Habermas wondered aloud why all the beacons of the German intellectual world treated Scholem with so much respect and humility, and what the world leaders in Jewish studies saw in him.[8]

As the conversation went on, I noticed a growing dissonance regarding the person we were talking about. Habermas described a nice and attentive person with a keen sense of humor, who was a loyal friend and whose only human weakness was an uncontrollable love for sweets. The portrait of Scholem I had brought with me to Munich from Jerusalem was that of a formidable tyrant, who was deeply admired yet tremendously feared. Scholem was portrayed by many in Israel as a grim gatekeeper of the academic world of Jewish studies, who ruled the Hebrew University of Jerusalem with an iron hand. That Scholem decided single-handedly who would be accepted to the small community of elite scholars on Mount Scopus and who would be condemned to an academic life of mediocrity in the purgatory of the one of the other Israeli universities. Yet in the Munich café, right in front of my eyes, a second Scholem was born and took shape, whose temperament and essence contradicted those of the man I thought I knew. How could the two opposing Scholems exist at the same time?

Given that Scholem was probably the most prominent scholar of Jewish studies in the twentieth century, his biography took on a quasi-mythic meaning. Many scholars in Israel and around the world sought to understand his German Zionism according to their own ideological and emotional needs, some to fortify their own Zionist convictions and some to criticize Jewish nationalism and Israeli politics. For both groups, Scholem's authoritative figure and his research on Kabbalah was a symbol of the Zionist enterprise. The consistencies and continuities in his life story were emphasized, whereas the doubts, disappointments, and interruptions—which were less evident and did not befit the image of a towering scholar—were downplayed.

Other scholars, some of them from the circles of Scholem's students and their students, chose to concentrate mainly on interpretative readings of his daunting scholarly work, on new readings of the sources he had interpreted, or on the topics he chose not to touch in his Kabbalah research. The tendency of some of these scholars was to distinguish between the person and the scholar and to refrain from looking for the relevance of Scholem's life story to his work.

The story told in this book falls in the gap between the two images of Scholem and the wish to understand their relationship. My research brought me to the conclusion that the difference between these images lies in the geographical and temporal aspects of Scholem's life. These aspects underlie the different roles he played in different contexts: Scholem was at the same time an Israeli scholar and a German writer, with the social and intellectual aspects that accompany the two roles. This book tells the story of the parallel existence of these two images of Scholem that he and others had, how they came into being, and how they motivated Scholem's positions and actions while he stood at central points of Jewish and European intellectual life. The tension between Israel and Germany and between the scholar and the writer were formative forces during his participation in different social networks in Israel and in Europe after World War II, including his place at the Hebrew University, in the Eranos conferences, and among the circles formed in Germany in the 1960s and 1970s around the Suhrkamp publishing house. Scholem was always aware of the role he was playing, yet he chose to omit this from the life story he told in his autobiographical work.

Scholem is considered one of the most prominent intellectuals of the twentieth century, and his work and intellectual life are the subjects of increasing examination. This book is the first biography of Scholem since his death and the first comprehensive effort to present him as a man who acted in historical and social circumstances and interacted with them, and it sheds new light on one of the towering figures of Jewish scholarship and intellectual life.[9] This study shows how Scholem navigated the challenges of Jewish life and the Jewish worlds of his time, from his aliyah through the riots between Arabs and Jews in 1929, the Holocaust and its aftermath, and the political developments in Israel during the 1970s. Scholem's writings and presentation of his life do not reveal its whole historical context to the reader, and this book aims to offers insights and nuanced understandings that enable a deeper and fresh interpretation of his life's work.

This book is divided into three parts, the first of which deals with the years between Scholem's immigration to Palestine and World War II. The second part treats his attitude toward the Holocaust, covering the period of the war and his trip to Europe in its aftermath. The third part discusses his connection with the German-speaking intellectual world during the postwar decades.

The first part of the book presents Scholem in the framework of the great cultural project that characterized Jewish national rebirth, the Zionist project of *kinus*. In this context, I examine Scholem's relation to the Hebrew University, the Hebrew language, and two of the central Hebrew writers of his day, whom he knew: Hayim Nahman Bialik and Shmuel Yosef Agnon. The part also examines Scholem's place and participation in the Jewish cultural rebirth in Berlin during the 1920s and the demise of that world in the 1930s. At that time, Scholem published much of his scholarship in Jewish venues in Germany and in German. The first part of the book goes on to discuss Scholem's role in Brit Shalom, the political circle in which he took part during the 1920s. His participation in this circle, which was largely composed of German-speaking Zionists and which conducted a large part of its activities in German, left him disappointed with the path of the Yishuv and its attitude toward the question of the Arabs of Palestine. This part of the book also discusses Scholem's attitude toward the religious dimension of Judaism, as it took shape at that time: on the one hand, through his understanding of Kabbalah, his field of research, and, on the other hand, through his conception of the independent religious person, who is not subject to any religious authority.

The second part of the book is devoted to two central aspects of Scholem's attitude to the Holocaust. First, it treats Scholem's response to the Holocaust while it was taking place in the context of the general response of the Yishuv—for example, by analyzing his 1944 essay, "Reflections on Modern Jewish Studies."[10] Second, this part examines in detail Scholem's search between February and August 1946 for Jewish books that had been stolen by the Nazis and were located in the American-occupied sector of Germany. During this journey Scholem was forced to confront directly the results of the Holocaust and World War II. The journey had an important symbolic meaning for Scholem and made a deep impression on him, which can be understood as a turning point in his life—in his relationship both to Zionism and to Germany.

The third part of the book examines Scholem's increasing activity in Germany and in the German language after the war. Here I discuss the Eranos conferences, which were held in Ascona, Switzerland, and which Scholem attended frequently between 1949 and 1979. Scholem's place at these conferences, mainly during the 1950s, and his relations with his colleagues are examined against the background of his relationship to German culture. The discussion then focuses on three episodes central to Scholem's intellectual activity in the 1960s: his dispute with Hannah Arendt about her book *Eichmann in Jerusalem*; the discussion about the existence of a Jewish-German dialogue before the Holocaust; and his part in the reception of the writings of his late friend, Walter Benjamin, in Germany. Here the discussion focuses on the two volumes of Benjamin's correspondence, edited by Scholem and Theodor Adorno, that were published in 1966. The editors' collaboration on Benjamin's correspondence was also the basis of an important collaboration with the Institut für Sozialforschung and with the Suhrkamp publishing house in Frankfurt, which became a decisive factor in Scholem's entry into the German intellectual world. The final chapter of this part of the book deals with Scholem's reception in Germany during the 1970s and up to its peak in 1981, when he was appointed a fellow of the new Wissenschaftskolleg zu Berlin and which was also the last year of his life.

The afterword of the book discusses Scholem's autobiography, which he wrote in the autumn of his life. Examining this book as a document that moves on two different axes of time—the present, when it was written, and the past, which it describes in the light of all the events that took place in between—brings us back to the central questions raised at the beginning. By analyzing Scholem's life story as that of a man standing between his country of origin and an ideological destination, an important chapter in Jewish spiritual life in the twentieth century is recounted: the history of Zionism and its realization in Palestine and the State of Israel. In this context we come to understand the way personal utopias play out after they are achieved.

Although this biographical study picks up the thread of Scholem's life story at the time and place where he decided to set it aside, unlike his autobiography, it does not seek to present a complete and rounded picture. The biographer's knowledge of the subject of Scholem's research and the guiding principles of the dialectic between the visible and the invisible in his writing is entirely different from that of the man who wrote the story of his own life. The dialectic between the aspiration to discover as much as possible and the awareness of the limitations of time and the abstract and elusive essence of human nature and interpersonal relations guides the way this life story develops and is one of the many plotlines in Gershom Scholem's life.

PART I

"CONTINUITY OF THE CRISIS"

Zionism is the encircling of that crisis point where nationalism gleamed in our lives. The continuity of the crisis is what threatens us.

GERSHOM SCHOLEM, OD DAVAR

HOPE AND DISILLUSION (1923–1938)

CHAPTER 1

CULTURAL CONTEXTS

Indifference, on the one hand, and, on the other, unlimited glorification of the form, of spoken Hebrew, without any connection to the content of traditional Hebrew culture, even though it was what gave meaning to every word in Hebrew—these are the characteristics of the new Jewish settlement, the *yishuv*, in this matter, which is of supreme importance. There is apprehension, lest the younger generation of Hebrew speakers, growing up in this atmosphere, might perhaps be Hebraic in an extreme manner, but far less Jewish than its parallels in Germany and America, where outstanding teachers are at work. Though they do not speak and write in Hebrew, they are much closer to the sources of Judaism.

SHMUEL HUGO BERGMANN, "GEISTIGES LEBEN"[1]

Beginnings in Palestine

A Young German Jewish Man Arrives in Palestine

On the morning of September 20, 1923, Yom Kippur, a coastal steamer slowly approached the port of Jaffa in Palestine. The ship, "which bore freight and a few passengers and anchored in various ports between Alexandria and Istanbul," was arriving from Egypt one day late, after being unexpectedly delayed in Port Said.[2] Among the few passengers on deck were two young men who had been born in Germany, each of whom was to become, in his respective field, a pathfinder in the history of twentieth-century Jewish studies. One of them, the Orientalist Shlomo Dov Goitein, remained on the anchored ship and sailed on to Haifa, the next port. The other, Gershom Scholem—whose fiancée, Escha Burchhardt, had come to greet him—disembarked and arrived, for the first time in his twenty-six years, at his desired destination, in Zion. After spending ten days in Tel Aviv and Ein-Ganim, near Petach-Tikvah, where he spent the Sukkot holiday with friends from his Zionist youth movement in Berlin who had come to Palestine a short time before him, Scholem reached Jerusalem, where he lived until his death. Professionally speaking, Scholem's absorption into Palestine was easy and rapid. In his first week in Jerusalem he had two job offers. The first was to serve as a mathematics teacher in the teachers' college in Jerusalem, and the second was to become a librarian in the Hebrew Department of the National and University Library. The library's director, Shmuel Hugo Bergmann, was to become a close friend of Scholem. The two had already met in Bern, and Scholem lived in Bergmann's house immediately after his arrival in Jerusalem. After some hesitation, Scholem chose the librarian's job, though the salary was lower. In the library he could deal solely with topics that interested him, whereas he had some trepidation about being a teacher: "As a teacher I would have to correct papers in the afternoon as well, and who could say whether my pupils would not laugh at my Berlin-accent Hebrew?" he wrote in his memoirs.[3] Scholem worked in the National Library for about four years, until he received a full-time appointment as a lecturer in Kabbalah at the new Hebrew University of Jerusalem.

From a personal point of view as well it appears that Scholem's highly successful adaption to life in the Land of Israel took only a short time. On December 5, his birthday, he married his fiancée, Escha Burchhardt, on the roof of the Mizrachi teachers' seminary in the center of town. Rabbi Simcha Assaf—who later became a professor of Talmud, the rector of the Hebrew University, and a member of the Israeli Supreme Court—officiated at the wedding. (Gershom and Escha's marriage lasted twelve years. In 1936 they divorced, and Gershom married Fania Freud, his student—a marriage that lasted for the rest of his life.) In December 1924 Gershom and Escha lived in a rented apartment on Ethiopia Street, at the edge of the Meah Shearim neighborhood. At that time Meah Shearim was full of old Hebrew books, including works of Kabbalah, for which there was almost no demand, and they were sold very cheaply. Thus, Scholem, an enthusiastic book collector, was able to explore that "dialectical Paradise," as he called it, and enlarge his library without interference, at least until other book collectors arrived and expressed interest in esoteric Hebrew literature.[4]

In other ways as well, Scholem adjusted without significant difficulty. His body became used to the local climate without succumbing to any of the many diseases that ordinarily afflicted immigrants,[5] and in his memoirs he described his arrival in Palestine as entering a new social network that lasted for many years. He made friends with immigrants of longer standing, most of whom had come from Eastern Europe, and renewed old friendships, mainly with members of the Zionist youth movement in Germany who were working in agricultural settlements.

Thus Scholem's immigration and the beginning of his life in the Land of Israel was (at least as he described it retrospectively) a success story from the personal, social, and ideological points of view. Scholem wrote to his friend Werner Kraft

FIGURE 1 Escha and Gershom Scholem, Jerusalem 1924. From the collection of the National Library of Israel, Jerusalem.

in Germany about his impressions of the Land of Israel and life there about a year after his arrival. In his autobiography, Scholem quotes a Hebrew translation of a portion of this letter (without mentioning that it was addressed to Kraft). There he describes Palestine as an ambiguous place, but one that mainly inspired and excited him. In the second part of the letter, which was published only after his death, Scholem describes the local cultural life in a different tone, and far less enthusiastically:

> The waters of my life flow slowly here. I cannot speak at length about the conditions that determine my attitude toward the country. Without doubt I am among those who tend toward the most apocalyptic opinions with regard to the fate of the Zionist movement here. There is no way you can imagine the worlds that meet here. Life here is an open invitation to thinking people to go out of their minds, and in any event it is inevitably necessary to assume that there is a theological background for even the most ridiculous forms of life, if you don't want "to stand out"—standing out happens here openly, sometimes in the form of the messiah, and sometimes in the form of a labor leader, and sometimes in much more frightening disguises. Indeed one may say everything about the new Land of Israel, if you want to understand me correctly, especially bad things—and how could this not be otherwise—in the indescribable collisions of unrestrained powers of creativity from six continents including the upper world? However, it seems necessary to me to admit one thing, that more things are happening here than in other corners of the universe.[6] I personally

> suffer in the most catastrophic possible way from the attitudes toward the language [Sprachverhältnisse], about which it is impossible to write in a sober way. If I ever write an essay on this, I won't hide it from you.
>
> The intellectuals in this country are as bad as anywhere, as [bad as] Jewish intellectuals can be, but they aren't enigmatic like the ghosts you describe to me! In this country (a phenomenon that only developed completely at the Zionist stage) they are only one thing: stupid. Stupid in a surprising way, I tell you. The phenomenon of primitive, true (not to say original) stupidity of the Jews is apparently completely unknown in the Diaspora. This is one of the strongest impressions of the country. I don't say this as a joke. In this apocalyptic country, indeed only here, it is possible to encounter *Gartenlaube* figures in Hebrew,[7] a most exciting phenomenon. One can also meet the last of the kabbalists here.[8]

Along with the ambivalent feelings of wonder and amazement that his new city and its atmosphere aroused in Scholem, here he presents the cultural situation of the Yishuv (the prestate Jewish community in the Land of Israel) in unequivocally negative terms. In the latter part of the letter—which, as noted above, he chose to omit from his autobiography—one senses Scholem's disappointment with his encounter with the cultural and intellectual side of the Land of Israel. This disappointment is understandable and natural if we examine the place of Palestine in the world of Jewish culture at that time, especially in comparison to the situation that prevailed in Berlin, where Scholem came from. If the Land of Israel of the 1920s can be placed on the margin of Jewish intellectual life, Berlin can be called its omphalos. Scholem's passage from this vital center to the margin, even with the purpose of making the latter central, certainly entailed many difficulties and was neither unequivocal nor ideal, as Scholem depicted it years afterward. This process, with the disillusion inherent in it (as expressed in his letter to Kraft), can be better understood by examining Scholem's Zionist expectations of the Land of Israel, which had taken shape in the circles of Hebrew culture in which he had been involved in his youth. These circles fashioned the Hebrew cultural ideal that he brought with him when he immigrated and made a deep mark on the way he envisioned Zionist achievements in the land of his choice.

Bialik and Agnon

The Germany of Scholem's youth, during World War I and under the Weimar Republic, saw the renewal and flourishing of Jewish culture. The awakening and organization in the Jewish communities and the immigration of Zionist Jewish intellectuals from Eastern Europe who became active in Germany made a deep impression on cultural life there and made cities like Berlin, Frankfurt, and Bad-Homburg into vibrant centers of Jewish culture.[9]

For Scholem, as for many German Jews of his generation, the encounter with Jews from Eastern Europe was one of the formative experiences of his youth and had a deep influence on his path in Zionism. These encounters, both through the writings of Martin Buber, which Scholem both admired and criticized, and through his personal acquaintance with Buber, played a critical role in Scholem's progress on the path that led him to the Land of Israel. Indeed, if one traces the movement of Hebrew Zionist cultural centers from their origins in Eastern Europe through Germany on their way to the Land of Israel, one may say that the time of their flourishing in Germany, especially in Berlin, overlapped with the years when Scholem's Zionist consciousness was formed. This flourishing was accompanied, mainly among Zionist youth, by a strong feeling of nostalgia for Eastern Europe and its Jews.[10] Years later Scholem explained the essence of the attractive power of the Judaism and Jews of Eastern Europe as part of the process of forming an independent Jewish identity and part of the resistance to the assimilated German identity of his parents' generation, which was generally representative of German Jewry at that time:

> The more we encountered the not at all infrequent rejection of Eastern European Jewry in our own families, a rejection that sometimes assumed flagrant forms, the more strongly we were attracted to this very kind of Jewishness. I am not exaggerating when I say that in those years, particularly during the war and shortly thereafter, there was something like a cult of Eastern Jews among Zionists. All of us read Martin Buber's first two volumes about Hasidism, *The Tales of Rabbi Nachman* and *The Legend of the Baal Shem*, which had appeared a few years earlier and had made Buber very famous. In every Jew we encountered from Russia, Poland, or Galicia we saw something like a reincarnation of the Baal Shem Tov or at any rate of an undistinguished Jewishness that fascinated us. These contacts and friendships with Eastern European Jews have played a great role in my life.[11]

An encounter of this kind took place during World War I in Berlin and gave rise to a complex relationship that continued throughout Scholem's life. This was with a young author who was born in Galicia and named Shmuel Czaczkes —that is, Shmuel Yosef Agnon, who was living in Germany at that time. When Scholem first saw him in the public library of the Berlin Jewish community, at the beginning of the war, Agnon was already a famous writer and a well-known figure among the Zionist youth there. Scholem and Agnon were introduced in 1917 by a mutual friend, Max Strauss. They liked each other, and a friendship grew up between them. Agnon, who was about ten years older than Scholem, charmed the latter with his personal magnetism and unique style. "The Russian Jews with whom I lived in Pension Struck were by nature and by character intellectuals, basically enlighteners and enlightened people," Scholem wrote in his memoir. "Agnon, however, had come from quite a distance, as it were, from a world of images in which the springs of imagination flowed profusely. His conversations often enough were altogether secular in nature, but he spoke in the style of his stories' heroes, and there was something irresistibly magnetic about this rhetorical style of speaking."[12] Scholem described Agnon's arrival in Germany as "a great event,"[13] because Agnon was seen as unique in comparison with the other Hebrew authors who were known in Germany at that time. As he was both from Eastern Europe and also from the Second Aliyah (the second wave of secular Zionist immigrants to Ottoman Palestine), his foreign way of talking, the content of his conversation, and his behavior were entirely new, and in the eyes of the Zionist youth of Germany, he glowed with the light of the authentic Judaism of the East.[14]

Agnon was unique in Scholem's view and in that of his generation because Agnon belonged to foreign worlds they yearned for, and because of the special way that he described those worlds and made them available to the culture of the West—through his stories and tales. The worlds that were rendered visible to Scholem and his generation through Agnon's stories stood in contrast to the German Jewish bourgeois milieu, with its assimilationist tendencies, to which they belonged. This bourgeoisie, with whose values they had grown up, was alienated from and hostile to the Eastern European Jewry that the youth regarded as authentic.

Scholem's admiration for Agnon was great, and Agnon's personality and stories made a deep impression on the younger man. The huge emotional influence he had on the young Scholem is shown in an entry in the latter's journal from June 23, 1918, in which he described his feelings when he read the story, "Agadat Hasofer"[15] (The tale of the scribe) in the translation by Max Strauss, to his friends Walter and Dora Benjamin: "On Friday evening I read 'The Tale of the Scribe' out loud to Walter and Dora. I read it probably for the tenth time, but as I already knew, it touches me more deeply every time. From the very first word such excitement gripped me, that I could only keep my voice stable with great effort. I trembled as if I had to kiss a girl."[16] With Scholem's conscription into the army in the summer of 1917 and his wanderings in Jena and Switzerland after his rapid release from military service, the connection between him and Agnon was severed. It was renewed two years later, when Agnon was living in Munich. Agnon met Escha Borchhardt, Scholem's girlfriend and future wife, by chance. Following that meeting the two men remained in contact. Agnon implored

Scholem to come to Munich to translate his stories from Hebrew to German. And in October 1919 Scholem arrived in the city to study at the university there and to be with his girlfriend.[17]

The two men were in Munich together for about half a year, until Agnon moved to Leipzig and then Berlin. During their time in Munich, they became close friends and spent a lot of time in conversation and walks together in the city's streets and parks. Scholem did translate Agnon's stories, and four of them appeared in later years in *Der Jude*, the magazine founded by Martin Buber in 1916.[18] The many meetings and lively conversations Scholem and Agnon had also made an impression on the older man, and years afterward Agnon described Scholem as a person with insatiable curiosity: "It seemed to me that he saw everyone as though he had come into the world only for him, so he could learn from him, but that didn't prevent him from disagreeing."[19] Just as Scholem's view of Agnon was that of a young German Jew looking at someone from Eastern Europe who brought with him a new, authentic Jewish spirit, Agnon's view of Scholem was that of a man from Galicia and the Land of Israel who had encountered an extraordinary and special product of German Jewry, which he saw as degenerate.

Scholem's and Agnon's paths crossed again in 1923, a short time before Scholem's emigration. At that time Scholem was living in Frankfurt and was reading kabbalistic works in Hebrew with a small group in the framework of the Freies Jüdisches Lehrhaus (free Jewish study house of learning), which was founded by Franz Rosenzweig and focused on adult education. Agnon was living at the time with his wife in the spa town of Bad-Homburg. In his frequent visits to Agnon, Scholem became acquainted with one of the figures who was to play a very important role in his life, Hayim Nahman Bialik.

Bialik had arrived in Berlin in 1921, and he lived there for two and a half years. During this time he established two publishing houses: Moriah and Devir. His arrival in Berlin and his activities there, perhaps more than any other event, symbolized the emergence of the city as a center of Jewish and Hebrew culture.[20] The precarious economic situation of Weimar Germany attracted many Jewish cultural activists from Eastern Europe, who were able to take advantage of the galloping inflation with the foreign currency they possessed and establish important publishing houses such as Jacob Klatzkin's Eshkol and Simon Rawidowicz's Ayanot. Other publishing houses such as Stibel and Omanut moved their operations to Germany from Eastern Europe. Bialik's presence in Germany aroused interest and great enthusiasm among the Zionists, but this enthusiasm did not make Bialik interested in mingling with them.[21] In the summer of 1923 Bialik moved to Bad-Homburg, where Agnon had been living for about two years. At that time a lively Jewish cultural circle formed in Bad-Homburg, centered on figures like Agnon; Joseph and Shoshana Persitz, the owners of the Omanut publishing house; Jacob Fichman; Nathan Birnbaum; and Ahad Haam. Years later Scholem defined these Jewish intellectuals as "a brilliant circle whose like could be found only in prewar Russia and later in the Land of Israel."[22] After his arrival, Bialik became the central figure of this circle, axis around whom everyone else revolved.

Scholem and Bialik became acquainted through Agnon, who took Scholem with him to visit Bialik and Ahad Haam. When they first met, Bialik was drawn to the young Scholem and his interest in Jewish esoterica. In fact, there were two interconnected reasons for this attraction. One was Scholem's study of Kabbalah, a field that was close to Bialik's heart and that had a place in his anthologies, which will be discussed below. The second reason was that Scholem was a German Jew. Particularly because in general Bialik had little use for German Jews, he was struck by the young Scholem and "was interested in the phenomenon of a young German Jew who had set his mind on studying, of all things, the neglected and seemingly obscure subject area of Kabbalah."[23] Scholem was different from the people Bialik had met earlier in his exposure to German Jewry, and he made him into "the only *Yekke* [German Jew] in that circle"[24] of Zionist intellectuals from Eastern Europe who were living in Bad-Homburg. Bialik's fondness for Scholem never faded. He encouraged Scholem in his scholarly work, and he was among those who helped Scholem receive his appointment to the Hebrew University in 1925—the appointment that began his long and prolific academic career. Bialik continued to see Scholem as a German in their meetings in the Land of Israel. After Bialik's death in 1934, Scholem wrote an entry in his diary about their first meetings in Bad-Homburg, and he mentioned the nature of Bialik's interest in him: "He related to me, at the age of twenty-five, as though I were a new discovery, that testified to something about German Jewry for him, something he had not yet seen, and thus I remained for him an exceptional German until the very end."[25]

Bialik's name was of course very familiar to Scholem even before they met in 1923, and Scholem's first encounters with Bialik's writings made a great impression on him. In a journal entry dated December 25, 1915, Scholem wrote: "Bialik is great, because our hope is great. He honors our hope. As soon as I can, I'll translate Bialik."[26] Indeed, one of Scholem's first translations from Hebrew to German was of Bialik's essay "Halakha and Agada."[27] However, at the time that he translated the essay Scholem's acquaintance with Bialik's work was expanding and deepening. His attitude toward Bialik's poetry and effort to create a single lyrical space (*Lyrische Projektionsfläche*)—on which it would be possible to project simultaneously both the individual and collective Jewish self—became more nuanced and critical. In Scholem's opinion, this duality in meaning, which he called demonic, destroyed Bialik's poems from within, because the self—the individual element in them—repeatedly entered the semi-allegorical realm that belonged to the collective. Scholem saw Bialik as a victim who had to be sacrificed to the Hebrew language so it could be renewed. In Scholem's view, Bialik's poetry was eternally doomed to be the lowest point (*Talpunkt*) of the Hebrew language's decline, the point where it turned toward modernism and secularization. Scholem's view was interesting and problematic because Bialik's poetry was seen by Scholem's generation as at the height of Hebrew creativity, not merely at a transitional stage.[28] According to Scholem, Bialik's effort to bridge the gap between the individual and the collective, national self—a gap that, in Scholem's opinion was inevitable, and that was an essential part of Jewish existence in exile—was doomed to failure. However, by expressing the national feeling in the Hebrew language (or, in Scholem's words, by creating a Hebrew lyrical space in his poems), Bialik began to close this gap, though at the cost of the destruction of his poems. In this sense, Bialik was the victim of the renewal of the Hebrew language.

Although Scholem's opinion of Bialik as a poet was not high, his personal admiration for the man was great and increased over the years, until Bialik's death in 1934. In a journal entry probably from July 13, 1934, immediately after Bialik's death, Scholem describes him as an outstanding, charismatic teacher and educator: "He walked about like half a Socrates in the streets of Tel-Aviv." The secret of Bialik's charisma was his ability to make his interlocutor share his feelings, and for Scholem this ability made him, unlike other figures in Palestine, an object of expectation: "He belongs to the few in Palestine, to whom I owe something. . . . He was the embodiment of the Oral Law, and the only thing that he lacked to become a great reformer was perhaps the discipline."[29]

Scholem greatly respected Bialik as a human being and educator but thought less of him as a poet; he saw Agnon in precisely the opposite way. Scholem viewed Agnon as a great author and admired him as an artist but often harbored bad feelings about him as a person and a friend. In Scholem's opinion, Agnon's work succeeded in avoiding damage caused by the renewal and secularization of the Hebrew language, but the personal changes that took place in Agnon after he returned to the Land of Israel—chiefly Agnon's becoming religiously observant—disappointed Scholem greatly. This disappointment is clear in a diary entry dated June 22, 1948, in which Scholem refers to Agnon and "his truly insufferable" speeches about himself: "Often there is *truly* not a single syllable of truth in his speeches, just a vapor of mad self-reflection disguised as half-innocent modesty, which takes away his listeners' breath. I have often seen him recently, and, to tell the truth, each time I have also asked myself: What?!"[30]

The ambivalence in his attitude toward Agnon—greatly admiring his work but having problems with his personality—accompanied Scholem all his life. This distinction between Agnon the artist and Agnon the private individual is often expressed in the great gap between Scholem's public remarks about Agnon and the diary entries about him. As noted above, a similar dichotomy between the man and his work, though in the opposite direction, characterized Scholem's attitude toward Bialik. Nevertheless, despite his reservations, it appears that there were no Hebrew authors of his generation whom Scholem admired as much as Agnon and Bialik, to whom he attributed a critical role in the renewal of Hebrew culture and, above all, the process of renewing the Hebrew language.

The Renewal of the Hebrew Language

For its Passover edition in 1928, the German-Jewish magazine *Jüdische Rundschau* published the results of a short survey of the opinions of Jewish intellectuals. The central question was, what was the best and most important Hebrew book published in the past five years?" The survey was not asking for scholarly recommendations of academic books, but personal lists of literary works, explaining that the goal was answers "as someone who read a book that made an impression on him and recommends it to his friend. The survey addressed this question to intellectuals whose literary taste would be most relevant to the Jews of Germany. The magazine published responses by Scholem—his was the longest—as well as Bialik, Buber, Zvi Diesendruck, Zeev (Vladimir) Jabotinsky, Joseph Klausner, Klatzkin, Ernst Müller, and others. Writing five and a half years after his immigration to Palestine, Scholem mentioned Agnon's books and Bialik's children's books as the most beautiful and important Hebrew publications of the past years, in his view. In his explanation of this choice, Scholem emphasized the dangers awaiting Hebrew literature and the Jewish people in the process of renewing the Hebrew language and turning it from a holy tongue that existed only in written texts into a living language used every day. The process involved crossing a chasm separating the generations. Here, at this crossroads, lay the importance of Bialik and Agnon in Scholem's opinion, because in their Hebrew writings they were building a bridge between the world of the past and that of the future:

> The world of our fathers and that of our sons are the two great visions which, for those standing in the transition and [whose fate] in the spirit of the great poets is the sole guarantee for the renewal of our language, which has been oppressed by many speakers and has been made idle chatter by many authors, and nevertheless there is a need to retain its *healing power* (heilende Macht) for our children. . . . This is

> a good sign for our people, that the great poets once again draw close to the child's world: Bialik, who has consciously dedicated his creative power in the past years to the service of children's literature. And Agnon, in whose unique language and perfect expression and in his deep and exalted goal: to open, in the smallest way possible, the greatest of the greatest, has become a visionary too in the world of the Jewish child.[31]

The important place given to the world of children in the work of Bialik and Agnon made them, in Scholem's view, the most important and relevant writers for the present generation. To understand these remarks, written in 1928, in the context of Scholem's thought at the time—before Bialik's death and the recognition of Agnon as the greatest Hebrew writer of his generation, and when the process of renewing the Hebrew language in the Land of Israel was at its height—we must examine a contemporary document. I refer to Scholem's famous letter to Franz Rosenzweig of 1926, written three years after Scholem's arrival in Palestine. This letter, unlike the passage quoted above, was not published during Scholem's lifetime but was written as a personal message of congratulation to Rosenzweig on his fortieth birthday. It was published only in 1985 and has been interpreted in many ways.[32] As is clear from its heading, the letter is in fact Scholem's confession regarding the current situation of Hebrew and the great dangers inherent in the inevitable process of its secularization. The letter was written at the height of what Shelomo Morag, a scholar of Hebrew, has called the stage of "the breakthrough" of the Hebrew language, in which Hebrew received official status under the British mandate and its vocabulary grew and gained strength rapidly.[33] Scholem's letter is an analysis of the illusionary character of the language's secularization and a warning against the dangers inherent in it. In Scholem's opinion, the essence of the illusion is the belief that it is possible to disentangle the religious element that the Hebrew language has acquired over thousands of years and to make secular use of old words that had sacred meanings for so long: "The secularization of the language is merely empty words, a rhetorical turn of phrase. In reality, it is impossible to empty the words which are filled to bursting with meaning, save at the expense of the language itself."[34]

Three generations are central to the letter to Rosenzweig, and what that binds their fates together is their attitude toward the Hebrew language and the way it is used. Hebrew, whose renewal is inevitable in Scholem's opinion, is the link that simultaneously connects and separates them. The first generation is that of the fathers, whose Hebrew belonged to the age-old Jewish religious tradition, and for whom its use as well as its meanings belonged to the sacred realm. The second generation is that of national renewal, or the transitional generation that, by rebelling against the older generation, created a rift in the continuity of the Jewish tradition. That generation created a new godless Jewish national world, and as part of that project it tried to make Hebrew into a secular language and to remove the "apocalyptic sting" from it. As noted, in Scholem's opinion this is not possible, because the language can never lose its religious essence, which has been inherent in it for so many generations. This essence is liable to emerge anew and rebel against those who ignored it: "but if we pass on to our children the language that we have received, if we, the generation of the transition, revive the language of the old books that it may be revealed to them anew—will not the religious power [die religiöse Gewalt] latent therein one day break out against its speakers?"[35]

The third generation, which Scholem's letter focuses on, is that of the sons, who receive the language in its new secular and quotidian form as it is given to them by the generation of renewal, and with no knowledge of its original context. This generation will be the true victim of the process of secularization and will pay the price for the rebellion and hubris of the transitional generation. The founders of Zionism bequeathed to their children a holy tongue ostensibly bereft of all sanctity but gave the children no ability to cope with what is hidden behind the outer illusion—the language's religious content, which still exists and will burst forth even more powerfully in the future. The price of this bequest, in Scholem's view, was demonic courage, and it would be paid by the generation of sons: "This Hebrew language is *pregnant with catastrophe* (unheilschwer); it cannot remain in its present state—nor will it remain there. Our children will no longer have any other language; truth be told, they, and they alone, will pay the price for this encounter which we have imposed upon them unasked, or without even asking ourselves. One day the language will turn against its own speakers—and there are moments when it does so even now . . .—will we then have a youth who will be able to hold fast against the rebellion of a holy language?"[36]

The generation of renewal bequeathed to its children, by means of the language (and perhaps the language is merely a symbol here) separation from the generation of the fathers. However, in fact this separation is impossible, because the language itself does not comply with it and it is unwilling to divest itself, in Scholem's words, of the "heavy ballast of historical tones and overtones accumulated through 3,000 years of sacred literature."[37] The renewed encounter with the tradition, to which the younger generation is doomed because of the continuity of the generations, and from which there is no escape, will be (in the light of present developments) dramatic and fateful, almost apocalyptic: "When the power inherent in the language, when the spoken word—that is, the content of the language—will again resume form, our nation will once more be confronted by the holy tradition as a decisive example. And the people will then need to choose between the two: either to submit to it, or to perish in oblivion."[38]

Despite this pessimistic prophecy, the parallel reading of the two letters can help us understand more precisely how Scholem saw the place of these two great Hebrew authors in the process of the Zionist renewal of Hebrew culture and language. While he calls the Hebrew language bequeathed by the generation of renewal to the future generation "pregnant with catastrophe" (*unheilschwer*), a "healing power" (*heilende Macht*) is present in the language of the works of Bialik and Agnon, which can counteract the catastrophe by presenting the Hebrew language in its traditional form—including its context in the realm of sacredness—to the younger generation.

In these two letters Scholem sees the Hebrew language simultaneously as a connection between the generations of the fathers and of the sons and as a chasm separating them. The depth of this chasm derives from the secularization of the language. In the renewed Hebrew, words were wrested from their old context and placed in a new one, so that the vast religious element living in them was blurred, and ignorance of the original context contains great danger. Agnon and Bialik reduce this danger because they are a link between the generations and a bridge over the chasm. Through their works, the traditional Jewish world remains accessible to the younger generation, mainly because of their success in retaining the original context of the language while placing it in a modern, secular framework. Thus, for many years Scholem regarded Agnon and Bialik as the end of the classical tradition in Hebrew, because they were the last Hebrew authors whose raw material still followed the traditional Jewish patterns.[39]

Elsewhere Scholem called Agnon's work a "desperate incantation" and "an appeal to those who would come after him." Agnon's appeal to the generation of the sons, according to Scholem, rests exactly on this retention of the continuity of the generations through the Hebrew language: "It is as though he were saying 'Since you no longer accept the continuity of tradition and its language in their true context, at least take them in the transformation they have undergone in my work; take them from someone who stands at the crossroads and can see in both directions.'"[40]

Despite the significant difference in his attitude toward these two cultural giants and their work, throughout his life Scholem saw Bialik and Agnon as the most important Hebrew authors of the generation—as we see in the passage above. In his view they both stood at a point of critical historical change and played a central role in connection with the Hebrew language: bridging the generations and seeking to make sure that access to the vital source of Hebrew would not be lost for those growing up with the renewed language. By closing the intergenerational rift in their writing, within the secular Zionist rebellion, Agnon and Bialik helped protect what Scholem many years later called the delicate dialectic between continuity and rebellion—which in his opinion constituted the entire Zionist enterprise—from the danger inherent in falling into absolute secularization and separation from the Jewish tradition.[41]

Agnon and Bialik were the only contemporary Hebrew authors whose work Scholem translated into German. The attraction Scholem had for these two authors was based on the fact that they (two Jews from Eastern Europe) saw Scholem (a German Jew in the Weimar Republic) as a special type, entirely different from everyone else they had encountered in Germany—but they still regarded him as a Yekke. For Scholem, Agnon and Bialik were representatives of the true Jewish-Zionist tradition, which contrasted so strongly with the bourgeois, assimilated Jewry that he had known in Germany. In addition, Bialik and Agnon were two central figures in the volatile and rich cultural circle to which Scholem also belonged during the months before his immigration to the Land of Israel. Although both Bialik and Agnon moved to Palestine in 1924, not more than a year after Scholem did, a short time after his arrival in Jerusalem the city looked empty to him, devoid of everything he regarded as culture: European culture.

While Scholem himself was part of the process of the renewal of the Hebrew language and, despite the dangers he warned about, regarded it as necessary and unavoidable, he did not restrict himself to writing only in Hebrew. Along with his early translations from Hebrew to German—which testify to his interest in transmitting Jewish-Zionist culture to the Jews of Germany, most of whom could not read Hebrew—in the years after his immigration and almost until the outbreak of World War II, Scholem continued to publish articles and books in Germany, in the German language, along with his Hebrew publications in Palestine. In addition, the fact that the editors of the *Jüdische Rundschau* regarded the opinion of the thirty-one-year-old Scholem on Hebrew literature as relevant for the Jews of Germany, together with the opinions of the most important Zionist writers of the generation, shows the rather central place accorded to him in the Zionist intellectual life of Weimar Germany.

The return to the Hebrew language, despite the dangers inherent in it, was both a tool and a central goal of the Jewish renaissance that began in Europe and migrated to the Land of Israel. Morag regarded the revival of Hebrew as subordinate to the larger and broader Hebrew cultural renaissance, a process that was "from the outset a selective, eclectic continuation of heritage."[42] Viewed in this manner, the revival of Hebrew was part of the idea of *kinus* (ingathering or compilation), or the Zionist anthology project, which marked the literary and scholarly work of the intellectuals of the generation of national revival—in which Bialik, Agnon, and Buber were central pillars. Under their influence, extensive parts of Scholem's work on Kabbalah are marked by this project, which the following section discusses.

A Literary and Cultural Project

As noted above, shortly after his arrival in Palestine, Scholem formed a negative impression of the intellectual situation of the Yishuv, expressing his disappointment in his letter to Kraft of December 17, 1924. Less than a week afterward, on December 22, 1924, the first day of Hanukkah, the Institute for Jewish Studies of the Hebrew University in Jerusalem was inaugurated in a ceremony on Mount Scopus.[43] Perhaps more than any other event, the establishment of this institute, together with the inauguration of the Hebrew University itself on April 1, 1925, symbolized the path of Scholem's life in Mandatory Palestine and, later, the State of Israel. The degree of Scholem's involvement in the Hebrew University and the interweaving of his biography with its history as the emerging academic and intellectual center of the Jewish people were so great that the paths of his life and the development of the university were often nearly identical.

The Institute for Jewish Studies was the third to be inaugurated at the Hebrew University as it took shape, after the Institutes of Chemistry and Microbiology—which in fact functioned as a single unit. Great hopes were pinned on the Institute for Jewish Studies: the goal was for it to attract well-known Jewish scholars from the whole world and become a world center of Jewish studies. However, as Scholem recalled many years later, "already in the first year of the institute it became clear that the hopes for the arrival of major scholars of the generation in Jewish studies were unfulfilled,"[44] and the institute did not succeed in becoming, immediately after its establishment, a "'miniature temple' which, through its academic research, would offer a spiritual message to the Jews and the peoples of other nations of the world."[45] Some of the scholars who were invited did not want to settle in Jerusalem, and others who were willing to come were rejected for reasons of intramural Jewish politics.[46] Thus an opportunity emerged for young scholars, including Scholem, to receive appointments at the new institution. During the following forty years, until his retirement in 1966, most of Scholem's activities were in connection with or within the Hebrew University—from the time he was a lecturer and professor until his tenure as dean of the Faculty of Humanities, his two terms as the head of the Institute for Jewish Studies, and his appointment in 1968 as head of the Israeli National Academy of Sciences. Scholem also served the university in other ways at various times, at times representing it and acting in its name. To a great degree the university was the axis around which Scholem's life revolved, though in certain circles and various frameworks he sometimes criticized its functioning and tendencies. However, this was always from a position of identification with the university and its faculty.

Scholem's world at that time can be understood in the context of the university's consolidation in its early years, the factors that influenced it, the sources on which it drew, and the social and academic circles that formed within its walls or in proximity to it. The establishment of the university and the Institute of Jewish Studies were the first steps in a long effort to make Jerusalem an independent academic, cultural, and intellectual center in the Jewish world and in a struggle to alter the feelings of marginalization of its intellectual residents.

This effort was characterized by the tension between innovation and continuity in the new institution, which affected its character. The desire for innovation derived from the wish to build a new and creative national Jewish society in the Land of Israel, and the quest for continuity involved the use of Central and Western European academic practices, which served as a model for Western scholarship at that time. When it was founded, the Institute of Jewish Studies was intended to act solely as a research institute, following the model of the Academy for Jewish Studies (Die Akademie für die Wissenschaft des Judentums), which belonged to the German philological and historical tradition of Jewish studies and had been founded about five years earlier in Berlin.[47] The influence of the German academic world on the Hebrew University was an established fact in Scholem's view as well. He regarded the Institute of Jewish Studies and the academic activities pursued in it as a direct extension of the science of Judaism in nineteenth-century Germany, although Jewish studies took a different approach from that of its predecessor. The meaning of this new approach, as Scholem explained in 1937, was to examine Jewish history "by its original and innermost nature, by a proper estimate of the inner forces and movements which have brought about its external manifestations. This method of viewing Jewish history is different from that adopted by Jewish *Wissenschaft* almost a century ago. The latter was influenced by the attitude of apologetics, and possibly even more by the factors and political considerations involved in the Jewish struggle for political emancipation."[48]

In fact, the influences of German and German-Jewish scholarship on the character of the Institute of Jewish Studies can be seen from many perspectives, which reflect the various contemporary cultural trends that motivated the founders of the Zionist movement—who brought those trends with them from Europe to the Land of Israel. One of these cultural perspectives was the idea of kinus. As the discussion below will show, this idea was central to understanding Scholem's scholarly and cultural activity in its German-Jewish context, as well as the influence of European Jewish culture on the entire Zionist enterprise and on the Hebrew University and the Institute of Jewish studies in particular—institutions whose path and character Scholem played a decisive part in shaping.

The Idea of Kinus

As mentioned, the intention for the Hebrew University in general and the Institute of Jewish Studies in particular was that they would become world centers for Jewish culture and scholarship in the Hebrew language. The cultural roots of this idea reach back into the Jewish and Hebrew milieu of Eastern and Central Europe. It was characteristic of the revival of Hebrew culture in Europe, especially in the centers in Weimar Germany, that the desires for innovation and continuity work in parallel. The most prominent and perhaps the most important example of this, which had a strong effect on the cultural aspects of the Zionist enterprise and on Jewish studies was the idea of kinus.

The essence of this Zionist idea, like parallel romantic and nationalist trends in Europe, was to collect the treasures of Jewish culture and present them in modern editions to create a cultural continuum between the nation's past and present, in a manner that would serve its national goals in the future. In this ideological framework, at the end of the nineteenth century, Ahad Haam began the project called the Treasury of Judaism in the Hebrew Language. This treasury was intended to be a single encyclopedic volume, educational in nature, that would contain everything that the younger generation of that time had to know about Judaism, exactly as Rabbi Judah the Nasi, Maimonides, and Joseph Karo did in their time: "We need a new book again, which will be written in easy Hebrew and contain information about Judaism in all its specializations, with every special area written by experts in it, so that we can say of it what Maimonides said of his work, that if a person learns to read Hebrew first and then reads this book, he will learn all of Judaism from it."[49] This book was intended to present and interpret Judaism as a culture, just as Maimonides's *Mishneh Torah* summarized and clarified Judaism as Torah in a useful manner.

Bialik, a central figure in the project of kinus, was influenced by Ahad Haam's idea of the treasury, but he also criticized the idea and proposed developing and expanding it. Unlike Ahad Haam, Bialik did not envision a single encyclopedic volume composed of articles on various Jewish topics. In his opinion, the Hebrew reader "wants to and must know the divine presence of his people face to face, and not through an agent."[50] Bialik proposed the collection and "sealing" of those Jewish writings that were needed by the generation of national revival, along with the burial of all those that were of no use. He was conscious of beginning a new era, which required the summarizing the past and sorting out what was worth being preserved and taken into the future. Here, in his fine style, is his description of the necessary process: "Every act of sealing proclaims the closure of an old period, and at the same time it heralds the beginning of a new era. And none other than the excellent essence of the old, after it has successfully passed through the new atmosphere and emerged from it purified, itself becomes the soil for new plants, offering them moisture and succulence that assist their growth and flourishing."[51] Bialik also called the project of compilation "sealing," in reference to the earlier sealings of Jewish corpuses—the Bible, the Mishnah, and the Talmud.[52] Underlying the process was the same feeling that the times when it was performed were fateful for the Jewish people and its culture. However, unlike earlier "sealings," here what had to be done was "to go back and make a new 'collection,' national of course, not religious, of the best of Hebrew literature of every age."[53]

The goal of this project, therefore, was the canonization of the treasures of written Jewish culture of every generation. This new canon was supposed to determine what was marginal—and thus doomed to oblivion—and what was important and could serve as soil for the present and future growth of a new secular Hebrew culture.

In the secular national Zionist framework, which rebelled against the continuity of the Jewish tradition and called for separation from orthodox trends and frameworks as well as from trends toward assimilation, the fruits of kinus served as a bridge to the past, preserving the continuity of the generations within the separation imposed on the younger generation by virtue of the Zionist revolution.[54] Each editor determined the character of the continuity in his or her volume, and each compilation was subordinate to the ideological framework of the generation of revival, though its nature was also influenced by its being a contemporary canon—that is, an extension of the earlier sealings in Jewish history. The editors were placed on the same level as the anonymous canonizers of the Bible, Rabbi Judah Hanasi, and Maimonides. The parallel existence of tendencies toward innovation and rebellion and those toward preservation and continuity—which also are evident in the quotation from Bialik above—was one of the principal characteristics of the project of kinus, and it had an effect on what the editors produced.[55] The products of the kinus project include many volumes of anthologies, varied in character, that were published in Germany in Hebrew or German and in Mandatory Palestine and later the State of Israel in Hebrew. To a large degree one may see Israeli national cultural institutions like the National Library in Jerusalem as part of this project of kinus. In Israel Bartal's opinion, the establishment of the Hebrew University in Jerusalem can also be seen as part of the effort to fulfill this dream.[56]

Bartal called attention to the fact that the attempt to achieve the goal of compilation by means of the Institute of Jewish Studies was ultimately a disappointment, for it did not become a central factor in this area. Bartal found the explanation for this in the influence of the tradition of the rabbinical seminary in Germany, which demanded scientific distance and rigor. Therefore, most of the collections of Jewish and Hebrew sources were undertaken outside academe both in Palestine and in Europe, though some of the collections had a foothold in the academic world and influenced it over time.

Scholem was an exception. For him the idea of ingathering in Bialik's spirit was central, and his scholarship in the area of Kabbalah is marked by that project. The best and most important evidence of this is a letter he wrote Bialik, presenting his plans for research into the history of Kabbalah, and the way that he pictured the future of this area of research to himself. The letter was written on July 12, 1925, about three months before his appointment as a lecturer at the Institute of Jewish Studies. In it Scholem presented his view of the way in which research in Kabbalah should be carried out, in the spirit of kinus: "It is absolutely impossible to attain knowledge of the creation and development of Kabbalah as long as *seventy percent* of all the important texts are still in manuscript, scattered throughout the Diaspora. I am positive that there is no hope for restoring and researching Kabbalah if these manuscripts are not studied: the most important of them (and there are many) must be *published* in critical, analytical editions, to refine and clarify the truth from them about the development and antiquity of Kabbalah."

He went on to present his plans for research in Kabbalah, which he divided into two areas. The first was the study and publication of a significant quantity of kabbalistic manuscripts, and the second was the publication of scholarship and monographs from which a picture of the history of Kabbalah as a whole would emerge. "And at the end of such work and during it," Scholem emphasized to Bialik, "perhaps it would also be possible to prepare a true *anthology* from kabbalistic books that would not suffer from the randomness of printing."[57] Scholem's proposal received an enthusiastic response from Bialik, who encouraged him and promised to help in any way he could: "You are the man who, at the end of your work, will find the lost key to the locked gate of the palace of Kabbalah, and may it come to pass that I might find people in our camp who will realize how great the fruit is, which is hidden in the depths of this field of research, to which you plan to devote your life."[58]

Bialik's idea of kinus occupied a central place in Scholem's academic activities in Palestine and the State of Israel throughout his life, and it is possible to see the influence of this project both in his academic work in Hebrew and in the public positions he accepted. Among his academic works one may point to the editing of many manuscripts in the area of Kabbalah and Sabbateanism, and their publication with commentary in journals identified with the idea of kinus such as *Kiryat Sefer* (the journal of the National Library, which Scholem founded along with Ben-Zion Dinur) and *Kovetz al Yad* (the journal of Chevrat Mekitzei Nirdamim [Society of wakers of the slumbering], which was closely connected with the idea of kinus). In addition to these, one may also mention the volumes of an anthology in which manuscripts concerning Sabbateanism were collected and published and the publication of single manuscripts as separate books or pamphlets.[59] Underlying Scholem's scholarship one can also sense tendencies typical of the idea of kinus, as in his two central works on Sabbateanism.[60] Another research project connected to compilation, to which Scholem contributed a great deal over many years, was the *Encyclopedia Ivrit*.[61]

Scholem's connection with the project of kinus was not limited to the way it marked his scholarship. Along with his many publications in the spirit of ingathering, Scholem also held various public positions in institutions in the Land of Israel that were established in accordance with this idea. For example, in 1943 Scholem served as an honorary member of Chevrat Mekitzei Nirdamim and succeeded Agnon as the society's chairman in 1970. Though it was founded even earlier, the official date of the establishment of Chevrat Mekitzei Nirdamim was 1863, in the city of Lyck in East Prussia. The first purpose of the society, as its founders declared in the Hebrew newspaper *Hamagid*, was "to publish precious manuscripts that lie in archives and have never been printed, especially works of the Sages of Spain of blessed memory . . . and to distribute these books among the members of this society."[62] A decade later the society ceased operations, but they were renewed in 1885 in Berlin, as part of the beginning of the flourishing of Hebrew culture there that was mentioned above. At that time the society's journal, *Kovetz al Yad*, also mentioned above, began publication. In 1934 the society transferred its operations to Jerusalem, where it continues to operate. In a ceremony marking the centennial of the society's establishment, which took place on November 20, 1963, speeches were given by Agnon, its president; Ephraim Urbach, its secretary; and Scholem, a member of its executive board. In his speech Scholem emphasized the aspect of the society that he viewed as central: the preservation of "the golden chain of our fathers' tradition." In terms similar to those he used to describe the role of Agnon and Bialik in Jewish history, he said that Chevrat Mekitzei Nirdamim was none other than an assurance of "the continuity of the generations."[63]

At the inception of his academic work, even before his immigration, Scholem was already influenced by the idea of kinus, which marked the process of reviving Jewish and Hebrew culture in Germany at that time. A central figure—perhaps the most central—in his youth in Germany with whom Scholem maintained close personal and academic relations all his life was Buber.

Martin Buber and *Der Jude* (1916–28)

When Scholem was a youth in Germany, Buber was a well-known and much admired figure among young German Jews, including Scholem. Throughout his life he accorded a central place to Buber, both as an admired authority figure and as an object of criticism, mainly in the field of Hasidism.[64] Many years later Scholem described Buber's great influence on him and the rest of his generation:

> Here is Buber's voice, speaking from "Three Speeches on Judaism"[65] and from his first books about Hasidism. His voice had an enormous echo among us: he promised something, he enchanted, he demanded. To a petrified Jewish world he promised manifestations of revolutionary awakening from within, he promised manifestations of life hidden under the official, petrified forms, manifestations of treasures preserved in his archives, if only we knew how to cross the threshold and enter. He enchanted with his handsomeness and his full voice—Buber's power of expression was always huge. He demanded connection and identification with the heart of the nation, as he understood it then, he demanded of the youth that they become another link in the chain of hidden life, to be the heirs of an exalted and hidden tradition of uprising and revolt.[66]

This description also shows the spirit of kinus that was embedded in Buber's work, for his first books about Hasidism—which, as Scholem emphasizes, were highly influential on him and the rest of his generation—were written in that spirit. One of these books was a translation and adaptation of several of the stories of Rabbi Nachman of Bratslav, and the other was a collection and translation of selected legends about the Baal Shem Tov. Buber also dedicated a considerable amount of time to editing anthologies of Hasidic tales and legends, which made him very well known.[67] During his career in Germany, Buber participated in a number of efforts to collect and anthologize Hasidic stories.[68]

Scholem and Buber first met at the end of 1915, following a parody and caricature of Buber that were published in the almost-underground periodical *Die Blauweisse Brille*, whose first three issues were edited and printed by Scholem and his friend Erich Brauer and published in a small edition in the Scholem printing house, unbeknownst to his father. To the great surprise of the young editors, Buber invited them to visit him at home, greeted them warmly, and treated them with great fondness. Buber praised his guests for their work and courage and invited them to contribute to *Der Jude*, a new magazine he was putting out that was about to begin publication.[69] Scholem and Buber's cooperation on this magazine led to their long-lasting personal connection.

Buber founded *Der Jude* at the height of World War I, and he was its editor throughout the magazine's existence. The goal of the magazine was to provide a Jewish cultural framework for unifying the Jews of Germany and arousing them, following the war, to awareness of their unity and common fate that would overcome internal disputes and lead to the recognition of Jewry as a people and nation.[70] According to Paul Mendes-Flohr, even the name of the magazine was chosen with that goal in mind: "By boldly placing *Der Jude* on the masthead of his journal, he [Buber] sought to restore dignity to the term. From a badge of derision and shame, it would become anew an emblem of pride."[71] By publishing the work of the best intellectuals of the time, from across the broad religious and political spectrum of Jews in Germany, the magazine also reached non-Jewish readers and became an important intellectual forum in Weimar Germany in general. The founding of magazine also marked the beginning of the extensive correspondence between Scholem and Buber, which is now in Scholem's archive.[72] Scholem offered Buber a sharp critical article about the Jewish youth movement, which opposed Buber's Zionist path because it concentrated on Germany and not on the Land of Israel.[73] Their correspondence sheds light on the special relationship that began to form between the young Zionist and the philosopher and intellectual who was nearly two decades older. Buber related to Scholem with respect, admiration, and great sympathy in his letters, and at the beginning of the correspondence one also notes his forgiving and tolerant attitude toward Scholem's radical and immature declarations. Buber apparently detected the potential in the young scholar, and he encouraged Scholem to continue writing for the magazine despite—perhaps even because of—his approach to Zionism and Hebrew sources, which was different from and even opposed to Buber's. In that sense Scholem did not fit in very well with the general ideological scope of *Der Jude*, but during the years of its publication he maintained a close connection with Buber and helped him, by regularly contributing articles to the journal and bringing him up to date on the bibliographical details connected with Hasidic literature for his research.

After his immigration to Palestine, Scholem corresponded regularly with Buber, informing him about developments in his research plans, and even asking his help in publishing his work. In early June 1925, Scholem wrote to Buber about the difficulties he had encountered in his efforts to publish his research in the Land of Israel: "I am having no luck with my work: there is no place here, neither Hebrew nor German, where it is possible to publish scholarly research, neither general surveys nor essays, about Kabbalah. I have to wait a year and a half for the publication of a single work. . . . In Hebrew the situation is even worse, unfortunately. I would be very grateful to you if you could direct me to venues where I can publish my scholarship."[74]

Buber, an older and more prominent man, was a mentor or spiritual father for Scholem. He promoted and advised him, and at the beginning of his career gave him a venue for expressing his opinions and publishing his scholarship, even if these contained open criticisms of Buber. After Scholem's immigration, Buber enabled him to publish his articles in German—which was important, given the difficulties Scholem encountered in Palestine and the spiritual poverty to which he testified. Typical of relationships of this kind, Buber occupied a central place in Scholem's world, and the young intellectual had an ambivalent attitude toward the elder man of letters. "To engage Buber intellectually," Scholem wrote many years later, "meant to be tossed hither and yon between admiration and rejection, between readiness to listen to his message and disappointment with that message and the impossibility of realizing it."[75]

Jacob Klatzkin and the *Encyclopedia Judaica* (1928–34)

As part of his quest for a framework worthy of publishing his scholarship, Scholem took part in another project connected with the idea of kinus, the center of which was in Germany. In 1924 the Eshkol publishing house was established in Berlin by two men from Eastern Europe: Jacob Klatzkin, who was already known at the time as an author and Zionist intellectual, and Nahum Goldmann, who later became the president of the World Jewish Congress and the World Zionist Organization. In their plan for their publishing house—whose goal, according to its prospectus, was to publish "classical Hebrew literature in modern scholarly editions"[76]—the founders devoted much room to a series to be edited by Shmuel Abba Horodetsky, in which anthologies and manuscripts from Kabbalah and Hasidism would be published, but the project was never implemented.[77] They also gave a prominent place to Jewish mysticism in the great project that was the glory of the publishing house: the *Encyclopedia Judaica*, with its Hebrew edition the *Entziklopedia Israelit*. Originally Klatzkin and Goldmann envisioned a grandiose encyclopedia that was to be comprehensive and appear in German, Hebrew, and English. This plan was never completely carried out because of difficulties in obtaining sufficient funds and because the Nazis came to power. Nevertheless, ten volumes of the *Encyclopedia Judaica* were published in the period 1928–34, up to the letter L. The *Entziklopedia Israelit* began publication in 1929, but only two volumes of it were published. The task of preparing the English edition was never begun.

In the preface to the two editions of the encyclopedia, the editor, apparently Klatzkin, presented it as a contribution related to the anthologies, "one link in the long chain of the authors of our literary compendiums, who sought in all its periods to gather our spiritual property and cultural treasures, to preserve them from oblivion, and thus to help them to be mingled with the future." Under the influence and in the spirit of Ahad Haam's Treasury of Judaism in the Hebrew Language, the author of the preface regarded former acts of compilation and sealing in Judaism such as the Mishnah, the Talmud, the *Mishneh Torah* of Maimonides, and the *Shulhan Arukh* by Rabbi Joseph Karo as encyclopedias, in spite of the fact that "most of them [are] not in alphabetical order, though some are in that order."[78]

In addition to serving as with the historian Ismar Elbogen as editors in chief of the encyclopedia, Klatzkin wrote its article on "Philosophy and the Philosophy of Religion; Kabbalah; Hasidism," and this was the background of his connection with Scholem. As early as 1924, Klatzkin showed Scholem the plan for the encyclopedia and invited him to participate in it, along with contacts regarding the possibility of publishing his doctoral dissertation on *Sefer Habahir* at Eshkol.[79] In May 1925 Klatzkin asked Scholem to write some shorter entries and "a general monograph about Kabbalah, its essence, and its development for it."[80] This longer entry was meant to occupy a central place in the encyclopedia and be one of its major articles. However, in the letter he attached to the list of proposed entries, Klatzkin also explained the methodological and practical approach of the encyclopedia to Scholem, as well as its limitations: "Though I do not intend to offer authors a Procrustean bed, it is nevertheless impossible not to set the approximate size of each entry. A column—this means a column in the English Jewish Encyclopedia.[81] . . . I do not want to ignore the articles on Kabbalah in the *Encyclopedia Judaica*, and we must not slight them, as the other encyclopedias have done. However, encyclopedia articles are things that are limited and their brevity is their merit."[82]

Once again Klatzkin's words show the close connection between the encyclopedia and the focus on compilation in Germany at that time, and this connection belongs to the language he and Scholem shared. However, in spite of an understanding that was based on this connection, Scholem's relationship with the editors of the encyclopedia was not a smooth one. Klatzkin predicted some of the problems the editors would have with their contributors in the passage quoted above. The first rift between the two men opened because of changes the editors made in the first entries Scholem submitted. When Scholem complained, Jacob Naftali Simhoni, Klatzkin's assistant, answered that "the corrections and additions inserted in your articles were needed for the sake of objectivity, which is the foundation of our entire encyclopedia. In its original form your article on Abulafia was *absolute defense*, omitting the 'opposite side' . . . completely."[83] Scholem wrote a sharp letter in reply, protesting against the attitude of the editors and announcing that he would no longer work for the encyclopedia. Simhoni answered: "There are two kinds of knowledge: objective knowledge and subjective knowledge, but the encyclopedia can only use the first kind."[84] It is not clear why Scholem resumed writing for the encyclopedia—perhaps Klatzkin intervened, perhaps a third party mediated, or perhaps publication in such a venue was an opportunity for the young scholar that he could not easily forgo. In any event, after a while Scholem was once again advising the editors and agreed to write new entries, but on one condition: "From now on I will accept only those articles in the encyclopedia in which I can scientifically state something new, which cannot be edited by others from the known literature."[85] This condition contained the seed of the next disagreement: in his letter Scholem made it clear that in the few entries he was prepared to write, he could not accept Klatzkin's earlier stipulation that the columns of the entries in the encyclopedia be equal to those of the earlier American encyclopedia. If the editors insisted on cutting his future articles, Scholem would abandon the project completely.[86]

Indeed, the second crisis was not long in coming. When Klatzkin received the manuscript of the article "Bahir, Buch," in the mail, he wrote Scholem: "I was very pleased with your article, excellent in its kind, small but containing much, full to the brim with new research and insights—be that as it may, there is no room in our encyclopedia for such a long article about the 'Bahir.'" Fearing that the project would reach an excessive length of twenty volumes, Klatzkin asked Scholem to cut the article by half, especially in light of the fact that in his large article about Kabbalah he would also be discussing the same work (*Sefer Habahir*).[87] Scholem promptly dispatched a reply, containing a closely argued refusal. Klatzkin rejected this refusal, and after a short exchange of letters, Scholem asked Klatzkin to mail the entry back to him and once again withdrew from the project: "I seriously doubt whether in the present state of affairs, as it emerges from our negotiations, my work [for the encyclopedia] can still be productive. You can well understand that if we get that far, the fate of my summarizing article about Kabbalah will be identical to that of the entry on *Habahir*: you will praise it, but you will refrain from printing it."[88] A month later Klatzkin sent Scholem a short letter in which he informed him that, at the last minute, the editors had decided "to present your article on *Habahir* in full, since space was vacated in the volume for reasons that we could not predict in advance."[89]

In the following years Scholem continued to write for the encyclopedia, though to a smaller extent. In addition, the connection between him and Klatzkin survived, and he sent critiques of various articles by other authors. In fact, Scholem's most important contribution to the encyclopedia was his work on the entry "Kabbalah." After Klatzkin received the manuscript in the mail, he wrote Scholem, "It will be the crown of the following volume."[90] However, in an accompanying letter that was sent with the manuscript, Scholem explained why the entry greatly exceeded the limit he himself had set for it—two folios—exactly twice the length Klatzkin had asked him not to exceed.[91] In Scholem's opinion, the encyclopedia lost by dispersing the various entries relating to the field of Kabbalah in alphabetical order, and it was preferable to discuss them at length in one place: "If you aren't willing to print the article, I would like to ask you to return it to me as quickly as possible, since in this instance I have another plan for it. There is no way I can agree to have the article sent to any other master for possible editing or adaptation." In addition, Scholem asked that, as he had initially been promised, the article be printed as a separate booklet, and this was done in the end.

The collaboration between Scholem and Klatzkin ended at the end of 1932. In the wake of the world crisis of the early 1930s, the Eshkol publishing house encountered economic difficulties and was unable to pay the writers. At the end of December 1932 Scholem wrote his last letter to Klatzkin and the editorial board of the encyclopedia, announcing that, following the delays in paying him for the earlier entries that he had written, he could not continue working for the project.[92] Not long afterward the publishing house went bankrupt, and its offices closed.

In the years when he worked on the encyclopedia, Scholem wrote fifteen entries for the German edition and nine for the Hebrew edition. Although those numbers are not high, the entries that he wrote are important—especially the article on Kabbalah, which was the high point of Scholem's participation in the project—since this was the first time he discussed separately and comprehensively the area of scholarship he had chosen as his life's work. In the opinion of Michael Brenner, publication of the article on Kabbalah, which was the length of a book and the third largest entry in the entire encyclopedia, reflected "the will of the editors to allot to the new discipline of Kabbalah a prominent place in the project."[93] Scholem's character, his approach to his scientific scholarship, and his uncompromising attitude toward the publisher also explain the prominence accorded to his work. His refusal to accept changes or cuts in his work, along with his repeated threats to prevent publication of the article on Kabbalah, might have been what finally led to its publication at greater length than was planned by the editors of the encyclopedia. It is also important to emphasize that the editors' acquiescence to Scholem's demands points to the great importance they attributed to research on Kabbalah and to the fact that Scholem was the only academic dealing with that field as a scientific discipline.

For Scholem, it was very important to publish an encyclopedia article of this kind to establish his status and academic authority in the field of Kabbalah, thus laying the foundations and setting the boundaries of the field of research in a scholarly publication in the German language that attracted attention and was widely read.[94] Within the framework of the ambitious kinus project of the encyclopedia in Berlin, Scholem was given the rare opportunity to establish a small canon of his own, and by means of it both to set the future pattern of research in Kabbalah—which was to develop and become a discipline in its own right—and to create his own image as the founder of this discipline, ex nihilo.[95]

Salman Schocken and the Schocken Publishing House (1933–39)

Salman Schocken, who became one of the most important and influential figures in Scholem's life, was a wealthy merchant, man of culture, and patron. Born in Posen, Schocken was a Jewish businessman who owned a chain of department stores that bore his name, and from which his vast fortune came. Schocken had been interested in German literature and philosophy in his youth, and later he began to collect rare books in those fields. At the end of the 1910s, after reading Buber's adaption of the stories of Rabbi Nachman of Bratslav, a change took place in Schoken's life, leading him to focus on the Zionist renewal of Jewish culture and to invest considerable amounts of energy and money to that renewal. His activity in this area continued for the rest of his life, and through it he became one of the most central and influential figures in the world of Jewish culture in his time.[96]

Schocken's Zionist activity began in 1912 with the establishment of a local branch of the German Zionist Organization in the city of Zwickau, which was also the center of his business. Four years later he revealed his Zionist worldview in public, in a speech at a special convention of delegates to the Zionist Organization in the Savoy Hotel in Berlin. According to Schocken, the problem of Jewish existence was not political but cultural, and to return to the true soul of Judaism, it was necessary to rummage in the past and recover from it, by means of science, the treasures of Jewish culture hidden in ancient books.[97]

This Jewish cultural work (*jüdische Kulturarbeit*) had to be done by Zionist men, and its goal was to present the Jewish past in the perspective of the present by recounting Jewish history to the Jewish people once again. In addition, an institution had to be created that would provide financial support for the scholars who were engaged in this research and for publications. However, the work did not have to be done only in the halls of academe. There must be the publication of scholarly works, but also those of popular nature: "Our work will begin to be influential only when it is possible to place in the hands of every Jewish reader a report on the past of his nation and its present situation in the light of future developments."[98]

The first contact between Scholem and Schocken was occasioned by Scholem's reply to a general invitation sent to educated Zionist youth to take part in the activities of the Committee for Jewish Cultural Work, which Schocken established to implement his plan, and which he headed. In his letter, Scholem expressed hesitation about participating in Schocken's project, and in a meeting between the two at Schocken's home in January 1918, Scholem explained that the reasons for his hesitation were his studies and his plan to travel to Switzerland very soon.[99] "In any event," Scholem later wrote, "I went out with a strong impression that I had met a man of high standing."[100] Schocken was also impressed by the young scholar and offered to hire him as his full-time private expert in Hebrew, an offer that Scholem apparently rejected. In fact the collaboration between the two men began only in 1931, when Schocken founded Schocken Verlag, his publishing house. Much of Scholem's research was published there.

Schocken's cultural activities before the establishment of the publishing house were varied, but for the most part they were aligned with the Zionist idea of kinus. Thus, for example, anthologies occupied a central place in one of his best-known and most important activities, as Agnon's patron.[101] Another project in the spirit of compilation was first thought of in the framework of the activities of the Committee for Jewish Cultural Work. This project was an anthology of Jewish writing that was meant to offer the reader German translations of short items that reflected the essence of Judaism and Jewish life in various periods and fields. In 1931 this volume was published with the title *Sendung und Schicksal* (Mission and fate), and it was the first book produced by the Schocken publishing house, which had just been established. In fact, when Schocken Verlag was established in 1931, Schocken had a number of literary projects in hand. The first was the publication of an edition of Agnon's writing. Another project established by Schocken was the Forschungsinstitut für hebräische Dichtung (Institute for Research in Hebrew Poetry), whose goal was to publish sources from the Hebrew literature of medieval Spain in an accessible manner, in particular using a collection of about three thousand manuscript fragments from the Cairo Geniza, which Schocken had bought in 1928. In 1933 the institute transferred its activities to Jerusalem.[102] Another important project was Buber and Rosenzweig's translation of the Bible into German, a project that Schocken acquired from the Lambert Schneider publishing house, which had fallen into financial difficulties. Thus began Schocken's collaboration with Schneider, whom he hired as the administrative director of Schocken Verlag. Along with the Indologist, Moshe Spitzer, who was publishing house's chief editor, Schneider became one of its central pillars from the time of its establishment until the Nazis closed it at the end of 1938.[103]

A reprint of Scholem's doctoral dissertation was one of the first thirty-five publications of Schocken Verlag, as was a bibliography of scholarship in the field of Kabbalah that he compiled.[104] It soon became clear that Schocken planned to give Scholem a major role as an author in the publishing house. At the end of January 1933, Schneider wrote Scholem that with Buber's intervention and recommendation, Schocken had become highly interested in Scholem's research.[105] Scholem told Schneider he was interested in writing a comprehensive monograph on the field of Kabbalah as a long-range project, noting, "The composition of a comprehensive work of this kind is the main scientific goal of my life's work."[106] Thus began the productive collaboration between Scholem and Schocken Verlag that lasted for many years—though, as was the case with Scholem's relationship with the *Encyclopedia Judaica*, there were ups and downs that were connected with Scholem's temperament, among other things. The correspondence between Scholem and representatives of Schocken Verlag in Berlin, which is now housed in the Scholem Archive, shows the nature of this professional and personal relationship. Only part of the extensive preliminary plans of the collaboration were realized, given the times and Scholem's character. However, this part was considerable, and it laid the foundations for some of Scholem's large-scale future scholarship.

The first contacts between Schneider and Scholem solidified with the establishment of the *Almanach des Schocken Verlags* (the Schocken publishing almanac), which was published toward Rosh Hashana for six years, beginning in 1933. It was an anthology of various Jewish sources from various periods together with works by contemporary intellectuals. Its purpose was to describe Jewish life over the generations by presenting old and new texts of current significance and collect them in a single volume. In June 1933 Spitzer invited Scholem to contribute a historical or theological essay on a subject of his choice to the first volume of the almanac, which Spitzer was editing along with Martin Buber, on one condition: "In choosing the subject I wish you to pay attention only to the fact that the almanac and all the articles in it must express—of course indirectly—something innovative or original or at least by allusion (Anzügliches) about the present situation, the distress involved in it, and the hidden possibility that with some turning point it will end well."[107]

Thus, the first volume of the almanac contained an article by Scholem titled

"Nach der Vertreibung aus Spanien: Zur Geschichte der Kabbala" (After the expulsion from Spain: toward a history of Kabbalah), as well as a revised version of "Hakhshara," an article by Abraham Kalisker that had appeared in Buber's *Der Jude*.[108] The almanac was a great commercial success, and during the six years of its existence Scholem published another three articles in it: a translation of a poem by Nachmanides for Rosh Hashana, an article about Sabbateanism, and another one about Hasidei Ashkenaz.[109]

In September 1933 Spitzer announced a new project to Scholem: the inauguration of a series of books to be known as Bücherei des Schocken Verlags, which would be a Jewish parallel to the famous series published by Insel: "small volumes at a low price, intended for the widest circulation, which will include literary documents from every period in the history of the Jewish people, as well as non-Jewish works, which for some special reason deserve a place in a series of books intended for Jews."[110] This series continued the approach Schocken Verlag had taken with the almanac, though on a larger scale. The Jewish anthology here was not a collection of short texts collected in a single volume, but rather longer sources, dispersed over an entire series, in which each volume presented one type of source from various periods and fields to show the diversity of Judaism. In accordance with the principles of the idea of compilation, all volumes in the series had to be relevant to building a new Jewish culture in the present, in Nazi Germany, and both the content and the price had to make them accessible to a large readership.[111]

Scholem responded enthusiastically to Spitzer's invitation to include in the series Kabbalistic sources in German translation and proposed a number of possibilities. After consulting with Buber, Spitzer decided that the most appropriate option would be a kabbalistic-messianic anthology and selections from the Zohar.[112] Scholem took it upon himself to prepare the volumes and a broad anthology of kabbalistic sources with his scholarly notes. In the end only two books by Scholem appeared during the time that Schocken Verlag was in Berlin: a German translation of the first two chapters of the Zohar with an introduction, which appeared as volume 40 in the Schocken series, and the publication in Hebrew of a Sabbatean manuscript from Salman Schocken's collection, with a long and detailed introduction.[113] The first book was greeted by Salman Schocken with so much enthusiasm that he personally took charge of preparing it for printing and even republished it a year later in a private bibliophile edition of 150 copies.[114] The second volume was also published in this private series, and it was one of the few books that Schocken Verlag published in Hebrew during the time of its activity in Germany.

The reasons why Scholem was less productive than promised for Schocken

Verlag during those years can only be surmised. His correspondence reveals a number of points of tension, at least some of which could have been part of the cause. For example, Scholem and Spitzer's relationship had some of the same problems—related to Scholem's character—that had plagued the relationship between Scholem and Klatzkin. In November 1934 Spitzer heard from someone else that Scholem was angry at the publishing house and at Spitzer personally because he had been invited only at the last minute and by means of a telegram to participate in the second volume of the almanac, which did not give him enough time to prepare and submit an article, and this was why he had not responded to Spitzer's letters. In the same month Spitzer reported to Schocken about the many difficulties the editors had had in their relations with Scholem: "Scholem is one of the most difficult to deal with of all the authors with whom we are in contact. He always answers positively, but when things get serious, he cuts off all contact. Therefore we must try to renew relations every time. . . . In a personal way it is very hard for me to form a connection with him time after time. One gradually enters into the undesirable situation of someone asking a favor."[115] This rough spot in their relationship was smoothed over after Spitzer wrote directly to Scholem and asked him what was the matter. Scholem admitted his anger in his conciliatory reply, and their relations were restored to normal.[116]

Another possible reason for the relatively small number of Scholem's works published by Schocken Verlag at that time is connected to the relationship between the Hebrew and German languages during the Nazi regime. Throughout these years, as we find in various letters, Scholem sought to have the work that he sent to Germany published in Hebrew, or at least in both German and Hebrew. At the end of 1934 Scholem wrote to Spitzer about the language of publication of his planned monograph on Kabbalah: "As you can easily understand, in this period, and under the present conditions, I have great psychological impediments, as a professor at the Hebrew University, to seeing a comprehensive book on the field of my research published first in German. . . . I would be exposed to the accusation of disloyalty, if I published such a book in German, if there was available some opportunity to publish it first, or at the same time, in Hebrew."[117]

Scholem's position is understandable. To publish a monograph of this kind only in German would place him in the middle between Nazi Germany, the enemy, represented in the Yishuv by the German language, and the Yishuv itself, of which Scholem was a part, whose language was Hebrew. However, another factor may be more important than all of those mentioned above in explaining why many projects that Scholem proposed were not completed: the nature of academic work is such that, no matter how great one's desire or how ambitious one's projects may be, the daily life of a university professor contains other obligations that result in projects being set aside until they are forgotten or consciously abandoned. In addition, it was only six years after its founding that Schocken Verlag was closed by the Nazis, at the end of 1938. Despite its impressive achievements, many unfinished projects came to an end with the closing of the publishing house. For example, the Schocken series was meant to contain a hundred volumes. In the end, ninety-two volumes of the series did appear—an impressive achievement, given the circumstances in which the publishing house was functioning.[118] Furthermore, many of the ideas that arose in the first years of Schocken Verlag in Berlin eventually came to fruition after the publishing house opened new branches in New York and Jerusalem, and Scholem's contribution played a central role in the process of renewal of the Schocken publishing house.[119]

In 1934 Salman Schocken left Nazi Germany and transferred his official residence to Jerusalem. He settled in the Rehavia neighborhood, where the well-known architect Erich Mendelssohn designed his house, with a separate building for his library. The closeness between Schocken and Scholem at that time was a result of their being neighbors, as well as of Schocken's serving as head of the Board of Trustees of the Hebrew University from 1935 until he left the Land of Israel in 1940.[120] In addition to Schocken's friendship for Scholem, he provided financial support for Scholem's research. To supplement the honorariums and other fees Scholem received for his lectures, articles, and books, Schocken established the Schocken Institute for Kabbalah in 1939, which was headed by Scholem. The institute provided financial support for Scholem and his students Chaim Wirszubski, Isaiah Tishby, and Joseph Weiss and gave them free access to Schocken's private library and manuscript collection, where they could research Kabbalah and the history of the Sabbatean movement.

Schocken spent the last years of his life wandering between the United States, Europe, and Israel in increasing isolation, and the writings of Rabbi Nachman—which, in Buber's adaptation, had opened the door to Judaism and Zionism for him—accompanied him in his last days.[121] In August 1959 Schocken was found dead in a hotel room in Switzerland.[122] That summer Scholem wrote in his diary a kind of summary of his personal relations with Schocken and the complexity of the publisher's personality. Scholem felt that Schocken possessed "an absolutely unique combination of huge talents, sometimes simply impressive intuition, with greatness (and sometimes generosity) with which he himself could not entirely cope. Among few people dwells a Satan more bitter than in this man, who managed, by means of sadism, to make an enemy out of everyone he wished to benefit. And at the same time, a kind of insatiable desire to become well-liked and admired (more than esteemed, and that is all he achieved in the end)."[123]

Many years after writing this entry, Scholem wrote to his brother that in his view a very important part of the success and character of Schocken Verlag in Berlin derived from the anarchistic figures of the old Schocken and the young Spitzer.[124] According to this interpretation, it is possible to understand how Scholem saw himself as belonging to this enterprise, which flourished on the soil of Nazi Germany and in which he played a considerable part, both in its publications in the short term and in preparing the ground for his future research. Years later Scholem described the activities and significance of Schocken Verlag as part of the renewal of Jewish culture in Germany: "German Jewry never benefited from a summation of Jewish values in the broadest sense during all the years of its greatness, such as it received at the time of its destruction."[125]

Concluding Remarks

From Scholem's scholarship, translations, and bibliographical work the figure of a collector emerges, a man seeking to assemble and expose remote aspects of Jewish history that in his view were its very heart, and using academic tools in scholarly venues. The goal of his scholarship was, as he declared many times, "to raise up again, from the remnants of destruction that cover the field of our work, the image of the original structure of Jewish mysticism and to determine its changes and metamorphoses."[126] However, to understand fully the meaning of compilation for Scholem, it is not sufficient to consult his scholarship and the bibliographies. Perhaps more than any writing or scholarship of his, this ideal was fulfilled in his private collection of books, a task at which he labored for more than sixty-five years. The collection contained 25,000 titles at the time of his death. Scholem sold it to the National and University Library while he was still alive.[127]

In many respects one may view his library as the ideal embodiment of compilation in the field of Kabbalah, according to Scholem. The documents are lined up one after the other, testifying to the continuity of the cultural existence of Judaism, without any work of an editor or an intermediary, yet sometimes with Scholem's own annotations in the margins of the pages, and in any event after they were examined by the discerning eye of the library's owner. Books that did not survive Scholem's weeding-out process were not included in the collection, and he usually passed them on to his students as gifts. Scholem's special relationship with his library and the conscious and selective principles that guided him in building the collection were already expressed in his youth, when he had just begun collecting books. While he was staying in Munich in August 1916, he wrote in his diary: "I feel a strong yearning for my library. It is my best friend.

FIGURE 2 Gershom Scholem and his second wife, Fania. Photographer: Alfred Bernheim. From the collection of the National Library of Israel, Jerusalem.

Although it is not decent to give one's love not to life but to Torah. My library is Torah, in all its breadth. Everything that is not Torah is doomed to remain outside. The writings of the anarchists also belong to it. Oh, when will I sit at my desk again and let my gaze wander over the rows of books?"[128]

An examination of various documents suggests two central needs that contributed to Scholem's desire to collect books: a personal need and a public need. Underlying the personal need was, on the one hand, the goal of the collector to combat dispersal by striving for the general completeness of the collection and, on the other hand, the effort to view every single item in the collection as a world in itself. Scholem's close friend, Walter Benjamin, wrote of the latter need of the collector: "The most profound enchantment for the collector is the locking of individual items within a magic circle in which they are fixed as the final thrill, the thrill of acquisition, passes over them. Everything remembered and thought, everything conscious, becomes the pedestal, the frame, the base, the lock of his property. The period, the region, the craftsmanship, the former ownership—for a true collector the whole background of an item adds up to a magic encyclopedia whose quintessence is the fate of his object."[129]

Here, in his quest for a world order within the items themselves, Scholem's personal desire to collect books combined with a great public project, which was the national purpose of his library—the public aspect of his collecting. Here is how Joseph Dan phrased it: "It is very evident that the collection of books was not simply a personal project in Scholem's view, but a foundation stone of spiritual resurrection in the framework of his Zionist faith, and despite his zeal for his private library, he did not raise a barrier between it and the process of the development of Hebrew scholarship and creativity in the 1920s and 1930s."[130] Perhaps the most conspicuous expression of the mingling of Scholem's public and private areas in Israel was the sale of his library in 1965 to the National and University Library. After his death it was transferred to the Givat Ram campus, where it was given a separate room. This action, which touched directly on the area of compilation, was also Scholem's final act in his involvement in the activities of the library over many years: "He saw the assembly of all the written records of Jewish culture at the National Library in Jerusalem as a way of ensuring Jewish continuity, and he devoted himself fervently to that goal."[131]

CHAPTER 2

A POLITICAL CIRCLE

BRIT SHALOM

> Any report about intellectual life in Palestine must necessarily be fragmented and divided, like the intellectual life of Palestine itself. There is hardly any other place in the world where the residents live so thoroughly divided into groups, large and small, as Palestine, and there is no place where people know so little about one another. . . . Almost every household is world unto itself, and certainly every religion, every group from a shared country of origin. For years people among us have been speaking about drawing closer to the Arabs. They forget that for that purpose the most primitive foundation is lacking: a common language, and also only the possibility of meeting one another.
>
> SHMUEL HUGO BERGMANN, "GEISTIGES LEBEN"[1]

The Association

A small advertisement was published in April 1926 in the Jerusalem daily newspaper, *Doar Hayom*, and a short time later in the German Zionist magazine, *Jüdische Rundschau*. It was signed by five men, most of whom—including Yehoshua Radler-Feldman (known as Rabbi Binyamin), Shmuel Hugo Bergmann, and Gershom Scholem—were members of the Brit Shalom association, which had recently been established. The advertisement contained a short statement opposing a demand that the Revisionist movement had been voicing for years, and that had shortly before been granted by the British government—that a Jewish armed force should be created in the Land of Israel:

> With great sorrow we see that governments and nations continue to choose security in weapons over security by the creation of just and friendly relations, and that they value armament over raising the cultural and economic level of the masses. In our opinion, armament and feelings of mistrust and fear not only cannot protect against wars, but they create them. Our outlook, in accordance with the spiritual aspirations

of the Prophets of Israel, is that all of our efforts must be directed at uprooting from ourselves the military spirit and illusions promulgated in the name of the concepts of heroism and national pride.[2]

The government directive for the establishment of a Hebrew brigade—accompanied by a propaganda campaign waged by men of the Yishuv that, in the opinion of the advertisement's signers, contained distortion of the facts as well as "an address to the instincts of fear and national prestige"—created discrimination by excluding the Palestinian Arabs from this public service and caused tension between the nations. For these reasons, the signers "oppose[d] the creation of a Hebrew brigade for whatever reasons there may be" and demanded that the directive be canceled immediately.[3] This was Scholem's first public statement as part of Brit Shalom, the only organization with a declared political orientation that Scholem belonged to during his years in Mandatory Palestine.

Officially Brit Shalom was established in March 1926, though it had existed as a social club since the end of 1925. The founder of the association was Arthur Ruppin, who was its chairman until 1928. Other early members included Bergmann, Rabbi Binyamin, Chaim Margaliot Kalvarisky, Jacob Tahon, Joseph Lurie, Hans Kohn, and, of course, Gershom Scholem. In addition, Robert Weltsch and Georg Landauer were active members of the association in Germany, the former as the editor of *Jüdische Rundschau*, and the latter as the first director of the Palestine Bureau (Palästinaamt), the German branch of the Jewish Agency for Israel.[4] The purpose of the association, as its members declared in the first volume of its magazine, *Sheifoteinu* (Our aspirations), was "to pave the way for understanding between Jews and Arabs for forms of common life in the Land of Israel on the basis of complete equality of the political rights of both nations, with broad autonomy, and the forms of their common work for the benefit of the development of the country."[5] The association was intended to be solely a research organization, and its activities were carried out within the framework of the Zionist movement and in coordination with the Zionist leadership of the Yishuv. The association never had more than a few score members.[6] Almost all of them were Zionist intellectuals, but they differed vastly in their origins and their thinking, which makes it difficult to speak of Brit Shalom as a single homogeneous group.[7] The spiritual richness of each member led to a profusion of opinions in the association.

Aharon Kedar divided the association into two main groups. The first, which he called, "People of the Yishuv," was composed of Zionist intellectuals who had immigrated to Palestine in the early twentieth century, most of them from Eastern Europe, and their Zionism was chiefly political and pragmatic, although it had an aspect of personal fulfillment. Kedar's second group, the "Radical Group," was composed of intellectuals from Central Europe, and most of them were associated with the Hebrew University. This group included Bergmann, Kohn, Weltsch, Landauer, Shmuel Sambursky, Marcus Reiner, Ernst Simon, and Scholem.[8] This group was called radical because of their willingness to go farther than the other group in the effort to combine Jewish national aspirations with those of the Arabs, while recognizing the importance of ethical issues in building up the land. In fact, the ideas that characterized the activity of the members of this circle had been consolidated while they were still in Europe, and they had been influenced by the spiritual and intellectual climate in German-speaking Europe from around 1900 until the Weimar era. The political trends that characterized German Zionism at that time provided the background for the views of the members of this circle, the spiritual trends that influenced Zionist youth at that time, and the Central European spirit of *Bildung* and the advocacy of the members of the circle of moderate liberalism.[9]

Scholem's published and unpublished writings from that time show that the ideas of the members of the radical circle were largely consistent with the way he believed the so called Arab question should be solved and his understanding of its centrality for the fulfillment of Zionism. Through an examination of Scholem's activity in Brit Shalom during its existence (1926–33) and of his writings from that time, it is possible to arrive at a better understanding of his conception of Zionism as a personal attempt to realize his own Zionist utopia, as that had taken shape in his heart while he was still a youth in Germany.

The Utopia

Scholem's attraction to Zionism and Zion as a youth was influenced by the spiritual Zionism of Ahad Haam and the idea of a spiritual center that came from his school of thought. The essence of this approach is the idea that the central problem of Judaism was cultural, and therefore a territorial and political solution as proposed by Theodor Herzl—a Jewish state alone—could not supply an answer to the Jewish question. According to Ahad Haam, a small spiritual center needed to be established in the Land of Israel as a first stage, and over the years, it would become the center of the Jewish people and create conditions in Palestine favorable for the spiritual development of Judaism and the future establishment of a state with Jewish cultural content—not an organization of Palestine on an ethnic basis. In Ahad Haam's words, the purpose was to create "not merely a State of Jews but a truly Jewish State."[10] The future of the Jewish people depended, according to this approach, on cultural rather than political development. The spiritual center in the Land of Israel was meant to ensure the existence and perpetuity of Judaism itself, to be a firm foundation from which the Judaism of the Diaspora could receive its spiritual fare and a guarantee of its continuity. This small and high-quality center was also meant to be an ethical model for the entire Jewish people, and by virtue of this task it would also be in close contact with the Jews of the Diaspora, which was its periphery.[11]

The young Scholem compared Ahad Haam to Martin Buber. The charismatic figure of Buber aroused great enthusiasm in Scholem's heart as a youth, as was the case with many other members of his generation. But during World War I and in the light of Buber's support for the war, this enthusiasm became sharp criticism. Accordingly, the comparison that Scholem made between Buber and Ahad Haam emphasized Buber's importance in Scholem's early years. Thus, for example, in his opening speech at an evening devoted to a discussion of Buber in the Jung-Juda youth movement in January 1915, Scholem placed Buber alongside Ahad Haam as two of the most important and spiritually powerful men in Judaism.[12]

About a year and a half later, he contrasted them instead of comparing them. For Scholem, Buber had come to represent the negative side of German Jewry and the Zionist youth movement, which—because of Buber's influence—held the concept of experience (*Erlebnis*) in high esteem. In contrast, Ahad Haam symbolized the "true" spirit of Zionism, whose source was in Eastern Europe: "It is really and truly good that in Russia the greatest man is not Buber, but Ahad Haam, who does not speak of 'experience' at all, but of spirit. The Jews of Germany will be left far from Zion so long as they remain in Heppenheim [Buber's home in Germany since March 1916]."[13] For Scholem, Ahad Haam and his teachings represented the positive and "authentic" model of Eastern European Zionism, and Buber and his advocacy of "experience" represented the negative model of the German Zionists. Indeed, at this point Scholem's view of Buber was more negative than positive. "I was greatly impressed with Buber, but eventually I defined myself as an adherent of Ahad Haam," he wrote in his memoirs many years later. "It was his great moral seriousness that won me over."[14] At the same time, one should not underestimate Buber's influence on Scholem on other levels, which were connected to the idea of experience. I refer to the Buberian conception, which was influenced by Ahad Haam and regarded Zionism—that is, the way toward Zion—as a personal quest for fulfillment or actualization, in the background of which stands a personal and ethical decision.[15] Buber's famous three lectures on Judaism to the Bar-Kokhba circle in Prague—from whose ranks came many members of the radical circle of Brit Shalom—profoundly influenced the Zionist youth of Scholem's generation. These speeches were published in 1911 and were a systematic working out of the Orientalist tendencies that characterized Buber's attitude toward Zionism.[16] This appears to have been one of the central points where Buber made his mark on Scholem's Zionism.

As noted, Scholem's yearning for and attraction to the Orient had their roots in the spirit of the time of his youth in Berlin. These feelings, which are expressed in many places in his early diaries, have been discussed several times by scholars in the context of the establishment of Kabbalah as a field of academic study in the Hebrew University by Scholem and his students, or in the context of postcolonial Orientalist discourse, and mainly with the aim of linking the first context to the second.[17] Common to these discussions is the claim that Scholem arrived in the Orient as a representative of Western culture and with no real desire to assimilate into the Orient; instead, he wanted to remain in Western contexts. The kernel of these arguments is Scholem's allegedly ambivalent attitude toward the Orient, which is based on simultaneous feelings of "admiration and repulsion,"[18] while Scholem is taking from the Orient—which is presented as the source of "authentic knowledge"—the raw material needed to construct an essentially Western worldview that ignores the "true" context of that knowledge. According to this conception, "the Orient is both the source of the 'knowledge' and also the source of the apocalyptic danger, and the knowledge must be distanced from that danger—that is to say, the Orient itself—by setting it in the West as 'redemption.'"[19]

I am not convinced that the Orientalist perspective, which comes from postcolonial discourse and presents a dichotomy between the Orient and the Occident, is useful for understanding Scholem, his research, and the ideological background of his Zionism. Close examination of the sources gives rise to a far more nuanced picture, according to which Scholem was aware of the dangers inherent in Orientalism and kept them separate from his love and desire for the Orient. In the spirit of the times, many entries in his early diaries identify the Jewish people and the Land of Israel with the Orient, thus linking the desire for the East with his Zionism.[20] These entries were written in his youth, when Buber's influence on him was great. This influence is clearly evident in Scholem's conception of the Orient at that time, most of which he worked out in his personal struggle with Buber's teachings, his image, and his meaning for the members of Scholem's generation. Thus, for example, on December 11, 1915—shortly before his first visit to Buber, at the time when his critique of Buber's path in Zionism and his influence on the Jewish youth movements began to take shape—he wrote in his diary:

> Do I, Gerhard Scholem, have a desire for Palestine? Do I have the right and also—in my inner self—the obligation to go there? This is a hard question, and each of us

> ought to have answered it in fact with a decisive "yes." It is clear. I want to leave this place, but do I not want, [in] the same degree, to travel to Arabian countries, to Persia, to China, to *the East*? There is great love for the Orient within me, and I believe that the Land of Israel can celebrate its rebirth only in a covenant with the other Orient. But at the same time I certainly think that, while I wish to travel to the Orient, I want to live in the Land of Israel! That is the difference. I don't want to go in order to see Jerusalem, about which one may speak without shame, but I want to become a son of the old earth and a citizen of the future.[21]

In this passage Scholem places the Land of Israel and his desire to live there in the general context of the Orient, and he feels attracted to all of it. However, he brings out the uniqueness of Zion in relation to other countries in the East. Although in his view Zion can come to life again only in the framework of the Orient, the difference between the Land of Israel and the various other countries is clear: while the other countries arouse in him the desire to tour them, because of their exotic attraction, the Land of Israel is the only place to which he wishes to belong and where he wants to live. For the young Scholem it was also clear that Jewish renewal in the East, which will lead him to become "a son of the old earth and a citizen of the future," will also demand sacrifice, to make Western Zionism appropriate to the patterns of life in the place for which he yearns. The sacrifice, in Scholem's opinion, will be none other than his commitment to Western scholarship, to which he planned to devote his life: "If the sacrifice of science is demanded, to serve the renewal of the East within the spirit of the East, then there will be nothing to be said against that."[22] The sacrifice, according to Scholem's theoretical reflections here, is to give up intellectual life and become a tiller of the soil.

Scholem's awareness of the contradiction between his desire to become a man of the Orient and his attachment to Western culture and scholarship testifies to the complex and self-aware thought processes that accompanied his becoming a Zionist and moving to the Land of Israel. The utopia that he imagined was not a picture devoid of all Oriental elements or containing only Oriental elements that were adapted to meet the needs of the West (though it must be pointed out that the ideal of working the land, which Scholem presented here, is also rooted in the European West and not in the Orient). What is important is that this utopia contained the unknown, leading to apprehensions about the future in the Land of Israel and a consideration of the dangers inherent in the passage from West to East. One of the central dangers in Scholem's view was that the passage to the East would not be complete, and that the eyes of those in the center in Zion, including Scholem, would always look to the West: "Were I not to go to

Palestine, I would become a hypocrite of the first order here. By the way, in Palestine this possibility continues to exist: it depends on the people there, whether they glance in the direction of Europe, with two eyes, or to the East. I glance to the East. But in fact, I am not glancing. Rather, I am looking, I hope, I am burning."[23]

The rebirth of Zion, as Scholem imagined it before moving there, was meant to be in connection with the context of the Orient. Gazing from the East back to Europe seemed hypocritical to him, just as remaining in Europe did. This statement is consistent with the ethical conception that underlay Scholem's Zionism, through the influence of Ahad Haam. The Zionist decision to immigrate to the Land of Israel was a personal one whose motives were ethical, and it was incumbent on the handful of people who would build the spiritual center in the Land of Israel to be a model for the rest of the nation in their moral purity and creative life.[24] Of course, during the process of realizing utopia, it became clear that many of its elements could not be implemented. For example, the idea of a center implied a system of relations with the periphery and therefore constant connection with the West, and any person who uproots him- or herself from one world and moves into another encounters difficulties, which the young Scholem certainly did not anticipate fully. The reasons why Scholem chose to continue to pursue Western scholarship and gave up on the idea of a life on the soil—which he regarded in the passage quoted above as the solution to the paradox of Western existence in the Orient—belong to an area beyond the reach of the historian. However, it is important that Scholem's diary entries clearly show that he was aware of the tension between East and West and the complexity of Zion as the point of encounter between them. In addition, we may also emphasize Scholem's decision to learn Arabic as part of his preparation for immigration. Evidence of those studies is clear in the many books of Arabic grammar that he brought with him to the Land of Israel.[25]

In his utopian vision of the actualization of the Zionist idea in the Land of Israel, Scholem thus followed Ahad Haam's path. The idea of the spiritual center and the great emphasis given to ethics and individualism are important components of Scholem's Zionist background. The process of implementing Ahad Haam's ideas in the Land of Israel required coping with internal and external obstacles. Most important and, in the view of the members of Brit Shalom, the greatest test of Zionism, was an external obstacle: the relationship of Zionism to the Arabs and the inclusion of their needs in the Jewish national vision in an egalitarian and just manner. The internal challenge was coping with the Revisionist movement and its demand for Jewish exclusiveness, or at least a Jewish majority, in the country. As shown below, Scholem regarded this demand, which was based on Herzl's idea of a territorial solution, as a dangerous and potentially destructive extension of messianic aspirations.

The Fulfillment

In his letter to Werner Kraft, cited at the beginning of the previous chapter, Scholem drew an ambiguous picture of the spiritual condition of people in the Land of Israel in late 1924, about a year after his immigration. As mentioned above, Scholem's understanding of the reality into which he had immigrated was directly connected to his expectations of the country and the role he accorded it in the process of revival of the Jewish people—or, in other words, the way he saw Zionist politics. His complaints in the letter to Kraft about the situation of the Hebrew language in the country and about the quality of the intellectuals who wrote in it were repeated in much of what he wrote at that time and occupied a central place in his thinking and political positions. In the following passage, written at the same time as the letter to Kraft and similar to that letter in content, Scholem compares these aspects of Jewish national revival with trends in the Zionist movement in the Land of Israel:

> Zionism will survive its catastrophe. The hour has come when hearts must decide whether Zionism—whose meaning is preparation of the eternal—will succumb to the Zionism of the Jewish state, which is a catastrophe. The theocracy has proven to be too weak, and the nation's priests have not placed themselves in the breach. Now the worldly political Zionism of yesterday (*weltlich-vorgestrige Zionistenstaatlichkeit*) seeks to fill the vacuum left by the theocracy, which cannot be established. The vital forces of the nation, whose influence in Palestine is very small, are slowly dying, flowing into the veins of other nations, because we have not remained loyal to our destiny. In the name of God—this was not what we wanted. We believed inwardly in the fullness of the heart, and that thin and cold petit bourgeoisie, which links a pioneer with Klausner—his moral sermons, which I heard in Petach-Tikvah in 1923, when I happened on a lecture by him by chance, are unforgettable for me. And why? *Because the desiccation of the language withered our heart*, because we were not left with any expression (*Ausdruck*) that also made an impression (*Eindruck*)—because what grew here has not yet come to fruition, so long as it remains *before* its visible manifestation. We came with the intention of plunging into the fullness of the sea, not externally, but with the intensity of life that grows here, but we are based only in the mud of empty talk, which is spoken to us at assemblies full from wall to wall, no different from the pages of *Hashiloach*.[26] Hence we must proceed toward a crisis with our eyes open and still hope that it will come soon. *In metaphysical fashion* we

have lost the battle in the Land of Israel, which Zionism has won in the world. Thus it only remains to discuss which front before God will be the true one. We do not know it yet.[27]

This passage belongs to a collection of Scholem's writings and diary entries on Zionism that were written in the years after his immigration, most of which were never published.[28] Many of these fragments reflect Scholem's encounter with Zionism and the Zionist idea against the background of the situation in the Land of Israel, which was new to him, as well as the personal and political crises involved in his immigration and his disillusionment with the development of the Zionist movement in his new home. The passage quoted here is Scholem's first record of his feelings about Zionism after his arrival in Palestine. Hence both in the depth and the extent of the critique are surprising. The points and problems that he raised here were also central to his critique of the Zionist project during the following decade, the years of his involvement with Brit Shalom. During those years his critique would expand and touch on additional points, but its essentials are already to be found here, in the first year after his immigration—and most likely some of them had emerged earlier. One may suppose that Scholem could have anticipated some of his disappointment with the situation in the Land of Israel even before his immigration and could have prepared himself somewhat for the possibility that the situation in Palestine was moving in a direction different from the one he believed in.[29] However, as we shall see below, he could not have anticipated the extent of his shock at the direction that the Zionist movement had chosen to take. In any event, this passage is key for understanding Scholem's attitude toward Zionism in those years and his activity in Brit Shalom because it contains the kernel of his critique of Zionism, which he maintained during the following years.

In fact the opening sentence of the passage is complex: "Zionism will survive its catastrophe." This sentence assumes that the catastrophe is an integral component of Zionism, which is doomed to struggle with it. At this stage, Scholem believed that Zionism, as he understood it, would survive that struggle, which gives the passage an optimistic tone at the beginning. The essence of that catastrophe becomes clear to the reader immediately, as well as the significance of Zionism for the author. Indeed, Scholem juxtaposes the catastrophe and Zionism. On the one hand was the state of the Jews (the catastrophe), and on the other hand was "preparation of the eternal." Given the influence of Ahad Haam, for Scholem the "preparation of the eternal" was, clearly the establishment of a spiritual center in the Land of Israel. He calls the Jewish state a "theocracy," referring to the nationalist tendency in Zionism—which claimed that the Bible was the source of the Jewish people's right to the entire Land of Israel and held that this right was to be asserted by force of arms. This desire for territorial control and the view of how to achieve it were based on the messianic-biblical morality of the prophets, combined with contemporary European chauvinistic tendencies.[30]

Here Scholem was referring to the seeds of what would shortly become the Revisionist movement, established by Zeev Jabotinsky in 1925, almost at the same time as Brit Shalom was founded. Scholem called these tendencies in Zionism "the worldly political Zionism of yesterday," and he regarded them as a betrayal of the purpose of Zionism and a sign of the destruction of the movement from within. As a symbol of these tendencies Scholem points to Joseph Klausner, a prominent member of the Revisionist camp who was appointed to the Chair for Modern Hebrew Literature at the Hebrew University. As Scholem's note indicates, his first encounter with Klausner in Petach-Tikvah, during the first days after his immigration, made a negative impression on him.[31] Of course, Scholem saw the key to the future of the Jewish people and its eternal existence as the establishment of a spiritual center in the Land of Israel, and thus any expression of what he interpreted as lack of seriousness or charlatanism was a threat. In other words, if Jewish culture was a condition for the realization of Zionism and the revival of Judaism, then Zionism needed to take the form of the research into that culture. For Scholem, Klausner—who belonged to the Revisionist right and consciously linked his scholarship to his Revisionist political ideas—symbolized the danger lurking for Zionism in the Hebrew language and the way it was used: "Because the desiccation of the language withered our heart." This is the danger against which Scholem warned two years later in his famous letter to Franz Rosenzweig, discussed in the previous chapter. There Scholem stated that the revival of the Hebrew language entailed many more dangers than outside factors in the Land of Israel.[32] In the present passage we can discern the political background of the letter to Rosenzweig, implied in Scholem's pointing out that the danger for Zionism and its fulfillment was an internal Jewish matter and not closely connected to the Arabs of the land—the outer factor that the Revisionists viewed as a threat.[33] In the end, Scholem emphasizes the sentence that was to accompany his point of view on the realization of Zionism in the following years: in a metaphysical manner, in the Land of Israel Zionism lost the battle that it had won in the Diaspora. We can learn about the essence of this battle from what Scholem hints afterward: "Thus it only remains to discuss which front before God will be the true one. We do not know it yet." The metaphysical defeat of Zionism in the Land of Israel left open the question of religious ethics—which is the right moral side, or "front," in the eyes of God. Scholem's critique would grow stronger in the following years and reach its peak in 1930, in response to the Arab riots of 1929. As noted above, the great importance of this document, aside from its containing the essentials of Scholem's critique of the Zionist project during the following years, is its date. At the end of 1924, a year after his immigration to the Land of Israel and a year before the establishment of Brit Shalom, Scholem was already expressing the critique that would become the basis for that association's platform.

As mentioned above, Brit Shalom was founded in early 1926, and the first public declaration of its members was in opposition to the establishment of a Jewish armed brigade. The idea of creating a Jewish military force was one of the central guiding principles of Zeev Jabotinsky's political activities from a very early stage, and he succeeded when a Jewish Legion was established in the British army during World War I. The last of these was disbanded after the riots of 1921. In 1925 Jabotinsky founded a political movement, the Revisionist Zionist Alliance, which was a faction in the World Zionist Organization until it split from the larger group in 1935.[34] Jabotinsky had worked out the principles of the movement before its establishment. He addressed the relations of Zionism to the Palestinian Arabs in an article published in 1923, "On the Iron Wall"—a term adopted by the coming generations: "Our colonization should either stop or continue against the will of the native population. And this is why it may continue and develop only under the protection of a force, independent of the local population—an iron wall, through which the local population cannot break."[35]

The Zionist realization of the idea of Jewish nationalism was Jabotinsky's goal, and his approach was realistic both in its recognition of the existence of the Palestinian Arabs as a nation with aspirations for self-determination and in the solution that he proposed for the problem of the existence of two nations on the same land. In principle Jabotinsky had no objection to reaching an agreement with the Palestinian Arabs, but the way to that agreement was "the iron wall," meaning the unilateral strengthening of Jewish rule over the Land of Israel.

Brit Shalom was established largely as a response to Revisionism, and one may see the association's ideological position with respect to the attitude of Zionism toward the Palestinian Arabs as a mirror image of the position of the Revisionist movement.[36] Anita Shapira has pointed out that both opposing movements did not avoid the problem of the Palestinian Arabs, and both sought a practical solution, aware of the essential differences between the two nations and of the existence of Arab nationalism.[37] In addition, both movements understood that the solution had to be radical, and that any compromise or evasion, such as the policy of the Zionist establishment of the Yishuv, was inadequate. The great difference between the two movements was that the Revisionists thought the only way to ensure a Jewish majority in the Land of Israel and fulfill the Zionist project was through territorial nationalism that depended on the force of arms, while the members of Brit Shalom saw that majority itself as a disaster for Zionism and proof of its inner moral failure. To them, the danger for Zionism came from ignoring the needs of the Arab nation and from emphasizing hollow territorial and military nationalism instead of the revival of the spirit, ethics, and culture of the Jewish people. Instead of Revisionist nationalism, the members of Brit Shalom proposed the idea of binationalism, giving both nations equal weight and rights in the political formation of Palestine. Another essential difference between the groups was in their size and in the recognition they received within the Zionist movement over the years. While the members of Brit Shalom and their ideas remained marginal in the Zionist consensus, if not outside of it, the ideas of the Revisionist movement were adopted by the public in the Yishuv and continue to influence the policies of the State of Israel to this day.

In the long passage we have been discussing, Scholem predicted a crisis in Zionism and even hoped that it would come soon, apparently to alter what he regarded as the wrong path that Zionism had taken. In April 1926, the crisis began to take on form and substance in Scholem's private notes:

> Thus our movement will still confront a dreadful crisis, which will continue to live among us for a long time, the era when the Jews in Palestine will have to climb on the iron wall, defenseless, with their inner being undefended, because they fell into the original sin: *anticipation* of our victory. He who predicts his victory in spirituality will lose the power to gain it in materiality. We not only dreamed our utopia by ourselves, the beautiful hours when we believed we were ascending, but they drained the best of our strength to the marrow: we won too soon, because we are winning in the *revealed* world of the intelligentsia, before doing so in the invisible world of demons (*Dämonen*) who threaten the language of our rebirth, which is developing under duress and in assemblies.[38]

The iron wall—the physical power that, according to Jabotinsky, was a condition for the success of the Zionist project and Jewish existence in the Land of Israel—becomes for Scholem the main obstacle to the fulfillment of Zionism. The source of the future power and defense of the Yishuv was not in the physical exterior, but within it, and in that respect the Yishuv remained exposed and unprotected. Political developments during the first days of the Mandatory government, which showed a clear leaning toward the Jewish side and an understanding of the physical needs of Zionism, created great optimism in the ranks of the Zionist movement. The declarations of encouragement of Jewish immigration to the Land of Israel and the expansion of settlement there to create a national home for the Jews produced the feeling that an opportunity had been created to realize the dream of the Jewish state.[39] According to Scholem, this was the premature victory of Zionism, which was predicting a successful future for itself on the material and physical plane. As opposed to this exteriority, Scholem speaks of the hidden interior, which he calls demonic, which will defeat the Zionist movement, and which is expressed in the use of the Hebrew language. The demonic inner being is disobedient to the standards of ethics and the spirit that, in Scholem's opinion, are required from Zionism. The illusion of victory in the revealed world, the world of intelligence, led to neglect of the struggle on the hidden level, that of ethics. Hence it is possible to understand how Scholem saw the establishment of the Revisionist movement, which advocated ideas contrary to his own about the fulfillment of Zionism, as accelerating movement toward the crisis that he both feared and hoped for. Nevertheless, this passage lacks the optimistic tone that characterized the beginning of his comments from 1924, and the feeling of defeat has grown stronger.

The solution that Scholem found for this crisis, and that also characterized the policy of Brit Shalom, was silence and withdrawal from all public discourse. In deciding to adopt this passive path, the members of the association relied on its primary definition as a research group. At that time Scholem made no public declaration of his political positions, and the only evidence of the psychological turmoil aroused in him by the direction that Zionism was taking is in his personal writings. This situation changed in 1928. That was when the members of the radical group of Brit Shalom began to express their political opinion in public and thus to change the association's policy. Scholem was part of this trend as an editor of the new magazine *Sheifoteinu*, which was the organ of Brit Shalom, and in his publication of political articles taking issue with the path of Revisionism. For example, on November 20, 1928, he wrote in *Jüdische Rundschau*: "Only this bumpy road is left, to work for rapprochement within our camp and within that of the Arabs. Or else the path of the Revisionists is left, to depend on an imaginary sword and not to be deterred from oppressing the inhabitants of the land, to bring the Jewish state into being. But precisely this will be, if it is possible to implement this, none other than the absolute decline (*Untergang*) of Zionism."[40]

In 1928, for the first time Jewish messianism appears in Scholem's writings in a negative context. His first article about Sabbateanism was published in that year, in the final issue of *Der Jude*, which was dedicated to Buber's fiftieth birthday. This article, which deals with the Sabbatean Abraham Cardoso, concludes with the following declaration: "The messianic phraseology of Zionism, especially at important moments, contains no little of the Sabbatean temptation, and it has the capacity to bring about the shattering or renewal of Judaism and the steadying of its world in the spirit of the unbroken language. While all the theological structures, including those of Cardoso and Jakob Frank, faded away with time, the deepest and most destructive motivation of Sabbateanism—the hubris of the Jews—remains in place."[41]

According to his diary and personal notes before his immigration, messianism occupied a solid place in Scholem's inner world. The image and character of the messiah frequently preoccupied him, and he usually attributed a positive place and goal to Jewish messianism.[42] Throughout his life Jewish messianism interested him, and he devoted a good part of his intellectual energy to it as a historical phenomenon. But the positive and sympathetic tone that he used in writing about it as a young man faded in his later scholarship. Scholem presented the powers of renewal of the Sabbatean movement as breaking the traditional framework of Jewish society and heralding new forms of Jewish life such as Hasidism, the Haskala (Jewish Enlightenment), and secularization. Usually he accompanied this narrative with a warning about the price that Jewish messianism exacted and continues to exact from the Jewish people and the threat to the existence of a healthy and independent Jewish society in Israel.[43] Scholem saw this threat in every identification of Zionism with messianism, and not only in the Revisionist movement but in political Zionism in general.[44] In any event, 1928 marked the beginning of the change in Scholem's attitude toward messianism as he emphasized its dangers. As noted above, this change happened when he began his research into Sabbateanism, but his personal crisis with Zionism, which was also partly responsible for the change in his understanding of Jewish messianism, was the outcome of a long crisis that reached a climax at the end of the decade—after the events at the Western Wall.

The Events of 1929 and Their Aftermath

The decision of the members of Brit Shalom to break their public silence was connected to the increasing tension, starting in the autumn of 1928, about the question of control of the places in Jerusalem that were holy to Judaism and Islam. On the eve of Yom Kippur, the Jews erected a partition at the foot of the Western Wall to separate men from women. This action provoked a protest from the Supreme Muslim Council because the Jews had violated the status quo that had prevailed there. This event signaled the exacerbation of tension between the populations, as the Western Wall became, to a large degree, a symbol of the struggle between the two nations. In fact, the context of the friction was the Arabs' fear of the threat inherent in the rapid growth of the Yishuv and the declared support of the Mandatory government for Zionist policies. The tension between the two sides reached a peak on August 14, 1929, following a demonstration held in Tel Aviv and mass prayers at the Western Wall in which about 3,000 Jews took part. The next day a demonstration was held at the Western Wall involving hundreds of Jews, some of whom—members of Beitar, the Revisionist youth movement—bore clubs. After Friday prayers on August 16 and during the following days, until August 24, masses of Arabs rioted in Jerusalem, and Arabs attacked Jews throughout the country. In these riots 133 Jews were killed and 339 were wounded, and in efforts to protect the Jewish population and in acts of revenge, 116 Arabs were killed and 232 were wounded.[45]

The Yishuv was shocked by the extent and results of the riots. "For the first time," Anita Shapira writes, "the Jewish community in Palestine found itself caught up in a wave of violent disturbances that swept with a fury through Jewish settlements and neighborhoods throughout the length and breadth of the country. The danger now appeared to threaten the very survival of the entire Jewish community."[46] The feeling of danger brought about a change in Zionist policy in the Yishuv and its relations with the Arab population. The process of separation of the two nations was accelerated, and as the gap between them widened, their mutual hostility increased.[47] On the Jewish side a process began in which, "almost imperceptibly, a powerful identity was generated between self-defence, demonstration of force, and national revival."[48] This glorification of the use of force cast a negative light on refraining from physical defense and counterattacks. The new reality left the members of Brit Shalom outside the consensus. After the riots, there were harsh polemics in the Jewish press in the Land of Israel and Germany against the path of the members of the association, and Scholem and others defended their worldview against the criticism aimed at them. In responses that Scholem wrote in the association's magazine, *Sheifoteinu* and in *Davar*, the Histadrut daily newspaper, he reprimanded the Yishuv for what he saw as the great error it had committed and advocated what he regarded as the correct path for the Zionist movement.[49] In these publications Scholem sharpened his positions regarding Zionism and its development and clarified his opinions, which he had expressed until then only in his diaries and personal notes.

A central polemical article by Scholem appeared in *Sheifoteinu* under the title, "Bemai ka Miflagei?"—an Aramaic phrase found in the Talmud meaning, "What do we disagree about?" The main burden of this article was an effort to clarify the differences of opinion between the members of Brit Shalom and the Zionist majority, and what the relation of the former was to the latter. This article became, in a way, a reflection of Scholem's understanding of the development and failures of Zionism, which he believed had led to the crisis of 1929.[50] According to Scholem, the controversy about the Arab question was related to an internal Jewish question about the path of Zionism in general, and the debate was actually a struggle over what the essence of Zionism was and how Zionism should be fulfilled.[51]

According to Scholem, the effort to create a center in the Land of Israel, in the spirit of Ahad Haam—which was, as noted above, intended to guarantee the eternal existence of Judaism and to be a source of spiritual inspiration for Jews in the Diaspora—had failed.[52] Zionism had been active in the Diaspora before the spiritual center was established in the Land of Israel, and therefore Zionism used its best energies, especially in the light of its great success in the Diaspora, for the wrong purpose: to ensure the renewal and continued existence of Jewish life in the periphery—the Diaspora—rather than investing in an effort to establish a national home at the center. The Land of Israel and the Diaspora were separated from each other, and the proper order of things had been overturned. The place that was supposed to be the center of Zionism had become its periphery, and the Yishuv could hardly continue to exist without Zionism in the Diaspora.

In Scholem's opinion, Zionism should be exclusive and particularistic to the extent of becoming sectarian, and this was the true way to achieve its goals.[53] The sect represents the esoteric, hidden, and invisible side of Jewish spiritual renewal, one of whose characteristics—as noted above—was the revival of the Hebrew language, and only after this process of renewal can the exoteric and universal stage come. The early success of the Zionist movement had brought it to a crisis, for it no longer had anywhere to advance: its political goals had been achieved before everyone's eyes, before its esoteric task was accomplished. Here is how Scholem expressed this in a letter to Walter Benjamin on August 1, 1931:

> In the empty passion of a vocation become public we ourselves have invoked the forces of destruction. Our catastrophe started where the vocation did not maintain itself in its profanation, where community was not developed in its legitimate concealment, but where instead the betrayal of the secret values that lure us here became transformed into a positive side of the demonic propaganda. By becoming visible our cause was destroyed. The encounter with Sleeping Beauty took place in the presence of too many paying spectators for it to have ended with an embrace. Zionism disregarded the night and shifted the procreation that ought to have meant everything to it to a world market where there was too much sunlight and the covetousness of the living degenerated into a prostitution of the last remnants of our youth. That was not the place we had come to find nor the light that could enflame us.[54]

In "Bemai ka Miflagei?" Scholem saw the "original sin" of Zionism as depending on the great powers and joining the side of the victors after World War I. In Zionism's choice of the winning side as a partner in the Zionist project, as expressed in the Balfour Declaration, it betrayed one of what Scholem considered its most important principles, being a revolutionary movement. The revolution must come from below, from the weak, and therefore the correct allies from the ethical and historical point of view, those with whom the Jewish people shared a common fate, were not the British but the Arabs. By choosing British imperialism as its partner—a choice that Scholem calls "a counterfeit victory" —Zionism was destined to lose: "either it will be washed away along with the waters of imperialism, or it will be burned in the fire of the revolution of the awakening Orient."[55]

In this article Scholem espoused a practical political line that rejected the Revisionist territorial approach but also opposed the approach of the young MAPAI (the Hebrew acronym of the Worker's Party of the Land of Israel), which had been established in 1930 and was on the fence with regard to the relationship of Zionism to the Palestinian Arabs. The criticism of MAPAI, which represented the central stream of Zionism and was closer in its socialist principles to the views of the members of Brit Shalom than to those of the Revionists, was a response to the Seventeenth Zionist Congress, which took place in Basel in 1931. At this congress Jabotinsky initiated a debate on the matter of the final goal of Zionism, in the wake of the controversy with Brit Shalom. And during the congress Chaim Weizmann, who later became the first president of the State of Israel, gave an interview in which he said that he did not support the existence a Jewish majority in the Land of Israel. The content of this interview aroused a great turmoil among the delegates, in which Jabotinsky publicly tore up his entry card to the congress. This episode marked the beginning of the separation of the Revisionist Zionist Alliance from the World Zionist Organization, from which it was completely severed in 1935.[56] After these events MAPAI was called on to abandon its vague approach to the matter, provide a clear definition of the goal of Zionism, and decide whether or not it supported the establishment of a Jewish state. The party's great fear was that any proclamation that the goal of Zionism was a Jewish state, which meant a Jewish majority in the Land of Israel, might cause a conflagration in the region. Therefore delegates to the Congress decided to issue a milder and more general statement, according to which the goal of Zionism was "continuous immigration and settlement and renewal of full national existence in Palestine with all features of normal Jewish life."[57] This declaration, along with David Ben-Gurion's accusation that the members of Brit Shalom were responsible for the flaring up of the controversy that the Revisionists had aroused and for pushing MAPAI into a corner with their demand for clarity, provoked a vehement response from Scholem. In an editorial in *Sheifoteinu* he accused MAPAI of advocating a hawkish ideology, which was disguised for strategic reasons with ostensibly dovish declarations: "Here is revealed the dreadful psychological reality which must bring destruction and disintegration to the [Zionist] movement: the great majority of the Zionist Congress wants a Jewish state, but it does not want to admit it openly."[58] Scholem's fear was that this strategic declaration would in time become the MAPAI creed, a creed to which Brit Shalom objected strenuously. Scholem protested strongly against the accusation that Brit Shalom intended to diminish Zionism: "Our wish is not to diminish the image of Zionism, but to rouse Zionism from the superfluous and dangerous nightmare, a dream that does not belong in any way to the essence of Zionism as the movement of renewal of the Jewish people, and we must continue this battle with greater intensity and strength. If this is the dream of Zionism: numbers and 'borders,' if it cannot subsist without it, then it will fail in the end, or, rather, it has already failed."[59]

Scholem's battle against the calls for a Jewish majority in the Land of Israel was not limited to his public activity in Brit Shalom or to publishing articles in Palestine and Germany. His position and opinions after the 1929 riots were expressed in a practical way in his unwillingness to participate in the propaganda efforts of the Yishuv following the violent events or the struggle to gain the sympathy of the British. In the wake of the 1929 riots, the Zionist movement established a committee whose purpose was to examine material about the Western Wall and the question of Jewish rights to it, and to present that material to the international commission whose members were going to come to the Land of Israel to investigate the subject.[60] As part of its activities, the committee asked Scholem "please to help it with its work by examining all the material that exists in Kabbalah literature regarding the Western Wall and on a Jewish synagogue on the Temple Mount."[61] Scholem did not answer this letter and refused to cooperate with the committee. A year afterward a letter to the editor was published in *Doar Hayom*, which was identified with Revisionist views at that time. The author of the letter, A. Babakov, presented a highly inaccurate account of what had happened and expressed his disapproval of Scholem's actions and asked that steps be taken to prevent him from "continuing 'to preach Torah' in Israel."[62]

Three days later, the newspaper published Scholem's reply. He stated that his refusal to help the committee was a refusal to take part as a private individual "in scientific work for juridical and political purposes." His reason for refusing to cooperate was still valid: "Since I thought and still think that the entry of Jews in a judicial trial regarding the Western Wall is a great disaster for the Jewish people, I demand for myself, as for any private individual with a conscience, the elementary right to refrain from active participation (as was asked of me) in preparing steps that I regard as damaging and destructive. In my humble opinion, the question of the Western Wall cannot be resolved by legal deliberations before a third party."[63]

This episode demonstrates how Scholem applied his political opinions on the practical level. In his criticism of one of the main political principles shared by MAPAI and Jabotinsky, Scholem expressed his opposition to the view that depending on the British and cooperating with the Mandatory regime was the key to achieving the political goals of Zionism, whatever they might be. Not only did Scholem oppose the political aspect of Zionism, but he also felt that the way to achieve the Zionist dream was to come to an understanding with the Arabs of the land—who, in his view, were the main ally instead of the British. He saw the importance of dialogue with the Arabs and did not recognize the authority of the British as mediators in any controversy in Palestine.

Testimony to the great break with Zionism that took place within Scholem after the events at the Western Wall can also be found in his more personal writing, which became increasingly gloomy as time passed. At the end of June 1930 he wrote a poem in German titled "Begegnung mit Zion und der Welt (Der Untergang)" (Encounter with Zion and the world [the decline]), in which one senses bitter disappointment and disillusionment. The poem ends with the following two stanzas:

> This was the darkest hour:
> waking from the dream.
> And though the wounds were mortal,
> they were never what they seemed.
>
> What was within is now without,
> the dream twists into violence,
> and once again we stand outside
> and Zion is without form or sense.[64]

Scholem also expressed the crisis that was brewing within him in correspondence with friends and colleagues who were in Europe at the time. Along with the letter to Benjamin, mentioned above, Scholem wrote about his feelings to Martin Buber, a man who was close to the members of Brit Shalom and an authority figure for them. The sharp change in Scholem's outlook is evident in that letter:

> We must say to ourselves that there is no longer any importance to the way we interpret Zionism, now that its face has been revealed (and now the hour is decisive, no one can deceive himself anymore), even when it is turned toward itself, like the face of the Medusa. Of course: this is the moment because of which many of us, and I in any event, are found here: we believe that this is unbearable, if we are forced to say to

ourselves that our cause has failed without our being actual partners in it. The inner situation is horrible, the demoralization is complete. This is evident to everyone here, leaving almost no hope that it is still possible to do anything, because it is not the way of historical moments to turn back, and nothing can be saved of what was lost during the past half year for the sake of the renewal of Judaism.[65]

These were not just words written in the heat of the events. Instead, they signaled a turning point in Scholem's attitude toward Zionism and Zionist activity in the Land of Israel, or—to be precise—his acute realization that the Zionist movement had undergone a change that distanced the manner of its implementation from the utopia that had been its heritage. In the decades following the disbanding of Brit Shalom, and indeed for the rest of his life, Scholem refrained from all political activity. For example, he did not take part in the pacifist Ihud (Unity) Association established by Judah Leib Magnes in 1942, though some of the members of Brit Shalom did.[66] The years of his membership in Brit Shalom were the only time in his life when he belonged to an organization with a clear political direction and was active in it. Afterward, Scholem shut himself off in his academic research and lived his life, as Joseph Dan states, "according to the conventions typical of a professor at a German university, distant and shut off from current events and from the community around him."[67] After this, Scholem took a practical approach toward Zionism, at first to defend and represent the positions of Brit Shalom, and then to explain his Zionist motivations in the State of Israel. For example, in an interview many years later about a lecture he gave in Germany on behalf of Brit Shalom, he said:

> I was once asked, when I was abroad, I was asked to speak about Brit Shalom, they asked me in a very stormy dispute, in Frankfurt am Main in 1932, "What do you actually want?" I told them, and I was known as supposedly one of the radicals of Brit Shalom, "What I want is very simple, I want the Jewish state on both banks of the Jordan." You know that was the Revisionist slogan. If you ask me what I want—I want a Hebrew state on both banks of the Jordan. But the question isn't what I want. The question is what in effect, in the reality that exists in the country, it is possible to want. And not just what you want in a dream. In a dream I want a Jewish state. In reality, I don't believe that a Jewish state in that form is possible. So I take the line of Brit Shalom.[68]

Scholem's realistic and practical approach was anchored in the fact that the question of a Jewish state in the political situation of that time "was an unrealistic question. No one in the camp we were arguing with, the members of the governing body of the Histadrut, thought that the question of the Jewish state in 1929 was a question of our generation."[69] In the political situation in the Land of Israel during the 1930s the realistic possibility, in Scholem's opinion, was the establishment of a small spiritual center that would act in cooperation with the Arabs and that eventually might become a binational state. Hence, as noted above, came Scholem's conception of Zionism as a nonmessianic movement, and his understanding of the hope for the political realization of Zionism as dangerous messianism. As early as 1929 he regarded the idea of political redemption in the Land of Israel as a threatening mixture of religion and politics: "I absolutely deny that Zionism is a messianic movement, and that it has the right . . . to use religious language for political purposes. The redemption of the Jewish people for which I strive as a Zionist is not at all identical to the future religious redemption for which I hope."[70] He supported the principle of separation of religion and state all his life, and as a corollary to that he believed that Zionism was not messianic, even after the establishment of the State of Israel. In later years Scholem saw Zionism as the entry of the Jewish people into history and the Jews' assumption of responsibility for their fate—a responsibility that included accountability for their actions. He regarded the realization of Zionism as an event taking place in history and not—like the redemption—at its end.[71]

Regarding his personal relationship to Zionism and the reason for which he chose to move to Palestine, in later years Scholem developed that could be called a "no-alternative Zionism," meaning that he understood his immigration and his action for the realization of the Zionist utopia solely as attempts for which there was never any guarantee of success. However, his motivation was the recognition that there was no option except to try. The first signs of this approach appear in his early notes, some of which are discussed in this chapter. Scholem repeated his position clearly in interviews years after the establishment of the State of Israel. For example, in late 1964 he said:

> If you asked me, when I immigrated to the country, whether I had a political interest in Zionism, I would doubtless have answered: No. If you asked me: Why did you immigrate? My answer would doubtless have been: . . . I immigrated because I thought there was no hope except here. I didn't think we had assurance that this project would succeed here. . . . I was pessimistic with regard to the Jewish cause, but I wanted it to succeed, that is, I wanted and I thought that I had to live in the Land of Israel, in any event, that I had to try. *There is no other way*. If you asked me: Are you interested in building a new society and expecting it? What is more important to you, *the building of a living social organism*, or a political framework? Without doubt I would have answered you in the years of my youth, and I would answer today, that the first matter is the more important.[72]

Scholem's deterministic attitude, signs of which already appeared in his early writings, was clearly expressed only after the establishment of the state. The purpose of this conception was to resolve the conflict that arose within him in the light of the way that the Zionist idea had developed and was implemented in the following decades—as will be discussed in the following chapters—and in view of the Holocaust and its meanings for the Zionist project. "No-alternative Zionism" enabled Scholem to live in the country in spite of the disappointment he felt because of the direction of the historical development of the Zionist movement, which leaned toward nationalistic Revisionist ideas and turned away from the path of Ahad Haam. This disappointment or disillusionment was certainly a natural phenomenon in the process of immigration and adaption to a new life in the Land of Israel, and not something that differentiated Scholem from other members of his generation.

Perhaps to be able to continue calling himself a Zionist and to reconcile himself to the political reality in his home in the Land of Israel and the State of Israel, Scholem needed to bring out the deterministic side of his understanding of Zionist and develop a "no-alternative" position. Similarly, in later years he refrained from passing judgment (either favorable or unfavorable) on Brit Shalom and from commenting on its historical contribution or the correctness of its path in his view, and this is consistent with his withdrawal from political involvement. For example, looking back on the historical role of Brit Shalom in an interview in 1972, he said, "I am not prepared to say today, 'we sinned,' or 'I sinned,' and I am not prepared to say that we were righteous or that we say that this was precisely the path."[73]

In fact, the ideas that were the basis of Brit Shalom's platform appear in Scholem's diaries and notes even before his immigration to the Land of Israel, as well as immediately afterward. The fact that in 1924 he had already noticed the political trends that were relevant for him after 1929 also points to his great political sensitivity, the way the Yishuv was developing, and his involvement in that development. The events of 1929 were a turning point in Scholem's relationship to the Zionist project, but the crisis had arisen before then. Many years later, in another interview, Scholem described the 1920s as "a plastic hour" in the history of the Yishuv and of Zionism, when "perhaps we could have made certain decisions which would have affected our relations with the Arabs."[74] But in accordance with what he hinted at in the passage above, the rise of the Nazis in 1933 and the influence of that on Zionism put an end to the sense of miscarriage: "But after Hitler, there was nothing to be done but to save as many Jews as possible."[75] Brit Shalom ceased to exist in 1933. From then on Scholem withdrew from the political field into the academic world and the private realm—taking part only in more intimate social circles[76] or circles based on academic inquiry.

CHAPTER 3

RELIGIOUS CONTEXTS

It is impossible to speak in the "true" language, just as it is impossible to effectuate the absolutely concrete.

GERSHOM SCHOLEM[1]

The Chain of Kabbalah

As we saw in the first chapter, the idea of ingathering was a very important component in Scholem's development, especially after the outbreak of World War II. In his scholarly work in those years, he tended to regard the anthology as a genre that combined the cultural and national aspects of Judaism. Like Shmuel Yosef Agnon and Hayim Nahman Bialik—whom Scholem regarded as the epitome of ingathering—he wanted his work to build a bridge over the chasm between the generations and to find through research in Kabbalah, the vital marrow of Judaism that continued to exist despite severance from the previous generation, and to convey it to following generations in the way he understood it.

However, in spite of the influence of Agnon and Bialik, as discussed at length in chapter 1, Scholem's conception of ingathering was unique in several ways. His insistence on scholarly, philological accuracy distinguished him from the popular trends that typified the project of ingathering in Bialik's sense and also underlay Scholem's reservations about Buber's approach. Scholem differed from Bialik, though not from Buber, in not insisting on Hebrew as the sole language to be used in the ingathering.

Scholem's attitude toward Hebrew was the opposite of his public position regarding the study of the language in the years prior to his immigration. The subject of Hebrew was a central part of his criticism of Buber and the Jewish youth movement in Germany. Years afterward, Scholem summed up his youthful criticism of that movement: "All of my preaching was that these young people should first of all study Hebrew and something about their past and present instead of being given over to worlds of romantic experience."[2] Although his departure from Germany, which entailed consciously giving up an academic career there, and his immigration to Palestine were accompanied by harsh criticism of the ways of German Jewry and disgust with Germany, throughout these years Scholem continued to publish in the German language. His German translations of Hebrew literature, his literary criticism, and the many articles he published in various venues in Germany—accounting for a considerable part of his publications in these years, in terms of both quantity and quality—all indicate his need to receive recognition from the Jews and Zionists of Germany, the audience of which he was contemptuous before his emigration. This contradiction cannot be resolved, and in my opinion, it is inherent in the inner dialectic that constantly plays out in the soul of a person who uproots him- or herself from one world to be planted in another. The first and most conspicuous difficulty in such a transition, of course, is the change in language. It may be assumed that writing in German was far easier for Scholem in those years than writing in Hebrew, and, therefore, publication in German was more accessible. Another possible reason was the scarcity of Hebrew venues for the publication of scholarship, a situation from which Scholem suffered. "I have no luck with my works," Scholem complained to Buber in 1925, about two years after his immigration. "There is no place here, neither Hebrew nor German, where it is possible to publish scholarly research, neither general surveys nor essays, about Kabbalah."[3] Also at the end of his famous letter to Bialik from July of the same year, Scholem mentions this problematic situation when he complains that his books "are being published in German, since I found no possibility of publishing them in Hebrew."[4] The great majority of people in Scholem's social and professional networks were still in Germany, and the possibilities for him to create a broad social network in the Land of Israel were limited. Hence, his connections with the Jews of Germany remained strong, despite—perhaps because of—his abrupt transfer from the center to the periphery. In this context, we should note the dialectical process by which the margins become central. By definition the center and margins are interdependent; in fact, they define each other. The fact that throughout these years Scholem published in German shows, in my view, that the center of Jewish culture was still in Germany, but it is important to remember that the margins can never become the center without receiving appropriate recognition from the center itself. In other words, the publications in Germany by Scholem, as a scholar from the Land of Israel and a professor at the Hebrew University, played a large role in giving the Land of Israel recognition as a developing Hebrew cultural center—recognition that was a significant part of the process by which the margins became the center. However, these publications were still a concession that Germany was the cultural center at that time, and scholars had to gain recognition there.

In any event, underlying Scholem's need and desire to publish in German lay the great gap between Germany as a center of Jewish culture and the Land of Israel, which still stood at the cultural margins of Europe. Indeed, the mid-1920s, when Scholem wrote the two letters quoted here and his letter to Werner Kraft cited at the beginning of this part of the book, were a period when an independent literary center began to be consolidated in the Land of Israel. In the opinion of Zohar Shavit, the beginning of this process is indicated by Bialik's immigration in 1924 and the transfer of the Devir publishing operation to Palestine. This symbolic event, according to Shavit, put an end to a four-year stasis in cultural life in the Land of Israel and symbolized the beginning of a process that "confirmed the status of the Land of Israel as the leading center of Hebrew culture."[5] The increase in immigration, especially from Germany after 1933, and the gradual elimination of Jewish cultural life in Germany laid the basis for the center in the Land of Israel. Scholem played a part in this process—for example, in his contribution to the establishment in 1924 of the bibliographical journal *Kiryat Sefer*, and in the steady flow of his publications in that venue and others that were established in the Land of Israel at that time. However, in 1925 it still seemed to Scholem that in the Holy Land he was meeting with the "primitive, true (not to say original) stupidity of Jews," as expressed in the level of the Hebrew-speaking intellectuals in his surroundings: "In this apocalyptic country, indeed only here, it is possible to encounter *Gartenlaube* figures in Hebrew, a most exciting phenomenon. One can also meet the last of the kabbalists here."[6]

The question of Scholem's relations—or, to be precise, lack of relations—with the kabbalists of his time and the reasons for his attitude toward them has already been discussed by other scholars.[7] For the present discussion, what is important is the estrangement that Scholem expresses toward the kabbalists of his generation. The source of this feeling lies in his view that the tradition of the religious kabbalist was parallel to that of the academic scholar of Kabbalah: parallel and never meeting. Scholem takes the kabbalist to be the opposite—like a photographic negative—of the academic scholar, who belongs to a traditional system:

> The Kabbalist himself lives entirely in his world of cryptic secret knowledge. He knowingly and joyously identifies himself with the long chain of Kabbalist tradition and views it from within. As a result he acquires the privilege of participating directly in those spiritual values of Kabbalah, which still have relevance to his own generation. Yet, at the same time, he necessarily relinquishes many of the possibilities of dispassionate inquiry which the scholar cannot relinquish without violence to his innermost self. He lives within the realm of Kabbalah, but even that only to an

> extremely limited degree. . . . Thus, in the opinion and belief of the Kabbalist, Kabbalah (which literally means "tradition") is the tradition that was first received in the days of the creation, concerning matters divine and human and which was entrusted to Adam or, according to others, to Moses, the man of God. A sense of history and historical criticism were never among the strong points of the mystic sages.[8]

Here Scholem depicts the kabbalist as someone closed within a world possessing a chain of kabbalistic tradition—in other words, the canon—of its own, with laws of its own that he must obey without question. For that reason his outlook is uncritical and lacks historical perspective. In contrast to the kabbalist, Scholem presents the man of science—himself. According to Scholem, the kabbalist typically has a narrow vision that seeks unity in the world of phenomena. In contrast, the task of the man of science is to ask questions and emphasize the multiplicity of phenomena and the dynamic of the mystical tradition. Thus, Scholem compares the passivity of reception to the activism of research. The contempt that he expressed for the local intellectual life emphasizes the fact that in his opinion he had moved from the center to the margins, even if they were only at the beginning of the process of cultural development and still on the way to become an independent center. Indeed, Scholem's awareness that he had moved to the periphery was bound up with his utopian and Zionist aspiration to make the margins into a center.

As for the kabbalists themselves, in the opinion of Boaz Huss, the fact that Scholem did not appreciate Kabbalah as it had been interpreted by the kabbalists of his time derived from his rejection, in the spirit of the basic assumptions of modern scholarship in Kabbalah, of the importance of mysticism within the religious realm. Huss argues that Scholem's view emerged within the framework of modernistic, Zionist, and Orientalist discourse.[9] Thus, according to Huss, Scholem regarded academic scholarship in Kabbalah as an extension of the Jewish mystical spirit in its desire "to reach the metaphysical and mystical foundations of the Kabbalah through the use of philological and historical methods."[10] Huss believes that this approach is well represented in Scholem's famous letter to Salman Schocken of October 29, 1937:

> The mountain itself—the things themselves—does not need a key at all; it is only the misty wall of history (*Historie*) that surrounds it that must be penetrated. To penetrate it—that is the task I have set for myself. Would I remain stuck in the mist, suffering a professorial death (Tod in der Professur), so to speak? Yet even if it demands sacrifices, the compelling need for a critique of history and for historical criticism cannot be provided in any other way.

> It may, of course, be that fundamentally history (*Geschichte*) is no more than an illusion. However, without this illusion it is impossible to penetrate through temporal reality to the essence of the things themselves. Through the unique perspective of philological criticism, there has been reflected to contemporary man for the first time, in the neatest possible way, that mystical totality of Truth (*das Systems*) whose existence disappears specifically because of its being thrust upon historical time.
>
> My work is sustained today, as it was at the very beginning of my path, by the virtue of this paradox, and in anticipation of being answered from the mountain, through that slight, almost invisible motion of history (*Historie*) allowing the truth to break through from what is called development.[11]

These words show clearly that the ultimate goal of research in Kabbalah is of metaphysical or religious value. But in my view Scholem is not referring to a system meant to add a layer to the religious tradition or to replace or cancel it, but rather to a parallel tradition. In opposition to the long chain of the Kabbalistic tradition, in which the kabbalist lives, it is possible to present a chain of Kabbalah to which Scholem belongs—this is the Zionist literary canon discussed extensively above, and the effort to determine its guiding principles is made in the framework of the ingathering project. In this spirit we may also understand Scholem's unequivocal statement in his letter to Schocken quoted above that "the compelling need for a critique of history and for historical criticism cannot be provided in any other way." Like any tradition, this one has strict laws regarding the way it is possible to understand the world. Its laws or tools for examining the past, which characterized the academic tradition to which Scholem belonged, were the absolute opposite of those of the kabbalists, and the sources of authority that gave validity to the laws that guided the paths of these two traditions were also diametrically opposed. If—according to Scholem—for the kabbalists the source of this authority is the reception of Torah, for the researcher the source of authority is in historical research whose ancestry is the *Wissenschaft des Judentums*. However, the goal of the academic scholar's work, like that of the kabbalist, is to return to the primal and authentic understanding of the origins of things. Thus in 1938 Scholem described his work as an effort "to raise up again, from the remnants of the ruins that cover the field of our work, the image of the original structure of Hebrew mysticism and to determine its transformations and metamorphoses."[12] In the light of these words, in my opinion one should not see the historiography and research in Kabbalah according to Scholem as the secular heir of the kabbalistic tradition itself, as suggested by Huss.[13] As I understand Scholem's words, the relationship between the two worlds is that between two parallel traditions that neither meet nor touch each other. In this manner one can also explain Scholem's lack of interest in Kabbalah of his time and the small importance he attributed to it and to the circles of kabbalists in Jerusalem during the years following his immigration. Scholem's words explain also the clear boundary he drew publicly between science and religion in the concluding paragraph of his major book on the Kabblah, published in 1941: "To speak of the mystical course which, in the great cataclysm now stirring the Jewish people more deeply than in the entire history of the Exile, destiny may still have in store for us—and I for one believe that there is such a course—is the task of prophets, not of professors."[14]

However, at the same time it would be an error to see Scholem as an entirely secular person, from whose heart God and faith were distant. As the letter to Schocken cited above shows, Scholem did believe in a hidden truth behind the visible world of phenomena, which is connected to it and guides political and moral behavior in it. However, for Scholem, unlike the various religious streams in Judaism, this religious sentiment was fundamentally subjective and not submissive or bound to any religious framework, tradition, or authority. He frequently called this sentiment religious anarchy, and one may see it as the essential characteristic of Scholem's position with regard to religion and as the point at which the political and religious planes of his thinking meet. An example that probably demonstrates Scholem's anarchical religiosity in the most appropriate way for the present discussion is his attitude toward a religious circle to which he did not belong, though he was closely connected with it and its members. This circle, which was also composed of German speakers in the Yishuv, was called Ha'Ol (the yoke).

Ha'Ol Circle: Religious Anarchism

Very little is known about the short-lived Yoke circle and its meetings. However, it is known that the goal of this circle was to discuss current religious issues. The scholarship of Paul Mendes-Flohr on the circle shows that it was established by Judah Leib Magnes and Martin Buber in the spring of 1939, and its regular members included Yitzhak Fritz Baer, Shmuel Hugo Bergmann, Julius Guttmann, and Akiva Ernst Simon.[15] Except for some isolated references in Magnes's notebooks and two letters from Magnes and Buber to Mahatma Gandhi, the central remaining testimony about the meetings of the circle are the minutes of a meeting that took place on July 13, 1939, in Magnes's home.[16] Scholem was invited to make some opening remarks as a guest at this meeting, which mainly dealt with the complex meaning of Torah for the current generation.[17] He was somewhat apprehensive about the meeting, so he prepared himself well in advance by reading background material on the subject. When he arrived at the meeting, he discovered that his prior preparation had been unnecessary, and that he could manage very well without the scholarly background, but he was very cautious in expressing his positions. A large audience attended this meeting, and he was apprehensive that the listeners take him as a kind of new theologian, which could create misunderstanding and anger in many of them. However, this fear proved to be unwarranted: "I thought I would arouse opposition—but that was not the case. Everyone fell upon me with questions."[18] In his diary Scholem noted that the remarks of Guttmann, Baer, Simon, Buber, and Magnes stood out, though for him they "were not good for the cause."[19] The minutes of the meeting contain an abstract of Scholem's opening remarks and the comments of his friends and colleagues. Though partial and written in the laconic style characteristic of such abstracts, it is an important and highly interesting document for understanding Scholem's position on religion in those years and the way he understood the role of religion within Zionism, against the background of the opinions of his friends and colleagues.

Central to Scholem's introductory remarks about the meaning of Torah was the concept of commentary. In Scholem's opinion, the word "Torah" had two different meanings: one was "designation of a path," and the other was "transmission of something," or tradition. Torah also assumes the existence of a supreme authority and stands between it and humanity. Therefore, there can be no Torah without commentary on Torah—or, in Scholem's words, "there is no written Torah without the oral Torah." In fact, in his opinion, the true Torah cannot be attained at all, nor can it be expressed. The only thing that can be communicated is commentary: "Were we to desire to restrict the Torah to the Torah transmitted in writing, we would not be able to read even the Pentateuch but only the Ten Commandments. It follows that even the Torah (i.e., Scripture) is already Oral Torah. The Torah is understandable only as Oral Torah, only through its relativization. In itself it is the perfect Torah without a blemish, and only through its mediation, the Oral Torah, is it rendered intelligible."[20] This dialectical character of Torah makes the understanding of it into a dialogue, a series of questions and answers that inevitably is dynamic and flexible and formed according to the generation that interprets Torah. In accordance with this understanding, which is parallel to the orthodox tradition of commentary, one must wait for an authoritative tradition of commentary that is appropriate for the present generation: "We must therefore wait for *our* own Oral Torah, which will have to be binding for us, leaving no room for free, non-authoritative decision." Scholem concludes: "There is no Torah without revelation (*matan Torah*), and there is no Torah without heteronomy, and there is no Torah without an authoritative tradition."[21]

As noted above, in his diary Scholem wrote that his words were received enthusiastically by the audience, but they also met with criticism from members of the Yoke circle, and the minutes note the various points of criticism voiced by the participants in the discussion. Guttmann argued that "Scholem's position leads to utter subjectivism" and that there was no mention of the content of the Oral Torah in his talk, content that must be sought. Simon objected to the idea of the heteronomy of Torah. In his opinion one must also depend on the interpretive autonomy of every single person, which is based on ethics. Baer objected to the theological dimension of Scholem's talk, arguing that Torah demanded "the creation of a social order that is in consonance with the Hebrew [conception of] justice." Buber emphasized the concept of revelation in this context and a person's ability to awaken revelation by his actions. Finally, Magnes objected that in fact Scholem denied Torah when he denied any religious authority: "According to the accepted understanding, the Oral Torah is a fence around the Torah [that is, the written Torah and its mitzvot]; according to Scholem it is liberation from the Written Torah. This is the position of the Gospels. This position constitutes negation of the Torah."[22] Scholem responded to this criticism with the following words:

> To a known degree we are all anarchists. But our anarchism is *transitional*, for we are the living example that this [our anarchism] does not remove us from Judaism. We are not a generation without mitzvot, but our mitzvot are without authority. I do not have a feeling of inferiority toward those who observe [the Law]. We are no less legitimate than our forefathers; they merely had a clearer text. Perhaps we are anarchists, but we oppose anarchy . . . I believe in God, this is the basis of my life and faith. All the rest [of Judaism] is in doubt and open to debate.[23]

This is the first expression of Scholem's concept of religious anarchy, to which he would return on various occasions throughout his life. The essence of this anarchism is the rejection of the existing religious authorities coupled with belief in the existence of God. To phrase this in the terms that Scholem used here, it is belief in pure Torah—as it is—but not in the Oral Torah, or the authority of the existing commentary. Scholem repeated this principle many times in conversations and interviews.[24] Important for the present discussion is the fact that at this point, in the summer of 1939, one can detect a certain turning point in Scholem's political and religious views that is connected with the idea of anarchism. Scholem did not use the term "anarchism" for the first time in his speech to the Yoke circle. Even in his early diaries, Scholem—more than a little influenced by his brother Werner—frequently expressed revolutionary political ideas in the spirit of socialism and anarchism. During his youth in Germany,

Scholem used "anarchism" to describe his understanding of the correct path for the political implementation of Zionism.[25] In his memoirs he speaks of the influence of Zionist theories from the school of Leo Tolstoy and Gustav Landauer in his early years: "The social and ethical views of anarchists like Tolstoy and Landauer were of no little importance in the work of influential groups, who came from Russia and German-speaking countries, in creating a new life in the Land of Israel. My own development also tended clearly in that direction, in the years under discussion here, although the possibility of setting up an anarchist society appeared more and more dubious to me."[26]

When Scholem saw and understood that these radical doctrines could not survive the test of reality and could not be implemented in the Land of Israel in the way he had advocated in his youth, he internalized the concept of anarchy, as reflected in Scholem's words at the meeting organized by the Yoke circle. When he saw that Zionism was being fulfilled in a materialistic, institutional, and nationalist manner, which depended on the great powers and ignored the needs of the Arabs of the land, he abandoned his identification with anarchism as a political doctrine, which had taken shape within him during World War I, and transferred the concept of anarchism to the personal realm—the realm of inner religious faith. Most likely this process was connected to the political developments of the late 1920s and the early 1930s, which were discussed above and will be discussed further below, and to his withdrawal from all political activity after the dissolving of Brit Shalom. Perhaps his identification of Zionism as a movement that had shifted to the side of the victors instead of clinging to the idea of revolution by the weak and oppressed lay behind the change in his application of the concept of anarchism. The minutes of the meeting discussed here is the first expression of that change, and it could be an expression or the result of Scholem's prolonged disappointment with the way Zionism was being actualized. In contrast to the members of the Yoke circle, whose religious position led them to call for activism,[27] Scholem felt that what was needed was not political activism but rather withdrawal from political activity to the individual, private religious plane. This was also the point that differentiated Scholem from the members of the circle, and perhaps for that reason he was also exposed to criticism by most of them. The fact that Scholem did not join the Ihud Association—which was established in the summer of 1942, three years after this meeting, and whose mainstays were Magnes, Simon, and Buber—strengthens this interpretation.[28]

The impression the meeting made on Scholem was ambiguous. In his diary he summed up his interaction with the audience: "Because the others did not bring ideas of their own but were yearning for 'Torah,' I left there with a heavy feeling that I had stood on the wrong pedestal."[29] What disturbed Scholem during his lecture, as he wrote in his diary, was the expectation that he felt in the audience that he should be the bearer of a certain religious message, whereas his intention was to prompt them to think for themselves. This feeling placed him in an uncomfortable position in his own eyes, and one may assume that he felt he had been expected to stand in the shoes of a prophet, a role that he rejected frequently in his life and that was connected in his mind to the figure of Buber, whom, as already discussed, he criticized harshly.[30]

Hence, Scholem left the meeting with a certain feeling of a missed opportunity, because he sensed that he had not succeeded in communicating his ideas to the other participants, and that his thoughts had not received the response he hoped for. His disappointment can be understood against the background of the central place that religious anarchism had in his life, which distinguished him from Jewish secularism and humanism like that of Ahad Haam.[31] In fact, for Scholem, the idea of religious anarchism involved important religious and theological questions that touched on religious authority, Torah and its interpretations, and God and his revelation—all of which were overshadowed by the great paradox of the effort to express in words and identify in historical reality what actually cannot be expressed and stands beyond history.[32] The effort to transmit that which cannot be conveyed from generation to generation is central to this process in that it "renders the word of God applicable in time."[33] Here we find the complexity of the relationship between Torah and Oral Torah, between the idea and its interpretation, between God and the world, and between the signified and its signifier in the Hebrew language. At this point the three strata in Scholem's life—the cultural, political, and religious—come together.

Concluding Remarks

Discussing each of these three strata in Scholem's life before the Holocaust separately, as I have done here, is essentially an artificial constraint. The cultural, political, and religious aspects of his life were so interwoven that it is impossible to discuss them without thinking about how they are bound to one another and the dynamic relationship among them, as reflected in Scholem's letters and his relations with people around him. A model may help explain this dynamic relationship.

The model is an equilateral triangle, and the sides of the triangle move counterclockwise. The side extending from religion to culture is labeled ingathering because that is how Scholem translated terms that belonged to the world of religion into the secular, cultural world to create a new tradition. The side extending from culture to politics is labeled ethics to represent the ideas behind

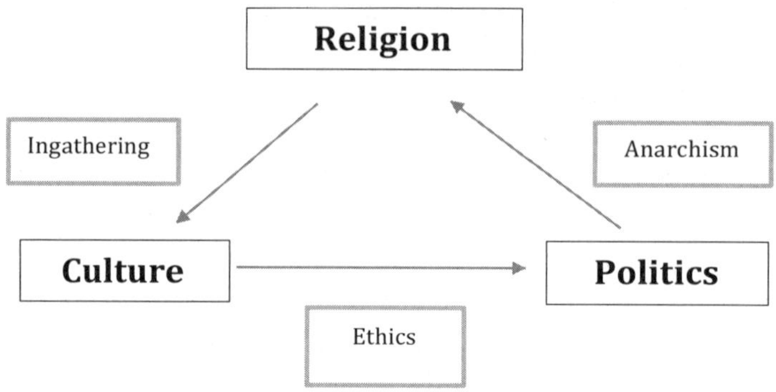

Brit Shalom—the ethical and social ideas anchored in Hebrew culture that were translated into political action. The third side, leading from politics back to religion, is labeled anarchism.

Each side of the triangle is linked to the others. Thus, for example, the side labeled anarchism expresses, on the one hand, the process of internalization that took place in Scholem's political worldview, which included withdrawal from the political realm to the religious, and on the other hand, the central way in which the political and religious dimensions in his life became connected at that time. The area formed by the triangle is utopia—Scholem's Zionist dream, which was bounded by the sides of the triangle.

To construct a complete model, we would need to add another element that would represent the dynamism that nourished the tension in each side of the triangle and among the sides and drives their movement. This movement keeps the triangle from imploding and makes it possible for utopia to exist. The missing element is the Hebrew language, whose existence, according to Scholem, is the condition for the existence of Judaism and Zionism.

The triangle and the tension among its components are what create the utopia, bound it, and make its existence possible. Scholem's radical position with regard to Zionism, which demanded all or nothing with respect to the realization of its utopia,[34] requires adding to the model a layer expressing its internal contradiction. Like any utopia, Scholem's could not be realized without damaging its delicate tissue. The various elements in it cannot withstand the radical demand that exists at the moment of actualization. In other words, the effort to actualize Zionism demanded compromise, which was opposed to Scholem's radical demands. Thus, the seed of its self-destruction was inherent in the moment of the utopia's realization. As long as the Land of Israel was a utopian center and a political periphery, Scholem could hold Zionist positions. But the moment it became a political center, the utopia ceased to exist. Perhaps this dynamic, among other things, is what caused disappointment for Scholem, disappointment that would appear to be inevitable.[35]

An additional element that might be inherent in Scholem's utopia was the idea of the succession of generations and continuity in Judaism. In his eyes, the threat to the existence of this continuity increased as long as the implementation and political actualization of Zionism continued and solidified. A later expression of this utopian aspiration that is also linked to the three apexes of the triangle in the model can be seen in remarks that Scholem made at the ceremony to mark the thirtieth anniversary of the establishment of the Institute for Jewish Studies at Hanukkah, 5715 (1955): "If only the love of the Jewish people and the heritage of its past might not be less than love of the Land of Israel; and if we have become free people in our land, let us bind ourselves with thick cords to love and understanding of the chain of generations, and let us not forget the vision of the defeated in the hour that we have become victors."[36] These words were spoken after the establishment of the State of Israel, one of the peak moments in the process of the realization and victory of Zionism. The establishment of the Jewish center in the Land of Israel took place in the shadow of the historical developments of the 1930s and 1940s, which brought about the dramatic and violent end of the center of Jewish culture in Germany. Such an end could not have been anticipated by the builders of Zionism, including Scholem, in the 1920s and 1930s, when they were trying to bring their utopia to life as they established a new center from the margins in the Land of Israel.

PART II

THE UNPARALLELED CATASTROPHE

I am very skeptical whether we indeed wish to bind ourselves, as people proclaim from every hill and mountaintop, to the memories of the millions who were killed in Poland and Lithuania, etc. I am very doubtful as to whether this is possible without directly confronting the great problematic of our life. We must confront the reality which forces us to interpret an unparalleled catastrophe. We do not know what answers we can give, but there is no way to escape the question.

GERSHOM SCHOLEM, "MEMORY AND UTOPIA IN JEWISH HISTORY"

DESPAIR (1939–1948)

CHATER 4

RESPONSES TO THE HOLOCAUST

Once he said to me: Hitler came and mixed up all of Zionism.

JOSEPH WEISS, "DIVREI SHALOM"[1]

Zionism and Zion after the Holocaust

The existence and role of the Jewish settlement in the Land of Israel in relation to the Holocaust and the degree of the Yishuv's awareness of what was happening in Europe between 1938 and 1945 have been widely studied. Today 1942 is usually seen as the turning point with regard to the relation of the Yishuv to the destruction that was occurring at the time.[2] From the beginning of World War II to this turning point, information arriving about the murder of multitudes of Jews in Europe was limited to rumors whose truth could be doubted, especially in the light of their dreadfulness. Moreover, until that time the existence of the Yishuv was threatened by the Nazi army under the command of Field Marshal Erwin Rommel, which was advancing eastward in North Africa and had reached the borders of Egypt, distracting the Yishuv from more distant troubles.[3] Rommel's defeat at the end of October 1942, in the second battle of El Alamein, removed the threat and also the terrible fear that had gripped the Yishuv. This defeat, along with the defeat of the Nazis in Stalingrad, indicated the beginning of the shift in the tide of war in favor of the Allies and was a harbinger of the end of Nazi Germany.

In tandem with these events, the partial information that had reached the Land of Israel until then became, at the end of 1942, incontrovertible proof that the systematic and organized destruction of the Jews was taking place in Europe. The testimony of sixty-nine citizens of Mandatory Palestine, who were returned from Europe to Palestine in November as part of an exchange agreement between the Allies and the Nazis, and who had been witnesses to events in Europe, shocked the Yishuv deeply and was another step toward realization of the dimensions of the Holocaust. Shortly after the return of the citizens, the Jewish Agency for Palestine published an official announcement in *Haaretz* confirming the horrible news. In mid-December 1942, the international media published a joint official statement from the Allies that condemned the destruction of the Jews of Europe by the Nazis.[4] As information continued to arrive from the areas conquered by the Nazis, which received considerable space in the daily press, the Yishuv began the slow process of absorbing the bitter truth.

As part of the effort to cope with the events, November 30 to December 2, 1942, was declared a three-day mourning period in the Yishuv, to include fasting and protests. Calls for action were voiced, and the possible actions by the leadership were discussed. Throughout 1943, additional days of mourning and assemblies were declared, but the first three days of mourning were the central and most important ones, and Dina Porat regards them as the watershed for the Yishuv between the first three years of the war, a period characterized by lack of full awareness of the events, and the last three years.[5] These last three years were marked by tension between what the Yishuv and its leaders did and expectations for them to try to rescue the Jews of Europe, and also by the Yishuv's helplessness, given its position in the international arena. In addition, there was tension between awareness of the present horrors, which—since most of the people in the Yishuv had relatives in Europe—personally affected the Jews in Palestine, and their physical distance from the events combined with their psychological need to continue with the routines of daily life. People responded in many ways to these tensions. Some of the responses were public expressions of the distress of the Yishuv, and some were efforts to understand and analyze the tensions and to explain, either critically or defensively, why the Jewish residents of Palestine continued their ordinary patterns of life, at least superficially. Along with these efforts one also finds both expressions of despair and strong feelings of guilt about failing to realize earlier the seriousness of the situation and calls for public action on a worldwide scale.[6]

Among the voices heard in the Yishuv at that time, the voice of a small group of intellectuals stood out. The group was called Al-Domi (No to silence), and it was formed when the harsh news arrived at the end of 1942. This circle—whose members included the author Rabbi Binyamin, the psychiatrist Fishel Shneerson, Joseph Klausner, Shmuel Hugo Bergmann, Judah Leib Magnes, Martin Buber, and Ben-Zion Dinur—held an assembly and observed days of mourning, initiated various information campaigns, and called for acts of rescue by the Yishuv. The members of the group wished "to impress upon the leadership and the public at large the need to enter into intense rescue operations" and "to reinforce 'a positive climate for rescue' that would remain constant and prevent the Yishuv, world Jewry, and intellectuals in the free world from sinking into despair and a sense of powerlessness."[7] With its activities, the group tried to break the silence and paralysis that had gripped the Yishuv, which—in the opinion of the group's members—was very dangerous.

Despite their intentions, the members' opinions and actions went largely unnoticed, and they did not succeed in spurring the Yishuv to take action on a significant scale. In fact, most of their initiatives were never implemented.[8] After failing to influence the Yishuv, they restricted their activities to small meetings, in which the members conversed and discussed the meaning and possible consequences of the Holocaust. The course of at least one of these discussions, indirectly connected to Scholem, was documented by Dinur.

In late 1942 or early 1943 several members of Al-Domi met to discuss various responses to the dire reports that had recently reached the ears of the Yishuv. Dinur made notes of the contents of the meeting, which he presented in a speech given at the Teachers' Seminary in Jerusalem and published.[9] At the meeting five men spoke, whom Dinur did not mention by name but described by their professions. They were the "philosopher" (Buber), the "hasid" (Shneerson), the "historian" (Dinur), the "author" (Yitzhak Yatziv), and the "soldier" (Ben-Zion Yisraeli).[10]

When his turn came, Dinur emphasized the public's feeling of guilt about the failure of Zionism to understand the historical events preceding the Holocaust and anticipating it: "The very fact that this dreadful Holocaust came down upon us so suddenly that we were confused and bewildered, not knowing whence help would come, as though we did not expect it and were not afraid of it—therein lies a severe and dreadful indictment of us all, of the people, of the generation, and of every single one of us. We sinned, we are guilty, we have trespassed against the people, against mankind, against God. Our first and sacred duty of life, of those who remain alive, is: to give an accounting of our guilt."[11] The Holocaust, according to Dinur, was not actually sudden or unexpected. In fact, there had been many warning signs, such as the pogroms in Eastern Europe and the violence directed against the Jews from time immemorial—especially the antisemitic laws of Nazi Germany. Although "prophetic seers" had arisen within the Zionist camp, "people with open eyes, courageous hearts, and soaring vision"[12] who had warned against the imminent catastrophe, the Zionist movement was guilty of not heeding them, not dealing with reality, and ignoring its historical duty to take immediate action to get the Jews out of Europe and bring them to the Land of Israel, especially when the political conditions in Palestine still made that possible. The Zionists of the Yishuv had abandoned the path of Theodor Herzl, and people were working for their own good alone.[13]

The sin of the Zionist movement was its pride and the self-assurance of the present generation, "the generation of the *magshimim* [those who carry out the task]," which saw itself as the generation heralding the advent of redemption and which, being so focused on itself, wanted to enjoy the virtues and advantages of that status without accepting the responsibility bound up with the status. Thus, ironically and tragically, this was also the punishment of the generation of revival: "Is there any punishment harsher or crueler for this generation than to make it drink to the full of the cup of destruction and extinction?"[14] In conclusion, Dinur emphasized the need to do everything possible to save the Jews of Europe.

As noted above, shortly after writing down the contents of the meeting, Dinur published the written version. It appeared in a pamphlet titled "Our Fate and Our War: Five Voices from the Day of Mourning and Warning," which was published in March 1943.[15] One of the addresses to which the pamphlet was sent was 28 Abarbanel Street, the home of Dinur's friend Scholem. Scholem read the pamphlet carefully and responded to it in a letter that so far is one of his few known direct responses to the Holocaust as it was happening:

> April 1, 1943
>
> My friend Mr. Dinaburg,[16]
>
> I have read the pamphlet you sent me with great interest, and I even tried to follow the thoughts of those speakers, whose faces seemed almost familiar to me. And I will not conceal from you the feeling that takes hold of me when I read these words: How much we do *not* have the power or the words to respond. . . . But there is no wonder about it: At the time of the catastrophe there are no teachings (*ein torah*), and words were given only to those who could observe from a certain distance, and the one standing at the eye of the storm must always be silent. This is my feeling, although I always wonder how my friends could express what the mouth could not utter and the ear could not hear. But we are all *inside* the calamity (*betokh hamapolet*) and we do not have the required mental distance (*hamerchak hanafshi hadarush*), and maybe this is what contributes to the unhuman appearance of the words of some of the speakers (*lefartzufam habilti humani shel kamah medivrei hapotchim*). I could *understand* the philosopher and maybe also the historian, although I cannot agree with his assessment of the Zionist movement as if it had foreseen the *catastrophe*—this does not seem to me compatible with our experience through the last thirty years. *Not one* of the Zionist prophets and none of us who listened to them . . . could have imagined *such* a role for the *Rebirth* [underlined twice instead of just once] Movement (tenu'at hatchiyah). No, my dear—not you nor I, not Herzl nor [Max] Nordau, saw the Jewish crisis in its true light, and we are not to be blamed for it, since nobody thought of such an eruption of evil (*sitra achra*). And what would have been the benefit of such thought—*such* a vision would have taken our breath away, and I am afraid it would

have paralyzed instead of encouraging us. And this is actually the whole tragedy: Zionism, which did not dream of such an elimination of the Diaspora, is not at all an answer to the events. It *was* an answer to events of a completely different nature and character, and why should we pretend now to be wiser and richer than we actually were? Excuse me if I tell you that in my opinion the historian will have to speak in a different way in the future, and his account will have to be *even* much more *desperate* than your account. And for such an account we will have to prepare ourselves.

Yours, Gershom Scholem[17]

Scholem's strong opposition to Dinur's pamphlet is extremely important for understanding his attitude toward the Holocaust as it was perceived in the Yishuv at that time, and on how that attitude compared to the various responses of the Yishuv. In his letter Scholem expresses two objections to the pamphlet that Dinur published. The first is to its very existence of the pamphlet and to making any statement at such a tragic time. According to Scholem, speaking and reflecting about such a catastrophic and unprecedented event can take place only from a distance, with a certain historical perspective, and a contemporary who experiences events personally that are inconceivable and inexpressible cannot evaluate them and therefore should remain silent.

Scholem's second objection is to Dinur's words themselves—or, to be precise, to Dinur's charge that the Jewish people and the Zionist movement did not heed the warnings of certain leaders of the movement, who had predicted the imminent catastrophe.[18] Scholem firmly rejects this charge, saying that in his opinion none of the founders of Zionism could have predicted such a radical turn of events. The generation of rebirth—as noted above, Scholem underlined "rebirth" twice, pointing out the irony of the word's meaning in its new historical context—was destined to assume a role other than that of a small group of survivors who will bring the destroyed nation back to life. Furthermore, not only could none of the theoreticians of Zionism or the shapers of the movement have predicted the disaster, but any prophecy of such a shocking fate could have weakened the Zionists' creative powers. Here, according to Scholem, lies the root of the true tragedy of the Zionist movement in view of the Holocaust: Zionism, which he believed had been established to respond to other problems in a different historical situation—specifically, the founding of a Jewish spiritual center in the Land of Israel, which would assure the eternal existence of Judaism—could not be a response to the present events, whose horror (the physical destruction of the Jewry of the Diaspora by the Nazis) is unimaginable. The conclusion to which Scholem's letter to Dinur leads is that the destruction of the Jews of Europe as a historical event ineluctably led the entire Zionist project into a trap: not only could Zionism not have anticipated the event, but in retrospect it could never have been an answer to this new reality. Thus, it lost its power and relevancy as a basis for the spiritual rebirth of the Jewish people and as a political solution to the Jewish question. In such a trap, the only thing left to do is keep silent.[19]

In principle, Scholem's position, as expressed here, stands in opposition to that of the vast majority of Jews in the Yishuv—who, like Dinur, understood and interpreted the Holocaust as proof of the correctness of the Zionist way. In this context, Yechiam Weitz emphasizes that "it was a common unequivocal feeling throughout the Yishuv, that the victory of Zionism was the central moral of the Holocaust."[20] At the same time, despair and loss of confidence in the path and goals of the Zionist movement were also expressed by some people of the Yishuv, especially in the period central to the discussion here, when revelation of the magnitude of the Holocaust aroused great psychological turmoil and a sense of crisis.[21]

However, unlike others who were disappointed by the passivity with which the Yishuv responded to the destruction and who regarded this as a contradiction of the Zionist aspiration to provide an answer to the Jewish question, Scholem despaired at a much deeper level—he reacted to the bitter and unavoidable fate of Zionism itself, as seen in retrospect, in the tragic turn of history for the Jewish people. As noted in an earlier chapter, Scholem's despair about the realization of the Zionist utopia began even before his immigration. The events of 1929 were a turning point in his attitude toward the Zionist enterprise, and after that he withdrew from all political engagement, adopting a deterministic attitude toward the goal of Zionism. As seen in the letter to Dinur, Scholem's deterministic position grew stronger as the magnitude of the Holocaust grew clearer, and it was expressed in his view that silence was the most appropriate response. His feelings about the place of Zionism in the shadow of the Holocaust also appear in a diary entry written about three months before the letter to Dinur. This entry, one of the few in which Scholem refers to the destruction of the Jews of Europe, contains harsh criticism of the Zionist movement, the way in which the Zionist idea was realized, and the Yishuv:

> Land of Israel:
>
> January 9, 1943
>
> In Europe my people is perishing physically, and if something will remain of it, mentally—the people, whose true sad fate I actually *came here* to share. I came, because I could not bear the notion that we did not *try* to save it, and thought: [even] if [it] fails, you should not [try to] slip out of it. Now we are dwelling here in a Zion

which is not one: 500,000 people (Jews)—so one must perhaps say—and of them maybe 50,000 of those we were thinking about. The rest are lies and deceptions (*Lug und Trug*)—and here is also *the* crucial point that these lies and deceptions "run" the "building" on a *large* scale and attained it, if this *overnight shelter in the homeland* (*Nachtasyl in der Heimat*) for a people that is being slaughtered in the meantime, is an *achievement* at all. And the frenzy from trembling continues.[22]

This diary entry, whose style shows that Scholem was addressing himself, does not display the linguistic clarity and coherence in content that one finds in Scholem's finished essays or letters. However, the entry is quite informative about his attitude toward Zionism and the leadership of the Yishuv at the time. The first important point in this entry is the motivations for Scholem's immigration to the Land of Israel, as he understood them at the time. At the moment of writing the entry Scholem saw his immigration as taking part in the tragic fate of the Jewish people, as an effort to rescue something that he does not name specifically, but that may be assumed to be Jewish culture, and to preserve it by the establishment of a spiritual center in the Land of Israel according to the vision of Ahad Haam. Scholem's deterministic outlook—what I called "no-alternative Zionism" above—is evident in what follows in the diary entry. However, this personal solution to dealing with the goal of Zionism did not change the difficult problem posed, in his opinion, by political Zionism, after it emphasized the immigration of Jews and not the Jewish cultural character of the Jewry of the Land of Israel. Only 10 percent of the Jews in Palestine were the type of people he imagined in his vision of Zionist, and "the rest are lies and deceptions." It follows that this majority (the "lies and deceptions") built up the land, did everything that had been done up to that time, and shaped the spirit of political Zionism in its image and character. Hence, what had been built was actually neither a true home nor a homeland for the Jewish people, with the spiritual significance that would entail, but rather an "overnight shelter in the homeland." As if that were not enough of a problem, this shelter has now become entirely worthless, since it was intended for a people that has already been murdered and no longer exists. Scholem's name for Palestine contains much bitter irony regarding the image of the Yishuv and the Zionist leadership in those years, because an overnight shelter is what Nordau famously called Uganda when the Sixth Zionist Congress supported Herzl's controversial plan in the summer of 1903, in the wake of the pogroms of Kishinev, to establish a Jewish homeland in the African country. Nordau used this name to emphasize the temporary nature of Uganda as an interim solution, which would meet the Zionist leadership's obligation to save Jews wherever they were from the dangers threatening them and as a station for Zionists on the way to the Land of Israel.[23] In the diary entry Scholem also refers to immigration as an effort at rescue, but given recent events, the goal of attempted rescue receives an additional, ironical, meaning. In place of the fear that Uganda would become a final destination rather than an interim one and lead to the loss of Zion, which aroused such powerful opposition to Herzl's plan, here the final goal—Zion itself—has become only a Jewish territory with no spiritual content, merely an "overnight shelter in the homeland," and the ultimate purpose has been lost. Thus under the historical circumstances Zion had become a Uganda in the Land of Israel or, in Ahad Haam's words, not a "Jewish State" but a "State of Jews."[24] These words bear witness to Scholem's great disappointment and despair, not only because the Yishuv was not the achievement of the Zionist vision of a Jewish center in the Land of Israel, so that the homeland had lost its meaning as such, but also because the Jewish people, who were supposed to arrive at a later stage of the establishment of Zionism in the Land of Israel, had already been murdered and no longer existed. Zion was left a center with no periphery, and thus deprived of its validity as a center.

The substance of Scholem's critique of the Yishuv during the war and the reason for his viewing it as "lies and deceptions" will be discussed at length in the following pages. Important for the discussion at this point is the impression left in the reader's heart that the words that Scholem wrote in his diary expressed his consciousness of a personal crisis. Indeed, in many places in his diary one finds expressions of a steadily worsening mental state during the war years. The reader of these passages cannot ignore the centrality of comments about his inability to work, his difficulties in forming connections with his friends and other people around him, and a great feeling of isolation. Thus, for example, at the beginning of the passage quoted above from January 9, 1943, he wrote about the difficulties he encountered because of his condition while beginning to write a book about Sabbateanism,[25] and about his existential state: "Now I see for the first time, in true and absolute fashion, that my youth, in which I believed until now in such a paradoxical way, is over. This is something that it's hard for me to grasp. My youth has ended, but I can't grasp the other life. The situation has gone so far that I am no longer able to read in a concentrated way: this is the most serious symptom in me."[26]

A conspicuous public expression of Scholem's psychological state at that time was his article on Jewish studies that was published in *Luach Haaretz*, the annual literary supplement of *Haaretz*, in 1944 and has been much discussed by various scholars. Here I propose to read it as reflecting Scholem's psychological turmoil at that time and his attitude toward Judaism and the Jewish people in regard to the Holocaust. Scholem's response to the Holocaust is expressed through the prism of his understanding of Jewish history as it is reflected in the development of Jewish studies—a field so close to his heart.

Reflections on Modern Jewish Studies

The article was titled "Reflections on Modern Jewish Studies (an Introduction to a Jubilee Lecture That Will Not Take Place)," and it was to become one of Scholem's most widely discussed articles and a central text for both scholars and critics of Scholem to use in understanding his conception of history.[27] As the subtitle indicated, the article contained a speech that he might have been planning to give in honor of the twentieth anniversary of the establishment of the Institute for Jewish Studies at the Hebrew University. The circumstances behind the cancellation of the ceremony or of Scholem's participation in it, if such a ceremony was even planned, are unknown. However, the article's subtitle is important since its reference to words written for delivery at an event that never took place, or potential matters that never became actual, suggest a negative attitude and helplessness that are typical of the entire essay.

In the guise of penetrating criticism of the scholars of Jewish studies—the practitioners of the Wissenschaft des Judentums in nineteenth-century Germany and the following generation of Zionist scholars—the essay is actually a bitter personal account of the developments in the scientific scholarship of Jewish history. Throughout, Scholem's article gives evidence of the harsh impression that the Holocaust made on him, and it is clearly written by someone who already saw the fate of the Jews of Europe and who was making a historiographical accounting in the light of the new situation. As a result, both the language that Scholem used and the images he chose for his descriptions of Jewish studies were dark and morbid.

The basic assumption from which Scholem started is that the process of innovation in Jewish studies was a complete failure, especially in the way that it envisaged the Zionist movement and in the way that it was expressed with the establishment of the Institute for Jewish Studies at the Hebrew University in Jerusalem—an effort toward the "building of the present while raising up the past as a vital power."[28] The purpose of his written reflections was to seek the root of that failure and the cause of the deplorable condition of Jewish studies.

Scholem proposes to examine the development of the Wissenschaft des Judentums in the nineteenth century and the contradictions inherent in the nature of Jewish studies. He discusses three essential contradictions that are important for understanding the role of Jewish studies as a force in the history of the Jewish people, and he devotes the first part of his article to those contradictions. The first one is between the proclamation of a pure science for its own sake and of scientific objectivity and the political role that Jewish studies explicitly played, as a tool in the Jews' struggle for equal rights. The second contradiction is that the scholars of Jewish studies were rational intellectuals by nature, but at their approach to the analysis of history and the goal of their research were romantic.[29]

The third contradiction, according to Scholem, was the most central to the substance of Jewish studies, and its essence was that "the conservative tendencies and destructive tendencies within this discipline are interwoven with one another."[30] Although in every renewal movement there is the potential for a dialectical use of historical criticism for the purpose of innovation and construction, in Jewish studies this dialectic gave rise to a dreadful paradox. The essence of this paradox was that the way in which the scholars of Judaism in the nineteenth century understood history made it impossible to use the constructive potential of scholarship and science, and the goal of their romantic approach to scholarship was actually to provide "a hasty burial" for Judaism.[31] To explain this claim, Scholem hints at the historical connection to current events in Europe:

> In recent times we have occasionally tended to ignore too much the tendency toward historical suicide, of destruction and dismantling, which were operative within the Jewish Haskalah. The demon of destruction assumed a dozen different shapes among the nations of the West, both hidden and revealed. We tend to forget that the science of Judaism also played a great role in the tendency towards destruction, and that it was primarily in this role that its practitioners became accepted by those forces which stood at the head of the community.[32]

Whether or not this was intentional, the direction scholars of Jewish studies in the nineteenth century took in their research was toward "destruction" and "death," so that Scholem sensed something satanic, "coming from the other side" (from the sitra achra), in the deceitfulness of their optimistic tone and opinions in comparison to the practical consequences of these opinions.[33] He went on to describe, in a very picturesque way, what he called "the metaphysical platform of the Science of Judaism" as a kind of frightening purgatory. Scholem described those who attempted to make Jewish studies, in which the spiritual and rational aspect of Jewish history is emphasized, attractive to Christians as "spirits which have been uprooted from their bodies and made abstract wander about in desolation. They dwell next to the fields of the living and gaze at the world with longing eyes. How they would wish to walk there too, and how weary they are of the wanderings of generations, wanting only to rest."[34] He calls the scholars Leopold Zunz and Moritz Steinschneider "giants who, for reasons best known to themselves, have turned themselves into gravediggers and embalmers, and even eulogizers. And now they are disguised as midgets, gathering grasses in the fields of the past, drying them out so that there [does] not remain in them any of the juice of life, and putting them in something which one does not know whether to call a book or a grave."[35]

With these words Scholem describes the apologetic goal of the Wissenschaft des Judentums, which was intended to justify Judaism to German Christian society of the nineteenth century and to adapt Judaism to that society so as to facilitate the acceptance and assimilation of Jews within it. Scholem describes this process as mummification and the extraction of the marrow of life from Jewish history by ignoring phenomena that were not consistent with the political purpose of the Wissenschaft des Judentums. This process deprived it of the creative dialectical tension between the destructive and preservative forces in Jewish culture that act alongside each other, and this lack in tension led them to the sin of bourgeois complacency and the "orgy of mediocrity."[36]

A great change came with the flourishing of Zionism, when the entire Jewish people gained a new historical perspective, according to which one must examine the history of Judaism from the inner, not the outer, context. This perspective "has no other accounts to make than the perception of the problems, the events and the thoughts according to their true being, in the framework of their historical function within the people."[37] The role of the new Jewish studies in the generation of rebirth was to produce a new model of the history of the Jewish people, which would be free of all apologetics toward the non-Jewish world. The goal of the new Jewish studies was "not the washing and embalming of the dead body, but the discovery of its hidden life by removing the masks and curtains which had hidden it, and the misleading inscriptions."[38] In other words, the function of Jewish studies in the generation of national rebirth was to lay bare those phenomena in Jewish history that endowed it with vitality—the very phenomena that had revolted the previous generation, which had tried to embalm, desiccate, and bury them because they were inconsistent with its political goals: "It may be that what was considered by them to be degeneration will be perceived by us as a revelation of light, while that which they saw as the delusions of the powerless will be revealed as living and powerful myth."[39] The result of such a discovery was the construction of a new and broader picture of the history of the Jewish people that was free of the contradictions that typified the Wissenschaft des Judentums in the nineteenth century and that would make it possible to present the "interrelationships between the body and soul of the nation" in the correct light, as well as the problematic relationships between the Jews and their non-Jewish surroundings.[40]

Here Scholem came to the essence of his critique. In fact, he was disturbed by nineteenth-century Jewish studies only because it was the background of and explanation for the present condition of Jewish studies, whose scholarship ought to have undergone the same change as that of the generation of rebirth. Although he concedes that there was a reason for the national arousal, and that many things had indeed been done since then, his verdict on the other members of his generation was essentially negative: "But we are obliged to admit that we still remain stuck somewhere along the path between the vision and its realization. We have not applied the critical scalpel to everything that was crooked, grotesque, and embarrassing in the heritage of the Science of Judaism which we set out to renew. We declared programs, but we were satisfied with generalizations. In practice, regarding innumerable details we accepted the same form of perception which we held in contempt in our earlier declarations. We came as rebels and found ourselves to be heirs."[41]

Scholem found in the current scholars of Jewish studies the same flaws that they had identified in their predecessors. The central difference is that the apologetics of the Wissenschaft des Judentums in the nineteenth century had been replaced by Jewish nationalism in the present generation: "All these ills have now assumed a national dress. From the frying pan into the fire: following the emptiness of assimilation there comes another type, that of the contentious nationalist phrase."[42] In other words, despite the change in the language and historical context of the writing, what had not changed in the generational transition was the distortion of Jewish studies by making it a political tool in the service of worldly and utopian goals and, it may also be said, messianic aims—whether assimilationist or nationalist. However, Jewish studies was not far from achieving its goal in that respect. The Holocaust that struck the Jews of Europe also threatened the hope for reform:

> The time has not yet come to sing our own praises. The Science of Judaism requires repair both of its head and limbs. Who knows whether we shall manage to complete that which is imposed upon us, for we had hoped for healing, and received instead terror. In the total destruction of our people in Europe, there were also destroyed the majority of those fresh forces with which we had hoped to continue this enterprise. Or perhaps we do not at all realize the extent to which we are orphans and alone in our project. Could we be rebuilt from the power of the surviving remnants? At times, it seems that when we stand before the great vision of a renewed discipline of Judaic Studies our stance is like that of the angels who were called upon to recite praises to God and did not manage to finish their chapter, for their power expired and they were denied the right to stand before the Creator, like the spark which expires in the coals.[43]

No reader of this article by Scholem could fail to notice the negative attitude and feeling of helplessness expressed in it. Michael Brenner notes that "no representative of Jewish Studies ever made such a radical statement regarding the origin and development of the discipline."[44]

Indeed, from beginning to end, in both form and content, this article radiates pessimism, passivity, and fatalism in the face of the historical situation Scholem discusses in it: the failure of Jewish studies during the generation of national rebirth to change and reform the tendencies of the previous generation. The previous generation was satanic, and in its works something that comes from "the other side" was evident and the smell of death rises from its "tendency to abolish," which is expressed in the scientific "burial ceremony" of Judaism. The present is the failure of Jewish studies to change anything. Despite the good will that characterized the beginning of the field, ultimately the powers of continuity overcame those of the hoped-for rebellion, and what might have seen as a change turned out to be a change of form alone, not of content. And the future held absolute destruction, orphanhood, isolation, and uncertainty about whether the important task of saving Jewish studies and Judaism from their fate can be accomplished. The metaphor that appears in the passage above and that concludes Scholem's article intensifies the reader's feeling of aporia: Zionist scholars of Jewish studies, including Scholem, are compared to angels called upon to sing before the Lord, but they are too small, their strength is insufficient, and they are tired out by a responsibility too great for them, so they do not manage to finish what they began.

The feeling of despair that emerges from this article, which still reaches the reader after so many years, was clear to Scholem's generation and colleagues at the Hebrew University, who were central to his criticism, and in some cases it aroused discussion and a spiritual accounting. In a diary entry dated October 5, 1944, Bergmann reports on a discussion he had with Nathan Rotenstreich and Hanoch Reinhold (Rinot) on a trip to the cities of southern Samaria with a group of youth leaders:

> On the way I had a conversation with Rotenstreich and Reinhold about Scholem's moving article in *Luach Haaretz*. I said that the article could in fact be a motivation for suicide, since it came to such discouraging conclusions. If so, *why* didn't we succeed in creating Jewish studies that would be free of glances to the right and left? Why is the scholarship written in the Hebrew language so apologetic and idealized, and not true in its depth, like that which was produced in foreign languages? This must be something deep within, that does not enable us to look openly and directly at our own face, some feeling of guilt about ourselves. It appears to me that this is because

> we do not know where we are standing in the spiritual sense, because we also have not consolidated a position with regard to national Judaism, upon which we can lean, and from which we could, in good conscience, say yes to our existence and not have to be ashamed of Jewish robbers.[45]

Bergmann, who had also been a member of Brit Shalom, understood Scholem's article as relating to the political sphere and not just to the historiography of Judaism and Zionism. The root of the problem, in Bergmann's opinion, was the hidden feeling of guilt at the inability to find a spiritual position within Jewish nationalism from which it would be possible to exist in tranquility without repeating the errors of the earlier generation or being ashamed of the internal Jewish negative phenomena. The feeling that after twenty years of living in the country, they had not found a place from the national perspective—either on the personal or the collective level—was not easy to live with for Zionists like Scholem and Bergmann. Their disappointment as members of Brit Shalom with political developments until that time and with the rise in power of radical and national-messianic trends in the Yishuv was great. This disappointment was central to Scholem's article.

Scholem's opposition to the political direction in which the Yishuv was heading is seen in a letter that he had written to Walter Benjamin about four years earlier, two months before the outbreak of World War II and about a month after the publication of the White Paper issued by the British government in reaction to the Arab Rebellion that limited Jewish immigration to Palestine and the rights of the Yishuv to purchase land. The White Paper aroused strong opposition in the Yishuv:

> The chance of salvaging a viable Palestinian settlement over the course of the next world war is being endangered just as much by us as by the Arabs and the English. Abominable things occur from among our ranks as well, and I shudder when I try to consider what the sole consequence must be. We are living in terror; the capitulation of the English in the face of this terror leads the fools among us to believe that terror is the only weapon with which we, too, can achieve something, notwithstanding our special conditions. But such fools are too prevalent to be acknowledged as such. So that is the reason why the things that are happening are happening. I never believed the English could do much to us, as long as we ourselves did not abandon the civilized foundation on which our cause here rests. But we are well on the way to doing precisely that.[46]

This letter shows Scholem's response to the historical events and the upheavals that the Yishuv was undergoing at the time of his writing. The Arab Rebellion of 1936–39,[47] which included a general strike of Arabs in Palestine and violent attacks by Arabs on Jews and British administrators, led to a change in the attitude of the Yishuv about the necessity of using force to obtain political goals. When the riots began, the vast majority of the Yishuv adopted a policy of restraint in response to the violence of the Arab population. They had both practical political motives and also ethical reasons for doing so.[48] As time passed and the riots continued, especially after publication in 1937 of the plan for the partition of Palestine recommended by the Royal Inquiry Commission headed by Lord Peel, the Haganah's policy of restraint, which had characterized opinion in the Yishuv, gave way to the activist policy of the Irgun, the Revisionist military underground that left the ranks of the Haganah in 1937: "The use of force ceased to have a functional importance and became a value in its own right. The objective of force was 'the conquest of the homeland Israel by the sword of Israel.'"[49] The Irgun challenged the leadership of the Yishuv, which was made up of people from the labor movement, and its great success among the political opponents of that leadership threatened to take over the leadership of the Yishuv.[50] At the same time a change took place in the view of the Yishuv's leadership about the essence and meaning of restraint. The establishment of many settlements—known as "Tower and Stockade" settlements—in outlying areas where there had been no Jews was a response to the partition plan and intended to determine the future borders of the Jewish part of Palestine by means of territorial expansion and seizure by force of areas in the north of the land.[51]

At this time views that opposed the use of force and advocated an ethical and tolerant solution to the conflict, in the spirit of Ahad Haam, were shunted aside, to be replaced by the view that Jews must defend their lives and honor, and that the control of the Jews over the Land of Israel could be obtained only by the use of force. During World War II, the understanding of the use of force as a defensive measure was replaced by the view of "power as a legitimate means for ensuring the further development of the Zionist project. Force was to play a central role in realizing the political aims of the Zionist movement."[52]

When the dimensions of the Holocaust became known to the Yishuv at the end of 1942, and the responsibility for preventing the entry of refugees into the Land of Israel was placed on the British, opposition to them grew stronger, and public support for violent action against them increased. In 1944, when Scholem published his essay on Jewish studies, the leaders of the Yishuv felt that there was an immediate need for an aggressive and revolutionary change that would achieve the Zionist movement's ultimate goal. This feeling arose from an understanding of the dimensions of the Holocaust, the realization that war between the Jews and the Arabs was unavoidable, and the assumption that the approaching end of World War II would bring with it a new world order.[53] Consequently, terrorist attacks against British targets by the Irgun and the Stern Gang, another splinter group, increased, and the British imposed punishment on the whole Yishuv. The Stern Gang tried to assassinate Sir Harold MacMichael, the British high commissioner, on August 8, and at the end of September they tried to kill a British intelligence officer. The Irgun attacked various British targets in Palestine at that time, including police stations in Beit Dagon and Hadera in September.[54] These actions increased the popularity of and support for these splinter groups in the Yishuv, whose members disliked the perceived helplessness and inactivity of the leadership—which was busy planning the absorption of refugees in the Land of Israel and rejected the idea of actively resisting the British until the end of the war in Europe.[55] Scholem's criticism in the article on Jewish studies was directed against this mood in the Yishuv, which had been spreading for a long time and was gaining strength. In this context, Scholem's essay expresses his opposition to a policy based on power and violence in the Yishuv, which was "forcing the end" (a traditional expression for trying to force the messiah to come, a forbidden action according to the Jewish tradition). Against this background, Scholem's criticism can also be understood as directed against Zionist and Revisionist historical research, which served a nationalistic political approach and expressed that approach in scholarly terms.

It is also possible that the object of Scholem's criticism was himself and his scholarly achievements. His part in the Zionist scholarly project of ingathering was discussed in chapter 1, along with his plan for publishing a scholarly edition of kabbalistic manuscripts, presented in a letter to Hayim Nahman Bialik written in July 1925, when Scholem was twenty-seven. Scholem's plan was extremely ambitious and included many kabbalistic sources. Scholem not only told Bialik of his willingness to take this task on but also gave Bialik an estimate of how long it would take to finish the task: "I am prepared to take these tasks upon myself, and there is a hope of finishing them not in one or two years, but over twenty years!"[56] Perhaps twenty years after writing that letter, Scholem was taking himself to task for finishing only a very small part of the task he had assumed. In fact, this failure had more than academic significance, for one may also see in it the tension between utopia and reality, which also was present in most of Scholem's criticism regarding the political situation in the Land of Israel. As discussed in chapter 1, Scholem's intellectual aspirations, as he envisaged them in his early and hopeful letter to Bialik, were not free of Zionist motivations, both political and utopian. In addition, Scholem's original plan was written after he had lived in the Land of Israel for only two years, immediately after the inauguration of the Hebrew University, and a short time before he was appointed as a lecturer there. Most likely, at that time Scholem could not foresee either the difficulties of life in the Land of Israel or the great strength necessary for adapting to that life, nor could he anticipate how demanding it would be to teach at the university. Scholem wanted and perhaps expected of himself far greater productivity in Jewish studies than he was able to accomplish, and it is possible that twenty years after laying down the general outlines of his plan, he was blaming himself for giving in to the demands of daily life and neglecting the rebellion against the nineteenth-century Wissenschaft des Judentums, remaining stuck "along the path between the vision and its realization."[57] Being "enthused by a great idea" naturally gave way to the routine of daily life and its problems, and Scholem identified in his own work not only tendencies toward rebellion, but also those toward continuity: "Have not a few souls from this world of chaos entered and sown confusion in the world of correction with which we have been engaged?"[58] In this spirit, perhaps, one may also understand what Scholem wrote to his friend Shalom Spiegel regarding this essay: "In truth—I am shattered between taking on the yoke of 'rebels who proved to be successors' and rebellion against it. Here is the place of great weakness, just as here is the source of heroism."[59]

So far, the analysis of Scholem's critique of the scholars of the Wisssenschaft des Judentums has pointed out two possible ways of understanding it. The first is as criticism of the political situation in the country and the political messianism of certain circles, which was taking hold among the people of the Yishuv. The second is as self-criticism in the form of a personal accounting of his scholarly achievements and the difficulties in realizing the utopian idea, even if only on the academic level.

A third possible way, which is interwoven with the first two and which may be the most important for this discussion, is the expression that Scholem gives in this article to his despair because of the Holocaust taking place in Europe and the consequences of this historical situation for the entire Zionist enterprise. As noted at the beginning of this discussion, Scholem treats Jewish studies in this article as tantamount to Judaism itself, and the condition of Jewish studies and its direction can be seen as a metonymy for the situation and direction of Judaism. Thus, the tendencies of the nineteenth-century Wissenschaft des Judentums "toward historical suicide, . . . destruction and dismantling"[60] are part of the historical development that led to the Holocaust. The tragic development of history is what led him to make a spiritual accounting of Jewish studies and to point to its part in the process that led to catastrophe. It is possible to understand Scholem's accounting of the people of the Yishuv in similar fashion. This was the generation that began with innovation but remained stuck on the way from the vision to its realization and lost its way and its powers. Thereby it sinned against the process it had begun, and instead of rebelling it found itself continuing the process of destroying Judaism by its violent political behavior in the Land of Israel. Scholem saw this behavior as the result of pursuing a national messianic dream and ignoring the situation of the Jewish people in the Diaspora (whose continued physical and spiritual existence was in danger) as well as in the Land of Israel (where, according to Scholem, there was a danger to the continuity of the Zionist enterprise because its moral aspect was being ignored). The human beings on whom the Zionist enterprise depended to accomplish what it had begun had been annihilated, and that disaster—along with the Yishuv's ignoring of the Arabs of Palestine, who constituted an obstacle to the realization of the Zionist dream—shed an ironic light on the tendencies of the generation, in Scholem's opinion. In this regard, the generation was similar to the previous one.

Scholem admitted many years later that he had written his article "in a moment of linguistic fury,"[61] and that "its formulations were so tempestuous that I could never bring myself to present the original version to readers not familiar with Jewish affairs."[62] Nevertheless, in 1959 Scholem gave a lecture in German titled "The Science of Judaism—Then and Now" to German Jewish immigrants at the Leo Baeck Institute in London.[63] In this lecture he presented a far gentler and more balanced position on the place of Jewish studies in the history of Judaism, and his comments about the past and the present were far more moderate. On several later occasions Scholem said he was sorry that he had given this lecture, calling it "a very watered-down, overly compromising German speech on the subject, . . . and I regret it to this day."[64] In fact, in Scholem's lecture, the critique of nineteenth-century Wissenschaft des Judentums is much milder, and the bitter, critical tone toward his own generation has entirely disappeared. Instead, Scholem treats the Holocaust and the establishment of the State of Israel as representing "two sides of a single vast historical event," and he emphasizes that "we ourselves—considering our close proximity to the events—have as yet scarcely been able to rationalize and understand in a scholarly manner the meaning of what we ourselves have lived and suffered through."[65] Nevertheless, toward the end of his lecture he pointed out that, following the establishment of the State of Israel, Jewish studies had yet to free itself from the danger of writing Jewish history from the viewpoint of Zionist ideology, a tendency that he called "apologetics in reverse" here, alluding to the "sin" of the generation of the Wissenschaft des Judentums.[66] Scholem's article on Jewish studies can thus be read as a personal document that reflects the various aspects of the psychological turmoil he experienced at that time. Placing his words in their historical context sheds light on his attitude toward the events of his time while they were happening. The article ends without expressing any hope or proposing any solution, leaving the reader with an impression of helplessness and aporia. This was not a mere stylistic or artistic way of writing, but rather an outward expression of his feelings—the great despair he felt. In fact, "Reflections on Modern Jewish Studies" is a historian's interim evaluation of the Zionist movement toward the end of World War II, after the dimensions of the Holocaust had become clear. Central to this evaluation is despair at the current state of Judaism in the world as a whole and in the Land of Israel, based on a critical analysis of the development of Jewish studies—the instrument Scholem regarded as so central to building up the land—in an effort to cope with the tragic situation. One might also regard this article as a historian's assessment of the future, given what Scholem wrote in the letter to Dinur quoted above. Scholem's assessment of the state of affairs was bitter and discouraged, and it expressed his disappointment with the situation of Zionism and his own Zionist path. However, whereas in his personal letter to Dinur, the assessment is directed at historical circumstances and fate, in his article, it also deals with the residents of the Yishuv and the political situation in the Land of Israel.

On December 6, 1944, immediately after his forty-seventh birthday, and a short time before the end of the war, Scholem made an entry in his diary that expresses the deep despair and loss of faith that he felt at the time: "Is it true that God is revealed in the isolation of a broken life? Why, then, is everything in my life so dark, without any way out, and jarring? . . . Sometimes I still struggle desperately with the remnants of the great dreams that once inspired me, as if I could still write them on some piece of paper or another—and I've lost faith in the strength needed for that. Everything is so much in vain, so hopeless."[67]

When Germany surrendered, Scholem wrote a kind of summary in his journal, or a private accounting of the place of the world, the Jewish people, and himself after the long years of war:

> On May 7, 1945 Germany surrendered—the greatest sin was atoned for, if this may be called atonement at all. We have become insensitive, almost more than we can yet feel the consequences of the events, which mean for us "only" the death of the Jewish people. . . . How will we find our way? Another world, which certainly does not exist, not even a better [world]. Only a world without Hitler and Goebbels. What will come now? Only God knows. All the prophets, almost without exception, were mistaken. I am alone—Fania is still in Tiberias for a cure and will come back the day after tomorrow. How alone I am is hard to say. I went through this war alone. Friends in the true sense are no longer. Few significant feelings.
>
> I fight in vain against the tempest that rages within me, that keeps me farther and

> farther away from friends, yes, [a storm] that condemns me to muteness. This is a central and unpleasant (*unheimliche*) fact in my life, that became more and more clear to me during the years of the war. And it is no longer connected to a *moral* decision. In any event, am I still capable of moral decisions? Desperation dwells too deeply, and for years it has been the sole object of my most private thoughts. Alas for the defeated (*Vea Victis*).[68]

During the years of the war, there were changes both in Scholem's attitude toward the realization of the Zionist idea and in the way the war and Zionism were connected to his personal situation. His relative optimism in 1933 and his belief that Zionism was the correct response to events gave way to a loss of confidence in the Zionist path and personal despair, a feeling of intense isolation, and loss of faith "in the great dreams that once inspired me." Scholem saw the decision to bring the Zionist idea from potentiality to actuality by immigrating to the Land of Israel as essentially an ethical decision, but after the war he doubted his ability to make moral decisions in the light of the weakening of his faith in that path. This weakening of faith came in the wake of his understanding that Zionism could never have offered an answer to historical events as they developed in Europe at that time. As a Zionist and an intellectual, Scholem was deeply wounded by historical events, which led him to eschew future political action and to reject his Zionist utopia, which had already suffered from those events for two decades. Thus, at the end of the war he was left with a feeling of loss, which he expressed in his diary with the words "Alas for the defeated."

CHAPTER 5

THE JOURNEY TO SALVAGE LOOTED BOOKS AND MANUSCRIPTS

> His interest in handwritten and printed books went beyond their function as the sole sources of the historian. . . . He had a unique sort of emotional relationship with books, where the distinctions between function and essence, between the vessel and its contents, became blurred.
>
> MALACHI BEIT-ARIÉ, "GERSHOM SCHOLEM AS BIBLIOPHILE"[1]

> "The books' fate was no better than that of the people," said Scholem.
>
> BARBARA HONIGMANN, "DOUBLE BURIAL"[2]

The Diaspora Treasures Committee

At the end of World War II, after Europe was liberated by the Allies, enormous collections of property were discovered in the conquered countries—mainly libraries and smaller collections of books that had been plundered by the Nazis. Before the war these books had belonged to communities that were persecuted under the Nazi regime such as the Freemasons, but mainly what was found was books that had belonged to Jews, along with ritual objects and other Jewish cultural treasures.

The source of most of the stolen books was the Jewish communities of Germany, and about a third of those communities had been transferred to Germany from the countries conquered by the Nazis.[3] The work of stealing and keeping this property was done by so-called research institutes, which were established by the Nazis and carried out pseudo research about Judaism and the Jewish question. The central institutes were the Reichssicherheitshauptamt (RSHA, Reich Main Security Office) and the Einsatzstab Reichsleiter Rosenberg (ERR, Reichsleiter Rosenberg Taskforce). In the American occupation zone many collections of books were found, and these were taken by the US Army to a central collection point that was established in July 1945 in the Rothschild Library in

Frankfurt. After that became too small to contain all the books, they were transferred to Offenbach, a city on the other side of the Main River, where they were kept at the Offenbach Archival Depot (OAD). This was a five-story building at Mainstrasse 169 that had belonged to the I. G. Farben company and had been converted into a storehouse. The OAD was opened on March 2, 1946 under the command of Captain Seymour Pomrenze—an American Jew who, before being conscripted in the army, had been an archivist at the US National Archives—and it became the center for the collection and identification of stolen books, with the aim of returning them to their owners.[4]

The process of returning the property would have been relatively simple, had it been possible to identify and locate the legal owners of the books or their heirs, but what was to become of books that had been Jewish communal property, or whose owners could not be identified or had been killed? Who was the legal heir to this property? Within contemporary Jewish centers these questions became critical, and they became an urgent matter for the great powers that ruled Europe and the non-Jewish world because the status of the Jewish people was not anchored in international law, and thus it was impossible for them to demand compensation collectively. Beyond that, according to accepted judicial views, property with no living owners or their heirs that had been taken as plunder in war either belonged to the country within whose borders it was found or to the occupying power, or it had to be returned to the country where it had originally belonged.[5] Hence, there was reason to fear that this property might remain in Germany or that it would be transferred to the United States or to the countries in Europe where Jewish life no longer existed, and whose governments had collaborated with the Nazis. At the same time this situation led to confusion within the Jewish collective. Indeed, the question of the fate of these books was bound up with many questions in that collective, which gained intensity after the war: Who was the true representative of the Jewish people, to whom the treasures of Jewish culture and spirit belonged? Where was the center of Jewish life, from which continuity would emerge after the great catastrophe?

Even before the end of the war, when the imminent defeat of the Germans was anticipated and the dimensions of the destruction of European Jewry were already known in the West, the world's Jewish centers began trying to determine the future of Jewish cultural treasures that had been stolen and remained in Europe with no heirs to claim them. The problem was first discussed in England, in a lecture given by the historian Cecil Roth in April 1943 at a conference of the Jewish Historical Society of England, which was published a year later.[6] Roth proposed transferring the books without owners to the Hebrew University in Jerusalem, where they could be preserved, and in his conclusion he recommended the establishment of a committee that could continue dealing with the subject.[7] Such a committee was formed, and its functions were to remain in contact with the Allied authorities regarding stolen property and to take care of other matters connected with the restoration of Jewish cultural life in Europe. The members of this committee included Roth and the jurist Norman Bentwich.[8] Similarly in the summer of 1944, the Commission on European Jewish Cultural Reconstruction (CEJCR) was established in the United States, headed by the historian Salo Baron. The purpose of this commission was to rehabilitate and rebuild the Jewish communities in Europe and elsewhere in the world by, among other things, restoring stolen cultural treasures to the Jewish people and distributing those treasures among various Jewish communities. The commission was organized and administered by Jewish American academics and intellectuals such as the philosopher Hannah Arendt, the historian Joshua Starr, and the jurist Jerome Michael.[9] In 1946 the commission published an initial list of Jewish cultural treasures that had existed in Europe before the Nazi period as a first step toward obtaining information about their location.[10] In the United States there was interest in the books that were found in the American occupation zone in Germany, particularly the Jewish books, and as a result a delegation of librarians from the Library of Congress was formed and sent to Germany for the purpose of enriching the collections of that library and those various others in the United States by acquiring books from the American occupation zone.[11]

People at the Hebrew University in Jerusalem began to lay the groundwork for possible action that would lead to the transfer of the books' ownership to the Jewish people. The approach of the university was that the worthiest destination for the books was the National and University Library in Jerusalem, because the communities and institutions to which the books had belonged no longer existed, their restoration was unclear and would be prolonged, and at the Hebrew University "the attempt is being made, and with considerable success, to create a Central Library for the Jewish People, and in Jerusalem there are gathered a larger number of distinguished Jewish scholars than in any other place, for whom these libraries could be of great use in their work of research."[12] On May 6, 1944, two days after the letter quoted above was written, the Diaspora Treasures Committee (Hava'adah Lehatzalat Otzrot Hagolah) met in Jerusalem to discuss actions that could be taken to recover the stolen books.[13] According to the minutes of the meeting—in which senior people from the Hebrew University, including Scholem, took part—the members were in agreement that the Hebrew University should promptly send an official emissary to Europe who would be in contact with Jewish organizations in England and the United States and represent the interests of the university. "It is important," stated Martin Buber, "for us to appear in the list of claimants as soon as possible." Scholem emphasized the danger that Jewish organizations in England and the United States might demand the books for themselves. "The university must appear as the custodian of the deposit," he argued. "A delegation must be formed to go to Munich and Frankfurt. Treasuries of stolen books are located in those two places. If an agent of the university does not appear soon, they will decide without us. We must address England and America."[14]

On January 4, 1946, an article by Robert Weltsch appeared in *Haaretz*, in which he reported on his impressions after a stay in Frankfurt.[15] Weltsch wrote about a visit to the collection point in the Rothschild Library and his meeting with Koppel Pinson, the director of the education department of the Joint Distribution Committee (JDC)—the central American Jewish relief organization—in Germany. Although most of the books had already been transferred to the OAD, although it was not yet open, the visit to the Rothschild Library was enough to convince Weltsch that this was "the largest Jewish library in the world." The books were not arranged in any order, so it was difficult for Weltsch to estimate the importance of the various items. "Most of the books that I opened have no value for libraries," he admitted, "but it is always impossible to know whether a highly valuable Hebrew book is lying next to a trashy Yiddish romance." Nevertheless, he estimated that "the main treasures are still lying in Offenbach, and no one knows whether more cartons, which had been hidden somewhere, will be discovered."[16] He called for action on the part of the Jewish center in the Land of Israel, both internally and internationally:

> Here the Land of Israel must receive the role it deserves: it is sad that very little of what was possible has been done about this as yet. World public opinion must be informed that the Land of Israel is the spiritual center of the Jewish people, and it is appropriate that the treasures of culture, which were stolen from the Jews of Europe, should be brought there, for no one can claim them now. . . . Care must be taken to send experts to Germany to work on the material. This is our right. The National Library in Jerusalem must demand it for itself. It must send a group of chosen officials to Frankfurt to examine the books, appraise them, arrange them, and catalogue them. It is absurd that until now this task has been assigned to Aryan German officials, who have no knowledge of Jewish literature. It seems to me that I was the first person with a scientific interest in the matter to enter this library. . . . This entire vast collection was abandoned until now, and no one paid attention to it. It is necessary to try immediately to obtain permission from the American military administration, which usually responds to such matters with great understanding, to send Jewish experts from Jerusalem.[17]

Weltsch's call from Frankfurt did not fall on deaf ears in Jerusalem. Two days after his article was published, the administrator of the Hebrew University, David Werner Senator, sent a letter to the rector, Michael Fekete, along with the clipping from the newspaper.[18] Senator felt that the time had come to do something about the books and put the university in contact with the American authorities in Germany. Weltsch's suggestion to send experts and librarians to Germany to sort out the material there seemed extremely sensible to Senator, and he felt that doing so would definitely assist the university achieve its long-range goals. He wrote Fekete: "You know that there is a weekly airplane from Palestine to the American zone. I would therefore suggest that the committee dealing with the matter should have a meeting as soon as possible and should elaborate definite and concrete proposals in the direction outlined above."[19] Indeed, the pace of work was accelerated. The Diaspora Treasures Committee met twice in January 1946 to discuss ways of increasing the efforts to send representatives to Europe as soon as possible. At the second meeting, which was held on January 24, three significant decisions were made.[20]

The first decision was to establish a subcommittee to discuss relations between the committee with other institutions in the world, both Jewish and non-Jewish. This subcommittee, whose members were Shmuel Hugo Bergmann, Gotthold Weil, and Scholem, met once, on January 31. It recommended the establishment of a small international commission headed by a representative of the Hebrew University, which would speak for the Jewish people to the Americans and demand a decision regarding the distribution of stolen Jewish property. The subcommittee also determined criteria for future distribution, according to which priority would be given to Jewish institutions in England, which had suffered from German bombing, and equal division between the United States and Palestine. The division would be determined by two adjudicators—one from Palestine and the other from the United States.[21]

The second decision adopted at the meeting on January 24 was to create a legal committee alongside the Diaspora Treasures Committee, whose task would be to investigate the legal problems involved with the recovery. Three senior jurists from the Hebrew University were appointed to the legal committee: Norman Bentwich, Nathan Feinberg, and Abraham Haim Freimann. Its first meeting was held on January 29,[22] and on February 26 it issued a nine-page memorandum examining the legal aspects of the stolen Jewish property.[23] This memorandum laid down the guidelines for future actions of the Diaspora Treasures Committee. After a short survey of the present situation of stolen Jewish cultural treasures in Europe, the memorandum discussed the question of the ownership of this property. The main problem that emerged in the report was the legal principle, accepted in most countries, that "the private property of missing individuals, who left no legal heirs passes by inheritance to the state treasury."[24]

However, in the case under discussion, it was not possible to recognize Germany's legal right of inheritance, because estates in its territory had been left without heirs as a result of the systematic murder of Jews.[25] The legal committee argued:

> In light of what is known about the systematic campaign of destruction carried out by the German state against the Jewish people, it would only be just and correct according to elementary human decency that the abandoned estates of the Jews who were murdered without leaving any heirs would pass, instead of to the treasury of the state of Germany, into the hands of the Jewish people, the creator of this cultural property. The Jewish people, which is coming to life again in the land of the Patriarchs, has a unique and vital spiritual connection to the treasures of its culture, [and a duty] to honor and keep them in its national and spiritual center in the Land of Israel.[26]

The transfer of this property to Palestine also was in keeping with the principles of the laws of inheritance, which seek to honor as much as possible the wishes and intentions of the person leaving the property. In the opinion of the legal committee, the victims certainly would have wished to make the property available to the "Jewish community which is involved in Jewish culture and literature."[27] Since the Hebrew University in Jerusalem was the only Jewish university in the world, and since its library was the national library of the Jewish people, available to all Jews, "therefore there is no place or institution in the Jewish world that has a better right, from the cultural, moral, and human points of view, to be appointed as the trustee for the cultural estate of the destroyed Jewish Diaspora than the National and University Library on Mount Scopus in Jerusalem."[28] The Hebrew University and the National Library were willing to receive this property, to ensure its protection, and to serve jointly as the trustee of it for two years, after which all items still lacking other owners would be owned by the National and University Library in Jerusalem, which would be responsible for distributing surplus books among Jewish communities around the world. With regard to cooperation with other Jewish institutions, the committee recommended forming a united front with them and having the Hebrew University appear as the sole claimant. For this purpose, agreement had to be reached with various cultural institutions in the United States, England, and Europe on the distribution of the books in accordance with the specific requirements of the Jewish communities in each country. The final item in the memorandum addressed the possibility of making another claim against the state of Germany for "certain compensations from the cultural treasures of public libraries in Germany." The purpose of such a claim would be to have transferred to the Jewish people Hebrew and Jewish manuscripts, publications, and archives connected with Judaism, as well as a certain number of general and scholarly books. There were three reasons for making this claim: first, their behavior toward the Jewish people proved that the Germans are not fit to preserve the treasures of Jewish spirit and culture; second, "an irreparable loss has been caused to the Jewish people and its culture, and the German people owes the Jewish people payment for damages for this wicked destruction";[29] and third, that German cultural institutions had received many contributions from Jewish philanthropists and, given the mass murder of German Jews, the Jewish people was entitled to be compensated for those contributions. The general guidelines laid down by the memorandum directed the future efforts of the Hebrew University to claim ownership of stolen Jewish property that had no other owner. However, this demand for sole trusteeship was softened later on, given the urgency of removing the books from Germany. As will be discussed below in this chapter, this urgency reduced the competition among the various Jewish centers around the world and ultimately helped them form a united front.

The third decision made at the meeting on January 24 may have been the most significant one: the choice of the members of the delegation that would leave for Europe to rescue the treasures of the Diaspora and take the first steps in implementing the basic principles laid out in the memorandum. Avraham Yaari, the librarian of the National Library, and Scholem were chosen for this mission.[30]

The Story of a Journey: January–August 1946

Preparations in Jerusalem (January 28–April 10)

After receiving news of his appointment to the delegation, Scholem began preparations for the trip. On January 28 the Hebrew University officially requested a visa to Germany for the two delegates through the American consul in Jerusalem, but this request was rejected in early March.[31] The refusal did not discourage Scholem. A letter to Senator dated February 21 shows that Scholem was planning for an imminent departure. He asked Senator to obtain visas for him to Czechoslovakia, Italy, Holland, France, England, Poland, and Switzerland. Moreover, after his trip to Europe he planned to continue directly to the United States for the purpose of giving a series of lectures there.

During the preparations, disagreements arose between Scholem and Yaari regarding the division of responsibility and authority during the mission. While Yaari insisted that the members of the delegation must have equal authority in making decisions, Scholem argued that one of them had to have the final say in case disagreements between them could not be resolved, and since he was the senior member of the delegation, this right should be accorded to him.[32] Yaari sensed that Scholem was not including him in the preparations for the trip, and he appealed to Judah Leib Magnes. Magnes asked Scholem to cooperate with Yaari as much as possible on a basis of equality, though he agreed with Scholem that if the need arose, the final decision should be his.[33] In response Scholem asked to meet with Fekete, Magnes, and Yaari to remove any shadow of doubt regarding the division of authority during the trip, concluding his letter in a personal tone that indicates the tension between him and Yaari that existed even before the trip: "I am certainly prepared to work with Mr. Yaari [Scholem crossed out the words "with Mr. Yaari"], on the basis you wrote of, but I cannot help but see his attitude to personal questions with great concern. His behavior forces me, uncharacteristically, to adopt great caution in my relations with him, and I regret this."[34] The issue was resolved at a meeting between Fekete, Senator, and Scholem, based on the compromise suggested by Magnes, and it was formulated in a letter sent by Fekete to Yaari and Scholem. The letter emphasizes the equality between the two members of the delegation in terms of responsibility for the mission, but "in a case when it is impossible for them to reach a decision, it will be the right of the senior member of the delegation, Professor Scholem."[35] At the end of March, the Hebrew University sent an official letter of appointment to its delegates, which set out their functions and the nature of their task:

> A. You have two principal functions:
>
> 1. You must seek to gather all information that you can obtain about Jewish collections, libraries, archives, and other accumulations, etc. that are in the hands of the Germans and to seek as much as possible to examine the collections themselves to the best of your ability.
>
> 2. You are to be in contact with local Jewish institutions, communities, or other organizations, which can be regarded as important to clarify the fate of past and future collections and clarify all the questions involved in the matter with them, and you should try to discover the fate of the owners of personal collections, to the degree they are present in the countries where you will visit.[36]

The letter of appointment emphasized the informative nature of the mission: the task of Scholem and Yaari was to gain as much information as possible about the books, but not to begin any judicial or official negotiations. Furthermore, it specified the need for close cooperation with delegates of the Jewish Agency and the JDC who were active in Europe. It continued: "In case of need, you have the power of attorney to present yourself as emissaries of the Jewish Agency in any matter touching upon this mission."[37]

Making connections and depending on international Jewish organizations, especially the JDC, were necessary for success, because the JDC had access to the American occupation zone, and its leaders were closely connected to occupation authorities. Magnes wrote to Joseph Schwartz, the manager of the JDC in Europe, who was based in Paris, asking the JDC to assist the representatives of the Hebrew University as much as would be necessary for them to carry out their mission. In reply, Schwartz's assistant, Arthur Greenleigh, wrote Magnes that the JDC would help as much as it could, but—in a hint of what was to come—Greenleigh emphasized that traveling from Paris to Germany was no simple matter at that time, because decent accommodations and meals were scarce.[38] On April 10, the two delegates of the Hebrew University set out with letters of recommendation and information they had collected in advance, but without permission to enter Germany.

London and Paris (April 10–May 15)

Scholem and Yaari arrived in Paris on April 14 on a flight from London, where they had stayed for two days. Scholem took advantage of that stay to visit the family of his brother Werner, who had been murdered in Buchenwald six years earlier, and to meet with representatives of the JDC and Bentwich, who were in England. Bentwich tried to help Scholem and Yaari and connect them with the JDC in Paris. In a letter to Magnes, sent after Scholem and Yaari had left, Bentwich reported on their visit and on the tension among various Jewish organizations regarding ownership of the stolen books. Roth had expressed to Bentwich his dissatisfaction about the conduct of the Hebrew University regarding the books. Roth supported the establishment of a common organization representing the Jews of England, the United States, and Palestine to recover the books and distribute them fairly, and he had protested the idea of appointing the Hebrew University as the trustee responsible for distribution. At the same time, Bentwich foresaw that the Americans would be the greatest obstacle to the university's achieving its goals. According to a document that had come into Bentwich's possession, Pinson had tried to arrange the transfer of the book collections to the United States in trusteeship of American institutions. Bentwich wrote: "As he is the person to whom S[cholem] and Y[aari] turn, I expect he will not be very helpful."[39]

After the end of World War II, Paris was full of displaced people and others returning home. Prisoners of war, exiled forced laborers, and political exiles created an entirely new society in the city with their return. Great optimism prevailed, but at the same time that society was bruised and fragmented. The Jews of Paris, who had hoped to return to their homes and find there the property that had belonged to them before the war, often discovered that their property had been stolen and that its recovery was not a simple matter. Disappointment with the situation and with the indifference of the non-Jewish residents of Paris, as well as physical deprivation, created a grim atmosphere among the Jews of the city.[40] But in 1946 the leadership of the Jewish institutions in the city had already been restored, and the JDC was working intensively, becoming a central factor in shaping the renewed life of the Jews of France.[41]

Immediately after their arrival in Paris, Scholem and Yaari contacted the office of the JDC and the director of the local office of the Jewish Agency, Ruth Klüger (later Aliav). During the war, she had been a member of the Mossad Le'aliyah Bet, helping to rescue the Jewish refugees of Europe and smuggle them into Palestine. Scholem and Yaari began trying to obtain entry visas for Germany and Austria, a task that proved to be far from simple. Starting on April 1, restrictions had been imposed on entering Germany, and at this time, in contrast to the previous arrangement, special authorization to enter Germany had to be received from the American military authorities.[42] On April 17, Scholem and Yaari filed their request for entry visas, and it was sent to the American Office of Military Government in Berlin, from which the Americans directed their operations throughout Europe.[43] While waiting for a response, Scholem and Yaari began to gather preliminary information regarding the condition of the books in Frankfurt. News that Pinson was trying to transfer the books to the United States as a temporary refuge had already reached them and aroused concern, as did rumors that many books had been stolen from the warehouses where they had been collected.[44] This information, which increased the urgency of their mission, did not make the waiting for visas any easier. The situation gave them the feeling that they were already too late, and that the chance of reaching the books had been reduced through the American intervention. They were also disappointed by the attitude of the JDC toward them—although it was supposed to be helping them, it was not, in their opinion, trying very hard to do so. As Scholem wrote in a letter to Senator:

> Two things have become clear here: (1) That we are at least two or three months too late, and people are bitter about this. They say that it would have been possible to remove a lot of things that we had come for just a short time ago, but meanwhile several Jewish and non-Jewish parties have arisen, to steal whatever is possible for America. (2) The attitude of the JDC is not unequivocal. On the one hand, they want to help without doubt, and they have helped us in small matters here, but on the other hand they are very bureaucratic, and we feel very well that we are disturbing them. . . . We have the impression, though I can't prove it to you one hundred per-

FIGURE 3 Scholem in a US Army uniform with an unknown woman, Paris 1946. From the collection of the National Library of Israel, Jerusalem.

cent, that the JDC, for reasons of its propaganda in America, would be very favorably disposed to transferring the books to America so they could say: Look what we did for the Jews of America![45]

Despite the discouraging situation and the difficulties in obtaining visas, preparations for Scholem and Yaari's trip to Germany continued. On the recommendation of people from the JDC and the Jewish Agency, they bought US Army uniforms in an officers' store, after it became clear to them that if the visas arrived, they would only be permitted to circulate in the American occupation zone in military dress. "A very ridiculous appearance," Scholem reported to Senator, "like in an operetta."[46] In addition, Scholem and Yaari spoke to authorities at the United Nations Relief and Rehabilitation Administration (UNRRA), asking for the agency's help in entering Germany by inviting them to do so—a request that was answered in the affirmative—and they submitted a request for a visa to Czechoslovakia to travel to Prague. At the same time, a negative answer came from the authorities in Vienna in response to their request for an entry visa to

Austria. On May 3, they received notice from Berlin that their request for an entry visa to Germany had been denied, despite the invitation arranged by UNRRA.[47]

Scholem and Yaari believed that the denial was connected to the general policy of the Americans with respect to the collections of books in Europe, which was essentially to close the book warehouses in the army's possession—including the one in Offenbach—as soon as possible. The Americans wanted to accomplish this by returning the books whose owners—individuals or institutions—could be identified and to the states from which they had been stolen, leaving it to those states to find the legal owners. The Americans planned to send the remaining books to the United States and to keep them until a final decision about their fate was made. The result, according to Scholem and Yaari, would be that the Jewish people would lose the books. They believed that American Jewish institutions such as the CEJCR were behind the plan to transfer the books to the United States, through the work of Pinson in Germany and other people: "It seems there were several appeals from Jewish figures and institutions in America to the military authorities in America, and lacking a united front and coordinated steps on the part of the Jewish institutions has so far done damage and is likely to cause even further damage, bringing about the absolute loss of these treasures for the Jewish people. We express our opinion that there is an absolute need to establish in America, without any delay, a united front of the Jewish institutions."[48]

Following the rejection of their request for entry visas to Germany, the two members of the delegation decided that Yaari should return to Palestine and Scholem should stay in Paris and wait for developments on the diplomatic level,[49] as well as for a reply to the request for a visa to Czechoslovakia—and seek to enter Germany disguised as an educator for the JDC giving lectures in displaced person (DP) camps.[50] However, waiting for the visa to Czechoslovakia also seemed to be in vain to Scholem. "They won't let me in," he wrote in his journal on May 7, "as if particularly bad luck hangs over this entire mission. Everything is as though really under a spell."[51] On May 10, before Yaari's return to Palestine, information reached Scholem that, thanks to Schwartz's efforts, the authorities in Berlin had decided to reverse their decision and authorize the delegates from the Hebrew University to enter Germany.[52] Despite this positive development, and against Scholem's recommendation, Yaari decided to abandon the mission and return to Palestine. The documents provide no explanation for his decision. Perhaps it was connected to the slow pace of developments in Paris and the exhausting wait, and perhaps it was also connected to his personal relations with Scholem and the tension between the two since even before the trip.[53] In any case, Scholem decided to stay in Europe and later explained his decision in this way: "I thought (and I still think) it was a severe error to leave this great matter in the middle, as long as there was a true *chance* for some degree of success. In any event, I myself decided to stay here and see how things would turn out."[54] On May 15, Yaari left Paris on his way back to Jerusalem.

Paris (May 15–24)

Scholem's apprehensions about the Americans' intentions to transfer the Jewish books to the United States were not unwarranted. On May 17, a memorandum from the CEJCR to Rabbi Philip Bernstein, the advisor on Jewish affairs to the US Army in Europe, recommended transferring to the United States the book collections whose owners had not been identified because of the danger threatening the collections from the Soviets, who were demanding the return of property to the countries of the Soviet bloc.[55] According to the memorandum, not only would an official demand from Palestine not be recognized by the powers, but it would also support Soviet claims for the books, because none of the book collections had come from Palestine and no one recognized the legal right of the Yishuv to them. Therefore, the memorandum recommended returning to their owners the books that were privately owned and whose legal owners could be located and placing the books belonging to communities temporarily in trusteeship, until the renewed communities in Europe could grow and be able to use the books. Books without owners should also be placed in trusteeship until their fair distribution among various Jewish communities could be arranged. The most appropriate institution to act as trustee and remove the books from Germany quickly, in the opinion of the CEJCR, was the Library of Congress in Washington, which had already agreed to accept responsibility for the transfer of the Jewish property to the United States—where it would be sorted and redistributed according to the needs of Jewish communities in the world, with the cooperation of the CEJCR. As for the claims of the Hebrew University, the memorandum recommended that "the erection of a Memorial Library at the Hebrew University to commemorate the millions of slaughtered European Jews should be seriously considered."[56]

These developments exacerbated Scholem's sense of urgency. He was still in Paris, waiting for an entry visa, and the news did not make the wait any easier. The hope that had arisen in his heart when he heard of the imminent arrival of the much-desired visa dissipated within a short time. In fact, the promised visa disappeared in the labyrinth of US Army bureaucracy. What he received was not an official visa from Berlin, as he had been told to expect, but only a limited and temporary visa. To obtain a real visa, he had to address the authorities in Berlin once again, though they knew nothing about the temporary visa and had just rejected his previous request. Again the chances seemed slim. After racing around and making many arrangements, Scholem heard that he had to wait for three more weeks for a final answer to his request.[57] Nevertheless, he decided not to return to Palestine but to wait in Paris as long as there was a ray of hope, as he wrote to Magnes: "At any rate I have decided to stick it out, and would return to Palestine only if I have to give up all hope of doing any real business here."[58] Meanwhile, as he had been doing since he arrived in Paris, he met with the Jews of the city and gained an impression of their situation after the war. For example, he wrote in one of his first reports to Senator: "What I have seen in several conversations with French Jews is very depressing. I have already met with several people, some of them distant relatives of mine who had their children baptized. They explained to me that they had to make their children forget they were Jews."[59] The meetings with the younger generation of Jews in France also disappointed him with regard to their ability to continue Jewish life or to serve as a human reserve for strengthening the Jewish center in the Land of Israel. As he wrote to Magnes, "they are not at all in the state of mind that we supposed them to be and the trends leading away from Judaism are stronger than the opposite ones, as far as I can see."[60] Scholem also learned that his mother had died. Betty Scholem had fled to Australia in 1939 and been living there with her two elder sons.[61] This sad news deepened his gloom into apparent depression:

> May 17. Yesterday night I learned that Mother died on May 5 while we were touring Versailles! At the moment we were talking about her with a friend of Pflaum's father,[62] she breathed her last. I was expecting this news for several weeks and now I still feel like a fossil, petrified to the heart. I don't know—what a horrible feeling of petrification, of loss is gradually increasing in me, and it won't let me take a proper accounting of my world. In the past years Mother was a larger matter in my life than earlier. Her figure grew clearer as she passed seventy and the lights glowed from there, and I was more connected with her soul in several respects. The suffering in Australia brought her close to us, and the courage of her spirit surprised us. I had an easy mother, who didn't try to intervene and also knew how to maintain herself with great wisdom. What distanced me from her in earlier years, about thirty years ago, was blurred and ceased to exist. . . . I imagine that her real life was very hard, and she prevailed with a strong spirit.[63]

Scholem found a friend in Klüger of the Jewish Agency. Their long meetings and conversations while he was in Paris consoled him in difficult moments. Klüger was also the one who suggested that he should go to Switzerland for a week and try to obtain a visa to Czechoslovakia from there. "In fact it is on my mind to do that," Scholem wrote in his diary, "because this evening I received an invitation *from there*, as it happens, from Dr. Hurwitz, a dentist, to visit him for a few days."[64] A week later Scholem arrived in Zurich.

Zurich (May 24–June 5)

"The enormous difficulties that I encountered in Paris evaporated as though by the wave of a magic wand when I finally went to Switzerland," Scholem wrote in a report to the Hebrew University.[65] Indeed, with the help of Siegmund Hurwitz, a dentist and Jungian psychologist who had personal connections with the assistant Czechoslovakian consul, Scholem immediately received visa allowing him to travel to Prague, with no difficulty. However, the trip had to be delayed by about ten days because there was no available transportation to the Czech capital.[66]

The stay in Zurich brought an upturn not only in Scholem's mission but also in his mood, as he once again saw sights familiar to him from his youth.[67] "Zurich is marvelous," he wrote in his diary, "and without chocolate, because two weeks ago *restrictions* on it were limited, and after that people stormed into the stores like savages and bought it all, and there is none to be found!!"[68] Scholem spent the days of waiting with his new friends, Hurwitz and Rebecca Schärf, who was also close to Carl Gustav Jung, talking about Scholem's work and research in Kabbalah. The two received him with more than a little enthusiasm: "They're really killing themselves for me!" he wrote in his diary.[69]

Through these new friends, Scholem met Jung on May 27 and spoke with him about Kabbalah. "An evening with Professor Jung, the psychologist," he wrote in his diary on the day following the meeting. "Meir warned me about his suspicion of him regarding his previous Nazi inclinations. . . . [But] he listened carefully."[70] The meeting left Scholem with an equivocal impression of Jung, especially with regard to his earlier connections with Nazi ideology and the Nazi movement, as Scholem wrote in his diary several days later: "Yesterday with Dr. Schärf, a conversation about Jung and the Nazis. An effort to cleanse him of the accusations against him—apparently accused justly according to what I learn from his defense."[71] The meeting with members of Jung's circle and the long conversations with Schärf and Hurwitz reached a peak in an evening in Scholem's honor at Hurwitz's home, where Scholem spoke about Sabbateanism with a group of local intellectuals.[72] These initial connections and Scholem's attraction to Jung's associates grew stronger over the years and were expressed in his regular participation in the Eranos conferences, which are discussed at length in the chapter dealing with Scholem's participation in Eranos. As Scholem stated, the stay in Zurich was a time of "*recovery* in all of the confusion and nerve-wracking disappointments of this journey."[73]

Prague (June 5–24)

A few days after Scholem and Yaari left Palestine on their way to Paris, a letter from Bergmann was received by Senator in Jerusalem, containing details about large collections of books in Prague and Bratislava. According to Bergmann's investigations, the only difficulties to be anticipated in transferring the books from Prague to the Hebrew University would be not with the local authorities, but with the Jewish community.[74] This information was quickly conveyed to Scholem, who was already in Paris,[75] and it was a decisive factor in his decision to travel to Czechoslovakia.

The source of the collections of books that Bergmann had reported on was not Czechoslovakia, but they had been transferred there from Berlin by the Nazis. The libraries stolen from the conquered countries had been collected and sorted in Berlin by Jewish forced laborers at the RSHA and the ERR. Transfer of the collections from the capital to border areas of the Third Reich—mostly to castles in small towns in Silesia and Czechoslovakia—began in 1943, to find shelter for them and save them from Allied bombing. In that way a very large collection of Jewish books and manuscripts, about a quarter of a million volumes, had reached the Niemes (Mimoň, in Czech) castle in northern Bohemia. A smaller collection of about 60,000 books had been transferred from Berlin to the Theresienstadt concentration camp by the RSHA, preserved there, and sorted by Jewish experts. The concentration camp also had its own library, which was built by the Nazis for propaganda purposes. This library served the prisoners as part of the illusion of relatively normal life that characterized that camp.[76] In September 1945, the books were transferred to the Jewish Central Museum in Prague. This museum had been established by the Jewish community of the city in 1906 but was closed by the Nazis in 1941. In 1942 it was reopened as a repository for objects of art, ritual objects, and books that had belonged to exterminated Jewish communities. It is not clear whether this reopening was an initiative of the Jewish community to preserve Jewish property until the end of the war, or of the Nazi authorities as part of their effort to preserve evidence of the existence of what they called the Jewish race as they destroyed it.[77] In any event, during the war the museum served as a kind of warehouse for stolen Jewish property, and after the war it contained 213,096 items, about a third of which were books. Books from Theresienstadt were added to this collection.[78]

Scholem arrived in Prague on a flight from Zurich, which he described as "two and a half hours, uncomfortable seats like in a tram, in a Czech plane, but with God's help the weather during the flight was excellent."[79] Almost two months after leaving Palestine, Scholem could finally devote his time to the task for which he had been sent: locating stolen Jewish books and examining the possibility of transferring them to the National and University Library in Jerusalem. Since he arrived in Prague on Shavuot, which overlapped with the Christian holiday of Pentacost in that year, a lot of people were on vacation, and he could not move forward until June 11. However, he managed to meet with Paul März, the Jewish Agency's representative in Prague, who expressed willingness to help in any way he could. He also met with the historian Rabbi Otto Muneles, with whom he visited the Jewish museum and who estimated that there were about a hundred thousand books there from Bohemia and a similar number from Theresienstadt. The collection's condition concerned Scholem, as he wrote in a report to the Hebrew University on his activities in Prague: "Almost all of it is still packed in boxes, and direct examination is impossible. Storage in stinking cartons in half-damp cellars gives reason for concern."[80] Scholem was very impressed by the museum's enormous art collections, which he said could fill many museums. But he saw little chance of successfully bringing these collections to Palestine because of their fame and the great interest already shown in them by various art historians. He suggested leaving a discussion of the art objects to a later time.[81]

Scholem spent the following days in conversations with the heads of the Jewish community of Prague and with the president of the council of the Jewish communities of Bohemia and Moravia. Through these conversations he managed to persuade them to send the books from Theresienstadt, which were in Prague and had come from Germany (that is, not the books from Bohemia and Moravia) to the Hebrew University in Jerusalem, which would become their trustee.[82] He also made use of his time in Prague to hunt for valuable books in the collections of the museum, but the content of the books he found was not what he had hoped for. "A few valuable collections, but nothing exciting," he wrote in his diary.[83] His visit to the Smichov quarter of the city on June 11 also failed to lead to significant discoveries: "In the afternoon, a visit to the Smichov quarter, where, in the hall of the cemetery, the books of the Jews of Prague are piled up, tens of thousands of volumes, 80%–90% prayer books and Bibles, in fact it's all worthless. It's stored badly, by the way. Halls with no windows, broken bookshelves, moisture, and mice can do as they please. In comparison, the things from Theresienstadt are stored better."[84]

On the morning of June 22, after a three-day trip to Bratislava and Vienna, he received the happy news that his request for the much-desired visa to Germany had been approved. Diplomatic efforts and pressures in the United States and the endeavors of the JDC in Paris had borne fruit. In Berlin an entry visa was granted with the help of authorizations from UNRRA, allowing Scholem to travel to Germany as an educator from the JDC, dressed in a US Army uniform.[85] Two days later he flew back to Paris.

The books that Scholem had seen in Prague did not constitute the large and precious collection he was seeking, and thus they were a disappointment. He did not get to the large repository in Niemes in this trip, though according to some accounts he was able to determine that very important books and manuscripts had been sent to this collection—if it was still there.[86] Nevertheless, he wrote to the Hebrew University that "my actions here mainly succeeded more than I had estimated at first."[87] His success was in making a preliminary connection that eventually led to the transfer of many books to the university.[88]

Paris, Bad Arolsen, Frankfurt, and Offenbach (June 24–July 18)

In Paris Scholem made final preparations for entry into the American occupation zone in Germany. He had no idea of the length of the planned trip and what he would find there, as he wrote to the Hebrew University from Prague: "How long I will stay in Germany I cannot say in advance. It is hard for me to imagine that it will be less than a month. Everything depends on what can be done there, and it will also be impossible for me not to spend a lot or a little time camouflaging myself as someone from the JDC, who has come to look into matters of culture and education. In any event, I will of course visit the [DP] camps. First I will go to Frankfurt, and from there to Munich. Apparently my authorization is also good for the British zone."[89]

A week later, in a personal letter to Magnes from Paris, he wrote in a different tone: "If it were possible, I would return to the Land of Israel from there [Germany], because I am very tired." He went on to tell about his preparations before the trip. For example, he had learned from further conversations with JDC people that their attitude toward him and his mission had not changed: "The heads of the JDC announced 'unofficially' to me that in their opinion, and to their deep regret, *I should not* expect energetic cooperation from Professor Koppel Pinson in Frankfurt. I took the hint [the sentence is in English in the original]." At the end of the letter he added: "I thought that my mission would end on July 1, and I could return to my work, but it's just beginning to develop! A person who travels in Europe now has to be prepared to lose a lot of time!"[90]

On July 1, Scholem left Paris on a night train to Frankfurt. "I couldn't sleep," he wrote in his diary the following day, "because of the snoring of the man sharing the compartment."[91] Upon his arrival in Frankfurt he discovered that he could not begin working before he was in possession of the appropriate residence permit. To get one he had to go to the American military headquarters in the spa town of Bad Arolsen, which was near Kassel. For technical reasons, Scholem had to stay in Bad Arolsen for two additional days, and he used the delay to travel in the area in a military jeep. "A charming town," he wrote in his diary.

"The landscape is so beautiful, the peace all around—and the Germans stare at you."[92] The next day, on July 4, he returned to Frankfurt with the proper papers.

Frankfurt became a divided city after the war. The American part, on one side of the city, was restored, busy, throbbing, and full of vitality, as Weltsch described it in his notes from the city on the trip to Europe he made in 1946: "American vehicles of all types fill the streets, army people and administration officials in uniform rush about and liven up some parts of the city, the important American offices are the centers and crossroads. . . . All the houses that were worth repairing have been properly repaired and equipped with modern conveniences, including (even excessive) central heating." In contrast, the larger part of the city, where the Germans lived, lay in ruins: "There entire streets have been wiped off the face of the earth, but in all the dark alleys, that the people have dug through the piles of debris, people are walking: and you wonder, how and where can people live there?"[93] Nevertheless, the trams were running even in that part of the city, and while Weltsch was there a production of Beethoven's *Fidelio* was put on at the city's opera house. The separation between the Germans and the Americans in the city was almost absolute: except for those Germans who came to work and serve the people living in the American part, the two groups did not mix at all.

The focus of Scholem's interest in Frankfurt was actually on the other side of the Main, the OAD in Offenbach. When Pomrenze, its director, began working in the OAD, there were more than a million and a half books to be sorted out and returned to their owners.[94] Many years later he described his feelings at the sight of the books on taking up his new task: "My first impressions of the Offenbach Collecting Point were overwhelming and amazing at once. As I stood before a seemingly endless sea of cases and books, I thought what a horrible mess! What could I do with all these materials? How could I carry out my assignment successfully? Beyond the mess, however, was an even larger mission. Indeed, the only action possible was to return the items to their owners as quickly as possible."[95]

Indeed, under Pomrenze's direction, the work proceeded efficiently and quickly during the six weeks when he was responsible for sorting and returning the books. At that time large consignments of books were sent back to their countries of origin, when it was possible to determine where they belonged. The first shipment, a truck with 371 crates of books, left for Holland on March 12. In that month books were also sent to France and Belgium.[96] At the same time, as material was discovered throughout the American occupation zone, more books continued to arrive at the warehouse, and as of May 1, the OAD became the only place where books and printed matter were to be collected for the purpose of restitution.[97] On April 15, Pomrenze was replaced by Captain Isaac Bencowitz,

FIGURE 4 Books at the Offenbach Archival Depot. 1946. From a photo album of the OAD made by Isaac Bencowitz. Yad Vashem Photo Archive, FA2 73 2/18.

a chemist by profession, who was also Jewish and who remained as the director until October. When Bencowitz assumed responsibility for the warehouse, about 30,000 books were being identified and sorted per day. This was done by eleven sorting teams consisting of German citizens. Since none of the German workers could read Hebrew letters, the books in Hebrew and Yiddish were set aside, awaiting separate treatment.[98]

Upon Pinson's intervention, 25,000 Yiddish books whose owners could not be identified were lent to the JDC for use of the residents of the DP camps throughout Germany, where there was a great lack of material for educational and cultural activity. By the end of April, the JDC had received 20,000 volumes from the warehouse.[99]

By the time Bencowitz became the director, more than a million items had already been returned to their owners, and about 800,000 remained in the warehouse.[100] The fate of these books was to be determined in accordance with official policy, which the American occupation authorities had yet to determine. The origins of some of the books were unknown or only partially known; some of them were from Germany or regions conquered by the Soviet Union, whose governments that the Americans did not recognize.[101] The examination and sorting of the roughly 500,000 books in these categories were Scholem's purpose when he reached Offenbach. At the end of June, warehouse workers had sorted 267,400 unowned books, and of them 43 percent (114,800) were in Hebrew and 16 percent (42,000) in German, with Jewish content.[102] Moreover, just before Scholem's arrival, items from the library of the rabbinical seminary in Breslau had been identified in the warehouse, as well as items from the libraries of the Jewish communities in Frankfurt and Berlin and from the library of the Yidisher Visnshaftlekher Institut (Yiddish Scientific Institute YIVO) in Vilna, community registers, and about six hundred manuscripts (including a significant collection of manuscripts of Habad Hasidism).[103]

As soon as he arrived in Frankfurt, Scholem met with Pinson, who was going to leave Germany in two weeks, and Bencowitz. In contrast to Scholem's expectations, Pinson greeted him cordially. At their meeting, Pinson "spoke copiously about his great heroism in saving and transferring books,"[104] and he immediately suggested that Scholem should work in the warehouse to identify and sort the Hebrew manuscripts there. Pinson complained to Scholem about the JDC people, who, in his opinion, had no interest in culture or Jewish cultural treasures, thus revealing some of the internal tensions in the organization. "Pinson poured out his anger at the JDC, just as they poured out their anger at him," Scholem wrote in his diary on July 5. "It's interesting to hear both sides."[105]

On July 6, almost three months after his arrival in Europe, Scholem reached his destination, the OAD. His first survey of the building gave him an impression of the situation: "First visit to Offenbach—for two hours I wandered around the building with Pinson and saw all the arrangements. Masses of books and disorganized heaps, instructions that make *anything* possible! But we are entirely *too late*. Something could have been done a few months ago, if we had sent the right people to them. The two heads [of the warehouses] are Jews who want to help but are more afraid of the authorities than the people in Prague. The only one who manages to get along with them—Pinson, who can in fact take the really *precious* things away from here!!"[106]

That evening Scholem spoke with Bencowitz about the aims of the Hebrew University and its hopes of transferring the books for preservation to the National Library in Jerusalem. Bencowitz opposed the university's general guidelines and agreed to help Scholem only to transfer books to the United States, on condition that he received appropriate authorization to transfer the YIVO books to the organization's branch in New York. At the same time he advised Scholem to remove the books from the warehouse quickly, as Scholem noted in his diary: "The only thing that [Bencowitz] is willing to do is to smuggle a few thousand books [out] along with the YIVO books, when an official order is given for their benefit (which still doesn't exist). About all the things that are important to us in the Land of Israel he said: Forget about it! [Bencowitz's remark is in English in the original]. My advice is to hurry very very fast to reach a decision in Washington, because after him a German director will come, and he will do whatever he can to transfer the books to German ownership."[107]

Scholem's meetings with Pinson and Bencowitz during the first three days of his stay in Offenbach made the general condition of the various warehoused collections clear to him. His summary of these conversations draws a disappointing picture. First, he realized he had arrived too late, and most of the work of sorting the books and returning them to their owners had already been done, in the hope of closing the warehouse in the near future. In addition, administration of the warehouse was about to pass into German hands, which would prevent the remaining books from being transferred to Jewish ownership. In addition, contrary to reports that had reached Palestine, most of the books had not originally been owned by Jews, nor did they have Jewish content.[108] The large Jewish libraries of Germany and Austria were not in Offenbach. The situation was particularly dire with respect to manuscripts: "In Offenbach there were only a few hundred (about 400) Hebrew manuscripts, and without exception not a single one from the big collections, but from the communities of southern Germany and the Baltic countries. There is almost nothing of value, [no] really ancient thing—not at all."[109]

In light of these discoveries, Scholem later stated that "with respect to the search for cultural treasures in the sense of rare books, important manuscripts, or precious archival material, the depot in Offenbach is a disappointment."[110] The conversations with Pinson also left Scholem no room for doubt: there was no chance that all or even part the books would be transferred to Palestine. However, Pinson agreed to cooperate with the Hebrew University and told Scholem that the various Jewish organizations must first of all unite in their efforts to remove as many books as possible from Germany. As Scholem wrote in a report on his conversations in Offenbach that he sent to the Hebrew University: "In the present state of affairs, I am sorry to say he is right. In Paris or New York we, that is, the Jewish people, still will lose less of these things than if they stay here."[111] The main idea that arose was to prepare a repository of Jewish books in a Jewish center outside of Germany, to transfer the maximum number of books to that repository as quickly as possible, and only then to consider how the books should be distributed among the various Jewish centers. The most important thing was for world Jewry to present a single front to the American occupation authorities. These conversations seem to have effected a change in Scholem's approach to his mission in Germany and to the rescue of books. The danger threatening the books from the planned change in management of the OAD, as well as the thefts

FIGURE 5 Gershom Scholem at the Offenbach Archival Depot, summer 1946. From the collection of the National Library of Israel, Jerusalem.

of books by workers in the warehouse, convinced him that it was necessary to act quickly and in concert with the Jews of the United States to move the books somewhere that would be the property of the Jewish people. On July 9, the day when he dictated the report, Scholem sent a telegram to Magnes, who was in the United States, urging him to reach a decision about the books: "Unless decision reached before August danger imminent Jews lose all."[112] Scholem maintained that position at the end of his trip as well, as shown in what he wrote from Paris to Stephen Wise, the head of the World Jewish Congress, shortly before returning to Palestine:

> Everybody to whom I spoke, including the people of the Fine Arts and Monuments Commission, implored me to do what I could to work for one policy to be advocated. They say that if the Jews between themselves are divided, even the State Department will be afraid of making a decision, and the whole business may linger for years. To this must be added the fact that I have not found anybody who thinks it possible that a direct transfer of the libraries to Palestine may be achieved, and no decision on that line is within our reach. On the other hand, I consider it very important to get these collections, as far as they are still there, out of Germany as soon as possible. The longer they remain there, the greater the danger will be of losing parts of them. Any place outside Germany would be better than to leave them at their present place,

although they are now kept in boxes after having been sorted in a very summary fashion.[113]

Scholem spent the following days working in the warehouse in Offenbach, identifying and sorting various manuscripts and books. Since most of the books had already been placed in crates, which had then been sealed, the main task remaining was consultation and assistance in various areas, as well as sorting piles of books in German and Latin. During the days he spent in the warehouse, Scholem grew to understand the problems and limitations inherent in his mission, in the manner and timing in which it was undertaken, and the errors made in evaluating the situation from Palestine. As he wrote in a letter to Magnes:

> I dealt with organizing manuscripts and other special books. Next week I will deal with material from the border countries, and every day I weep, seeing how much I could have done, if I had come by April, as planned, when most of the books had not yet been returned to crates according to the new arrangement, and it would have been possible for me to have a large influence on the arrangement and the instructions issued for it. Now only limited possibilities remain to give good and acceptable advice, and that is what I am trying to do. . . . The main job that should have been done, and that I cannot do, is, in my opinion: *searching* for the vast buried and hidden material. That work would have required two conditions, which were not clear to us in Jerusalem: (1) *a very long time*, because this is a matter of "espionage," to find what the Americans and the English *didn't* find. (2) *total freedom of movement*, which was completely denied to me for reasons of the occupation authorities and of the conditions under which the JDC obtained my entry into Germany.[114]

Scholem's resentment against the JDC and its attitude toward him and his mission increased. "The JDC office is not cooperating," he wrote in his diary on July 9. "That is the director is not interested in my mission, and I have the impression she is sabotaging me politely."[115] Two weeks later, before his trip to Munich, Scholem wrote in his diary: "The bitterness of my heart and my disappointment about the attitude of the JDC to me is growing."[116] In contrast, good tidings arrived that reduced the sense of urgency: the American authorities decided that Bencowitz would not leave in August as had been planned, but would remain the director of the warehouse for three more months, which would delay its transfer to German hands as well as its closing. In addition, in response to proposals for the future of the books submitted by the CEJCR to the US War Department, the latter ordered the American authorities in Germany not to send any more shipments of books from the warehouse without authorization of the State Department.[117] This delayed the return of the books to their country of origin and gave the Jewish organizations more time to have the books sent elsewhere.

Heidelberg (July 18)

On July 18, Scholem went to Heidelberg for an eight-hour visit. He met three German intellectuals there: the Catholic publisher, Lambert Schneider; the Protestant philosopher and physician, Viktor von Weizsäcker, a friend of Buber; and the philosopher Karl Jaspers, whose pioneering book dealing with German guilt after the Holocaust was published in early 1946 by Schneider.[118] These three men all played an important and active role in rebuilding German culture after the war, and they had been close to Judaism and Scholem's friends from before the war—especially Buber and Ernst Simon, the religious philosopher and educator. Scholem sent Simon a long letter the day after his return to Frankfurt, reporting on his visit to Heidelberg in detail.[119]

In Heidelberg, Scholem spent the most time with Schneider. As mentioned in chapter 1, before the war he had owned a publishing house bearing his name in Berlin and had then worked with Moshe Spitzer for Salman Schocken's publishing house there, corresponding with Scholem about possible publication projects. After the war, Schneider opened another publishing house under his name, this time in Heidelberg.[120] Schneider was very pleased to hear from Scholem about their common friends in Jerusalem, especially Buber, Spitzer, and Schocken. Scholem told Simon that Schneider had left Berlin in 1943, after the last employee who worked under him in the Schocken publishing house, Erich Loewenthal, was sent to Auschwitz.[121] After the war Schneider settled in Heidelberg, and at the time of Scholem's visit he was the father of a three-year-old boy and three adopted children. The first big project of his new publishing house was a magazine, *Die Wandlung*, which was in existence from 1945 to 1949. This publication was edited by Jaspers; Dolf Sternberger, a political scientist; Werner Krauss, a scholar of Romance languages; and Alfred Weber, a sociologist of culture and the brother of the sociologist Max Weber.[122] Among those writing for this journal were Jaspers, Hannah Arendt, T. S. Eliot, Rudolf Bultmann, and Weizsäcker. The name of the journal can be translated into English as "the change" or "the metamorphosis." However, another possible meaning is rooted in Catholicism, as "Wandlung" also refers to the miracle of transubstantiation, wherein the consecrated bread and wine of communion are transmuted into the body and blood of Jesus. In any case, the name largely represents the self-understanding of the members of the circle, which was surprisingly similar to what could also be heard in those years in the Jewish DP camps. In his introduction to the first issue of *Die Wandlung* Jaspers states: "We have lost almost everything: state, economy, certain conditions of our physical human being and worse than this: the values and norms which bind us, the moral dignity, the united self-consciousness as a people. Yet Germany has not lost everything: We *survivors (Überlebenden)* are still here. We have no possessions but we are here. Indeed, we have no property upon which we can rest, nor have we the possession of memory; indeed, we are at a most radical point; nevertheless the fact that we are alive has to have some significance. From nothingness we will recover."[123]

The aims of the journal, as Jaspers presented them in his introduction, were to prepare German society for a change and then initiate that change, to renew Germans' sense of responsibility along with their feelings of mutual trust and commitment to the values of freedom and humanism, and to work toward the spiritual and physical reconstruction of Germany.[124] This publication was not the only one in postwar Germany that sought to build a new society. Rather, it was part of a general trend.[125] Scholem's German colleagues, like the survivors in the DP camps and the delegates of the Yishuv in Europe, confronted the ruin that characterized the present and an unclear future, full of dangers they would have to cope with. From different sides, many people were seeking to build a future out of the ruins. In addition, the people whom Scholem met had to deal with a hostile intellectual environment in Heidelberg, where there were many Nazis and former Nazis. At the time of Scholem's visit, the circle that had formed around *Die Wandlung* to achieve spiritual renewal had had limited success, as Scholem reported to Simon: "If the Americans were to leave tomorrow, the people connected with *Die Wandlung* . . . would be shot down in the street in broad daylight, . . . *Die Wandlung* is truly a matter of the veteran non-Nazis from before 1933, and the name has not yet been justified."[126] Although the situation in Heidelberg was difficult, Scholem heard from Schneider that he wanted to begin publishing books on Jewish subjects again, because of the large demand for them at that time among the non-Jewish Germans of the city.

After parting from Schneider, Scholem met with Weizsäcker and spoke with him for about an hour, mainly about Buber. Before the war Weizsäcker had been a neurologist in Heidelberg; during the war he had been a professor of neurology in Breslau; and after it, in 1945, he had returned to Heidelberg. His actions during the war were a matter of dispute, because in the city of Loben (Lubliniec, in Polish), which is near Breslau, a Nazi institution euthanized children and youths with physical and mental disabilities. To this day the degree of Weizsäcker's knowledge of what was done in that institution is not clear, though he definitely took no active part in it.[127] He was a friend of Buber and in 1926–28, along with the theologian Joseph Wittig, he edited *Die Kreatur*, a magazine that was published by Schneider.[128] Weizsäcker asked how Buber was and, because mail service in the American occupation zone was poor, he asked Scholem to tell Buber how he and their common friends were doing. Weizsäcker especially wanted to tell Buber that his two sons were assumed to be dead because they had not returned from the Russian front, but his two daughters were safe and sound.[129]

Scholem had dinner with Jaspers and his Jewish wife. There the conversation revolved around events in Palestine and their mutual acquaintances, Hans Jonas and Hannah Arendt. They also spoke about Scholem's work and about Jaspers's biblical theology. During this conversation, Scholem's driver, who was waiting in the car to take him home, honked the horn, and because Scholem did not want to accept Jaspers's invitation to spend the night there on his first visit, he decided to return to Frankfurt that evening. Scholem left Heidelberg with good impressions of the city and the desire to visit his acquaintances there again. He wrote to Simon, "But maybe I'll go there once again before returning to Paris, because there were a few people there, with whom it was good to converse."[130] Indeed, a month later, a few days before returning home, Scholem went back to Heidelberg for two days and stayed with Schneider. Scholem's visits to Heidelberg made a deep impression on Schneider, and the memory of them remained vivid twenty years later, as he wrote to Scholem: "Like you, my wife and I have not forgotten the three days in 1946 when you came to us, dressed in a uniform, and from every pocket you gave candy to the children. In your uniform you looked grouchy. You didn't suit the uniform, and the uniform didn't suit you. Thus the children saw the first Jew in their lives, in a strange disguise. You could write a novel about that."[131]

Frankfurt and Offenbach (July 18–24)

In the days following his return from Heidelberg, Scholem finished his work in the OAD, as he wrote to Magnes on July 22: "I've actually finished my work in Offenbach. I was able to give technical advice after looking over everything that was happening in this work. I hope it will be good. I don't think it's possible to do very much more."[132] During his time in the American occupation zone in Germany, in addition to his work in the warehouse, Scholem visited the survivors in the DP camps in the area of Frankfurt and Munich. These visits were part of his camouflage as an educational emissary to Germany of the JDC, but one may assume that he had a personal interest in educational activity among the refugees and in meeting with them. On July 11, for example, he spoke for two hours in the Zeilsheim Camp near Frankfurt. "I gave a lecture about the spiritual atmosphere in the Land of Israel," he wrote in his diary, "and this was met with great interest."[133]

Scholem's visit to the DP camp and encounter with its residents made a deep impression on him, and he lectured on the experience after his return to Jerusalem and wrote about it for *Haaretz*.[134] He wrote that Jewish life in postwar Germany had given him "a dreadful feeling of depression." In his opinion, the problem of the camps was not that they lacked material supplies: "People aren't hungry there the way the Germans are hungry. The residents of the camps receive twice as many rations as the Germans."[135] The problem was in the spiritual and psychological realm: the residents' severe demoralization derived from their long stay on German soil, lack of desire to work, and from idleness that led to friction among them—for example, about how each of them had survived the concentration and extermination camps, and whether anyone had acted immorally to save him- or herself. Many refugees had left the camps and gone to live in various cities of Germany, and some of them had begun to deal on the black market and integrating themselves that way into the German economy, "so that a new Diaspora is forming, not of German Jews, but of Polish Jews in Germany."[136] Another possibility open to the people in the camps was emigration to the United States, though this was not easy: the American consulates in Germany made it very difficult to obtain the necessary authorization. Emigrating to the Land of Israel seemed even more difficult because of the increased tension there between the British, the Yishuv, and the Arabs, and the latter two groups' acts of hostility toward each other. For those refugees who wished to move to Palestine, the waiting in Europe became unbearable. Here is how Scholem described to Magnes a meeting with young people in the Zeilsheim camp: "I saw some Jewish students who want to study with us, and all of them asked whether there was a way for a student to immigrate and study—and I had no answer. The mood here, which is created by the lack of any possibility of immigration soon—cannot be described in words. The damage is enormous and dreadful, and really everyone you meet weeps because of the spreading degeneration. And it is hard to see. I try to see something of the camps and I spoke in places where they asked me to speak, and for the first time in my life I gave a speech in Yiddish!"[137]

The fact that Scholem had to speak in Yiddish reflects the level of knowledge of Hebrew in the camp. After his return to Palestine, he said that at the time of his visit to the camp, of its 3,500 residents only 180 were studying Hebrew, and they did not keep at it, although there were good opportunities in the camp to learn the language. "I spoke with a few people," Scholem wrote, "and I said to them: 'After all, you're idle for eight hours a day—learn Hebrew eight hours a day for eight months, and when you get to the Land of Israel, you'll know the language perfectly.' They say: 'We will see when we get to the Land of Israel.' I say to them: 'In the Land of Israel you'll have other worries!' But they won't study."[138]

Like many of the emissaries of the Yishuv, who met the refugees at a relatively late stage in their liberation, Scholem was critical of them. Irit Keynan notes that the survivors made two different kinds of impressions on the emissaries. On the one hand, one finds expressions of idealization of the refugees and praise for their psychological resilience, and on the other hand, there are voices that emphasize the negative phenomena that developed in the camps.[139] Keynan attributes the differences to the time of the encounter between emissaries and survivors and its meaning for the Zionist enterprise: The closer the encounter was to the time of liberation, before the establishment of a routine in the DP camps, the greater was the emissaries' identification with and empathy for the survivors. And for Zionists from Palestine, the encounters were laden with great tension. To realize the Zionist idea, the Yishuv desperately needed immigrants, and the possibility of losing this human resource was a matter of life or death for the entire Zionist movement.[140]

According to Scholem, most of the refugees interested in moving to Palestine wanted to go there not because of Zionist motivations, but primarily because of their desire to leave Europe and not to live in non-Jewish surroundings. Their hope was simply to live their lives in tranquility from now on. When it became clear that the situation in Palestine was more complicated than they had thought, and their chances were small of obtaining the harmony and quiet they desired, they began to doubt the wisdom of immigrating, and the Zionists' efforts in the camps were undermined. The constant news about the rising tension in Palestine encouraged the refugees to seek other solutions for themselves. As a Zionist, Scholem's encounter with the refugees in the camps was disappointing, depressing, and worrying—these were not the sort of people through whom the Zionist idea was going to be accomplished. His impression was that most of them had no interest in Zionism but were concerned with the material problems of life, and those who were Zionists were troubled by the difficult situation in the Land of Israel. Nor was he pleased with the Zionists among the refugees who were living in camps described as training kibbutzim (*kibbutzei hakhsharah*)—groups of refugees who were preparing themselves in separate encampments in Germany for agricultural life in the Land of Israel. Scholem perceived a contradiction among the people living in the training kibbutzim, in that they yearned for the Land of Israel but at the same time were cultivating the hated land of Germany as farmers.[141] In general, he had a very negative opinion of most of these kibbutzim, as he wrote after his return: "As a matter of principle, the people refuse to lift a finger in Germany; and some of them go so far as to say: we won't even consider tidying up our room—let the *shikse* (non-Jewish woman) work. But they live together and call it a kibbutz. In general they misuse that term: five merchants on the black market, who live together and employ two *shikses*, are called a kibbutz. Of course, there are some real kibbutzim. But the term, as a magic word, is so common, that it has lost its real content in their use of the language."[142]

In the face of all these problems, Scholem felt helpless: "Who can give advice to a person after all he has undergone over the years, in the presence of the current events now?"[143] Indeed, the violent events in Palestine in the summer of 1946 put the emissaries in the camps in Germany in a difficult situation between two worlds. The first world had been destroyed, and the second, which was supposed to provide a solution for the catastrophe of the first, was in grave danger. Haim Avni, the emissary of the Histadrut, described this complex situation in notes from the summer of 1946, when he was sent to the DP camps in Germany by the World Zionist Organization: "It is difficult to understand this world if one draws a line in thought connecting this station, which is named 'UNRRA camps,' to our final destination—the Land of Israel. One's heart freezes, and one's eyes grow dull with huge magnitude of abysmal pain, while comparing these two pictures: the Land of Israel under siege and this horrible exile."[144]

Nor was Scholem indifferent to the troubling news that was reaching him about the situation in Palestine and the increasingly violent events there. He concluded a letter to Magnes with the following words: "The news from the Land of Israel is so depressing and makes all our work harder. How painful to read in sensational telegrams about the destruction of what we are building."[145] On that day, July 22, the Irgun blew up the King David Hotel in Jerusalem.

After returning from his first visit to Heidelberg and finishing most of his work in Offenbach, Scholem devoted his remaining time in Frankfurt to searching for Jewish books in the municipal library, which had been established and financed by contributions of the Jews of Frankfurt in the second half of the nineteenth century.[146] During Nazi rule the books in the library remained in place, because the mayor refused to deliver them to the national government. To Scholem's great disappointment, when he visited the library he learned that its valuable Hebraica department had been entirely burned in bombing attacks by the Allies on March 18, 1944.[147] However, the items in the Judaica department and several manuscripts owned by the library were saved. This news encouraged Scholem, as did an important conversation he held with the recently appointed director of the library, Hanns Wilhelm Eppelsheimer. A socialist, Eppelsheimer had been married to a Jewish woman and refused to divorce her during the entire Nazi period (she died of illness in 1946). Nehemya Allony, who met Eppelsheimer in January 1952 to discuss the possibility of photographing the Hebrew manuscripts for the National and University Library, described him as "a man with graying hair, tall and solidly built, with a nose like a potato and one lip drooping down. A man of open and fluent conversation." Eppelsheimer made a very favorable impression on Allony: "This man is a liberal of the decidedly good and fine type of the Germany before Hitler and before Kaiser Wilhelm," he wrote in his notes.[148]

Scholem proposed to Eppelsheimer that the Frankfurt municipal library transfer its Hebrew manuscripts to the Hebrew University. This request to give up the treasures of the library was based on the fact that all the manuscripts and books had been purchased for it and contributed by Jews—or, as Scholem wrote, "they were all bought with Jewish money." He said that the transfer would "be a simple step to repair the injustice that cannot be described in words."[149] Scholem's proposal was in fact an extension of the policy recommended in the memorandum of the legal committee of the Diaspora Treasures Committee submitted in February, a policy of demanding that Hebrew books and manuscripts in German public libraries be transferred to the Jewish people.[150] Scholem felt that Eppelsheimer's response was very positive. "He was very sympathetic and willing to consider it with his municipal authorities," Scholem wrote.[151] During the conversation, the two men agreed that giving the books and manuscripts to the Hebrew University must be a moral gesture of restitution to the Jewish people via the university. In this spirit, Eppelsheimer insisted that all the steps to be taken had to be made by the Germans, not by the Jews.[152] When he went to Munich, Scholem pursued this line of action—making contacts with the local authorities for the purpose of transferring Jewish cultural treasures from public libraries in Germany to the Hebrew University.

Munich (July 24–29)

In the introduction to an English guidebook to the city, the first to be published after the war,[153] Karl Scharnagl, mayor of Munich in 1946, described the situation in the city this way: "The Munich of old, the pride of Bavarians and the Mecca of visitors from all over the world, is no more. Instead, we have desolate wastes, and ruins that gaze on us accusingly from hollow eyes; the bitter heritage of an age of horrors. And yet life does not stand still, if it does not of itself give up the struggle, nor has the Munich heart, as the saying has it, 'the golden Munich heart,' ceased to beat."[154] To a great extent, Scharnagl's words represent the way in which Munich's citizens saw their city at the end of World War II. On the one hand, there is a romantic nostalgia about its past, before the Nazi regime, and on the other hand (sometimes simultaneously), there is a look toward the future of the city and a call for its physical and cultural reconstruction.

Interestingly, a similar situation prevailed among the Jewish population of the city and in the DP camps around it. Despair in the face of the vast destruction of the present left the refugees in the area with the same two possibilities: basking in memories of the distant past as a way of coping with the difficult experiences of the more recent past, or yearning for—and sometimes acting to bring about—a utopian future. Avni described the state of the Jews of the city and its surroundings this way:

> In the narrow street you'll always find people, mostly young men, roaming about and looking for something. I believe that they are seeking content in their lives. In the morning they get up and don't know what for. The day passes and night comes. If you look a a youth like that in the eye, and you know how to read his soul—you'll understand that his soul is still wandering in the past. He remembers yesterday and yearns for tomorrow. The present is superfluous and its only purpose is to bridge [the gap] between the life that once was and that which will be. The feeling that everything is provisional is felt at every step. There is no stability—either material or spiritual. Yesterday they were in hell on earth, and tomorrow they will be in paradise on earth—and between one and the other there is a void and idleness.[155]

The refugees who were settled by the US Army in many camps in and around the city, together with the representatives of Jewish relief organizations who came in the refugees' wake and established offices in the city, made it temporarily into a large Jewish center on the liberated soil of Germany. For example, the JDC set up an office in Munich. Thus it was not surprising that Scholem, who was traveling around Germany in the guise of an employee of the JDC, included Munich in his plans. His visit to the city is also not surprising from the personal angle. He knew Munich very well from his days as a student there, in 1919–22. He had written his doctoral dissertation on *The Book Bahir* at the University of Munich, based on a manuscript of that mystical work in the Hebrew manuscript collection of the Bavarian National Library. It was also in Munich that he prepared himself for emigration to the Land of Israel.

When he arrived in Munich in 1946, Scholem began searching for collections of Jewish books, holding meetings with central figures who could help him. With the assistance of Leo Schwarz, the director of the JDC for refugee affairs in the city, he found a place to sleep in the JDC offices. Schwarz made a very good impression on Scholem and displayed a willingness to help him, unlike the people in the JDC office in Frankfurt. The day after Scholem's arrival, he met the head of the renewed Jewish community of Munich, Julius Spanier, who told him about the dismal situation with respect to locating Jewish books: many of them had been burned in the Allied bombings; the community library had disappeared without a trace; and the community archive had been moved somewhere, along with other general archives, and all of them had been burned there as early as 1943.[156] A few valuable items had been buried in the Jewish cemetery, but the work of searching for them and removing them had not yet been done. According to Scholem, Spanier understood the need to transfer the items that still might be found from Munich to Jerusalem, because of the present situation of the community: "*Here* there are *three* couples, both of whose members are Jewish, and all the rest are intermarriages, of which one spouse declared his Judaism and desire to belong to the community."[157]

Scholem recorded in his diary his impressions of the conversations he had with various people in Munich: "There are some Nazis who still know where the things disappeared to, especially university people, like the former professor of Semitic languages. . . . The amount of information possessed by all these people is minuscule. But I got information . . . that I hadn't thought of before, that [Hans Ludwig] Held was still alive, and he was again the head of the *municipal* library."[158]

Several times in his trip, Scholem had opportunities to find out about the fate of Jewish books from Nazi sources. On several occasions he heard that there were still collections of Jewish books in hiding places known only to former Nazi officials. These officials were willing to share the information in their possession, but they insisted on one condition, which Scholem mentioned in the report that he wrote after his return home: "The question is how much it is permitted to be involved with people like that in order to obtain information, which of course is connected to the demand made by these gentlemen to be given a certificate of merit as philo-Semites (*ohavei Israel*)."[159] Scholem decided to refrain from depending on such sources of information, and he did not meet with those officials, but he indicated that there was reason to believe the reports, because many Nazis had plundered valuable Jewish books on their own account. "Thus it is possible," Scholem wrote, "that in time things of this kind will be put up for sale in Germany."[160]

One of the pieces of information that Scholem received in his conversations with people of Munich encouraged him greatly: Held was in Munich and the director of the city's municipal library. Held—whom Allony described a few years later as "short and broad of build," whose "appearance is impressive and leaves an impression"[161]—had been the director of that library from 1921 until the Nazis came to power in 1933, when he was dismissed because he was a socialist. He was restored to this position in 1945. Scholem was on friendly terms with Held, and the two had exchanged a number of letters before the war and apparently met when Scholem visited Munich in 1927. Held was interested in Judaism and had even published a number of works on Jewish topics, including an adaptation of a collection of Talmudic tales with an introduction and a book on the Golem.[162]

Scholem met with Held after an unsuccessful meeting with the director of the Bavarian National Library, who had shown little willingness to help. However, Scholem did discover in this meeting that the important and famous collection of Hebrew and Jewish books and manuscripts owned by the library had been saved in its entirety and was awaiting rearrangement. Scholem was very familiar with this collection from his student days in Munich, and he had even published corrections to the important catalogue of manuscripts in the library written by Moritz Steinschneider.[163]

In his meeting with Held, Scholem presented the idea that the Germans should compensate the Jewish people, which he had been discussed with Eppelsheimer in Frankfurt. According to this idea, the city of Munich would transfer the important Hebrew manuscripts in its collection—chiefly the famous Codex 95, the only complete manuscript of the Talmud, which Steinschneider had estimated to be the most valuable in the collection[164]—to the Hebrew University. Scholem reported to the Hebrew University on his conversation with Held: "I said that it might be an important moral gesture if German authorities, of their own free will, would turn over certain of this objects, and especially the Munich manuscript of the Talmud, to the Hebrew University in Jerusalem as a symbolic act towards the Jewish people and as a *first step toward bridging the awful abyss* that has been created between the two peoples."[165]

Although Scholem's approach in the two cities had been similar, there was an important difference between the collections in Munich and Frankfurt: whereas the manuscripts in the municipal library of Frankfurt had been contributed or purchased with funds provided by the local Jewish community, the books in Munich were legally owned in full by the Bavarian state, and there was no judicial basis for the claim that they belong to the Jewish people. Any negotiations about transferring part of this collection could proceed only on an ethical and political basis, rather than a legal one. Hence in his conversation with Held, Scholem raised Eppelsheimer's idea that such a step could be taken only at the initiative of German agents, without any Jewish intervention. "The Germans who are prepared to deal with this matter are decidedly anti-Nazi and of a pure ethical character," he declared in the report written after his return, referring to Eppelsheimer and Held. "They are interested in seeing the matter proposed by Germans and not as a claim of the Jews."[166] Held expressed one concern: if such a gesture were to encounter refusal on the Jewish side, this would cause great distress among the Germans, and Scholem wrote his thoughts on this point to the university as well: "I, personally, expressed the opinion that the university would give a decent and encouraging answer to such a symbolic act of restitution of the important Jewish treasures which are legally in the hands of the Bavarian government. I said that the university might recall the *existence of two Germanys* and, at any rate, would take an attitude in line with general humanistic and liberal principles which it has always stood for."[167]

Scholem's remarks on building a bridge over the abyss that had opened between the two nations and on recognition that there were two Germanys came much before their time for both sides, and that could be why the plan to convey the precious material to the Hebrew University was never carried out. The Hebrew-language collection, including Codex 95, remains in the possession of the Bavarian National Library.

Scholem's efforts to obtain other important manuscripts and books from collections in German libraries for the National Library in Jerusalem had a practical purpose internal to Jewry: to fill in the huge gap created by the disappearance of a large number of the manuscripts that had been owned by Jews. The fate of the lost manuscripts was unknown, and the likelihood that they had been burned in Allied air raids was as great as the possibility that they might be found in the future. In his letter to the Hebrew University, Scholem called this uncertainty "one of the worst aspects of my experience here."[168] Indeed, his efforts in Munich to find information about book collections produced no results: "Everyone gives me different addresses, which are of little use, and sends me from one person to another who knows even less!" he wrote in his diary on July 26.[169] This situation and his oppressive mental and physical fatigue reinforced his sense that there was a fundamental error in his mission—specifically, the estimated time needed for seeking and locating the books. This error, he felt, placed him in an impossible situation. On Sunday, July 28, on the eve of his departure from Munich after visiting the DP camp in Landsberg, he wrote in his diary: "A huge storm toward evening. I feel so bad and unfit for the mission here! My insomnia comes of course with this constant feeling and incessant reflections. Every little thing requires a long time, and I cannot do anything because of lack of unlimited time!"[170]

Frankfurt and Berlin (July 30–August 11)

Scholem left Munich with a bitter sense of disappointment. "A bad feeling upon leaving here," he wrote in his diary on July 29, on the eve of his departure on the night train to Frankfurt. "I didn't succeed in finding even a few things, and who can find them?!"[171] On a one-day visit to Frankfurt, on the way to Berlin, he managed to leave his belongings and civilian clothes in the Jewish Agency offices, for fear that they would be stolen in Berlin. This short stay in Frankfurt also allowed him to form a gloomy picture of the disorganization and disunity in the ranks of the various Jewish agencies active in Europe: "The tension and

FIGURE 6 Friedrichsgracht Street in the Spittelmarkt quarter of Berlin, May 1945. Bundesarchive Deutschland, 183-R77870.

mutual bitterness among all the camps is very great. From every side I hear people complaining about each other, some seem justified, and others don't even have the appearance of justification. We have not formed a united front at all!"[172]

On August 1, at nine o'clock in the morning, Scholem's train from Frankfurt reached Berlin. His first quarters in Berlin were in the JDC building, but because it was outside of the city, he looked for somewhere else to stay. He spent the first days in meetings with various people regarding his mission, but the day after his arrival he also visited the DP camps in Schlachtensee and Tempelhof "to see the people coming from Russia."[173] Immediately afterward he went to see the center of Berlin and the scenes of his childhood for the first time after the war: "I saw our apartments in Neue Grünstrasse, [and] Friedrichsgracht *Everything* is destroyed!! The inner part of the city—*dead*. We went as far as the synagogue on Oranienburgstrasse. In the evening, *greeting the Sabbath* with Rabbi Rosenberg and with Hermann Landau from Fürth. A strange impression—*Shabbat Chazon* in Berlin after 14 years!"[174]

The situation in Berlin while Scholem was there suited the season according to the Jewish calendar—the season of days of mourning for the destruction of the Temple and the sorrow and distress that followed it. It was not by chance that Scholem emphasized the fact that the Sabbath of August 3 was Shabbat Chazon. The reading from the Prophets on this Sabbath, the last one before the fast day of the Ninth of Ab, is the following verses from the book of Isaiah: "Your country is desolate; your cities are burned with fire; your land, strangers devour it in your presence, and it is desolate, as overthrown by floods. And the daughter of Zion is left as a booth in a vineyard, as a lodge in a garden of cucumbers, as a besieged city. Except the LORD of hosts had left unto us a very small remnant, we should have been as Sodom, we should have been like unto Gomorrah" (Isaiah 1:7–9).

On that Sabbath Scholem moved into a "small and dreadful" room in a hotel in the Dahlem neighborhood of southern Berlin.[175] After another walk around the center of the city, he met with Ernst Grumach, a Jewish scholar of classics who had worked as a forced laborer in Berlin from 1941 in the library of stolen books that had been established by the RSHA.[176] Scholem received important information from Grumach about Jewish libraries that had been transferred to this Nazi library in Berlin, including the fact that Grumach had sent most of the books that passed through his hands to the Niemes castle in Czechoslovakia. When this meeting ended, late at night, the JDC car that was supposed to pick Scholem up and take him to his hotel did not appear, and he was forced to walk for an hour and a half until he found the hotel.[177] His attitude toward the JDC people became increasingly negative and bitter. The next day he wrote in his notes that, among the JDC people in Berlin, "a bad attitude toward me is brewing, and I feel it through the mask of a skewed smile. I don't know what caused it, but I see and feel it."[178]

The next day, after a sleepless night, Scholem resolved to end his journey and return home. He decided to give up on the effort to enter the English occupation zone and to cancel the trip to the United States that he had planned to take with Fania. The fact that in Berlin he had failed to find any hint of the location of important book collections, especially because of the limited time and the restrictions that had been imposed on his movements, as well as his generally gloomy mood, led him to feel that he had exhausted all the available possibilities and was himself close to exhaustion. Scholem spent the eve of the Nine of Ab at prayer with refugees in the Schlachtensee camp. Scholem recorded his impressions of the evening in his diary on August 5: "[Rabbi Mayer] Abramowitz read the dirges, and it was very impressive—nevertheless I felt the public's lack of response to this text. As though they had been turned to stone."[179] Scholem had known Abramowitz since the time he had studied with Saul Lieberman at the Jewish Theological Seminary in New York and with Scholem when he was there in 1938. Now Abramowitz was serving as a US Army chaplain.[180] While serving in various places in Germany, Abramowitz had visited many DP camps and provided the residents with religious services and material assistance (food and other basic necessities), and he helped some of them in their efforts to reach Palestine. He was stationed in Berlin in 1946 and took part in organizing the flight of Jews from Eastern Europe and tended to the residents of the Schlachtensee and Tempelhof camps. Perhaps Abramowitz's most important achievement in Berlin was the establishment of a large Jewish and Hebrew school for the Jewish children in the region, especially in the two camps. At the same time he created a teacher training program, in which a group of educated people from the camps took part. The teachers met every Thursday evening to learn Hebrew and educational methods and to discuss problems in the camps, as well as to have a social gathering at which they sang, danced, and ate.[181] On one Thursday evening, August 8, about a hundred teachers from the camp gathered at Abramowitz's house. He had just returned from a visit to Palestine, and he told the group —with a pinch of pathos and exaggeration—about the situation in the Yishuv in general and about the attitude toward them, the Jewish refugees waiting in Germany for the opportunity to immigrate to the Land of Israel. Two weeks later, the Yiddish magazine of the Schlachtensee and Tempelhof camps described the event: "He spoke . . . in warm words, telling us how well the Yishuv was organized. How every Jew knows what he is fighting for. From large to small, they do not pay heed to the difficulties, they do not dwell on their worries, everyone is occupied with a single task: to make preparations for thousands of new immigrants. Without commotion, without noise. Life proceeds in its course. Not a minute is lost, not a second of Jewish work for our cause."[182]

The audience eagerly drank in the charismatic rabbi's utopian descriptions of the Land of Israel, which were meant to inspire confidence and faith in the teachers, and in which they could also find consolation for their present situation and a goal to strive for. The magazine article described the effect of Abramowitz's words on his listeners: "The rabbi spoke, and his words were full of enthusiasm, soothing our miserable souls, like the best balm of all. The Yishuv is full of hope. Our victory—Abramowitz cries out—is assured. No power can stop the sweeping current."[183]

When Abramowitz was finished speaking, everyone ate together in a festive mood and spoke about their work, their purpose, and their future in the spirit of the rabbi. After the meal Scholem, the professor from the Hebrew University in Jerusalem, who had been present throughout the evening, rose and also spoke to the teachers in Hebrew for about half an hour. He praised them and tried to inspire them with hope and courage to pursue the goal they had chosen for themselves. The magazine article noted that "it was a special pleasure for us to hear the words of Professor Scholem, who, in Hebrew full of life, expressed his joy at seeing before him such a group of teachers and educators, who were standing on guard and doing everything to be the educators of a generation as firm as rock, to teach youth who must be filled with the spirit of our heroes. A generation that will know its own value and be prepared for action."[184]

Scholem's meetings with the refugees and the spirit of his talks in Frankfurt and Berlin, as presented here, indicate the way he understood his mission—as related to the Yishuv in general and not just to the Hebrew University and the National Library. His purpose was not only to bring ownerless books to Palestine to make it a spiritual center of Jewish culture, but also to encourage the stateless refugees and arouse their Zionist tendencies, which would lead them to immigrate and contribute to making Palestine a Jewish center.

In addition to his meetings with the Jewish residents of postwar Berlin, and despite the signs of fatigue and psychological distress that are evident in his diary, he also spent time searching for books, but without great success. At a meeting with Reuben Peiss, the head of the delegation of the US Library of Congress in Europe, Scholem spoke about Gestapo files and Nazi literature, which he wanted to transfer to Jerusalem, and thereby he aroused Peiss's interest in them, probably making it impossible to transfer them to Palestine. "The man is not friendly," he wrote about Peiss in his journal, "and he acts according to 'the letter of the law'!"[185] Another meeting with an American officer convinced Scholem of the uselessness of that avenue of activity: "Of course there would be no benefit to working with them unless I had *a great deal of time*," he wrote, "then they could arrange something for me, through official channels."[186]

Scholem had very little success in finding important books in Berlin. His investigations showed that all the Jewish community libraries had been transferred to the Gestapo. Books on general subjects had been sent to German public libraries, and locating them was very complicated.[187] As for private libraries, Scholem wrote in his report: "Only in very few cases did a few Jews, who lived in mixed marriages and were saved by a miracle from the destruction of their apartments by bombing, succeed in keeping their private libraries, and I saw no more than two like that with my own eyes, and their owners were very pleased."[188] The Jewish community of Berlin had been left with almost none of the libraries and archives that had been in its possession, but in this area Scholem did achieve something important: an agreement in principle with the head of the community to transfer to the Hebrew University in Jerusalem the books that it had owned and that, as Scholem surmised, had been sent to the Niemes castle in Czechoslovakia.[189]

On August 9, he went to the head of the Jewish community to receive an official letter to this effect. On his way to this meeting, Scholem was involved in a traffic accident: in the center of the city, at the corner of Unter den Linden and Friedrichstrasse, a motorcycle ran into the military jeep he was riding in, and he got a deep cut on his right arm. The initial treatment and x-rays at the community hospital showed that, fortunately, he had not broken any ribs. "The pain is very great, as is my weakness," he wrote in his diary the next day, "but I hope that in a week the wound will heal, if it is not infected. A souvenir of Berlin. My coat and my uniform were torn, and I don't have another!"[190] The wound made things difficult for Scholem, both physically and psychologically, and intensified his feelings of despair at not accomplishing much in Berlin. As he wrote in his diary: "I haven't yet sent telegrams about canceling my trip to the US. There is a cruel inner laziness that's worse than anything, because of the feverish activity that brings no benefit."[191]

Frankfurt, Heidelberg, Paris, and Jerusalem (August 12–26)

On the morning of August 12, Scholem returned to Frankfurt and began to prepare for his return to Jerusalem and the cancellation of his planned trip to the United States. Though he felt that his physical condition was improving slightly and that his wound was healing, his psychological condition continued to decline. "I have no 'holy spirit,'" he wrote in his diary, "something has been broken in me, and I am very depressed, something of the creativity and strength I had [is gone]. This mission has eaten me up, *and it did not bring with it the inner salvation (hapdut hapnimit) I had thought of.*"[192] His hopes for recovery from his wound also proved illusory, and it began to worry him again: "This morning my wound opened, which had not been bandaged tightly enough by the aide yesterday. A big mess."[193]

At that time Scholem held his last meetings with Pinson and Eppelsheimer, and he also worked for a few hours with Bencowitz in the OAD. A two-day visit to Heidelberg on August 17–18 did not improve his gloomy mood. At that time he stayed with Schneider and met again with friends. "Sad days in Frankfurt," he wrote in his diary, "a dreadful feeling of isolation."[194] On August 20 he returned to Paris, and on August 26—almost four and a half months after the beginning of his journey from Paris—Scholem returned to his home at 28 Abarbanel Street in the Rehavia neighborhood of Jerusalem.

A Famous Thief: The Manuscript Operation in the Offenbach Archival Depot

A few months after Scholem flew from Paris to Tel Aviv via Cairo, a special shipment traveled across the Mediterranean on its way to Palestine. In the hold of a ship that had sailed from England, along with the private library of Chaim

Weizmann, were five crates containing a large number of rare and valuable Hebrew manuscripts and books, making their way to the National and University Library in Jerusalem. The story of how which this rare collection from the OAD ended up in the hold of a ship sailing eastward from Europe is directly connected to Scholem and to Herbert Friedman, a young rabbi who was serving as a chaplain in Frankfurt and Offenbach.[195]

While working in the OAD, Scholem had sorted out the rarest and most precious Hebrew books and manuscripts that he found, putting them in five crates that were arranged according to the value of their contents.[196] His fear that these rare treasures might be stolen and sold on the black market led him to present an official request to the American authorities to take the crates with him to Palestine. This request met with refusal, behind which apparently lay an expression of interest in the books on the part of Jewish organizations in the United States. In particular, Louis Finkelstein, head of the Jewish Theological Seminary in New York, wanted some of this precious material for his library and had begun to try to obtain it.[197] In despair, Scholem spoke to Friedman, who sympathized with his situation and promised to help solve the problem. On New Year's Eve, more than three months after Scholem had left Europe, Friedman stole the crates of books from the warehouse, disguising them as a shipment of books borrowed by the JDC for the DP camps. Bencowitz turned a blind eye. Friedman signed the lending form in the name of Pinson, who by that time had already been in the United States for a few months.

Around midnight, when the warehouse workers were drunk as a result of celebrating the new year, Friedman loaded the crates into a windowless ambulance belonging to the JDC and then transferred them to a military truck that was parked nearby. He drove from Offenbach to the office of the Jewish Agency in Paris, to send the crates on to Scholem in Palestine through it. The people at the Jewish Agency refused to accept the stolen crates or take part in the plot, but they provided Friedman with important information: Weizmann's private library was being sent from England to Palestine on a ship that was then anchored in Antwerp. The ship was about to depart, and for Friedman this seemed to be the most secure and easy solution: "Hiding my five crates among his dozens would be the easiest way to smuggle the merchandise to Palestine and Scholem," he wrote in his memoirs many years later.[198] So he drove from Paris to Antwerp; scattered the crates intended for Scholem, which bore his name, among the crates of books from Weizmann's library; sent a telegram announcing the shipment to Jerusalem; and returned to Offenbach, where he continued his regular life.

A few weeks later Friedman was interrogated by the military police, who showed him proof of his responsibility for the disappearance of the books.

Knowing that he would face a court-martial, Friedman divulged the details of the affair to Bernstein, the advisor on Jewish affairs to the US Army in Europe. Bernstein arranged for an immediate meeting between Friedman and General Lucius Clay, commander of the US forces in Germany, and Friedman told him the whole story. Years later, in an interview, Friedman remembered his answer to Clay's question about what had motivated him to steal the books: "I said I didn't want the stuff to get stolen and lost the second time. Those boxes wouldn't be secure in that warehouse, somebody would rip them open, somebody would see the stuff, somebody would recognize it. An antiquarian would be approached, the stuff has value. And it was lost once. Its owners are gone. The Jewish people collectively is concentrating in Palestine. Palestine will be free one fine day. These should be in the National Jewish Library in Palestine, that's the successor, inheritor of all that stuff. That's why I did it."[199]

Friedman convinced Clay that he hadn't intended to sell the books on the black market, and that his chief concern had been to keep the books from being lost. It might be that the evident conviction with which Friedman spoke had an effect on Clay. In any event, he canceled the court-martial that had been hanging over Friedman's head, but he also ordered Friedman sent back to the United States immediately and discharged from the army. As for the crates, Clay ordered that they be returned to Europe immediately. At the end of the conversation, Friedman urged Clay not to move these valuable cultural treasures again, but to leave them in Palestine under the trusteeship of the Hebrew University.[200]

Further developments in this affair over the following months are revealed in a series of telegrams from Jerusalem, Frankfurt, and Paris, which are in the archives of the Hebrew University.[201] In mid-January the existence of the shipment was first reported to Senator, who tried to clarify the matter with Scholem—but the latter had known nothing about Friedman's actions and had no information about the exact contents of the crates. His surprise on receiving the information is shown in his letter to Senator in early March. Scholem wrote about his efforts to clarify the exact contents of the shipment before it arrived in Palestine. He reported that he had sent a man associated with the university to the ship—which was apparently then docked in France on its way to Palestine—to find out more about the shipment: "The difficulty is that I have no notion of the identity of these mysterious things, just one or two conjectures, and I have to wait until our friend opens them for examination." In the same letter he expressed apprehension about the likely consequences if it became known that he had been involved in stealing and shipping the books. In early 1947 a discussion had been held at the Hebrew University about sending a new delegation to Europe to organize the transfer of many books to Palestine. Without much enthusiasm, Scholem had agreed to join the delegation, if no other appropriate person could be found. "But now," he wrote Senator, "you must understand that if there is anything in it, and my name is known in high places, *it should not even be considered* that I can go there again, because they will reject me of course in the examination office. And this is of great concern, because I don't know who will go [instead]."[202] Scholem's apprehensions about the anger that the affair would provoke among the American authorities and the difficulties it would present for his continued efforts to rescue books were warranted, at least in the short term. For example, an official request by the JDC to the American authorities to remove additional books for the DP camps encountered many difficulties.[203]

News that the crates had been stolen was spreading among the Jewish figures who had an interest of their own in the books, which required the American authorities to locate the stolen books to return them. At the end of March a telegram from Frankfurt reached Scholem, in which Friedman informed him that the books would apparently have to be sent back, and that he would have to confirm receipt of the crates and promise not to open them except on further instructions.[204] Two days later another telegram arrived, this time from Bernstein, who corroborated Friedman's message: the crates must be returned to Frankfurt immediately, and this should be done personally, at any price, by Charles Passman, the new director of the JDC in Europe, who was visiting Palestine at that time. The problem was that the crates had still not reached Palestine.[205] Finally, on April 8, the crates were received by the Hebrew University in Jerusalem and, as promised, were left unopened. Scholem promptly sent a telegram with the news to Bernstein and received instructions from him to keep the sealed crates at the university for the time being, to inform Clay directly of their arrival, and to await further instructions.[206] A month later instructions were received from the US consulate in Jerusalem to transfer the crates to it, so they could be flown back to Europe.[207] On May 7, the crates were conveyed to the consulate, where they were opened and their contents were examined cursorily. The receipt given by the consulate to the Hebrew University after delivery of the crates stated: "Four cases which are apparently full, one case which is practically empty."[208] But a few days later, and without any clear evidence from the documents for the reasons for the change, the decision was reversed, and instructions were given to leave the books and manuscripts in Jerusalem and to appoint the Hebrew University as their trustee.[209]

When the crates were examined, a brief list in English of their contents was made by a librarian from the National and University Library, in the presence of a representative of the American consulate.[210] At the end of the list a short affidavit was appended, confirming delivery of the collection to the Hebrew University on June 22, 1947, and the university's acceptance of the consulate's conditions: "We undertake to return any and all of them [the items in the collection] on first request from that office."[211] Thus in the summer of 1947, a collection of Jewish cultural treasures from Europe—treasures that had been plundered by the Nazis, collected by the American occupation authorities, placed in the OAD, sorted by Scholem, stolen by Friedman, and sent to Palestine—found its way to the National Library on Mount Scopus under the trusteeship of the Hebrew University in Jerusalem. As mentioned above, Scholem's and Friedman's fear that the books in the OAD were liable to be stolen and sold illegally in Germany was not without foundation. Moreover, under the American military regime in Germany, stealing and bending the law by chaplains to fulfill Jewish interests was not a unique event. Abramowitz, Scholem's friend and former student, encountered difficulties when he wanted to print textbooks for the school he had established. To accomplish this task, he stole paper from a military warehouse and used threats and bribery in the form of cigarettes and military coal to get the printing done in a shop in the French occupation zone in Berlin.[212]

Thus Friedman's action was not exceptional, and if he hadn't been caught, the story would probably not have aroused any attention. Moreover, there are solid grounds for assuming that if he had not taken these valuable manuscripts illegally and sent them abroad secretly, most of them would have disappeared. At the same time, because of the significance of his operation in the international arena and the sensitivity of the subject for the various Jewish centers around the world, Friedman's actions could not have remained a secret, and the story would inevitably have been publicized in the Jewish world as well as in the American military.

On December 9, 1947, almost a year after the theft of the books from the OAD and their illegal shipment to Palestine, an article about these events was published in *Stars and Stripes*, the American military newspaper.[213] The story had reached the journalists from Clay. They performed a short investigation and published its results without mentioning the names of the men involved in the affair. The article reported the events in brief and inaccurately. Thus, for example, the journalists claimed that two American captains (one a chaplain) had committed the robbery, and that the crates were later and unexpectedly found in Jerusalem as a result of an investigation initiated by the US consul there. In any event, two central and important items of information about the affair appeared in the article: the estimate that 1,100 stolen items had been in the crates, and an appraisal of their value at between $3 and $5 million. The authors based this appraisal on a list of the items supposedly written by Scholem. Toward the end, the article criticized the US military regime in Germany for the way in which it had handled the matter, claiming that leaving the items in Palestine was contrary to "present

MG [military government] regulations which state that all looted materials must be returned to the country of origin."[214] A few months later the article reached Magnes, who immediately passed it on to Scholem, along with a short letter asking him to respond to it. The need for a proper response arose from fear that the article would arouse renewed interest in the books and the desire to come to a final decision regarding them, a decision that would imply their removal from the temporary trusteeship of the university.[215]

Less than a week later, Scholem sent a detailed reply to Magnes, which was mainly related to the article's estimates of the number of the books and their value.[216] Scholem denied that he had made a list of the items or estimated their value. In fact, he claimed that his criteria in sorting the books had been their value for a museum and the use to which they could be put for scholarship. He wrote that the monetary value of the items was not, in fact, high—at most about $10,000—though he knew very well that it was not really possible to estimate the market value of such unique items. Regarding the number of books that had been shipped, Scholem claimed that it had been greatly exaggerated. There were 350 items, not 1,100. Scholem attributed the exaggerated estimate to the way in which the books had been crated in Offenbach, where the average number of books per crate had been estimated to be 220—since the shipment had contained five crates, that explained the journalists' estimate.[217]

Scholem's claims were supported by the list of the contents made in the US consulate in preparation for their transfer to the university. That list contains 378 items and specifies which crate each had been in. The list is highly important for understanding Scholem's mission in Europe and his feelings when he examined the eclectic and abundant stolen cultural treasures in the OAD. The manuscripts and books in the crates symbolize the destruction of European Jewry and reflect the chaos that prevailed in Germany after the war. This small collection includes manuscripts from everywhere in Europe, mainly from Eastern Europe, which were listed with no internal order—exactly as they were crated by Scholem in Offenbach and found in the crates when they were opened in Jerusalem. The list is of writings from various places and periods, of different literary genres, and brought together by chance. At the same time, it is clear that chance alone did not produce the collection. Scholem's sharp eye redeemed it from absolute randomness and gave it a certain direction, and he relied on a kind of inner canon according to which he determined what was most worthy of being saved for the future of the Jewish people. All this was done, of course, within the restrictions of the relatively small selection of material gathered in the OAD.

Common to all the manuscripts in the crates—which varied widely in terms of place of origin, form, and content—was that they were written evidence of the rich and varied Jewish cultural life that had been exterminated in Europe. In addition, the arrival of these writings in various ways and after many peregrinations in a single collection that was illegally transported to Jerusalem is strongly reminiscent of the fate of the patchwork society of refugees who also arrived on German soil at the end of the war, after many tribulations and reversals of fortune, and who sought to continue to the Land of Israel. Like Scholem's encounter with the refugees in Germany and his first encounter with the writings in Offenbach, his renewed acquaintance with them almost a year later in Jerusalem was disappointing, as he reported to Baron: "I must say I am a little disappointed in the contents—from my own inspection I gather that there is nothing very ancient there, no medieval mss., most of it dating to the seventeenth or eighteenth centuries if not later."[218] The list indeed shows that the collection contained no truly ancient manuscripts or incunabula of great antiquarian value in 1947, but Scholem was also right in stating that it was impossible to assess the value of unique items, whose historical value as treasures of Jewish culture increases with the passage of time.

Magnes's fear that, after publication of the article in *Stars and Stripes*, they would be required to return the valuable collection proved to be in vain. To this day, these rare manuscripts remain in the National Library of Israel in Givat Ram —having been brought from Mount Scopus after yet another adventure. In 1949, at the end of Israel's war of independence, after the country reached a cease-fire agreement with Jordan, Mount Scopus remained an Israeli enclave surrounded by Jordanian territory. Within that enclave many books and manuscripts from the National Library were also cut off, including the collection from the OAD. Over time all the manuscripts were smuggled into Israel, a few at a time, by soldiers returning in the weekly supply convoy, and they were housed in the new National Library building in the campus of the Hebrew University in Givat Ram, which was inaugurated in the 1950s.[219]

This episode also had a happy ending for Scholem. He did not become persona non grata as he had feared, either in the American occupation zone or among the Jews of the United States. Scholem played a central role in the continued work of the Diaspora Treasures Committee and went to Europe a number of times in search of additional collections of books. Moreover, he was appointed the vice chairman of Jewish Cultural Reconstruction Inc. (JCR), the New York–based successor of the CEJCR that served as an umbrella organization to deal with the restoration of Jewish property that had been plundered by the Nazis. A few years later he also helped establish the Institute of Microfilmed Hebrew Manuscripts at the National Library and prepare Allony for his mission to Europe to locate and photograph Hebrew manuscripts.[220]

However, not surprisingly, among Scholem's private papers there is almost no mention of this affair or the publicity it received, except for one entry in his diary, where he described his renewed encounter with the European director of the JDC, Joseph Schwartz: "August 4 [1948]. Yesterday evening with Senator at a kind of reception for Dr. Joseph Schwartz from the JDC, where I met Mr. Goldstein, whom I had known in Paris. We spoke about books. Schwartz greeted me with the words: 'Sie sind ja inzwischen a famous thief geworden [you have become in the meanwhile a famous thief].'"[221]

CHAPTER 6

THE HEART OF ODYSSEUS

Oh, Gerhard, glue the parts of your heart back together. Do it like Odysseus, to whom the gods could only give an impervious heart, because he was so full of cunning and renewed himself time after time. For you know this is not yet the end; something worse can always come. And we also have to be able to undergo the end (and that doesn't necessarily mean to survive it).

HANNAH ARENDT TO GERSHOM SCHOLEM, NOVEMBER 27, 1946[1]

In my heart, the city
Where God sent me.
Will the angel, the keeper of the seal
Be impressed by it?

GERSHOM SCHOLEM, "GRUSS VOM ANGELUS"[2]

After the Journey

Scholem's trip to Europe marked the beginning of the Hebrew University's efforts to rescue Jewish cultural treasures that had been plundered by the Nazis and restore them to Jewish hands, and many further trips to Europe were made on that mission. In the wake of Scholem's investigations and recommendations, and the promise he had received from the council of the Jewish communities of Bohemia and Moravia to transfer the books that arrived from Theresienstadt to the university, it was decided first to concentrate the efforts and searches in Prague and the rest of Czechoslovakia. The next three trips, the first of which was made by Shmuel Hugo Bergmann in November 1946, about three months after Scholem's return, were to that country.[3]

Apparently under Scholem's influence, in view of the insights on the state of the looted Jewish books in Germany that he had gained during his visit, the Hebrew University modified the official guidelines for action that had been set by the legal committee discussed in the previous chapter—no longer would the university demand to be the sole representative of the Jewish people and its self-image, serving as the legal heir to the stolen treasures of Jewish culture that remained unowned. Scholem's impressions of the storage conditions of the books in the Offenbach Archival Depot (OAD) and of the danger threatening them from thieves and international law led him to recognize that the various Jewish centers in the world should join forces to remove the books from German soil as soon as possible, without worrying about dividing them among the centers. At a meeting of the Diaspora Treasures Committee soon after Scholem's return to Palestine—which was attended by Salo Baron, the chairman of the Commission on European Jewish Cultural Reconstruction (CEJCR)—two important decisions were made. The first was to tighten coordination between the committees in Jerusalem and New York, which included having each committee inform the other of its plans. The second decision, reached unanimously by the members of the committee after hearing what Scholem had to say, was that the "removal of the books from Germany is urgent and precedes the issue of their distribution."[4] With time the Hebrew University developed a better understanding of the needs of various Jewish centers in the world, especially those in the United States, and the competition among the various centers on this matter died down—in part because priority was given to the National Library of Israel in choosing the books it needed.[5] The establishment in April 1947 of a united front on the part of Jewish institutions throughout the world, through the establishment of Jewish Cultural Reconstruction Inc., the umbrella organization for the recovery of stolen Jewish cultural treasures that replaced the CEJCR, contributed to this understanding. This organization worked to locate the treasures, collect them, and distribute them among various Jewish centers; it was disbanded in 1952 when its work had come to an end. Eventually, 85 percent of the treasures was divided between the United States and Israel, 8 percent went to Europe (half of that to Britain), and the remaining 7 percent was divided among the other Jewish centers in the world.[6] During the organization's existence, Baron was its chairman, and Joshua Starr, followed by Hannah Arendt, was the general secretary. Scholem was its vice chairman for a time.

Judged by any external standard, Scholem's trip to Europe had been a success. The information that he had found and the connections he had made with the Jewish communities in Czechoslovakia were extremely important for the continuation of the work and led to the transfer of many books to the National Library.[7] Moreover, the preliminary contracts Scholem had made with the directors of the German libraries in Frankfurt and Munich made it possible to hope not only for the return of stolen books but also for negotiations regarding compensation to the Jewish people in the form of Jewish manuscripts that belonged legally to Germany. In addition to all this, Scholem's intensive work in the OAD in sorting books and manuscripts, packing some extremely valuable ones in crates, and checking the possibilities for shipping them to Palestine ultimately led Herbert Friedman to smuggle the crates out of Germany.

Scholem's work gained him great respect on the part of his colleages at the Hebrew University. Werner Senator thanked him in an official letter: "Despite the many difficulties, you succeeded in bringing us a lot of information from abroad and to clarify the situation. You made important connections, and we hope that in the end we will succeed, because of your action, in obtaining very important material for our National Library."[8] Even Scholem stated in his final report to the Hebrew University that it "was possible to accomplish to a large degree" his main task in Europe.[9] In the weeks after his return, Scholem was still busy with matters connected to his mission. Letters reached him from various places in Europe with new information about books and expressions of willingness to renew academic and personal connections that had been disrupted by the war, and he sent letters to Europe regarding the continuation of his work there, as well as personal letters to people he had gotten to know on the trip. At that time he was also engaged in writing an article on his mission, which was published in *Haaretz* about a year later,[10] and in preparing a lecture on his impressions of Jewish life in Germany, which was also published in *Haaretz*.[11] Despite his great activity and apparent success, Scholem returned from his trip exhausted in body and soul. The wound in Berlin and what he had seen and experienced greatly weakened his body and spirit, and a week after his return the university administration allotted him fifty pounds for recuperation and a vacation.[12] Many years later, Fania described his serious condition upon returning from Europe:

> He returned to the Land of Israel physically exhausted and mentally depressed. He would lie down for most of the day, doing nothing, hardly speaking with anyone, and only occasionally repeat sentences like: "The Jewish people has been murdered, has ceased to exist, only smoldering stumps are left, with no strength or direction. Their source of nourishment no longer exists, the people has been cut off at the root. And we in Israel, a handful of people, the remnant (*sheerit hapletah*). Will we really find the strength to build the creative, free society, not materialistic, for the sake of whose formation we came here? Maybe we won't succeed in the task and we will degenerate, because we are bereft of our nation, we are orphaned." He was prostrate on his bed, going from couch to couch in his house, without finding repose for himself. Scholem refused to be consoled and he only became himself again and recovered a year later.[13]

One of the central feelings that Scholem repeated in his notes and reports during the whole time he was in Europe was his sense that his mission was a failure. His repeated complaints about the bad attitude of representatives of the Joint Distribution Committee (JDC) toward him; about his arriving in Europe too late, so that many items had already been lost; and about the lack of time available to him, which prevented him from finishing his work, reflect his increasing depression. These feelings are also clear in the diary entries and letters he wrote at that time. These documents indicate that the extreme worsening of his mental state began only after he entered Germany, his former homeland. In contrast, when he was in Paris and Czechoslovakia, his expressions of depression and despair were less frequent and extreme. His spirits reached their nadir during his visit to his home city, Berlin. The accident that he suffered there, immediately after his decision to return home, symbolizes the severity of the crisis he experienced.

The outward expressions of what appears to have been a deep depression reflect his internal responses to historical events. Thus, the effort to understand the psychological breakdown that deepened during and after his trip is also an effort to understand the influence of the Holocaust on his life. As a result, his mission should be seen as having two central aspects: the public one, involving his serving as an emissary of the Yishuv on a public mission and his movement through countries; and the personal one, involving his internal changes. The public journey is in fact an expression and symbol of the inner search.

The Public Aspect

As discussed in the previous chapter, Scholem went on his European mission disguised as an employee of the JDC, and his frequent trips to the displaced person (DP) camps in Germany show that he actually performed some of work that he was supposed to be doing for that organization. From his diary entries and letters, it is evident that he regarded this activity as an important part of his mission, and he was well aware of its public aspect. His delivering of lectures and their content, as far as records of them have been preserved, indicate that he was interested in influencing the refugees in the camps, encouraging and supporting those waiting for immigration visas and providing information to the residents of the camps about events in the Land of Israel from the political and spiritual points of view. In this respect, one may understand Scholem's activities in Europe in the context of the work of other emissaries from the Land of Israel and understand his responses to what he saw and experienced in the broader framework of the experiences of the other emissaries from the Land of Israel who were active in Europe at that time.

Indeed, for all of the emissaries the encounter with the Holocaust survivors in

Europe was complex and difficult, because through it for the first time the representatives of the Yishuv could understand the magnitude and depth of the tragedy. Irit Keynan has noted that "the emissaries went out on a Zionist mission, to bring 'the message of the Yishuv' to the refugees, and they saw themselves as bearers of the national vision. The real character and dimensions of the catastrophe of the Holocaust began to penetrate deep into their consciousness only after they reached the camps and met the survivors face to face."[14]

At the base of the Zionist purpose of the mission was the view of the survivors as the sole human reservoir that could provide the foundation for continuing the Zionist movement. The emissaries prepared for the encounter with the survivors from this position. Great apprehension about the future of the Zionist movement and the urgent need to bring the survivors to the Land of Israel charged the encounter with "the tension of high hopes from the survivors and strong fear that faith in Zionism and the force and willingness to enlist in a new struggle were not strong enough among them."[15]

The great gap between the goals of the mission as defined in the Land of Israel and the situation on the ground in Europe, as well as the great emotional burden that accompanied the encounter with the refugees, gave the emissaries a feeling of being caught between two worlds. On the one hand, they had a feeling that no one in the Land of Israel understood the situation in Europe properly, and on the other hand, they themselves found it difficult to understand the world of the refugees. Together with difficulties created by the poor state of the infrastructure in Germany after the war, which made it very hard to contact people in Palestine by mail or telegram, this situation often made the emissaries feel isolated and frustrated. In addition to the intense and exhausting work in the camps, there were often difficulties in communication and coordination with the American military authorities and the United Nations Relief and Rehabilitation Administration.[16] In Scholem's case, he had trouble obtaining an entry visa for Germany, and he complained repeatedly about lack of cooperation from the JDC and his disappointment with its representatives. Scholem's situation was harder in a certain sense than that of the other emissaries, and his isolation was greater. Scholem did not belong to any organization with a base in Europe like the Jewish Agency or the JDC, and no supporting institution or organizational network stood behind him. Perhaps this situation heightened his feelings that some people wanted his mission to fail and put difficulties in his way. These feelings were grounded in reality, based on the competition that arose among the various Jewish centers in the world to be the official representative of Jewry after the Holocaust and the legal heir of the property left ownerless. Though Scholem had a clear position on the matter, the conflict of interest between the Jews of the United States who were acting in the American occupation zone and the Jewish Yishuv in Palestine, which he represented, convinced him that the prognosis for continued Jewish existence was poor—a pessimistic attitude bound up with his fear for the fate of the Jews' cultural treasures. These feelings led him to change his mind during his journey and eventually support the establishment of an umbrella organization that would unite the interests of all the Jewish centers and create a united front in facing the world.

Another feeling that often arose in his writings during his trip was that he had arrived too late, and as a result great damage had been done to Jewish interests—many books had already been returned to their country of origin, and many others had disappeared. The emissaries from Palestine whose goal was the DP camps were in a similar situation. These emissaries frequently reported that the refugees accused them of having arrived in Europe very late, seven months after the end of the war. This disappointment affected the attitude of the refugees toward the emissaries and the Yishuv in general, and it also disturbed the emissaries.[17]

As a member of the Yishuv who had been sent to Europe by the Zionist leadership, Scholem found that his meetings with the survivors intensified his feelings of helplessness, as he wrote in a letter to Ben-Zion Dinur in 1943 that is discussed at length in chapter 4. As a Zionist who rejected coexistence between Jews and Germans and who was in favor of the renewal of the Jewish people in the Land of Israel, Scholem was appalled by the sights and sounds that confirmed the tragic end of European Jewry for him and made him feel helpless. As he wrote to Dinur, Scholem did not believe that any of the thinkers and shapers of Zionism (himself included) could have imagined such an end to the Jewish question. Even worse, in hindsight it was also clear that Zionism could never have been able to offer the correct solution, because none of its founders could have foreseen the problem in the correct light and its full extent, because reality had surpassed all imagination. The trap into which the Zionist movement fell because of the Holocaust appeared to him in its full power in his encounter with Germany and its residents in 1946. The helplessness of Zionism was demonstrated to Scholem by the ruins, the eyes of the refugees whom he met on his trip, and the pages of the abandoned books. But at the same time these were the remnants on whom the continuity of physical and spiritual Jewish existence was supposed to be based after the catastrophe. This paradoxical situation, containing both destruction and growth, extinction and the need for creation and continuity, characterized Scholem's personal situation during his time in Europe.

The Personal Aspect

It is impossible to completely separate the public aspect of Scholem's trip as an emissary of the Yishuv and the personal aspect of his journey, since Zionism had a central place in his life and played an extremely important role in shaping of his personality. Nevertheless, it may be said that Scholem's sojourn in Europe had great personal meaning for him, which also had consequences for his path in Zionism. The effort to understand this meaning opens a window on his inner journey and provides a way to understand the deep impression his experiences made on him. Here, perhaps, may be a reason for his increasingly serious personal state during the trip and after his return. To try to understand what this personal journey meant for him, it is necessary to shift the point of view from the level of external events to the symbolic level.

For Scholem, the stolen Jewish books were more than Jewish property that had to be recovered. They were the cultural heritage of the Jewish people and the key to its continued spiritual existence after the Holocaust. As discussed in the previous chapter, the question of whom the books belonged to, in the absence of legal heirs, was linked to the questions of who was the true representative of the Jewish people and where would be the future center and focus of its existence. The potential for the continuity of Jewish cultural and spiritual existence was embedded in the stolen books, which is what gave them such great significance in the Jewish world during and after the war and aroused such interest and competition among the various centers. Under these circumstances, the boundaries between the Jewish books that were to be found throughout Europe and their murdered owners were easily blurred, and the mission of saving the Jewish treasures of the Diaspora could be interpreted in light of the failure to save their owners.[18] These books could also easily become a symbol of the surviving Jews of Europe, who—like the books—became both a symbol of the hope for the continuity of Jewish existence and a monument to the millions who had been annihilated. The parallel between the books and Jewish people who had been saved from the Holocaust and were still in Europe in 1946 was also drawn by Scholem's contemporaries who visited the OAD. For example, the American historian Lucy Dawidowicz, who, in her capacity as an emissary of the JDC sorted books in the OAD about half a year after Scholem was there, described the experience: "The smell of death emanated from these hundreds of thousands of books and religious objects—orphaned and homeless mute survivors of their murdered owners. Like the human survivors, these inanimate remnants of a once-thriving civilization had found temporary and comfortless shelter in the land of Amalek. The sight of these massed inert objects chilled me."[19]

In contrast, the books were much more to Scholem than mute objects, and his attitude toward them was emotional. When he first immigrated to the Land of Israel, he worked as a librarian in the National Library, and all his life he worked on his own library, which today is the Scholem Collection in the National and University Library in Jerusalem. Malachi Beit-Arié described Scholem's special relationship to books in a talk after his death:

> Gershom Scholem never ceased dealing with books as the physical products of spiritual culture—with sensitivity, with spiritual tempestuousness, and with enthusiasm, whose outward expressions rose above the outward expression of any other subject that concerned him. One might compare Scholem's attachment to books, which would appear to be no more than the "sheaths of wisdom," to use Ibn Ezra's expression, and their place in his inner world to the status of the symbols of Kabbalah according to his definition—as a spiritual reality that has no other way of being revealed except in the symbol itself, in the books themselves.[20]

What, then, was the spiritual reality that was revealed to Scholem through the books that he went to seek in Europe? And what was their inner personal meaning for him? A hint of this can be found in a sentence he wrote in his diary toward the end of the trip: "This mission has eaten me up, *and it did not bring with it the inner salvation I had thought of.*"[21] Understanding what "inner salvation" he was seeking when he left could explain his motivation for undertaking the trip and sticking with it to the point of exhaustion. Though the historian's tools do not make it possible to fully answer a question of this kind, which belongs rather to the field of psychology, one may still try to understand Scholem's motivations by using a model of a human quest that includes a deep emotional experience, usually religious, and the search for a solution to material problems in the present, or salvation. I refer to a sacred journey or pilgrimage.

To understand Scholem's journey in this way, one may use the anthropologist Alan Morinis's definition of a pilgrimage as a journey made by someone seeking a place that, according to his faith, embodies some ideal. Morinis defines the goal of the journey as "an intensified version of some ideal that the pilgrim values but cannot achieve at home."[22] The special nature of the OAD, as a collection point for plundered Jewish books whose owners had been murdered, gave it and its contents special emotional significance—even a sanctity—for those who visited it or worked there. The huge halls, full of immense quantities of books, and the monotonous work of sorting them and repacking them by a relative small number of workers certainly contributed to this feeling. The blurring of the boundary between the books and people discussed above took place very easily within the confines of the warehouse, and it could cause its visitors and workers to idealize and emphasize the books' symbolic character, whether one looked to the past (seeing the books as symbols of a culture that had been destroyed), the future (seeing them as a symbol of the remaining survivors), or both. According to Morinis, the pilgrimage has more than a present importance: in his journey, the pilgrim aspires to join the present to the past and unite them. Thereby, Morinis claims, "all time is collapsed into an eternal moment in which perfection overcomes the incompleteness of mundane lived time." He immediately adds: "This is salvation."[23] The feeling of such inner salvation is described in Dawidowicz's autobiographical work. At the end of her memoirs, she once again compares books to people, this time in the context of her personal voyage throughout Germany and her activity in the OAD. Dawidowicz had had been a research fellow at the Yidisher Visnshaftlekher Institut (YIVO) in Vilna in 1938–39, and after the war she located and sorted Yiddish books in the OAD—including some that had been stolen from the YIVO library in Vilna—and sent them to the YIVO library in New York. She concludes her memoirs with the following words:

> Once the YIVO library had been shipped to New York, I felt that I had laid to rest those ghosts of Vilna that had haunted me since 1939. I had realized the obsessive fantasies of rescue which had tormented me for years. I had in fact saved a few remnants of Vilna, even if they were just books, mere pieces of paper, the tatters and shards of a civilization. The sweet memories of Vilna and of the people I had known and loved were still intact in my mind. I knew that nothing more was left to me. My fevered feeling of guilt for having abandoned them had died away. I was ready now to move ahead. I was ready now to start a new life.[24]

Dawidowicz, who had been born in New York, could be reconciled with herself, her past, and the feelings of guilt that gnawed at her at the end of her journey. She attained a sense of fulfillment, even of redemption, by joining the past to her present by performing what she saw as the rescue of the stolen books: their removal from the OAD and shipment to the United States. For her, this action was a substitute for rescuing her friends from the year she had spent in Vilna from the Holocaust, which she could not do. At the end of her journey, she says, she could start a new chapter in her life and leave her past behind.

In contrast, Scholem's inner journey to save the books was doomed to failure from the start. For Scholem, who had been born in Berlin and spent his childhood and youth in Germany, the books also symbolized his own destroyed past—the world into which he had been born and that before the war had been one of the most flourishing Jewish centers in Europe. The power and obstinacy with which he invested his strength in the task, until exhaustion, were connected to his private mourning. The great destruction in the present of the familiar landscapes of his past did not permit Scholem to look toward the future with hope. Instead, he was turned to stone in the face of the huge catastrophe, like the angel of history described by Walter Benjamin, who had committed suicide six years earlier, in September 1940, while fleeing from the Nazis.

Concluding Remarks

The years of the Holocaust were a turning point in Scholem's life, when tendencies that had begun years before grew stronger. The fact that one finds no direct public reference to the subject or any expression of a thought-out position toward it on his part does not indicate that it had little influence on him—perhaps just the opposite. The impressions made by such an extreme historical event on a person's soul and the degree to which he or she internalized those impressions cannot be determined by public speech or silence, and it is very difficult to judge the matter with certainty.[25] However, on the basis of a few facts and various documents one may assume that the events of the Holocaust touched very intimate and vital levels of Scholem's soul, and for that reason he could not relate to it in an organized and calm way. During the war, Scholem lost not only Benjamin, but also his brother Werner, who was the closest of his three siblings to him and who was murdered in Buchenwald in the summer of 1940. And Scholem's mother passed away a few months after the war. His letter to Dinur discussed in chapter 4 shows that he did not see himself as qualified or ready to discuss the Holocaust directly, because in his opinion he lacked the historical perspective needed for that. Perhaps his view of himself as someone who stands truly in the center of the historical events never completely left Scholem, and he never could approach the subject with the psychological distance required of the historian. Similarly, I have found no document containing a deep discussion by Scholem of the fate of Werner, or even an expression of emotion that indicates the influence on him of his brother's long imprisonment and death in a concentration camp. Of course, this does not show that he ignored the tragedy of his brother and his family, or that it did not touch his soul.[26] Those years were also important in determining Scholem's path in scholarship. Moshe Idel identified a fundamental turning point in Scholem's thinking during the war, which was expressed "in a radical rejection of Jewish scholarship of nineteenth-century Germany and in the call to see history as a primary subject both for the kabbalist and for the scholar of Kabbalism, and, implicitly, for scholars of Judaism." According to Idel, the years of the Holocaust caused a crisis in Scholem's faith in metaphysics, faith that had characterized his earlier thought, and transfer of the emphasis to history: "Out of the Holocaust Scholem's most dramatic transition took place—from the search for a transcendental metaphysics to historical scholarship of dynamic character, ruled by irrational forces."[27]

In the light of various documents and sources, one may point out two central changes that took place in Scholem during the years of the war and the Holocaust. On the personal level, his feelings of depression and of being cut off from his surroundings and the people around him intensified. Ideologically, the Holocaust wrought a change in his attitude toward Zionism because of the trap into which the events made it fall. The inability of Zionism to offer a response in the past or the present to the problem of Jewish existence in the Diaspora, as well as its inability to ensure Jewish existence in the Land of Israel and a base for the creation of a new society in accordance with Scholem's Zionist vision, caused him bitter disappointment. His journey on a mission for the Yishuv to save the treasures of the Diaspora made his situation even more extreme. In Europe he saw with his own eyes the dimensions of the human disaster, symbolized by the cultural disaster. His secret aspiration for an inner salvation that would come during the journey and help him overcome the influence of historical events and be reconciled with them was also disappointed. Instead of finding consolation and reconciliation with himself and the present, the encounter with Europe and especially with Germany, his birthplace, in 1946 only intensified his despair and exhausted him. In a letter to Arendt, he confessed: "I am afraid this trip merely broke my heart, if such a thing exists (as I suppose). In any case, my hopes, which I left behind in Europe. Where can I find them again? I would like to know myself."[28]

The feelings of despair and helplessness with which Scholem returned from Europe accompanied him during the months following his return, though the historical events that came later created a situation in which little room was left for passivity. The violent events that preceded the establishment of the State of Israel, the danger that it would be "lost in its first steps in a sea of slaughter,"[29] and the war that followed demanded the full mental and physical forces of the Yishuv. During the siege of Jerusalem in May and June 1948, Scholem worked sometimes on the city's fortifications and read the works of Franz Rosenzweig. With Emanuel Ben-Dor and Benjamin Mazar (later Meisler), new archaeological officers from the headquarters of the Jerusalem district, Scholem patrolled the Old City (where he helped a little in arranging the library of the Dormition Abbey, which had suffered during the war and had become a military post of the Irgun), the Protestant cemetery on Mount Zion, and the Yemin Moshe neighborhood.[30] Like most of the Jews in Jerusalem, Scholem met frequently with the besieged people of his city, and among his guests was the Haganah commander of the Jerusalem district, David Shealtiel. Shealtiel told Scholem that he been in the same bloc as his brother Werner during eight months of imprisonment in the Dachau concentration camp in 1936.

Scholem observed the imminent establishment of the state with cautious expectation and even some apprehension. He saw the course of events of the Holocaust and the renewal as a test that entailed danger for the Jewish people, by bringing the problem of Judaism to the surface in its full strength. In a letter to Hugo and Asha Bergmann in late 1947 his desperate worry is evident: "While it is true that if we attain the establishment of a state of the Jews and it is not lost in its first steps in a sea of slaughter, the question of Judaism or the Jewish tradition will stand before us for the last time, in a particularly harsh form, and who knows how things will fall out and where the Jews will turn in their state. I live in despair and cannot act except in despair."[31] On July 14, he expressed in his diary his expectation of the arrival of the fateful hour, writing that "in principle the partition is assured. The problem of the state and Judaism in the light of the last developments will quickly emerge."[32] Years later Fania recalled her husband's apprehensions: "When the state was established, he said that we would pay a heavy price for it. Two grave events—the Holocaust and the renewal—that struck the nation, one after the other, were more than a nation could bear . . . without being damaged. We can expect the spiritual and moral decline of the Jewish people, he said and added that if there is a sick body, and it has a wound in one of its limbs, all the blood flows to the wounded limb. With us, all the talents and powers flow to defense, and this is one of the reasons for the spiritual decline."[33]

Scholem also expressed concern about the direction the young state was going and indirectly criticized it in an article that he published in *Luach Haaretz* in 1948, in which he discussed the history of the Magen David—the symbol chosen to decorate the Israeli flag. In this article Scholem showed that "the hexagram is not a Jewish symbol, much less 'the symbol of Judaism,'" and that it received its true Jewish meaning during the Holocaust from "those who made it for millions into a mark of shame and degradation."[34] Thus, he tried to separate the national symbol from the religious contexts that had been attributed to it—in other words, to distinguish between the religious and political aspects of the young state. In addition, by means of his efforts to remind people, who had so quickly become victors, about the period when Jewry was defeated, Scholem tried to prevent the strengthening of the arrogance that had already penetrated the hearts of the residents of the new state.[35] For Scholem, the end of World War II, the realization of the dimensions of the Holocaust, and the fulfillment of the Zionist territorial dream in the figure of a Jewish state, which took place a short time afterward, paradoxically symbolized the beginning of a process of return to Europe.

PART III

EIN TIEFES HEIMWEH

There, in his valuable library, the witty and up-to-date Scholem gathered a dozen professors and authors, all of them German speakers, and all of them speaking in German, about German memories, about German literature, even about the politics of German literature. As Werner Weber used to say, they dispatch some rival from the distant past or one who is still living, and they raise up some chosen one to the stars. Everything is as it was fifty years ago. They are as knowledgeable as they once were, they are brilliant and express themselves articulately, but something entirely new is added to each of them, which they would like to deny: nostalgia, deep yearning (*Heimweh*), which endows even their critical remarks with a romantic (*verklärt*) tinge.

KARL BURCKHARDT TO MAX RYCHNER, NOVEMBER 19, 1962

NOSTALGIA (1949–1982)

CHAPTER 7

ERANOS

> Therefore—and may every sanctimonious German maiden roll her eyes in virginal surprise—I hope from the depth of my soul that Ascona will someday become a place of refuge for liberated or fleeing prisoners, for homeless, persecuted people, for all those victims of circumstances . . . , who wander with no direction, hunted down, tormented, and yet they have not lost their aspiration to live a human life among people who respect them as people like themselves.
>
> ERICH MÜHSAM, "ASCONA (1905)"[1]

The Eranos Conferences

Shortly before the establishment of the State of Israel, Scholem turned fifty. He was then at the height of his scholarly career, which had already made him one of the outstanding intellectuals and academics of Israel. He had taken part in many academic projects and would participate in even more, and his scholarly activity would eventually be honored with almost all the prizes and titles that the State of Israel could offer. The height of this recognition was his tenure as president of the Israel Academy of Sciences and Humanities, from 1968 to 1974. In addition to his activities in Israel, Scholem contributed scholarly energy and strength to the academic world of the United States, while in residence at various universities to pursue his research. By publishing giving lectures in English, and developing close ties with his colleagues overseas, Scholem also made his mark on American intellectual life.

The third place where Scholem was active was the Federal Republic of Germany, which was founded in the same year as the State of Israel. World War II and the Holocaust had abruptly put an end to his writing in the German language, though he had previously attributed great importance to doing so. In a letter to Walter Benjamin of August 1, 1931, Scholem stated his intentions regarding the language in which he would write: "It is my serious intention to write more in German because no historian of religion is capable of reading Hebrew."[2]

Though he ceased to do so for almost a decade, this intention was not forgotten, and after the war the place accorded to German increased in his intellectual life, with much of his creative power directed to a German readership. The first forum where Scholem presented his research in German after the Holocaust was at the Eranos conference in 1949, and the publication of his first lecture there symbolized his return to the German-speaking academic world.

The Venue: The Foot of Monte Verità

The history of the Eranos conferences begins even before their establishment in 1933. In fact, the root of the conferences—which are held to this day in the Swiss village of Ascona, on the shore of Lake Maggiore, which marks the border with Italy—lies in the intellectual and cultural phenomena that preceded them by several years. Until the period when the annual meetings discussed in this chapter were established, the focus of the social, ideological, and spiritual ferment of Ascona was on the mountain where the village is situated. The mountain (actually, a hill) is called Monte Verità, "the mountain of truth."[3] During the first two decades of the twentieth century, the history of Monte Verità was to a large extent the history of alternative and antibourgeois German culture of that time.

Monte Verità first became a center for alternative trends and marginal movements in the fall of 1900, when a group of seven people that had formed around Henri Oedenkoven, the son of a Dutch banker, and Ida Hofmann, a pianist and music teacher, arrived with the intention of settling on the hill.[4] In the following years the place became a center for antibourgeois movements whose members advocated the principles of *Lebensreform* (life reform) and opposed modern industrialization. A sanatorium was established on the hill, where vegetarianism and the eating of raw vegetables, sunbathing, physical labor, and nudism were practiced. The sanatorium also offered artistic and musical programs for its residents.[5] In a short time, the group that had established the first sanatorium broke apart, and some members established another convalescent home on the hill. In the following two decades, the hill attracted settlers from almost every alternative and esoteric movement in Germany at that time: vegetarians, nudists, anarchists, pacifists, modern dance groups, theosophical organizations, Freemasons, Rosicrucians, Anthroposophists, and advocates of psychoanalysis. The author Hermann Hesse stayed in one of the sanatoriums on the hill to treat his alcoholism; and the Jewish anarchist Erich Mühsam and two members of the avant-garde group of German painters called *der blaue Reiter* lived in the area at the same time. The hill was a refuge for opponents of World War I, and in 1917 an antinational congress was held there, at which lectures on cultural and esoteric topics were delivered. Monte Verità became a meeting place for proponents of various alternative trends and ideas, who met and influenced each other. Most of these people were members of the German bourgeoisie who were rebelling against their parents' way of life, but who were financially supported by those parents while in Ascona. Many of them belonged to Jewish families. Along with the spiritual content of the activities on the hill, the alternative convalescent aspect of it remained in existence, and many patients were treated there in body and soul. After World War I, the sanatorium and its hospital encountered economic difficulties, and during the 1920s the residents of the hill began to disperse.

Another element central to the activity in Ascona during its peak was the meeting between East and West. The esoteric doctrines of the Far East interested proponents of almost all of the trends that were represented in Ascona. For example, Martin Buber gave a lecture there in August 1924 on Lao Tse and the Tao Te Ching. This lecture was of decisive importance for the Eranos conferences.

One member of the audience at Buber's lecture was a widow named Olga Fröbe-Kapteyn. The daughter of a Dutch engineer, she had been born in London in 1881. Around 1900, the Fröbe-Kapteyn family moved to Zurich, and in 1915 her husband died in a plane crash. In 1919 she went to a sanatorium on Monte Verità for a cure, and because she liked the place, her father bought her a villa named Casa Gabriela, on the shore of the lake at the edge of Ascona. He also provided her with monetary support. At that time Fröbe-Kapteyn was connected with the theosophical and esoteric circles that were still active on the hill, and through them she ended up at Buber's lecture. Following the lecture, she resolved to establish a center for religious and spiritual renewal, which would also be a place where religions and philosophies from the East and West could be discussed. For that purpose, in 1928 she built a lecture hall with a seating capacity of two hundred attached to her residence, and a year later she built another house for guests.

In the following years Fröbe-Kapteyn formed connections in the United States and Germany with people interested in learning about Eastern and Western cultures. In 1930 she met Carl Gustav Jung for the first time—the man who, perhaps more than anyone else, influenced the direction of the first two decades of the Eranos conferences. In 1932 Fröbe-Kapteyn went to Marburg, Germany, to meet Rudolf Otto, a famous scholar of religion, and to consult with him about the possibility of holding a series of conferences centered on encounters between East and West. Otto was enthusiastic about the idea and helped develop and improve it, as well as suggesting the name by which the meetings have been called from the summer of 1933 to this day: Eranos.[6]

The name first appears in Homer's *Odyssey*, where it describes a social encounter centered on a banquet to which every participant brought some of the food. In its original context in the classical world, Eranos is a kind of potluck supper that takes place as a social institution, and it has a religious dimension as well, since the banquet is a sacrificial meal.[7] In the late nineteenth century, renewed use was made of the name Eranos to describe intellectual and spiritual groups in various places in Europe. An association in Vienna that was dedicated to the study of classical culture was founded in 1876, a journal of classical studies in Sweden was established in 1896, a circle of intellectuals in Heidelberg was created in 1904 to discuss of religious topics, and a Festschrift in honor of the Austrian poet Hugo von Hofmannsthal published in 1904 all bore the name Eranos. Recently Tilo Schabert has proposed regarding all of the phenomena as a single Eranos movement, a European cultural trend that could be considered to include the establishment of the Eranos conferences in Ascona.[8] Thus the Eranos conferences in Ascona can be seen as drawing on intellectual trends that existed in Europe and on cultural and spiritual trends centered at the foot of Monte Verità. However, at the time of the 1933 meeting—the first in a long series, whose subject was "Yoga and Meditation in the East and the West"—little was left of the vital life that had characterized the hill of truth for more than twenty years. Nevertheless, what did remain and memories of the past affected the local landscape and made it a symbol of the social role that the area had played in earlier years, as a meeting place chiefly characterized by social and political freedom. This symbol still had great resonance for the participants in the Eranos conferences, and it had a moderate and indirect influence on the spirit of the place, its *genius loci*.

The Spirit of Eranos

Among the bushes next to Casa Gabriella, Fröbe-Kapteyn's villa, is a small statue, a kind of stone monument, with the inscription: "Genio loci ignoto." This little monument was erected in 1949 in memory of what Jung and the theologian Gerardus van der Leeuw called "the unknown genius of Eranos."[9] This proclamation of the existence of an unknown spirit, perpetuated in stone, was also an effort to grasp a bit of that spirit and link it to the place where the meetings were held. Indeed, there are few intellectual events in which the setting and location played such an important role as in the Eranos meetings. From 1933 to 1988,[10] intellectuals from all over the world met every August in the two villas that look out among the cedar trees at the blue waters of Lake Maggiore, at the foot of Monte Verità and on the outskirts of the picturesque Swiss village of Ascona.

Each conference lasted ten days, and in the morning of each day a prominent intellectual in the field of religious studies delivered a two-hour lecture about his or her research. The rest of each day was devoted to conversation and to a common meal around a large round table on the terrace of Casa Gabriella. This part

FIGURE 7 The Eranos Round Table, probably in 1947. Photographer: Margarethe Fellerer. Courtesy of the Eranos Foundation Archives.

of the day, in which the boundary between lecturer and audience disappeared, was regarded by many of the participants as the most important one. While eating and drinking in a relaxed and informal atmosphere, they could meet each other and discuss the morning's lecture and various subjects of mutual interest. Adolf Portmann, a Swiss zoologist, was one of the regular participants and an organizer of the conferences for many years. He described the setting evocatively:

> In the shade of the great cedar tree whose branches extend over the balcony of Casa Gabriella the meal is served to the lecturers at the conference. Around the large, round table, they meet at noon and in the evening, along with some guests of the house, in colorful succession. The landscape extends in the direction of Lake Maggiore. At noon the breeze from Italy moves the surface of the water; the evening passes with the vivid colors of the slopes of Monte Tamaro in view, and from the calm lake the last light is reflected. For everyone who has taken part in the conferences, these hours around the Eranos table are a significant part of the whole. The personal conversation deepens the impression of the lecturer by means of the broad

experiences of the people who meet here. The multitude of languages and ways of thinking, the treasures of the world that each and every person brings from his various origins, all of these make the event flourish and ripen, in a way that the larger appearances in the lecture hall alone could not supply.[11]

The social atmosphere described by Portmann is reflected in the very name of Eranos. Along with the lectures, the personal encounters among the participants were the heart of the annual conferences. The encounters took place in a relaxed atmosphere of leisure in both of the villas. Mircea Eliade, a Romanian scholar of religion and another regular participant in the meetings, described this well: "Eranos is like a dance that begins anew every year, but always with different dancers."[12]

These words of Eliade are also reminiscent of the bourgeois leisure and health culture at Central European spas, where people returned each year to the same spa and, in a relaxed atmosphere, improved their bodily and mental health and enjoyed merry festivities.[13] Such visits to spas were common among the German bourgeoisie before World War II, when the health resorts—including Ascona—offered their visitors temporary refuge from the worries of the modern age and everyday concerns. This cyclical structure was resurrected in the academic Eranos conferences, at the heart of which was a combination of intellectual activity, the culture of relaxation and leisure, and contact with spirituality in the midst of a breathtaking landscape. Over the years the Eranos conferences became a territory in their own right, a kind of separate space ruled by its own summer rules. Sometimes these rules were aligned with the outside world, and sometimes they contradicted it. Henry Corbin, a French scholar of Islamic mysticism and another pillar of the conferences, saw the significance of the encounters and believed their secret lay in their being a time in itself, not subject to time: "What we should wish to call the *meaning* of Eranos, which is also the entire secret of Eranos, is this: it is our present being, the time that we act personally, our way of being. This is why we are perhaps not 'of our time,' but are something better and greater: we are our time."[14] This definition points to the central role that the participants in the Eranos conferences played in constructing the image of the meetings and the way they constructed their own identity as members of Eranos. This quotation also reflects the views of other Eranos participants, who felt that the meetings belonged to a separate temporal and geographical dimension. Like Monte Verità in its early years, the Eranos conferences created a protected space or alternative world, related to prewar Europe. In this separate world, people whose youth had been spent in the age of imperialism met every summer and had an intellectual experience of a type that had been familiar but that had disappeared in the aftermath of World War I. All the aforementioned components played a part in creating the special atmosphere of the conferences, known among the participants as well among researchers of the phenomenon as the spirit of Eranos. This was the atmosphere that awaited Scholem in the summer of 1949, when he gave his first Eranos lecture on "Kabbalah and Myth."

The Path to Eranos

Scholem's long connection with Eranos began a few years before he gave his first lecture in Ascona, and it is directly connected with Jung. This fact is important for the present discussion, since Jung was one of the most influential people on the conferences and their character in the years preceding Scholem's participation in them, and since Jung had been a Nazi sympathizer in the early years of the movement. Jung and his psychological theory were a challenge for Scholem, with which he had to cope when he was asked to clarify his relations with the participants in Eranos.

As noted in chapter 5, Scholem met Jung for the first time in Zurich in 1946, through Siegmund Hurwitz and the circle of Jung's disciples there. In spite of Scholem's suspicions regarding Jung's Nazi past, once Scholem had returned to Jerusalem, he sent Jung a copy of the second edition of his book on Jewish mysticism, which was published in New York in 1946.[15] Jung thanked Scholem via Hurwitz at the end of April 1947 and asked for Scholem's address so he could send him one of his books.[16] In early May, at Jung's instigation, Scholem received a letter from Fröbe-Kapteyn containing an official invitation to lecture at the conference in August 1947. Fröbe-Kapteyn told Scholem that Jung had also suggested a possible topic for Scholem's future lecture: "The Central Ideas of Lurianic Gnosis."[17] In his reply, Scholem accepted the invitation willingly, but financial problems stood in the way of his participation: the organizers of the conference paid only the cost of the trip from the border of Switzerland, and he was unable to pay for the trip from Palestine to Europe. In any event, Scholem asked Fröbe-Kapteyn to write to him again in a year and invite him to the conference in the summer of 1948.[18] The invitation, dated September 10, 1947, is in the Gershom Scholem Archive, but without Scholem's reply.[19] A letter from Scholem to Hurwitz indicates that, along with the financial difficulty, historical events—the establishment of the State of Israel and the ensuing war—also prevented his participation in 1947.[20] But Scholem did give a lecture at the conference in the summer of 1949, attending it with Fania on their way back from a stay of several months in the United States.[21] The meeting that year was devoted to the subject of "Man and the Mythical World," and Scholem's lecture was titled "Kabbalah and Myth."[22] Scholem's participation in the Eranos conferences extended over three decades.

After Jung's death more than ten years later, Scholem was asked by Aniela Jaffé, Jung's last secretary, how and why he had agreed to take part in the Eranos conferences, although Jung's Nazi past was well known to him. In his reply, Scholem attributed his willingness to lecture to a conversation he had had with Leo Baeck in the summer of 1947, in which he expressed his doubts about participating in the event. Baeck had urged him to accept the invitation, telling him how Jung had sought him out in Zurich, after Baeck had been liberated from Theresienstadt, and how they had met in Baeck's hotel though Baeck had tried to avoid him. On the emotional conversation between Jung and Baeck, which lasted more than two hours, Scholem wrote to Jaffé: "Jung defended himself, referring to the special situation in Nazi Germany, but at the same time he confessed to him: 'Indeed, I stumbled,' in connection with Nazism and his expectations, that maybe something great would burst forth here. Those words—indeed, I stumbled—which Baeck repeated to me, I remember with great vividness. Baeck told me that in this conversation they settled everything that stood between them and parted reconciled with one another. On this basis of Baeck's declaration I also accepted the invitation to Eranos, when it came a second time in 1947."[23]

Scholem's later account differs at some points with findings that emerge from his archive. As noted, in his letter to Fröbe-Kapteyn of May 1947 he had already accepted the invitation, and his writing shows no essential hesitancy, merely regret that he could not finance the trip that year. By contrast, in his subsequent letter to Jaffé, Scholem reports having doubts about participating in the conferences in the summer of 1947. Of course, there is reason to assume that Scholem would not have divulged any hesitations to Fröbe-Kapteyn, but to the same degree one may assume that Scholem's description in his letter to Jaffé was written with apologetic intentions, to explain after the fact why he took part regularly in meetings that were directly associated with the name of Jung.

The matter of the degree to which the Eranos conferences were marked by the figure and ideas of the prominent and controversial psychologist is extraneous to the present discussion. However, it may be said that the extent of the influence of Jung, his theories, and his disciples on the Eranos conferences has not yet been sufficiently investigated. Certainly Jung was one of the central figures of Eranos during the first years of the conferences, and he had a strong influence on Fröbe-Kapteyn, who administered the encounters on her private property and who alone determined what topics would be discussed and which speakers would be invited.[24] However, in 1951, only two years after Scholem first lectured at Eranos, Jung gave his last lecture there. He was present at the Eranos meeting of 1952, which is discussed at length below. At that conference he left the lecture given by Herbert Read, a British scholar of art history, in a fit of anger, and he also expressed discontent with the lecture given by the philosopher Karl Löwith.[25] But Jung never again attended an Eranos conference. He died in 1961, and after Fröbe-Kapteyn's death in the following year, Portmann took over the administration of the conferences. Scholem never heard Jung lecture at Eranos, and Jung could not have heard Scholem lecture more than three times.[26] These facts contradict the statement made by William McGuire that there was a warm intellectual friendship between the two men in those years.[27] Thus, it is very doubtful that Jung exercised high-handed control over the proceedings at Eranos and determined their character in an arbitrary fashion. Examination of the sources clearly shows that one of the things that can be said with certainty about Eranos is that it was a broad and varied cultural phenomenon, and that over the years there were changes in the composition and character of its meetings. The effort to confine this rich phenomenon within the Jungian mold and to argue, as Joseph Dan has done, that Eranos was a "conference of Jung's disciples,"[28] diminishes it, in my view, and makes it difficult to understand its complexity and diversity. Moreover, in my opinion it is not possible to refer to the participants in Eranos as a single circle. Rather, they were part of a network of personal, intellectual, political, and emotional connections among various circles and individuals. The Jungians were one of these circles—perhaps even the central one, but doubtless not the only one. In the introduction to the printed edition of his journal, Eliade wrote: "Jung was the *spiritus rector* of Eranos, but one cannot say that the lecturers constituted a Jungian group. Most of them were only superficially acquainted with the problems of modern psychology."[29]

An examination of the list of participants in Eranos over the generations supports the view that they were a diverse group, many of whose members were decidedly individualistic. They included Karl Kerényi, a scholar of classical culture; Ernst Benz, an evangelical theologian; Erich Neumann, an Israeli Jungian psychiatrist; Gilles Quispel, a Dutch theologian and scholar of Gnosticism; Max Knoll, a German physicist; Portmann, a Swiss zoologist; Paul Tillich, a Protestant theologian; Helmut Wilhelm, an American sinologist; Chung-Yuan Chang, a scholar of Taoism; Daisetsu Teitaro Suzuki, a scholar of Zen Buddhism; Paul Radin, a Jewish anthropologist of native Americans, who was influenced by Jung; and many others.[30] In addition, guests were invited to hear the lectures every year, and they took an active part in the social activities. Sometimes there were fifty to a hundred guests, including authors, artists, intellectuals, and physicians. This heterogeneous group, which was certainly not composed solely of Jung's disciples, also affected the atmosphere, though very little written evidence of this exists. Hence, it is very hard to find a single political or theological idea that could define Eranos. The only stable framework according to which it is possible to identify the regular participants in the conferences is the *Eranos Jahrbuch*, the scholarly organ in which the lectures given at the conferences were published, accompanied by introductions by Fröbe-Kapteyn or Portmann. These annual publications, a landmark in the history of the twentieth-century study of comparative religion, were published in Zurich by Rhein Verlag, which was owned by the Jewish publisher, Daniel Brody.

In addition, an examination of what can be called the inner circle of Eranos shows that its connection with Jung and his theories was doubtful. In the end of 1960, Portmann sent a letter to Scholem and five other regular participants in the Eranos conferences: Corbin, Eliade, Read, Wilhelm, and the musicologist Viktor Zuckerlandl. It appears that the death of Neumann, who was a central figure in the conferences and regularly gave the opening address during the decade before his death,[31] led Fröbe-Kapteyn, now elderly, to think about the future of the conferences when it would beyond her ability to organize them. To that end Portmann called upon the six men who received his letter to take part in an inner circle of Eranos, which would decide the fate of the conferences in Fröbe-Kapteyn's absence: "At this stage, the formation proposed here of an inner Eranos Circle, indeed the Kernel of Eranos, is meant to create the possibility that the faithful participants in the forum and its shapers can decide on the continued existence or cessation of Eranos."[32]

Although no reply to this letter has been found in Scholem's archive, it shows the central place accorded to him at the Eranos conferences and indicates his feeling of belonging to them. At the same time the participants whom Fröbe-Kapteyn chose to be the inner circle shows that at the end of 1960, half a year after Jung's death and about two years before her own demise, the influence of Jung's theories on the participants in the conferences was not decisive. Steven Wasserstrom's book—which deals with Scholem, Eliade, and Corbin—shows that although the latter two maintained a certain connection with Jung and his theories, especially via the phenomenological approach that characterized their work, they cannot be regarded as Jungians.[33] The only one of the three other members of the inner circle who can be placed in Jung's school was Read, who edited the English edition of Jung's writings. But the letter of 1960 places the cart before the horse, and it is mentioned here to show not only that Eranos should not be viewed as a closed society, but also that one must doubt the extent of the influence of Jung and his theories on the conferences during the years when Scholem took part in them. Over the years, in part because of Scholem's influence, constant changes took place in the group of people who attended the conferences and determined their content. In 1949, after returning from his first Eranos conference and before realizing that these meetings would play such a central role in his life, and that he would play a role in determining their path, Scholem wrote Alexander Altmann about the experience and his impressions of his stay in Ascona. In his letter Scholem did not conceal the interest the event had aroused in him, especially its social aspect:

> The time I spent in Switzerland was excellent, and I enjoyed it greatly. The conference in Ascona was interesting though not shocking. My lecture was apparently a success, judging by the impression and echoes, but it is easy to succeed in this topic, which has a strong stimulus for a Jew and even for a gentile these days, especially if you come from the State of Israel and speak as a Jew, and nothing but a Jew. Kerényi was there and I found him to be a very special person in all his ways and interests, an attractive and strange mixture of deep science, excellent intuition, and outstanding fantasy—everything all together. They are imploring me to return next year, and if I can only obtain the money for the expenses of the journey, I would also like that, because it is worthwhile to meet with strangers and people close to one about matters of the study of religion. This time I got to know three or four people, just the acquaintance with whom made the trip to Eranos worthwhile.[34]

The enthusiastic tone in Scholem's letter is typical of his attitude toward Eranos in the long years that followed his first participation in the conferences. During the next thirty years, Scholem gave twenty-one lectures and attended a number of other conferences where he did not make a presentation. His fields of research and interest were perfectly suited to Eranos, and he also fit in well with the diverse group of the conference participants and the atmosphere of intellectual freedom, which encouraged original thinking and social exchanges between people. Nonetheless, it is evident that over the years Scholem had to cope with the inner and outward complexities that accompanied his participation in the conferences. Outwardly, because of the image in Israel of Eranos as a Jungian event, Scholem had to explain his close associations with Jung and Eliade, given their previous associations with the Nazis and the fascists, respectively. Inwardly, Scholem's participation in the events was, in many respects, a return to Europe after the Holocaust and the doorway for him into the postwar German-speaking intellectual world. The contradictory feelings that accompanied this process of return will be discussed at length in this chapter. Their outer aspect is discussed below, but the next section is devoted to the inner conflict that arose in Scholem during his visit to the Eranos conference in the summer of 1952.

Inner Contradictions

The 1952 Conference

To a large extent, the decision to focus on Scholem's visit to Switzerland in 1952 is because only during this visit did he record the events and his thoughts in his diary. An examination of the diary makes it possible to discuss the details of the visit and clarifies some of his impressions of the encounter. It may also be said that in many respects this year was important in the history of Eranos. It was the twentieth conference and the last one that Jung attended. To a certain degree this year signals the beginning of the departure of Fröbe-Kapteyn and Jung from Eranos and the renewal of the conferences.[35] As for Scholem, this was his third trip to Eranos, and it may be assumed that his time he felt more confident in his ability to participate in the scholarly and social activities, and he had begun to know the regular participants better and to feel that he was part of Eranos. In addition, unlike in previous years, he traveled without Fania. The conference of 1952 dealt with the subject of "Man and Energy," and Scholem gave a lecture on "The History of the Development of the Shekhina as a Kabbalistic Concept."[36]

As one may certainly assume that attending one of the conferences required preparation, and some of the lecturers who had become friends remained in contact with each other during the winter and spring in anticipation of the coming conference. Thus, in March 1952 Scholem wrote to Kerényi, who lived in Ponte Brolla, near Ascona: "The prospect of seeing your wife and you again, along with other friends, already gives me pleasure. In hopes that no impediment will arise, and that you won't depart exactly then on a worldwide trip! I offer, in return for coffee at Ponte Brolla, a report about the new mythology in the State of Israel! Please ask your wife what her opinion is about this? (Most regrettably, I can only come by myself)."[37]

Kerényi was not in Switzerland when the letter arrived, as he was giving lectures and doing research. Therefore, his wife, Magda, answered Scholem's warm words and discussed the dates of his visit to Ascona so that they could meet, because that year Kerényi was not planning to give a lecture at Eranos. She responded to Scholem's proposal with great friendship and affection: "Coffee in Ponte Brolla in return for a report on anything whatsoever is not a proportionate transaction. All the advantages remain on our side, but with a joyous welcome and gratitude for your human and spiritual glow, we will try to even out the situation."[38]

That year Scholem's trip to Europe included additional tasks. During the first days after his arrival in Zurich, along with visiting friends, he participated in meetings and negotiations as the vice chairman of Jewish Cultural Reconstruction Inc., the umbrella organization established to deal with the restoration of Jewish property that had been plundered by the Nazis.[39] On August 10, he met with two of his colleagues in the organization: Hannah Arendt, the general secretary, and Salo Baron the chairman. Scholem spent the following two days with Arendt, writing in his diary: "Relations with H. are very cordial, we don't talk about what separates us. We each make an effort to ease things for the other."[40] They spent their time in long conversations and in visits to mutual friends. In the evening they went to the circus together: "It had been thirty years since I was at a circus, and how we enjoyed it!! We were like happy children!"[41] The next day, Arendt invited Scholem to a formal meal in an exclusive restaurant in Zurich, after which they went their separate ways.[42]

In the evening of August 18, Scholem took the train to Ascona. On the way there he met one of the people who had attended a conference and was also on the way to Ascona: "On the train I traveled with my 'student,' who addressed me because she had heard me speak three years earlier. Miss Hégi is an expert on . . . bats! A pleasant conversation." Immediately after arriving in Ascona, Scholem spent two hours with Quispel and his wife, and immediately afterward he had a private conversation with Fröbe-Kapteyn. As he got out of the car at the entrance of his hotel, he met Brody and his wife, and they spoke at length, as Scholem accompanied them back to their house. When he returned to the hotel he ran into the Kerényis, who had come to find him: "Great joy, and we sat for another two hours until nearly midnight."[43] The intensity of social encounters continued in the following days. Scholem spent the next afternoon with Karl Kerényi. Scholem's impression of him was that "he is a most fair-minded gentile, and he doesn't understand a thing about what's happening in history." Scholem ate dinner with Portmann and was with the Kerényis and Brody until late in the evening. "I described what we eat in Israel and how we eat," he wrote in his diary.[44]

The conference started on August 20. Scholem's lecture began the proceedings, and his remarks on the concept of the Shekhina (the Divine Presence) made a strong impression. "It appears that I have succeeded greatly," he wrote that day. "[The hall] was packed, and the attention was close." In the audience were the Zionist leader Nahum Goldmann and his wife, with whom Scholem spoke afterward about German reparations and Israeli demands. After this conversation, they agreed that Scholem should join a meeting on this matter with Moshe Sharett, the Israeli minister of foreign affairs, which was supposed to take place two weeks later in Paris. After an hour's discussion with thirty of the people who had listened to his lecture, Scholem began a series of meetings with friends and acquaintances: Corbin, Erich von Kahler, Knoll, Löwith, and their wives,

FIGURE 8 During the Eranos conference in Ascona, August 1952. From *left to right*: Gilles Quispel, an unidentified man, Mircea Eliade, Stella and Henry Corbin, and Gershom Scholem. Photographer: Felix Thom. From the collection of the National Library of Israel, Jerusalem.

and of course the Kerényis. "I'm hoarse from so much conversation," Scholem summed up the day in his diary.[45]

Scholem spent the following days listening to the other lectures, eating, drinking, and conversing. Among the most important encounters of that conference was a conversation he had with Brody. Brody was a Hungarian Jew who had been a publisher in Munich until he was forced to flee from the Nazis, first to Holland and later to Mexico. After the war he returned to Europe and settled in Zurich, where he continued to be active in publishing and remained in contact with Fröbe-Kapteyn and the participants in Eranos.[46] Scholem wanted Brody to publish a German edition of *Major Trends in Jewish Mysticism*: "I sat with Brody and we discussed the publication of the book in German. Will something come of it? He wanted to look at the book and I gave him my copy."[47] This meeting was very important for Scholem's academic path in Germany after the war. Five years later Brody published a German translation of Scholem's book, and in 1960 he also published the first volume of Scholem's Eranos lectures—followed by another volume of the lectures in 1962.[48] During the 1960s, until Scholem moved to the Suhrkamp publishing house in Frankfurt, Brody was the main publisher of Scholem's writing in German. This was in part because Brody also published the

Eranos Jahrbuch, which contained the lectures given at the Eranos conferences. Despite the professional and social importance of Scholem's stay in Ascona, and despite the good atmosphere and the intensity of the participants in the conferences, he did not feel completely at home. On August 25, after Löwith lectured on "The Dynamic of History and Historicism," which Scholem found "very good," he wrote in his diary: "Jung was enraged by the 'abstract nonsense' and left after the first hour. A conversation with Jane Untermeyer and Erich von Kahler. Afterward with Corbin and his wife. Everything is very nice. I feel very well, but it disturbs me, how foreign our matters seem from here. No one pays attention to them. My influence here depends more on my Berlin-ness (*auf meinem Berlinertum*) than on the opposite side, I should say."[49]

The ambivalence described in this diary entry relates to questions about Scholem's feeling of belonging in Ascona. The foreignness of Eranos with relation to the reality from which he came—presumably he was referring to Israel—both charmed and disturbed Scholem. In his view, his arrival from a non-European environment into a world entirely nourished by European culture, and his awareness of the gap between these worlds, separated him from those around him in Ascona. This diary entry shows that what most disturbed him was that none of the other participants noticed his Israeliness, and that he fit into the group by virtue of the "opposite" aspect of his life, his Germanness. The fact that at Eranos he was less identified with Jerusalem than with Berlin made Scholem uncomfortable. Yet the source of this discomfort actually arose from the fact that he felt quite at ease and comfortable in the European environment. In other words, the extreme physical and psychological change of his transition from Germany to Israel in his youth and in his effort to replace his German sources with Zionist Jewish roots was not evident to his colleagues in the extraterritorial space of Eranos, and this change played no role in his great success there. As a consequence, contradictory feelings arose in him. These feelings persisted during his participation in the conference and were expressed again in a diary entry dated August 26, two days before the conclusion of the conference: "I don't think I'll come here next year (the subject: man and the earth!!!), despite the hint that my expenses will be covered in full by the Bollingen Foundation. I have to restrain myself a bit. Despite and because of the clear success. Mrs. F[röbe-Kapteyn] told Portmann in a preliminary conversation: I very much want Scholem next year, with him you know what to count on (she said: [you know] what there is). Was her meaning 100 percent positive as I understood it? That would surprise me!"[50]

The following year, Scholem gave a lecture at Eranos titled: "The Image of the Golem in Earthly and Magical Contexts."

Identification and Distance: Henry Corbin

In the summer of 1979 Scholem lectured at Eranos for the last time. In fact, he did not deliver a prepared lecture but rather made improvised remarks in place of Portmann. For years Portmann had been accustomed to conclude the ten-day conference with a lecture, but that year he suddenly felt weak at the beginning of his speech, and Scholem immediately rose from the audience and took his place. Portmann and Scholem were the two most veteran participants at that conference, and Scholem took advantage of the opportunity to present his reflections on the three decades in which he had taken part in Eranos conferences and their meaning.

Along with the words of praise he had for Portmann and his contribution to the organization and spirit of the conferences, Scholem pointed out something that had struck him over the years and created a certain difficulty for him in relation to Eranos:

> There is a difficulty that exists for all the participants in Eranos and also for most of the lecturers, perhaps all of them. This is the necessity to speak from within the tension between distance from the subject under discussion and identification with it. For Olga Fröbe this was almost a decisive consideration. She sought speakers who identified with the topic of their lecture. She wanted lecturers who were engaged in the subject of their research (*ergriffene Redner*), not professors, though they were all called professors. This was a sort of deception. The identification that led Olga Fröbe to choose us might perhaps have depended—more than once—on an error; because most of us—and I have to include myself among them—spoke specifically from the tension between these two extremes, that means, from this distance as well, without which scientific knowledge is impossible. Indeed, I believe that someone who identifies completely with the subject of his research loses the scientific standard, and without that it is not research. A scholar (*Gelehrter*) is not a priest (*Priester*); it is an error to aspire to make a scholar into a priest. But the tension between distance and identification, which became so vital for us here at Eranos, is the factor that characterized my activity, for example, in these meetings over these many years.[51]

Scholem was objecting here to Fröbe-Kapteyn's demand, which was also to a great degree the criterion by which she chose the participants in the conferences, that the lecturers be absolutely identified with the subject of their scholarship. In place of this demand, Scholem proposed that there be a tension in the scholar's attitude toward his subject, which derives from the dialectic between identification and distance. The question of how much one may identify Scholem with his scholarship has been widely discussed. One approach tends to regard Scholem's work as a camouflage for his personal, political, or theological tendencies; the other tends to separate the ideological side of Scholem's character from his scholarship.[52] A good example of the way in which Scholem understood his relationship to his field of scholarship and the material he was studying can be found in his friendship with Corbin.[53] The way that Scholem saw Corbin's attitude toward his work can help us understand Scholem's conception of himself in the light of the great closeness he felt for Corbin, as well as the connection between his field of study and that of his colleague. Late in his life he wrote about this in a letter to Stella Corbin, after he learned of the death of her husband in October 1978:

> For me he was not only a friend and a fellow but a man who devoted a life to understand, to penetrate as a scholar a world as near to the one which I had devoted a life to understand. We were in the truest sense honest and possibly the first scholarly excavators in the world of esoterical imagination such as Islamic and Jewish Gnose. Of all the speakers at the Eranos [Conferences] it was he to whom I felt the greatest affinity. He alone had that kind of inner sympathy that enabled him to light up the dark and difficult ways of the mystical world which I considered essential to do really important, and at the same time scholarly work in these spheres. His passing away means to me the loss of a spiritual brother.[54]

Like Scholem, Corbin was a researcher and intellectual who gave the imagination a place in his scholarship, and whose creativity derived from within the tension between the two extremes: identification with the subject of his research and academic distance that gave his scholarship scientific validity. In the remarks Scholem made in 1979, immediately after touching on the tension between distance and identification, he pointed to Corbin as an example of someone whose work lies within this tension. One may easily surmise that, in speaking of his late colleague, to a large degree he was also referring to himself: "We heard lecturers like Corbin, who spoke with a primary feeling of penetration to the essence of things, of near identification with them, but at the same time with the distance of a profound scientific spirit. He did not appear as the representative of a particular interest, but as an observer, as a person who acts out of contemplation and distancing consciousness, which would be impossible without this distancing."[55]

Corbin's "near identification" with the subject of his research, which existed together with a distance from it, also had a practical religious meaning, which he did not conceal from his close friends among the circle of participants in the Eranos conferences to which Scholem belonged. The religious value of Corbin's scholarship is shown in a letter he wrote to his colleague David Miller on February 9, 1978, shortly before his death, after reading Miller's recently published book on polytheism: "I believe our researches open the way, of necessity, to angelology (that of a Proclus, that of Kabbala) which will be reborn with increasing potency. The Angel is the Face that our God takes for us, and each of us finds his God only when he recognizes that Face. The service which we can render others is to help them encounter that Face about which they will be able to say: *Talem eum vidi qualem capere potui* (I am able to grasp such as I have seen). . . . But let us understand clearly that for yet some time we shall be few in number and that we shall have to take refuge behind a veil of a certain esotericism."[56]

Corbin's words to Miller recall Scholem's understanding of religious anarchism to a large extent, with a personal belief in God and his manifestations while denying any single general religious authority.[57] However, unlike Corbin, Scholem understood the role of the scholar of religion as being entirely different in essence from that of a clergyman, even if they are similar to one another at many points. "A scholar (*Gelehrter*) is not a priest (*Priester*)," he stated in 1979. The points of similarity between the scholar and the mystic are reflected in his essay "Zehn unhistorische Sätze über Kabbala" (Ten unhistorical aphorisms on Kabbalah), which published in the Festschrift for Brody.[58] For this volume Scholem was asked "to contribute something that I would not consider publishing at all under ordinary circumstances,"[59] and he sent ten aphorisms that convey his thoughts about his field of research from a personal point of view, rather than from the professional position of an academic. The first of these related directly to the researcher's attitude toward the subject of his research:

> There is something ironic in the philology of a mystical field such as Kabbalah, since its concern is the veil of fog which, with respect to the history of the mystical tradition, surrounds its body, its space, and the matter itself, and the fog bursts out of its very self. Is anything left to the philologist of the workings of the matter itself, or, in fact, does its essential foundation disappear in this projection into the historical realm? The uncertainty in offering an answer to this question is bound up in the nature of the way the philological question itself is presented, and therefore there is something ironic in the expectation from which this work is nourished, and this irony cannot be removed from it. But is this element of irony not found already in the subject of Kabbalah itself and not only in its history? The kabbalist claims that there is a tradition of truth, which can be transmitted from generation to generation. This claim is ironic, because the truth spoken of here is everything except transmittable. It is possible to become aware of it, but it is impossible to convey it. Indeed, that part of it which can be conveyed no longer contains the truth. The tradition of truth remains hidden; but the tradition that has disintegrated is crammed into one matter, and in its disintegration it is known to its full extent.[60]

In this passage Scholem expresses an idea that appeared in preliminary form in a letter to Salman Schocken in 1937,[61] referring to the question of the religious meaning of the attitude of the man of science to the subject of his research. In fact, the irony that Scholem pointed out is shared by both the kabbalist and the scholar, since it is immanent in Kabbalah itself: the effort to express in language that which cannot be expressed—or the effort to convey something to someone else that cannot be conveyed but can only be a personal experience—and that therefore loses its force during the effort to remove it from the realm of the esoteric to the exoteric as a subject of human communication. According to Scholem, the irony here lies in the fact that both the historian and the kabbalist belong to a tradition that requires communication as a condition for existence, and their goal is to ensure the continuity of the tradition across generations. This tension, in his view, is the common aspect that makes the historian and the kabbalist parallel figures, but different from one another in essence and purpose. The paradox lies in the effort to grasp that which cannot be grasped without absolute identification with the object of study, and to express in words what cannot be expressed at all. The necessity of doing this to satisfy the common rules of communication in the academic community produces the tension that makes scientific consciousness and creativity possible. It is this tension to which he referred at various points in his life, including his last remarks at Eranos.

In Corbin's letter to Miller the same tension appears: between the scholar's search for the countenance of his personal God and marking out the personal path of others, without the ability to convey the experience itself. Here an important difference between Scholem and Corbin should be pointed out. They both referred to two opposing poles, the historian and the mystic, but Scholem was closer to the side of the historian and Corbin closer to the mystic, or prophet. However, they were both aware of the tension in the need and desire to convey to others what cannot be communicated. Perhaps one may also say that both men (and perhaps participants in the Eranos conferences in general) were aware that creativity, whether in science or in religious experience, is born of this paradox.

Now, what is this tension shared by Scholem, Corbin, Eliade, and many of the other intellectuals who took part in Eranos? If it can be characterized in the area of theory and research, then one may say that it is the phenomenological approach to the history of religions. However, while the phenomenological approach underlay Corbin's scholarship,[62] Scholem's commitment to phenomenology was not so complete. Moshe Idel has suggested viewing Scholem, under the influence of his participation in the Eranos conferences, as "the founder of the phenomenology of the Kabbalah."[63] Indeed, it appears that in his scholarship

Scholem did accord a large place to the phenomenological study of the history of the Jewish religion, but this was always as a method that complemented historical and philological research, building on a scholarly foundation anchored in the sources. In April 1955 the Swiss magazine DU devoted an entire issue to the Eranos conferences. The issue included many articles by participants in Eranos, some of them about the conferences themselves and their personal and experiential side, and some about the participants' areas of research. Scholem contributed an article whose title was "The Thoughts of a Scholar of Kabbalah," in which he referred to the dialectic between closeness and distance in his research:

> The endeavor to understand what was here enacted at the heart of Jewry cannot dispense with historical criticism and clear vision. For even symbols grow out of historical experience and are saturated with it. A proper understanding of them requires both a "phenomenological" aptitude for seeing things as a whole and a gift of historical analysis. One complements and clarifies the other; taken together they promise valuable findings. The scholars who gathered for the Eranos conferences contributed greatly to uniting these two approaches. Research in Kabbalah, whose serious undertaking began in our generation, "came home" here, in the good sense of the word, though it is only a guest from Jerusalem.[64]

These words of Scholem's once again show that the tension between identification and distance did not exist solely in his relationship to the area of his scholarship within the confines of Eranos but rather in the way he understood his complex place at the conferences, simultaneously at home and a guest.

External Criticism

Carl Gustav Jung

In addition to the inner and personal ambivalence that Scholem felt in Eranos, a complication arose because of the way his participation was perceived by those around him in Israel and the Jewish world as a whole: it aroused tension because of Jung's influence on the proceedings. As we have seen, the assumption that all of the Eranos conferences were a stage for Jung and his theories is a dubious one, and the collection of individuals involved in the conferences was too rich and complex to be called a circle of any sort, let alone a Jungian circle. Nevertheless, the claim was made that Jung's influence on the conferences was paramount—mainly within the Jewish intellectual world, where criticism was also leveled at Scholem for participating in them. Idel, who began participating in them many years after Scholem did, observed: "The unfortunately strong rightist affinities and affiliations of Jung and Eliade before the Second World

War created in Israel a negative reaction against their scholarship, and by extension, a reticence towards *Eranos*."[65]

Scholem's way of dealing with the fact that he had been invited to the conferences by Jung, a former supporter of Nazism, so soon after the Holocaust, has been discussed above. For this reason, Scholem had to explain not only his personal relationship with Jung, but also his attitude toward Jung's ideas. This need became acute after the publication of Jung's *Antwort auf Hiob* in 1952, for the book evinces an antisemitic worldview.[66] Scholem read the book when it appeared and was aware of its antisemitic element. In a short diary entry dated May 18, 1952, he wrote: "I read Jung's *Antwort auf Hiob*, which triggered extreme reactions (*auslösenden Affectreaktionen*). Schocken lent it to me. This is the way a man writes who is capable of combining gnosticism with the antisemitism of a Swiss peasant."[67] Nevertheless, as shown above, Scholem had no essential reason to abstain from participation in Eranos: the variety of the conferences made it possible for him to attend without intense interaction with Jung. Moreover, the conference of the year when Scholem recorded his impressions in his diary was also the last one Jung attended. Scholem's outward difficulty during his years of participation in the conferences was actually with the image of Eranos in Israel, which identified the conferences with Jung, his past, and his theories.

Scholem's most important and severest critic, who identified Scholem's research with Jungian psychology in the wake of his participation in the Eranos conferences, was Baruch Kurzweil, an Israeli literary critic who devoted a considerable part of his critical writing to Scholem and his research.[68] As part of this extensive critical project, which was published over the years in *Haaretz*, in 1967 Kurzweil published an article explaining the common denominator on the level of ideas that made it possible for Scholem to take part in Eranos. Kurzweil argued that Scholem's type of secular study of Kabbalah, which exalts myth without faith in God—that is, without belief in absolute morality—opened the way to a nihilistic theology that denied the uniqueness of Judaism and was fascist in character: "The absolute difference of the God of Israel is obliterated in Jung, and his theory makes possible a theology without God, which is a nihilistic theology. More than that: Jung also gave a writ of divorce to the absolute claim of morality. The deep nihilism that underlies his thinking . . .—the nihilism of the modern admirer of myths—is what caused him to be, for a certain time, a follower of the Nazi movement as well. . . . It appears to me that Jewish studies has found the terminus of its adventurous journey in the shadow of Jung. It would be impossible to decree a more bitter fate for the path of Jewish studies.[69]

Scholem did not answer Kurzweil's accusations directly,[70] but they certainly were one reason why he needed to clarify his attitude toward Jung's theories.

He explained his objections to those theories in an interview that he gave in the 1970s:

> In treating the history and the world of Kabbalah, using the conceptual terminology of psychoanalysis—either the Freudian or the Jungian version—did not seem fruitful to me. Even though I should have had a strong affinity to Jung's conceptions, which were close to religious concepts, I refrained from using them. For twenty-five years I lectured at the Eranos meetings, and in that circle there was a considerable Jungian influence. But in those lectures I deliberately shied away from all psychoanalytical and Jungian psychopathological concepts. I was not convinced that those categories are useful. I particularly avoided using the theory of archetypes, of which I remain highly skeptical.[71]

Scholem's unequivocal words here are slightly surprising, seeing that elsewhere in his writings and scholarship—especially in the published lectures from Eranos—he did make some use of ideas from Jung's school, such as the concept of archetype and the ideas associated with it.[72] Although Scholem did not make much use of Jung's theories in his scholarship, his ambivalence about the use he did make of them and his rejection of them point to the mixed emotions that he felt about them. On the one hand, it was natural for Scholem to be influenced by other theories that were central at the Eranos conferences, and nothing in the way he used Jung's ideas implies that he was deeply influenced by Jung. But on the other hand, it cannot be said that Scholem did not use and grapple with Jungian models at all.[73] In any case, what is important for the present discussion is that Scholem's extreme rejection of Jung's ideas had an apologetic and defensive tone, the purpose of which was to reduce the bewilderment in the Jewish world about his taking part in Eranos.[74] In addition, Scholem never sought to blur or conceal Jung's affiliation with the Nazi movement, although he doubted its depth and seriousness. Thus, for example, he responded to the criticism leveled by George Steiner on this matter in a letter to the Jungian analytical psychologist, James Kirsch: "Indeed I am convinced that Jung was not a full-fledged Nazi, and the reading of his works proves that to me. However, I do not wish to deny that he had 'ties' to the Nazis, and that he defended certain theses in a time and place when their evil influence was doubled and redoubled. [These theses] went far beyond what he ought to have permitted himself according to his own theories."[75]

Jung's influence on Scholem, therefore, had two aspects: one positive and the other negative. The positive aspect is noticeable in several places in Scholem's writings—especially in the published Eranos lectures—where he used Jungian categories and models to shed light on phenomena in the realm of religion. The negative aspect, which is more significant, is evident in his rejection of any hint of a connection between his scholarship and Jung's theories. Scholem's participation in Eranos was always accompanied by a certain need to excuse himself for it to the Israeli public by defining himself as intellectually foreign to the Jungian circles at Eranos. In other words, Scholem's regular presence at Ascona required him to demonstrate a skeptical approach to Jungian psychology. To a great degree this rejection represented the rejection of Jung's Nazi past and his antisemitic aspect, which enabled Scholem to accept Jung's physical presence in the summer of 1952 and the presence of his spirit and disciples in the following years at Ascona. For this reason, perhaps, Scholem always preferred to characterize Jung's Nazi past as a misstep, a minor episode that could not be excused but—seeing the remorse Jung expressed to Baeck—could be lived with. Scholem could not take such a forgiving attitude toward Eliade, another controversial figure in Israel.

Mircea Eliade

It was during his second visit to Eranos, in the summer of 1950, that Scholem met Eliade for the first time. Eliade had not participated in the conferences before, and he recorded his impressions in his diary, devoting considerable space to his acquaintance with Scholem. Eliade had known of Scholem and his scholarship before their meeting, and he was surprised to hear that Scholem had read all of his books. From the first Scholem made a positive impression on Eliade, who described it in his diary in an entry dated August 20: "A very pleasant face, with large ears that stand out from his head. He speaks broken English with a delightful accent."[76] Scholem's lecture, titled "Tradition and Innovation in the Ritual of the Kabbalists," also impressed Eliade greatly. As he later wrote in his memoirs: "The next day Professor Scholem lectured; he fascinated me from the moment I met him on the evening of my arrival. I had long admired his scholarship and perspicacity, but that evening what impressed me were his gifts as a storyteller and his genius for asking only essential questions."[77] In the following decade, Eliade became one of the regular participants in the Eranos conferences, and he was a member of the inner circle mentioned above in this chapter.

In the course of time, the two men formed a professional and personal friendship, whose peak is symbolized by Scholem's contribution to a Festschrift in honor of Eliade that was published in Chicago in 1969.[78] However, after that they grew apart. In 1972 the first issue of *Toladot*, a Hebrew journal for the study of the history of the Jews in Romania, published an article by the historian Theodor Lavi that vehemently criticized Scholem's participation in the Festschrift. Lavi claimed that between the two world wars Eliade had been a member of the Garda de Fier (the iron guard), a Romanian fascist and antisemitic organization "whose murderous activity is engraved in our history with the blood of tens of thousands of Jewish victims in Romania."[79] According to Lavi, Eliade had supplied the philosophical background for the heinous activities of the organization, and his membership in it had a decisive influence on its success because Eliade was one of the most prominent intellectuals in Romania at the time. Therefore, Lavi argued, there was an ethical flaw in the intellectual connection between Scholem and Eliade, who continued to adhere to his former opinions: "Professor Gershom Scholem cannot, therefore, justify his actions by ignoring Eliade's past. A few years ago he also took the initiative of inviting Eliade to give a series of lectures at the Hebrew University. Even then he had been informed of the political biography of the scholar from Chicago, but Professor Scholem was apparently of the opinion that these were merely youthful sins, which could be forgiven. In fact, even today Eliade is far from secluding himself in the ivory tower of scholarship. He contributes to various publications in the same spirit, which are published by former members of the Iron Guard in their places of exile."[80] As proof of this claim about Eliade's dubious political affiliations, Lavi quoted passages from the diary of Joseph Hechter, a Romanian Jewish author, for the first time. Hechter, known by his pen name Mihail Sebastian, was a close friend of Eliadeat that time.[81]

Scholem's reaction to the criticism leveled against him was twofold. He sent a letter to Lavi in which he cast doubt on the truth of Lavi's accusations, stating that neither the article nor the passages from the diary provided actual evidence about Eliade's past,[82] and at the same time he sent Eliade a copy of the issue of *Toladot* in which the statements were made, along with a personal letter asking him, in a friendly but insistent manner, for a convincing explanation that would refute the claims. After presenting Eliade with Lavi's accusations against him, Scholem explained the embarrassment to which he was subject as a result:

> You will understand that I am most concerned about these things, and I would like you to react to these accusations, to state your attitude at those times and, if necessary, your reasons for changing your mind. In these long years I have known you I have no reason whatsoever to believe you to have been an antisemite, and even more so an antisemitic leader. I consider you a sincere and upright man whom I regard with great respect. Therefore, it is only natural to ask you to tell me, and through me those concerned, the mere truth. If there is anything to be said on this score, let it be said, and let the atmosphere of general or specific accusations be cleared up. Of all your writings prior to 1940 I know only your scholarly work in the field of Indology and History of Religion. When we first met I regarded you as a close colleague and later even as a friend to whom I could speak unreservedly. I hope this

openness of mind and human relations can continue. I think, however, that we must answer this attack which, no doubt, will be given wide publicity in Israel, where untold thousands of Romanian Jews have bitter memories of "The Iron Guard" and its activities.[83]

The caution and decisiveness with which Scholem addressed Eliade demonstrate the great respect he felt for Eliade along with the great importance of the subject for Scholem. He placed himself on Eliade's side in the letter, as a fellow target of criticism, and at the same time he reminded Eliade of the openness of their relations as the basis for his demand to know the truth. Hence we may surmise that a detailed confession about the antisemitic chapter in Eliade's life along with an expression of remorse—such as Jung's—would have sufficed to sweeten the bad taste of these accusations for Scholem.

The importance of Israeli public opinion on this matter was intensified because Eliade planned to visit Israel. In a relatively short time, Scholem received a long and detailed letter from Eliade in which he denied all the claims raised against him in the journal.[84] Scholem confronted Lavi with Eliade's counterarguments in the letter, but in response Lavi stated once again that in Romania at that time, it was commonly known that Eliade belonged to the Iron Guard, and that it was not possible to be a member of that organization without subscribing to an antisemitic worldview. Moreover, Lavi claimed, Eliade avoided confessing and expressing remorse for his past because he "still maintains his close connections with the authors of the Iron Guard camp." Scholem recorded these words in his notes of the meeting with Lavi, which he wrote in his own hand, indicating the importance of its contents for him. Scholem summed up his conclusions from the meeting as follows: "Even now the matter is a draw. Lavi was unable to prove any concrete or literary antisemitic actions on his [Eliade's] part, though I asked him to tell me what he [Eliade] in fact *had done*."[85] Thus Scholem was not entirely convinced of the proof of Lavi's accusations, but Eliade's evasions made him uncomfortable, and perhaps for this reason he chose not to answer Eliade's letter. Eliade was uncomfortable with Scholem's silence, especially because he received indications from Corbin and other colleagues that Scholem was not entirely convinced by the explanations in the letter. In March 1973 Eliade wrote to Scholem once again, revealing that he knew about Scholem's doubts about his past. In this letter Eliade again summarized briefly the important points he had made in the longer letter, the first and most important of which being that he never had antisemitic views. "I have never been an antisemite," he wrote.[86]

In his reply, Scholem expressed pleasure about Eliade's planned visit to Israel and about a possible meeting, which would provide a good opportunity for a face-to-face conversation about Eliade's words in his letter, "which are, as I feel, in need of a friendly and openminded discussion and elucidation."[87] Scholem reviewed the claims made by Lavi in their conversation and described the feeling of discomfort he had felt after it, because of his inability to come to a conclusion about the subject, and he observed that this discomfort had prevented him from replying to Eliade's previous letter: "I did not know what to tell you especially since you had not been specific about the Jewish point which interested me most."[88] Scholem told Eliade that he had considered writing a public and well-grounded article in response to Lavi's accusations, but, lacking unequivocal information that would support Eliade's claims, he had not done so. At the end of his letter, Scholem laid what could be seen as a little trap for Eliade, before his visit to Israel: "I have the same personal feeling for you as before and I would welcome the occasion of a visit of you here. Perhaps there would be an occasion for you to meet Dr. Lavie [*sic*] and have a frank discussion with him."[89] Coincidentally—or possibly not—in his reply, Eliade announced to Scholem that, because of illness, he was forced to cancel his visit to Israel, though he would have been very pleased to meet Scholem in Jerusalem and clarify what he called the "*malheureux malentendu*" (unfortunate misunderstanding).[90]

Eliade's evasive answers did not allay Scholem's growing suspicions, and he received a long letter from Mihail Sebastian's brother, André, that confirmed what the published passages from the diary had said about Eliade.[91] Scholem's reply to Sebastian was typical of the way in which he related to the episode in general: despite the suspicions raised in various quarters regarding Eliade's past, and despite Eliade's evasive behavior, Scholem refrained from taking a position about him as long as he had not received official, conclusive proof. He concluded the letter to Sebastian with the following words: "But I found nobody who was ready to produce any tangible proof . . . answering Eliade's challenge to do so from among the hundreds of articles which, according to Eliade's own statement, he had published at that time. I am of course utterly unqualified to judge in these matters."[92] Thus Scholem took the middle ground, between the accusations leveled against him in Israel and his need to defend his connections with Eliade, on the one hand, and on the other hand, his own need to discover the truth and uncover further information about his colleague and friend. Outwardly his tone was defensive, as expressed by his backing Eliade and demanding conclusive proof, but inwardly his writing to Eliade is characterized by growing suspicion and mistrust, concealed behind expressions of affinity. The latter tendency is corroborated by the fact that Eliade's letter to Scholem of April 1973 is the last one in the correspondence between the two as preserved in Scholem's archive.

While Scholem apparently severed relations with Eliade in writing, this does not indicate that he had reached a conclusion in the matter and regarded it as resolved. In 1978 Scholem's colleague Zvi Werblowsky shared a letter with him that Werblowsky had received from Kurt Rudolph, the East German scholar of religion through whom Scholem had tried to glean further information about Eliade's past. Rudolf had told Werblowsky about the many difficulties in obtaining relevant material from the libraries and archives in Bucharest under the Communist regime.[93] At the end of 1979 Seymour Cain, an American scholar of the history of religion, asked for Scholem's assistance in uncovering further details about Eliade's past. Since Cain intended to research Eliade's thought, he was trying to gather information from people in Israel about the basis of the accusations against him. Because Cain was unable to obtain concrete evidence about Eliade's activities, he wrote a letter to Scholem, whom he had met in Israel, in which he defended Eliade and argued that the accusations against him recalled the system of guilt by association, so common during the anticommunist witch hunts in the United States during the 1950s.[94] Scholem answered him as follows:

> You are certainly right in saying that there is to this very day no precise documentation of any antisemitic activity on the part of young Eliade, but I must confess that there is an uneasy feeling which is partly based on the evasive nature of Eliade's own writings, especially the published diary from his first years in Paris, which I have read. . . . You say that you dislike the technique of "Guilt by association" practiced on Eliade. You may be right, but the case of the leading circle around the Iron Cross [*sic*] is indeed a problem which could be solved only by detailed knowledge about the persons concerned and their activities. In this respect, one cannot say that Eliade, who is a very vocal man, has been particularly responsive.[95]

One senses a tone of increasing skepticism in Scholem's words about Eliade's past. Eliade's evasions during the six years that had passed since the beginning of their correspondence on the subject, providing neither a clear answer nor proof to refute the accusations against him, apparently deepened Scholem's doubt despite his abiding admiration for Eliade as a scholar. Until the last year of his life, Scholem remained in contact with Cain about Eliade's past and kept up with every scrap of information that Cain gathered, though Scholem was unable to solve the mystery completely before his death.[96] Even today, after the libraries in Bucharest have been opened and it has become possible to examine documents touching on the matter, Sebastian's testimony remains one of the important sources in the search for an answer to the question of to what extent Eliade was involved in the activities of the Iron Guard—a question that has yet to receive an unequivocal answer.[97]

Scholem's relations with Jung and Eliade demonstrate his stance between the wish to regularly participate in Eranos and the need to explain this participation to a critical public opinion in Israel. However, the case of Jung should be distinguished from that of Eliade. Scholem's acquaintance with Jung was only superficial and was free of any personal involvement. Hence, the attacks on his connection to Jung did not touch him directly and were rapidly displaced to the level of scholarship: the question of whether or not there was Jungian influence on Scholem and his research. In contrast, Scholem regarded Eliade as a friend and close colleague, so that the criticism of Eliade and Scholem's relationship with him disturbed him more. The question of Eliade's fascist and antisemitic past vexed Scholem far more than that of Jung's past—both because of the fog surrounding Eliade's past and because he repeatedly avoided providing a clear and unequivocal answer. This point was particularly problematic for Scholem, especially because of the close relations, both intellectual and personal, that the two men had had.[98] In any case, both of these episodes express the ambivalence that accompanied Scholem's participation in Eranos, although the attractive force of the conferences outweighed the deterring factors. The effort to understand the essence of the attractive force of Eranos for Scholem will help shed light on the place and meaning of the annual conferences in his life and in the history of his attitude toward Germany and Europe after the Holocaust.

The Meaning of Eranos

Scholem became a mainstay of the Eranos conferences, and they were an important component of his intellectual, academic, and social life. However, the question still remains: what caused him to participate in the conferences and persist in attending them for three decades, despite the ambivalence that often accompanied them?

In an article about Scholem and Eranos, Joseph Dan writes about the dreadful crisis that struck the Jewish world in the wake of the Holocaust and the difficult political position of the young State of Israel, which influenced the possibilities for research, as the principal reason for Scholem's attending his first Eranos conference in 1949. In addition, Dan mentions the attraction of the chance to use German in an academic framework after more than a decade, when Scholem had refrained from doing so. According to Dan, Scholem had no alternative: "Scholem did not go to Ascona because he chose that place and that circle from among many other possibilities. At that time there was almost no alternative to this type of circle."[99] Though I agree with the explanations Dan

FIGURE 9 Gershom Scholem lecturing at Eranos, undated. From the collection of the National Library of Israel, Jerusalem.

offers for Scholem's participation, I disagree with his negative conclusion. In my opinion, Scholem's choice to go to Ascona was deliberate and derived from positive motives. Though it is true that at that time Jerusalem was undoubtedly on the margins of the international academic community, and not only was the Hebrew University cut off from scholarly activity in the rest of the world, but also its library was inaccessible, surrounded by Jordanian territory on Mount Scopus. However, if Scholem had wanted one, he had an obvious and excellent alternative to Switzerland—the United States. Sooner or later, research in the United States and acceptance there would have provided a forum no worse than that of the Eranos conferences.[100] Scholem's conscious choice—despite the alternatives available to him over the years and despite the contradictions accompanying his participation—to continue to appear at Eranos conferences indicates the special place that they occupied in his life. The return to the German language of course played an important role in this choice, and here we may consider the language as representing the whole of German culture and its intellectual world, which remained an important part in Scholem's personal world even after World War II.

Furthermore, at that time Switzerland constituted a neutral territory for him, where he could present his research in his mother tongue to an audience that belonged to his native culture, for two uninterrupted hours. The large number of scholars and intellectuals who took part in Eranos and the great popularity of the Eranos yearbooks among scholars of religion offered an appropriate platform for him and a stopping point for him on his way back to Germany after the war, as well as a place where he could make connections and get to know colleagues with whom he had much in common. And perhaps more than anything, Eranos had nostalgic value for Scholem.

In her book on nostalgia, the sociologist Janelle Wilson notes the various aspects of this term and the complexity that characterizes it as a symbol of a human emotion. For example, one characteristic of nostalgia is its belonging to leisure activity, and another is its being an emotion that can be communicated to and shared by other individuals or groups. Indeed, nostalgia is yearning for a place or time identified with a certain degree of security for the person who feels nostalgic—a person whose present life lacks that element of stability.[101] Yet another characteristic of nostalgia is that its aim is to connect the past with the present and create the continuity needed to construct a personal or collective identity. This need usually arises at times when that continuity is in jeopardy because of a lack of security in the present, often following a traumatic experience or crisis that threatens the present. Here are the criteria proposed by the sociologist Fred Davis in his book on the subject: "(1) The nostalgic evocation of some past state of affairs always occurs in the context of present fears, discontents, anxieties, or uncertainties, even though they may not be in the forefront of awareness, and (2) it is these emotions and cognitive states that pose the threat of identity discontinuity (existentially, the panic fear of the 'wolf of insignificance') that nostalgia seeks, by marshaling our psychological resources for continuity, to abort or, at the very least, deflect."[102] The continuity of identity made possible by nostalgia is central to the research of Davis and Wilson, and its significance lies in the ability of the person who experiences nostalgia to create an empathic connection with his or her former self, which, for some reason, is no longer accessible in the present, and thereby to create a clear continuum of identity for that person between past and present, aimed toward the future.[103]

It is possible to identify strong nostalgic elements in the Eranos conferences in the period after World War II. The annual cycle of vacationing, the creation of a separate space for an academic event combined with leisure and communication among the participants, and the location in a place that had been a center of alternative spiritual trends before World War II—all of these looked, to a large degree, toward the past, toward the imperial era in Central Europe. Hence they fit the hypothesis advanced in Wilson's book, that nostalgia is "longing for a Utopia, projected backwards in time."[104] For Scholem the nostalgic aspect of the conferences was inordinately important. To a great degree, the shock that he experienced because of the Holocaust and his trip to save the treasures of the

Diaspora, along with the establishment of the State of Israel, undermined his confidence in his surroundings, and without doubt they contradicted the manner in which he had understood the meaning and function of Zionism. Through Eranos he was able to heal the rift that had opened in his identity and ensure continuity in it, by the ability to create an empathic connection with an important part of his life that had grown dim after his emigration to the Land of Israel and been lost to him after the Holocaust: German culture and language as he had known them, before the deep changes that took place under Nazi rule.[105] Thus Scholem himself stated in 1974, in a lecture given in Munich after he received a prize from the Bavarian Academy of Fine Arts:

> In 1946 I was sent to Germany with the special mission of examining the destiny of the Jewish libraries, to report on those remnants which survived, and to present overall proposals pertaining to their care. It is difficult for me to describe the shock that I experienced in my encounter with the German language of those days. There was in it something Medusa-like, something paralyzing, something that had absorbed the events of those years in a manner which cannot be explained. And if, in 1949, I began to write more extensively in the German language, this too had a certain bearing upon that selfsame shock. My lectures at the Eranos Conferences in Ascona were an additional factor. There I was given the opportunity to arrive at a synthesis of things upon which I had worked for thirty years, without sacrificing historical criticism or philosophical thought. In the atmosphere of those conferences, I felt that I could once again express myself properly in the German language without submitting to the provocation originating in that same shock.[106]

In the 1950s the Eranos conferences provided Scholem with a transitional stage in his life, on both the temporal and the geographical level. With respect to time, the conferences renewed his direct connection with his past—with the German culture and language—that he had lost. Geographically, Ascona was a protected intermediary space, a German-speaking realm that had no direct connection with the events of the Holocaust. Furthermore, Scholem had a personal connection with the place, since Switzerland had been important for him in the past. He had spent family vacations there during his childhood and youth, and he had fled to Switzerland after being exempted from military service toward the end of World War I. He had also passed a significant period in his life there, in the company of the friend of his youth, Walter Benjamin. This was the place where, after the Holocaust, Scholem laid the groundwork for once again being active in the German intellectual world, with which he had maintained a close connection after his emigration to Palestine. Of course that connection was severed during the war, but it became important to him because of his increasing disappointment with the possibility of implementing his Zionist utopia in the Land of Israel. Symbolically, the nostalgic atmosphere of Eranos provided a personal intellectual refuge for him, to which he could transplant his utopia from the collective future to the personal past: from Israel to Germany.

CHAPTER 8

BETWEEN ISRAEL AND GERMANY

Once, years ago, I heard a provocative statement from Scholem: "After Hitler, there exists between every German and every Jew a necessary intimacy, which everyone can treat this way or that, but no one can deny it."

AMOS OZ, *KOL HATIKVOT*[1]

Eichmann in Jerusalem

A Correspondence

The capture of Adolf Eichmann in Argentina by Israeli agents; his abduction to Israel; and his trial, which was held in Beit Haam (now known as the Gerard Behar Center) in Jerusalem between April and December 1961, were formative in the Jewish world with respect to the memory of the Holocaust and the internalization of its significance. One of the results of these events was the storm raised by Hannah Arendt's *Eichmann in Jerusalem*, which was first published in 1963 and was based on her coverage of the trial as a correspondent for the *New Yorker*.[2] The series of articles that Arendt published and, later, her book provoked many responses—unprecedented in their vociferousness—from Jewish intellectuals, especially in the United States and Israel. In the opinion of Richard Cohen, the importance of Arendt's book for her generation was because her analysis "sparked an unparalleled public airing of historical issues relating to the Holocaust. For the first time since the war, laymen, journalists, intellectuals, jurists, social scientists, and historians—of both Jewish and non-Jewish extraction—placed the events of the Holocaust in central focus."[3] Critiques of the book itself generally revolved around the same axes, and Arendt's various opponents, most of whom were Jews, emphasized similar points in her book. The critics mainly addressed Arendt's writing style; her position regarding the actions of the Judenräte, the Jewish leadership appointed by the Nazis during the Holocaust; and the way she described the figure of Eichmann as demonstrating what she called "the banality of evil." These central points appeared in Scholem's famous letter to Arendt, in which he severely criticized her book and her motivations for writing it. This letter, dated June 23, 1963, and Arendt's answer, dated July 20, 1963, are among the most important documents in the dispute, both because of Scholem's arguments and because Arendt's answer (which Scholem published, with her grudging consent) is one of her few direct responses to the fierce accusations leveled against her.[4]

In his letter, Scholem analyzed Arendt's book as dealing with two central problems: Jewish leadership during the Holocaust and Eichmann's responsibility for his deeds. According to Arendt, if the Jewish leadership had not cooperated with the Nazis, fewer Jews would have been murdered in the Holocaust. One sentence in her book infuriated many people: "To a Jew, this role of the Jewish leaders in the destruction of their own people is undoubtedly the darkest chapter in the whole story."[5] She described Eichmann as a passive bureaucrat who was incapable of independent thought. In response to Eichmann's personality, as she understood it, Arendt coined the phrase "the banality of evil," which was also widely criticized.

Throughout most of his letter, Scholem struggled with Arendt's claims that the Jewish leadership shared the responsibility for the dimensions of the destruction. His criticism was based on the assumption that "our generation is [not] in a position to pass any kind of historical judgment [on the Holocaust]. We lack the necessary perspective, which alone makes some sort of objectivity possible."[6] Scholem's central accusation against Arendt dealt not with the content of her book but with its form and vehemence. In his view, the book lacked all empathy with the victims of the Holocaust and thus revealed more than a little of Arendt's inner world and motivations for writing. This understanding of her book led him to level one of the most famous accusations against her in the Arendt polemics:

> It is that heartless, frequently almost sneering and malicious tone with which these matters, touching the very quick of our life, are treated in your book to which I take exception. In the Jewish tradition there is a concept, hard to define and yet concrete enough, which we know as Ahabath Israel: "Love for the Jewish People . . . [ellipsis points in the original]." In you, dear Hannah, as in so many intellectuals who come from the German left, I find little trace of this. A discussion such as is attempted in your book would seem to me to require—you will forgive my mode of expression—the most old-fashioned, the most circumspect, the most exacting treatment possible—precisely because of the feeling aroused by this matter, this matter of the destruction of one-third of our people—and I regard you wholly as a daughter of our people, and in no other way. Thus I have little sympathy for that tone—well ex-

> pressed by the English word "flippancy"—which you employ so often in the course of your book. To the matter of which you speak it is unimaginably inappropriate.[7]

The confidence with which Arendt passed judgment on the Jewish leadership and actions of Jews in extreme circumstances that she had never experienced seemed to Scholem to both sin against the subject she chose to write about and violate the principle of ethnic solidarity, which he expected her to honor since he counted her as part of the Jewish people. This accusation of lack of love of Israel was the first point to which Arendt referred in her reply to Scholem, contrasting his demand for Jewish solidarity and the demand for it on a personal and human basis: "You are quite right—I am not moved by any 'love' of this sort, and for two reasons: I have never in my life 'loved' any people or collective—neither the German people, nor the French, nor the American, nor the working class or anything of that sort. I indeed love 'only' my friends and the only kind of love I know of and believe in is the love of persons. Secondly, this 'love of the Jews' would appear to me, since I am myself Jewish, as something rather suspect. I cannot love myself or anything that I know is part and parcel of my own person."[8]

In her letter, Arendt repeated several times that Scholem had not understood her book properly—meaning not in the way that she had it. Indeed, the central example presented here clearly demonstrates the incompatibility of their positions, which, in my view, was the reason for the absolute lack of understanding that created the rift between them. Whereas Scholem based his arguments on the emotional and tribal level, Arendt based hers on rational grounds. Scholem refused to judge the Holocaust as a historical phenomenon, stating that no one who had not experienced that extreme event in person could pass judgment on it. In contrast, Arendt felt that she could analyze a phenomenon with an enormous emotional burden under "sterile" laboratory conditions, solely by exercising her reason. An example of the lack of understanding between the two can be found in the fact that even the term "love of Israel," which was central to the dispute in the passages quoted above, was not understood by Arendt in the context that Scholem intended it to be understood. Arendt reduced the broad and slightly fuzzy term (one may assume that Scholem intentionally avoided translating it in his German letter, to keep it fuzzy) to the ethnic and political level, and in doing so she missed various levels of its meaning that certainly lay behind Scholem's choice of the term.[9]

In my view, the argument that this bitter dispute and the deep differences between Arendt and Scholem were based on great closeness between them accurately describes their relations.[10] Indeed, one can point out many similarities between the two on the surface. For example, they both had a German-Jewish background; they were both close friends and great admirers of Walter Benjamin; both of them had rebelled against the German-Jewish bourgeois world of their youth; their participation for a certain time in Zionist activity was based on similar values (as discussed below in this chapter); and they had both been disappointed with the direction taken by the Zionist movement and had shifted to a critical position regarding it. With respect to their public and intellectual activity, David Suchoff is largely right in stating that both Scholem and Arendt "created new models for the transmission of tradition and the relation between ethnic culture and political action."[11] However, despite these points of similarity, which are mainly external, there were abysmal differences between them that were connected to the essence of the tradition to be preserved and transmitted to the future. First of all, in this context, one must note the difference in their attitudes toward the Hebrew language. In contrast to the centrality that Scholem attributed to Hebrew as a vital force in Jewish existence and Zionist activity, Hebrew did not occupy a central place for Arendt, even during her years of Zionist activity. While Scholem, as a Jew, was drawn to the East and to the Land of Israel, on various occasions Arendt expressed sharp reservations about and even revulsion toward Eastern Jews—whether they be Jews from Eastern Europe or the Israeli police force at Beit Haam, who, in her opinion, cut Judaism off from its true source, which was Western European culture.[12] In the context of the Arendt-Scholem dispute, Dan Diner has shown that, in contrast to nationalism on an ethnic basis, represented by the Jews of Eastern Europe and Scholem, Arendt represented nationalism anchored in the culture of the West and the process of emancipation.[13] Unlike Scholem, Arendt never considered moving to Palestine, and after Hitler's rise to power she chose to move to Paris.

Hence, it may be said that, despite the similarity of their backgrounds and certain aspects of their lives, Scholem and Arendt were essentially very different, almost opposites. In their dispute, this prevented almost all positive communication and led to repeated misunderstandings. This is not to say that the two did not have a connection with one another or that they did not respect or influence each other. In the dialectics between closeness and distance, between the similar and the different, Scholem and Arendt stood opposed to each other as in a mirror, each reflecting the other. Steven Aschheim wrote that "paradoxically, their negative personal evaluations of each other also looked like mirror images."[14] Consciously or unconsciously, willingly or not, Arendt's counter-image helped Scholem determine where he stood on the questions of personal identity and membership in the collective within the Jewish world after the Holocaust.

In Relation to Zionism: Questions of Belonging

One of Scholem's principal arguments toward the end of his letter to Arendt was that in the way she described Eichmann, she made a mockery of Zionism. Indeed, it seems that the differences between Scholem and Arendt in their attitudes toward Zionism are central for understanding the bone of contention between them in the Eichmann case and also serve as the background of that dispute. In discussing the trial of a Nazi war criminal by a political body that represented world Jewry, Arendt's book linked the Holocaust and the establishment of the State of Israel as historical phenomena. It is therefore easy to understand the powerful emotions accompanying the polemics of both sides, such a short time after these two pivotal events. To better understand the background of the Scholem-Arendt controversy on Eichmann, one may refer to correspondence about an earlier controversy that in form and content was amazingly similar to the correspondence of 1963: the exchange of letters between the two following the publication in the United States of Arendt's article "Zionism Reconsidered," toward the end of 1945. To a large degree this article summarizes Arendt's position on Zionism, and it contains vehement and blunt condemnations of Zionist policies, because of which it had been rejected by the editor of *Commentary*.[15] Immediately the article was published, Arendt sent a copy of it to Scholem, and he responded with a long, fierce letter.[16] The arguments that Scholem made in this letter are very similar in character to those he raised in his later letter about her book on Eichmann. For example, in both letters Scholem did not conceal the deep disappointment and bitter feelings that Arendt's writing aroused in him; his tone was emotional; he argued that her argumentation derived from her belonging to circles of the German left; and Arendt's tone was central to Scholem's critique, for he saw it as mocking, contemptuous, and arrogant toward Zionism and Judaism.

In both letters Scholem also criticized Arendt's theories about the conscious and unconscious collaboration of the Jewish leadership, both Zionist and non-Zionist, with the aims of antisemitic regimes, especially the Nazis. Arendt's article is permeated by hints of what would be more clearly articulated in her book: the Jewish mentality and the Jewish leadership (in this case, Zionist) played a certain role—even if it was passive—in the dimensions of the destruction of the Jews of Europe. For example, in 1946 Arendt wrote that the Zionist ideology of Herzl and his followers, which regarded antisemitism as a positive factor binding the Jewish people together and something with which it was possible to negotiate, led to great confusion, because of which the Jews could no longer distinguish allies from enemies—which made their true enemy even more dangerous.[17] She went on to write that Weizmann's Zionism, which regarded settlement in the Land of Israel as the answer to antisemitism, had proved to be ridiculous when Erwin Rommel and his army directly threatened Palestine in World War II. In fact, according to Arendt, the Zionists' error lay in their hope that Palestine would be a place where the Jews could escape from antisemitism, and that their enemies would miraculously became their allies there:

> At the core of the hope which—were ideologies not stronger for some people than realities—should by now be blown to bits, we find the old mentality of enslaved peoples, the belief that it does not pay to fight back, that one must dodge and escape in order to survive. How deep-rooted is this conviction could be seen during the first years of the war, when only through the pressure of Jews throughout the world was the Zionist organization driven to ask for a Jewish Army—which, indeed, was the only important issue in the war against Hitler. . . . That an early instinct and demonstrable participation of Jews as *Jews* in this war would have been the decisive way to prevent the antisemitic slogan which, even before victory was won, already represented Jews as its parasites, apparently never entered their heads.[18]

The fact that the Yishuv was so focused on itself ostensibly caused its separation from the Jews of the rest of the world and led it to form ties with imperialist forces of all kinds—including the Ottoman Empire, which was slaughtering Armenians at that time,[19] and the British, who had their own interests. The motivation for this behavior was the desire to establish an elitist center that would be concerned only with its own survival for the future of Jewry as an ethnic group, and have no concern for the masses. Consequently, the Zionist leaders sought to rescue only the Jews who suited that ideology: "Zionists used to argue that 'only the remnant will return,' the best, the only ones worth saving; let us establish ourselves as the elite of the Jewish people and we shall be the only surviving Jews in the end; all that matters is our survival; let charity take care of the pressing needs of the masses, we shall not interfere; we are interested in the future of a nation, not in the fate of individuals."[20]

The failure of the Zionists lay in their being focused on themselves, so that they took no independent initiative in the form of establishing a Jewish army or cooperating "with the revolutionary forces in Europe."[21] Rather, in their limited efforts to be rescued, they reverted time and time again to the Diaspora Jewish practice of what she called "*shtadlonus*" (pleading with the authorities) in their relations to imperialism and the great political movements, including Nazism.[22] The implication here is that, because of the weakness of the Zionist movement in Palestine and the separation between it and the Diaspora, the Yishuv was indirectly responsible for the failure to assist the Jews of Europe during the Holocaust and for its dimensions. At least this is how Scholem understand her in his response to this passage:

> I think that meanwhile experience has proven that every one of us, in this situation, would have had to act the way the Zionist Organization acted, and the only thing to be regretted is that in a corrupt world no use was made of the possibility of saving Jews from fascism in time and more decisively. You ought to know—and if you don't know, then this must be emphasized to you—that we were prepared during the war to buy Jews from the Gestapo and for this purpose good and hard currency of the JDC [Joint Distribution Committee] and Zionists flowed to Germany in large amounts, and that the people who took this complex mission upon themselves did not betray the Jewish people as you would categorize them according to your logic. Rather, they were people who did their duty. I would like to know whether we were permitted to save Walter Benjamin by means of a deal of this kind, if it depended on that! I have to say that I believed you would have more understanding for a dialectical situation [of this kind], and your naïve bickering is out of place in this instance, as well as in a discussion of the values of Zionism in itself.[23]

Scholem made his position clear in his exchange with Arendt by referring to the Yishuv in the first person plural and unequivocally defending its actions during the war. His words indicated his need to confront Arendt as a representative of the Yishuv and to defend his reference group against her attack. He went on to declare, in response to Arendt's ironic interpretation of Weizmann's statement that the response to antisemitism is Zionist settlement in the Land of Israel, that he and Arendt had no common ground for discussion.[24]

These differences in how Scholem and Arendt understood the political realities of their day are extremely important, because they also shaped the personal relations between the two and the way in which Arendt appeared to Scholem in the following years until they broke off all contact in 1963, in the wake of the controversy surrounding *Eichmann in Jerusalem*. This article was a turning point in relations between them because, for Scholem, it placed Arendt for the first time as a figure absolutely alien to his world, despite the many things they still had in common. In relation to "us," the leadership of the Zionist Yishuv, which Scholem opposed domestically, Arendt was defined as other and alien. Scholem's later accusation that she lacked empathy for and a sense of human solidarity with the Jewish collective is expressed here in presenting the example of Benjamin as a worthy person to rescue. With this example, he was addressing Arendt's emotions, but in hindsight, given what she wrote him in 1963, it also seems to apply to her ability to love only her friends.

In his earlier letter Scholem did not conceal his disappointment with a woman whom he had called five years earlier "a marvelous woman and an excellent Zionist,"[25] and who now proved to be a person who had developed a "great anti-Palestinian complex."[26] In her reply, Arendt also emphasized that she had expected something different from him, and that she was disappointed with the position he had expressed in his letter: "I always thought and understood your position as a Jew politically, and I felt great respect for your decision to deal seriously with the political reality in Palestine. To tell the truth, I never would have dreamed of thinking that for that reason you would have a Zionist *Weltanshauung*, if only because of my hopes that in fact you do not have [such an outlook]."[27]

The great disappointment they each expressed about the other could have emerged only in the context of their realization that they shared a practical political worldview. That realization on Arendt's part could have been grounded in the similarity of her views to the ideas of the Brit Shalom circle, such as its critique of political Zionism and the dependence of the Zionist leadership on the strength of imperialist powers.[28] Scholem also criticized Zionism in this spirit in the years following his immigration. The two also shared a great concern for the fate of the Yishuv. As Arendt wrote in her response to Scholem's criticism in 1946, her article had been written "with great concern, bordering on panic, for the fate of Palestine."[29] However, the closeness of Arendt's view to the political line of Brit Shalom—which was expressed in her support of Judah Leib Magnes and the Ihud Association, which he founded in 1942—was after the time when Scholem was active in Brit Shalom. Arendt's leanings toward Zionism began only in 1933, after Brit Shalom had ceased to exist. Scholem's refusal to join the Ihud Association when it was established, despite a certain affinity with Magnes and his ideas, points to Scholem's retreat from the political line he had espoused until the collapse of Brit Shalom, with Hitler's rise to power.[30] The Holocaust caused a reversal in Scholem's conception of the purpose of Zionism and the Land of Israel, moving him even further from Arendt. He understood that a political solution to the Jewish question had become a matter of necessity. In fact, in the wake of their dispute about Arendt's reappraisal of Zionism after the Holocaust, she became a person of great importance for Scholem, who felt the ambivalence of being both distant from and close to her at the one and the same time. In the following years, Arendt espoused positions opposed to those of Scholem, which reflected for him his own place in the Jewish intellectual world, and more than any other colleague she helped him sharpen his opinions regarding his belonging to the Zionist collective. A feeling of belonging is naturally relative: for someone to belong to a certain group, he or she must be able to define one or more people as not belonging to it—especially if he or she has experienced a crisis in his or her relation to it. For Scholem, Arendt was that person who was outside the various groups to which he saw himself as belonging. By seeing her in this way, through emphasizing their differences despite the many points of similarity between them, Scholem was able to formulate parts of his Zionist and Jewish identity, and this helped him cope better with the crises and inner doubts that gnawed at him about the path of Zionism. An example of this can be seen in his response to Arendt's 1946 article, in which Scholem referred openly to how he positioned himself in the light of her remarks about the situation of Zionism in the Land of Israel and its future: "I never believed it would be easier for me to agree with Ben-Gurion than with you! After your article I have no doubt about the matter. I regard Ben-Gurion's political line as a catastrophe, but still a more noble catastrophe and a smaller one than what can be expected for us if we follow in your footsteps."[31]

In contrast to the figure of Arendt, which he defined as external to the groups he belonged to, Scholem identified with David Ben-Gurion, whom he placed inside those groups although he strongly opposed Ben-Gurion's path. Scholem also expressed his opposition to the central stream of Zionism and bitter disappointment with its path in "Reflections on the Science of Judaism," an article he wrote in 1944, toward the end of the war and the Holocaust and under their influence.[32] However, Scholem's critique in his article, which was also extremely vehement, was in his view internal to Zionism and thus legitimate. He identified Arendt's critique as external and thus rejected it categorically, although it had a few points of similarity to his own critique.[33]

The deep differences between Scholem and Arendt, along with their closeness and similarities, were also expressed in their personal relations. The dialogue between them appears to the reader as a kind of intellectual *Maskentanz* [mask dance] in which each of them acts out the reflection of his or her image in the view of the other—the opposite side (sitra achra) of his or her very self. In the course of this elusive, dialectal dance, which was not devoid of mutual provocations, one can sometimes feel moments of closeness and great honesty, which are quickly and repeatedly replaced by a mask of distance and alienation.[34] Perhaps the donning of these masks was necessary for them to overcome the feeling of closeness and focus on their estrangement, the source of which was political. Arendt sensed this tendency in her relationship with Scholem and even complained about it in a letter to Kurt Blumenfeld: "It is only natural, that I cannot manage with Scholem, especially in Fania's presence, no? The nationalistic speech, which he himself doesn't mean seriously and whose source is understandable fear, is something I can't stand."[35] In my opinion, Arendt's feeling that the nationalistic positions that Scholem presented to her again and again did not reflect his true opinions touches on the essence of what I have called a dance. In fact, along with his attacks on Arendt and even within his letters to her, the great admiration that he felt for her is also visible—an admiration that was sincere to the same degree as his critique of her. An example of this can be found in a diary entry of August 3, 1963, in which Scholem reports a long conversation that he had had in the home of the English philosopher Isaiah Berlin. Arendt's book was one of the subjects they discussed, and Berlin told Scholem that he had refrained from reviewing the book or even from reading it because it was "an obvious case of Jewish self-hatred." Scholem disagreed with this statement and, in parentheses, he wrote in his diary: "I don't think this is the kernel of the matter —coldness of heart, yes—self-hatred, no."[36] Later in the conversation Scholem expressed his opinion of Arendt to Berlin, taking an almost defensive position toward her. In any event it represented an effort to understand her in context and to alleviate the severity of judgment against her: "I said that I thought that H. A. was extremely gifted and in any event honest on a much higher level than Prof. [Bruno] Bettelheim, who is truly a scoundrel, whom I regard as the height of Jewish assimilationist charlatanism. In comparison to him, H. is quite a saint. [Berlin] wanted to read out our correspondence and to see whether it was appropriate for *Encounter*, where it can reach a broad readership."[37]

The fact that Scholem had taken a defensive and empathetic position toward Arendt indicated the closeness he still felt for her, in spite of the sharp criticism he leveled against her. Apparently with Berlin as an intermediary, an English translation of their correspondence was published in *Encounter*, where it received extensive circulation, despite Arendt's initial objection to its publication.[38]

For Arendt, too, Scholem was a figure who reflected her image, but he also represented everything she rejected in contemporary Zionism: the focus on itself based on a conception of the ethnic collective coupled with arrogance toward the Jews of the Diaspora and people of other nations (Arendt's husband, Heinrich Blücher, was not Jewish), and based on the belief that the State of Israel was the true representative of Judaism and therefore was the center of the world. No better example of this could be found than Arendt's famous remark about the impression Scholem made when he was in the United States in 1957: "He is very intelligent, but not really wise. Aside from that, he is so self-involved, that he has no eyes to see (nor even ears to hear). Basically he thinks: the center of the world is Israel; the center of Israel is Jerusalem; the center of Jerusalem is the Hebrew University; the center of the University—is Scholem. The gravest aspect of all this is the fact that he seriously thinks the world has a center. And just that, thank God, is what it doesn't have!"[39]

Bernard Wasserstein has recently showed how Arendt's mocking and amused view of Scholem was a double-edged sword that could just as accurately describe her own self-image: "On Arendt itself it might with no less truth be said that she saw the Jews as the centre of history, the German Jews as the centre of Jewry, the stateless, exiled refugees as the centre of German Jewry, and herself as the queen bee among those intellectual émigrés."[40] Although Scholem accused Arendt of heartlessness,[41] one aspect of their relationship was the powerful emotions —both positive and negative—they felt about each other. This dialectical relationship continued until the common elements that drew them together could no longer counteract the factors that separated them, which were expressed in Arendt's reporting on the Eichmann trial and Scholem's attack on it. Reading the two exchanges of letters discussed in this chapter allows one to say that for both of them, their dispute was based on the Holocaust, the way each of them interpreted the world after it in its shadow, and the way each understood how the other saw this point of crisis in Jewish and human history.

Facing the Holocaust: A Look toward the Future

The differences between the ways that Scholem and Arendt understood the Holocaust can be described in the context of their similar backgrounds. Both of them were active immediately after the war in efforts to locate and reclaim stolen Jewish property. They both made trips throughout Germany for the purpose of their work, and they both published accounts of their journeys.[42] To a great degree, a comparison of their reports on the situation in Germany shortly after the war points up the essence of the differences between the two: Scholem's report focuses on the situation of the displaced Jews (though he did not always view them favorably), whereas Arendt's deals with "the effects of twelve years of totalitarian rule on the German people,"[43] without mentioning the Jews who remained in Germany at that time.[44] To a great extent this difference in recording their impressions of the situation in Germany after the war also characterized their positions in the dispute over *Eichmann in Jerusalem*. Arendt's position regarding the Holocaust brought her closer to the experience of the German collective, as Diner has shown,[45] while the nature of Scholem's criticism placed him on the side of those who attacked Arendt's book, a group that included other Jews of German origin. The response of this group was so uniform in character that at a certain stage it seemed to Arendt that an organized campaign was being waged against her. In Richard Cohen's opinion, Arendt's feeling was not entirely mistaken: "Their past experience as Jews of German extraction was the formative factor in their almost uniform response. This lent their critiques an image of an organized response, but, in effect, it was their individual appropriation of and profound attachment to a collective past memory that provoked the similarity. Their perception was anchored in their German-Jewish past, and few turned to issues outside this purview."[46]

In contrast to Arendt's rationalistic and universalistic attitude in her book—

which derived from her feeling of affiliation with the German intellectual world, which was not necessarily Jewish—the Jewish position expressed by Scholem (like other Jews of German origin) was based on emotion, which to a great extent reflected his personal attitude toward the Holocaust. As Cohen wrote: "The response of Jews from Germany sheds light on a characteristic attitude of individuals who have undergone a major trauma and whose identity has become deeply intertwined with this experience. They deny the outsider's ability to penetrate authentically into their experience, perceiving that only someone who has experienced a similar event can reach the depths of true understanding."[47]

Thus Arendt's book touched a painful nerve for world Jewry and Scholem himself, which explains why his response was vehement and pointed. However, it would be a mistake to think that the Eichmann trial was not an emotional confrontation with the Holocaust for Arendt. Elisabeth Young-Bruehl has pointed out the feeling of mission that accompanied Arendt's desire to be present at the Eichmann trial and her view of a face-to-face confrontation with him as a retroactive cure.[48] If it is possible to imagine what that cure was, in light of Arendt's book, we may say that it was the ability to discuss events from a distance and rationally, and in a manner that would make it possible for her to maintain her connection with Germany and German culture. The solution Arendt reached was to divide the blame for the events between the perpetrator and the victim, removing the stigma of the aggressor from Eichmann and placing some of the guilt and responsibility on the shoulders of the Jews themselves. Thus, the Germans and the Jews could together bear the burden of guilt, which would be the shared basis of a future connection for them.

Scholem also struggled with the Holocaust and with the awareness of the need to renew the connections between Germany and Israel and between Germans and Jews. However, for him, the Holocaust was a living and painful event, and he was unable to observe it from a distance or with self-criticism. But as the next section of this chapter shows, for Scholem, too, the abyss that the Holocaust opened up between the two nations was paradoxically the basis for a renewal of the connection between them, which would follow new rules. An example of this can be found in Scholem's opposition to the execution of Eichmann, which he expressed in an article published in 1962.[49] In this short article Scholem presented both nations as victims: "the Jewish people, whose millions were murdered, and the German people, who became a nation of murderers when it allowed the Nazi doctrine to gain power over it."[50] Since the guilt was borne by an entire nation, the execution of an individual criminal, as central a figure as he was, created the illusion of the conclusion of a chapter, which was out of place. This act might create the impression in Germany that "something was done to 'atone' for the act, for which there is no atonement," which would be entirely contrary to the Jewish and human interest:

> As Jews and human beings we have no interest in such a phony "finis." It was an easy, slight ending in two senses: it was slight both in significance and judgment. This hanging was an anticlimax, the satyr play after a tragedy such as had not been seen before. One fears that instead of opening up a reckoning and leaving it open for the next generation, we have foreclosed it. What superficially seems severity of judgment is in reality its mitigation, a mitigation in no way to our interest. It is to our interest that the great historical and moral question, the question of probing the depths which this trial has forced all to face—How could this happen?—that this question should retain all its weight, all its stark nakedness, all its horror. The hangman who had to execute Eichmann's sentence added nothing to the situation, but took away a great deal. . . . He introduced the misplaced suggestion that this marked "the end of the story."[51]

Like Arendt, Scholem also saw a cooperation between the aggressor and the victim and the need to continue the connection between the Jewish and German peoples, especially in view of their shared catastrophe. In this respect, Arendt's book was consistent with Scholem's call for a spiritual accounting. Therefore her identification—which surprised Scholem—with the German side and her harsh criticism, in content and form, of the Jewish side, offended him. However, beyond the personal insult that Scholem saw in Arendt's words, especially their tone,[52] there was a paradox that accompanied him all his life: his saw the Holocaust both as a historical event that must be researched and as a living mystery that could be spoken of only via symbols, and whose profound essence could not be grasped. After Scholem's death, Nathan Rotenstreich wrote of Scholelm's attitude toward the symbol, which is meant to express something whose essence cannot be known or understood: "The symbol thus serves as a sort of a bridge between man and the universe, even as the individual realizes that it does not comprehend the mystery, either of his own existence or of that of the universe beyond."[53]

German-Jewish Dialogue

Before the Holocaust

In the fall of 1962, Scholem received a letter from Manfred Schlösser, the editor of a series of books called Agora, inviting him to contribute to a Festschrift in honor of the ninetieth birthday of Margarete Susman, a German Jewish author. In his letter, Schlösser asked Scholem to write something appropriate for general framework of the planned volume. According to Schlösser, the purpose of the book was to restore awareness of Susman and call attention to her writing. At the same time, he wanted the book to bring out a central aspect of Susman's work: "Beyond this, the volume seems to me to be an important contribution to a reflection on the indestructible spiritual symbiosis of German-Jewish intellectual life."[54] Susman had been born in 1872 to a Jewish family, and as a young woman she lived and studied in Munich and Berlin, among other places. In those cities she became acquainted with members of the circle of the poet Stefan George and studied with Georg Simmel, the famous Jewish sociologist. Afterward she was connected with the circle around Franz Rosenzweig and the Freies Jüdisches Lehrhaus, the adult education institution which he founded in Frankfurt. Susman was close to Jewish intellectuals and activists such as Martin Buber and Gustav Landauer, and in her writing she emphasized her connections and commitment to Judaism and to German culture, and the closeness between Christianity and Judaism. In 1933 she was forced to leave Germany and shortly afterward settled in Switzerland, where she lived until her death in early 1966.[55] Scholem had met Susman for the first time during his visit to Zurich in 1946, during his mission to locate the treasures of the Diaspora. She made an ambiguous impression on him: on the one hand, he felt close to her, and in his journal he wrote that his conversations with her gave him pleasure, but on the other hand, her attitudes toward Christianity distressed him. The fact that Susman almost converted to Christianity as a young woman and her deep emotional connection with Christianity, which was expressed in the book she published that year, *Das Buch Hiob* (The Book of Job) disturbed Scholem.[56]

Susman sent Scholem a copy of the book when it was published, and he quickly replied that, although the book touched his heart, he was unequivocally critical of the second chapter, which sought to connect her world of Judaism to Christian Europe (especially Germany): "According to my conception, the metaphysical equilibrium between these two worlds, upon which you work, cannot abide forever anywhere."[57] In the following decade and a half, the two remained in contact, and Scholem occasionally sent Susman copies of his books and articles. However, his criticism of 1946 still stood between them, and it certainly recurred in his memory when he received the letter of invitation from Schlösser to contribute to the Festschrift. The barrier between Christianity and Judaism, which Scholem maintained throughout his life—considering himself and most of what was precious to him to be Jewish or identified with Judaism[58]—was in absolute contrast to Susman's attempts to combine the two worlds in her work and life. Perhaps this contrast lay in the background of Scholem's refusal to contribute an essay to the volume. The goal of the book, as presented by Schlösser, was another factor in Scholem's refusal to take part, since it was defined as a "reflection on the indestructible spiritual symbiosis of German-Jewish intellectual life." Schlösser's pleas managed to change Scholem's mind, and a short time later he accepted the invitation and sent an open letter to be published in the volume, in which he fiercely criticized the view that saw conversation and dialogue in the relations between Jews and Germans before 1933 and called it a "German-Jewish symbiosis."[59]

This letter, dated December 18, 1962, provoked a short dispute between Scholem and Schlösser in their correspondence as well as in the pages of the *Bulletin des Leo Baeck Instituts*. Scholem's letter and his position in the dispute shows his attitude toward the relations between Jews and Germans before the Holocaust: "I deny that there has ever been such a German-Jewish dialogue in any genuine sense whatsoever, i.e., as a historical phenomenon."[60] According to Scholem, such a dialogue, which Schlösser presented as self-evident, never took place because the Germans did not respond to the Jews' call for it. In his opinion, the Jews tried to create a discourse of this kind in every possible way, but they always encountered a contemptuous and arrogant attitude: "The allegedly indestructible community of the German essence with the Jewish essence consisted, so long as these two essences really lived with each other, only of a chorus of Jewish voices and was, on the level of historical reality, never anything else than a fiction, a fiction of which you will permit me to say that too high price was paid for it."[61] Scholem revealed exactly what price had been extorted by this illusion from the Jewishness of the Jews of Germany in his article in answer to two polemical letters against him: "The liquidation of the Jewish substance by the Jews themselves must in large part be held responsible for the fact that this dialogue did not come to take place as a historical phenomenon. This liquidation certainly has deep and far-reaching reasons, only a part of which have hitherto been expressed, but the dialectical connection between this liquidation and the fate of the Jews in Germany, for good and for evil, seems evident to me."[62]

The order of things as presented here by Scholem is clear: the liquidation of the continuity of Judaism and the Jewish tradition by the Jews of Germany is connected, though indirectly, to their physical liquidation. This position is surprising, especially in view of Scholem's harsh criticism of a similar principle proposed by Arendt in her 1946 article, discussed in the previous section of this chapter. Arendt claimed that the similarity between the goals espoused by the Zionist movement and antisemitic tendencies in Germany deceived the Jews of Germany and prevented them from identifying their true enemy, and in *Eichmann in Jerusalem* she argued that the Jews bore some responsibility for their bitter fate during the Holocaust.[63] The similarity between Scholem's remarks here and Arendt's positions is unexpected, especially in the light of the severe criticism Scholem voiced against Arendt. In any event, both Scholem's and Arendt's positions were developed after the Holocaust and as a result of judging events according to their consequences. However, Scholem left open a small window open on the future, as shown in the end of his letter: "It is true: The fact that Jewish creativity poured forth here is perceived by the Germans, now that all is over. I would be the last to deny that there is something genuine about this—[which is] at once gripping and depressing. But it no longer changes anything about the fact that no dialogue is possible with the dead, and to speak of an 'indestructibility of this dialogue' strikes me as blasphemy."[64]

Scholem tried to distinguish between Susman and Schlösser, directing his criticism only to the latter. Moreover, in his correspondence with Susman from the publication of the book until her death in 1966, he attacked only Schlösser as representing a tendency in postwar Germany to see Jewish existence in that country before the destruction in a romantic light. In fact, the language of the invitation to contribute to the Festschrift for Susman was only one of the factors that motivated Scholem to respond as he did. Another factor was the figure of Susman, whom he saw as standing between two worlds, the Jewish and the German Christian. That figure and the sector of German Jewry that it represented for Scholem made him feel a need to have an accounting with the German Jewry of his youth, before its violent elimination.

As the previous chapters have shown, Scholem's youth in Germany was colored by his rebellion against the bourgeois milieu that characterized assimilated German Jewry and by his moral commitment to a separate Jewish culture in the Land of Israel. However, in none of his writings before his letter to Schlösser did Scholem address this issue separately and systematically, but after this episode it is evident that the subject had begun to preoccupy him, and in the following years he struggled several more times with the question of Jewish-German relations before the war in a more comprehensive way. The first time was shortly after the dispute with Schlösser, in a lecture Scholem gave at the plenary session of the World Jewish Congress in Brussels in August 1966,[65] and the second, which I discuss at the end of this section, was more than a decade later, in a lecture at a conference in the United States.[66]

In the 1966 lecture, Scholem expanded on the position he had expressed in his letter to Schlösser by surveying the stages in the history of German Jewry. Scholem presented one sentence that Susman had written in 1935 (she had died before the lecture) and that called on the Jew to abnegate himself at that time in history as an example of "a perversion whereby Christian ideas—rejected by Jews unto their dying breath—now presented themselves as the demand of the greatest Jewish minds."[67] Another passage at the end of the 1966 lecture was devoted to the future of relations between Jews and Germans, and there Scholem left an opening for a new beginning:

> Fruitful relations between Jews and Germans, relations in which a past that is both meaningful and at the same time so horrible as to cripple communication may be preserved and worked through—such relations must be prepared away from the limelight. But it is only through an effort to bring them about that we can guarantee that official contacts between the two peoples will not be poisoned by counterfeit formulas and demands. Already the worm of hypocrisy is gnawing at the delicate roots! Where love is no longer possible, a new understanding requires other ingredients: distance, respect, openness, and open-mindedness, and, above all, good will.[68]

As noted, Scholem's point of departure was after the Holocaust, and he projected the eventual destiny of the Jews of Germany onto their beginnings, and thus onto all their history. He judged this history retroactively, in view of the tragic outcome. However, along with his deterministic and negative attitude toward the past, another tone is perceptible in his words, emphasizing the future and the continuation of relations between the Jews and the Germans after the catastrophe and expressing his personal decision to try to build a bridge between the nations. Perhaps, paradoxically, one may postulate that, for Scholem, the trauma of the elimination of German Jewry in fact made an opening for future dialogue.

After the Holocaust

In two different periods during his life Scholem rejected the possibility of maintaining a productive connection between Jews and Germans in Germany. The first was before the Holocaust, especially in his youth, and the second was immediately after the Holocaust, during his journey in 1946, after meeting the remnant of the Jews of Germany and the displaced people living in temporary camps throughout the American occupation zone. His impressions and conversations during that journey led him to the conclusion that "there was no restoration for Germany Jewry," and he saw a moral flaw in the Jews who remained there.[69] Perhaps it is surprising that at the same time Scholem adopted a conciliatory tone toward Germany itself, during his efforts to transfer the manuscript of the Talmud from the Bavarian National Library to the Hebrew University during his visit to Munich.[70] In a letter to the university authorities he described this gesture on the part of the German authorities as "a symbolic act towards the Jewish people and as a first step toward bridging the awful abyss that has been created between the two peoples."[71]

This early statement about the continuation or renewal of relations between Jews and Germans, so soon after the Holocaust, was not a slip of the pen. Rather, it represented an important aspect of Scholem's attitude toward Germany and the Germans after the Holocaust and in light of it.

One of the first public discussions regarding cultural connections between Jews and Germans took place during a minor dispute that occurred shortly before the major disagreement surrounding the negotiations on reparations with Germany, which began in 1952.[72] At that time the young Israeli society felt anger and hatred toward Germany and the Germans in general, and there were calls for revenge. The official policy toward Germany of the State of Israel during its first years was guided by principles that rejected direct contact between the states as well as between Jews and Germans, especially on German soil.[73] Against the background of this atmosphere, in December 1951 Martin Buber was awarded the Goethe Prize by the University of Hamburg. When Buber, who had immigrated to Palestine in 1938 after years of Zionist activity in Nazi Germany, agreed to accept the prize, there was a public outcry in Israel, including condemnations in the daily press. In the wake of this pressure, Buber refused to travel to Hamburg to receive the prize and to speak publicly, and he donated the prize money to two Israeli journals.[74] In response to the public condemnations of those awarding the prize and its recipient, on December 30, 1951m Scholem wrote a letter to the editors of *Haaretz*, in which he defended the city of Hamburg. Scholem agreed with those who had attacked Buber that he ought to reject the prize, "as long as an abyss still yawns between us and them."[75] However, while the connection with the German collective was problematic, there was no reason to condemn the intentions of the individuals who had offered the prize to Buber, for their intentions might be pure, "to break through the tragic vicious cycle of guilt and shame and eternal sorrow":

> I believe that in the existing circumstances it is the duty of the Jewish side to be wary of any contact and negotiations with Germans, especially with those who speak not in their own name but in the name of the German *public*. All those among us—and I am one of them—who have acted in Germany after the war on missions for the Jewish public, have experienced this difficult problem. Individuals might be decent, and there were even, here and there, those who deserve to be called righteous, but the German public in this generation is not decent. However, for this reason must we spit in the face of such individuals, when an entire public supports them, or, shall we even say: exploits the purity of their heart? Acceptance of a prize from the German public is not conceivable, because that public necessarily includes a majority of people unknown to those awarding the prize, and certainly many among them

> are people with hands soaked with the blood of our people. But one may ask: must one therefore condemn the intentions of those awarding the prize, which might be exceedingly pure?[76]

Although he rejected any connection with Germany as a nation and collective, Scholem did not reject communication with individuals whose innocence during the Nazi period and pure intentions could be verified. At the end of 1952 Scholem received a letter from the editor of the *Deutsche Universitätszeitung*, asking him to write for it. Scholem refused to take part in this project, but he expressed admiration for the work of the editors of the newspaper, as members of a new generation acting to build a future for their nation. He explained his refusal by stating his view that many German academics would prefer to forget their activities during the period of Nazi rule, feigning innocence when confronted with questions. In Scholem's opinion, this tendency undermined any possibility of sincere conversation in the present. However, he hoped that the situation would be different in the future: "I wish wholeheartedly that you will be given the opportunity to take part in creating an atmosphere in which sincere words can have an influence once again, one in which a Jew can once again speak to an anonymous group of Germans, who are unknown to him, without reflecting on their past." This letter of Scholem's was printed in the magazine.[77] His rejection of cooperation at the time, along the empathetic and encouraging tone of his reply, heralds Scholem's tendency in the following years to build a new personal dialogue with Germany. In the beginning of this process, he often expressed admiration, respect, and closeness for individual Germans whose past was not suspect, and at the same time he avoided contact with anyone whose Nazi past was made known to him.[78] Perhaps this is why Scholem did not appear before the general public in Germany during the following years.

This attitude began to change in 1957. In July of that year Scholem gave three lectures in the Loeb series, devoted to the history of Jewish religion and thought, in the Philosophy Department of the University of Frankfurt. Scholem was invited to give the lectures by Theodor Adorno and Max Horkheimer, and they dealt with the history of Kabbalah in Safed during the sixteenth century. In the same year, the first German edition of Scholem's *Major Trends in Jewish Mysticism* was published. Although the book was published by Daniel Brody's Rhein Verlag, in Switzerland, Scholem wrote a few words in his introduction about his views on relations between Jews and Germans then and in the future:

> Between the German nation and the Jewish people a deadly earnest (*blutigen Ernst*) chasm opened up during the years of catastrophe and destruction, in the full meaning of the word, and any effort to ignore it would be in vain. The publication of this

> book in German only now is connected to this state of affairs. Whether scientific understanding and a historical outlook can do anything to bridge this chasm is difficult to say. However, I believe that deep discussion of significant phenomena in the history of the Jewish religion, such as I sought to present in this book, can be of special significance in this situation. A Jewish author cannot do very much by himself to change this situation, but he can provide tools and materials, and perhaps also insights, that can be important for the discourse (*Aussprache*) that might, perhaps, begin anew.[79]

The chasm between Jews and Germans during the Holocaust gave importance, in Scholem's opinion, to the publication of scholarship in German about Jewish history and the Jews, for examination of the past had the potential to provide tools for the creation of a future discourse. In other words, Scholem suggests that academic research in Jewish history can create an opportunity to build a bridge over the chasm and renew relations between Jews and Germans. This tendency toward a gradual approach to Germany through Scholem's academic work continued in the following years. In 1959 he wrote a short introduction to Georg Langer's book on Hasidism, which was published in Munich,[80] and in 1960 the first volume of his Eranos lectures were published in Zurich.[81] Also in 1960 Scholem gave a lecture on the Sabbatean Dönmeh sect at the Tenth International Conference on the History of Religions, which took place in Marburg.[82] And in 1962 the Berlin publishing house of Walter de Gruyter published an expanded version of his book on the origins of Kabbalah,[83] and the second volume of Scholem's Eranos lectures was published in Zurich.[84]

One of the most important years in the history of Scholem's connections with Germany was 1963, when for the first time he received an invitation to serve as a visiting professor of Judaism at the University of Heidelberg, an invitation he refused because of the Nazi past of several people at the university.[85] That was also the year in which the dispute with Arendt broke out and Scholem was invited to contribute to Susman's Festschrift. As discussed above in this chapter, this letter prompted him to begin to deal with the question of Jewish-German dialogue or its lack before the Holocaust. However, the most significant event in the development of Scholem's relations with Germany in that year might have been the publication of the volume *Judaica* by the Suhrkamp publishing house in Frankfurt.[86] This volume contained eight articles by Scholem intended for the general public and was the first book Scholem published with Suhrkamp. His long and close relations with the director of Suhrkamp, Siegfried Unseld, which are discussed in the following chapter, led to his publishing five other books with that publisher.

Thus it may be said that as early as the beginning of the 1950s, while Scholem severely criticized the view that Jewish-German dialogue had existed in the past, he was trying to promote dialogue of this kind—at first with individuals and gradually in a more institutional manner. In 1963, against the background of the Eichmann dispute and in response to the Susman Festschrift, Scholem objected to taking a romantic and nostalgic view of the past by presenting the end of the Jews of Germany—their destruction—as the point of departure for understanding their history. However, the Holocaust, the chasm separating Germany and the State of Israel was also a point of departure for him, opening up the possibility of renewed discourse or, if one accepts Scholem's claim that such a discourse never existed, the beginning of true dialogue.

This dialogue could begin and establish itself, as Scholem wrote in the introduction to his book quoted above, through study of the past, which would lead to knowledge of it. He also repeated this principle during his dispute with Schlösser: "I am not among those who altogether refuse and oppose the resumption of such relations. In order to render such a resumption fruitful in a serious sense, one requires, however, not only knowledge of what is, but also of what was."[87] The way in which the past was studied and understood was thus the key to improved relations between Germans and Jews in the future. Research into the history of Judaism and Jewish life created the possibility for Scholem of building a bridge over the abyss that had opened between Jews and Germans and provided an opportunity for renewal of relations between them.

If we understand Scholem's interest in the history of the Jews of Germany before the war in this context, then we may say that, paradoxically, his position and preoccupation with the lack of conversation between Jews and Germans in the past was the key for him to creating the possibility of such a dialogue. In other words, Scholem's views regarding the lack of dialogue in the past was at the same time a call for dialogue and expressed his hope for discourse in the present. Not coincidentally, his letters to Schlösser and others that were part of this dispute were published again in 1970 with a lecture about Jews and Germans in the beginning of his *Judaica 2*, the second volume in the series intended for the general public.[88]

In late 1972 Scholem received a letter from Martin Broszat, a historian of antisemitism and later of Nazi Germany and the director of the Institut für Zeitgeschichte (Institute of Contemporary History) in Munich. The letter contained an invitation to come to Munich in the following year and lecture about German-Jewish relations before the rise of the Nazis, as part of the annual meeting of the academic advising committee of the institution. The idea of inviting Scholem, who was at that time the head of the Israel Academy of Sciences, occurred to

Broszat after he had a long conversation with Scholem in the home of the historian George Mosse, during which Scholem told many stories about his youth, and after reading *Judaica* 2, which had just been published. Broszat proposed a possible subject for the lecture: "Judaism in Germany before the First World War. The social and social-psychological obstacles before German-Jewish cooperation. And it might almost be best, if you spoke about this subject through analysis of memories and reflections, which you often prefer in your writing."[89] Scholem immediately accepted the invitation and the proposed subject for the lecture, which was scheduled for March 15, 1973. The official title of the lecture was: "Judaism in Germany: the Social and Social-Psychological Problematics of Jewish-German Relations before Hitler."[90] He delivered it at the Institute of Contemporary History with great success, before representatives of the intellectual elite of Germany.[91] The enthusiastic audience's only disappointment was that no time remained after the lecture for discussion or questions. In his introduction to the lecture, Broszat presented Scholem and his work as evidence of the success of the renewal or creation of dialogue between Jews and Germans: "He, Gershom Scholem himself, has succeeded through his life's work—after the catastrophe of Hitler—as a Jew, in making the Germans faithful listeners. In changes such as these, after all, lies the best condition and the decisive condition for enabling dialogue between true partners."[92] From this lecture was born his last long and comprehensive article about relations of Jews and Germans before the Holocaust, an article that extended the lines of his 1966 lecture about Jews and Germans and that combined the style suggested by Broszat: incorporating Scholem's memories and personal impressions into the subject. In April 1976 Scholem gave a lecture in English in Saint Louis, Missouri, that was presumably a reworking of his German lecture in Munich. This lecture was published shortly afterward in English and German, and it is a deeper examination of the matter, combining the personal aspect with a general historical survey.[93] In the published version the emotional and extreme formulation that had characterized the dispute surrounding the Susman Festschrift more than a decade earlier gave way to a more balanced and cautious inquiry. The ambivalence that had characterized Scholem's attitude in the early 1960s toward the need to discuss Jewish-German dialogue before the Holocaust with Germans gradually disappeared, and Scholem found that his attraction to the German intellectual world and his desire for a place in the discourse with it overcame the resistance and doubts that he had harbored. In the published version of the lecture in English the issue of the renewal of dialogue between Jews and Germans was not mentioned, nor was the fact that a German version of the article had preceded publication of the English version by a year,[94] which shows that by the end of the 1970s Scholem already acknowledged the existence of post-Holocaust discourse of this kind. Incidentally, this last lecture has not yet been translated into Hebrew.

A History of Reception

From Zurich to Frankfurt

In the evening of September 1, 1952, immediately after participating in the Eranos conference in Ascona, Scholem arrived in Frankfurt on a flight from Zurich. A lot of work awaited Scholem in Germany in connection with the treasures of the Diaspora, and he had scheduled an important meeting with Salman Schocken about the Hebrew University. However, before turning to all that, he devoted a few days to visiting his friend Theodor Adorno, whom he telephoned as soon as he reached the city. Adorno had been known to Scholem before the war through their common friend, Benjamin. Adorno headed the Institut für Sozialforschung (Institute for Social Research, IfS), a research institute for Marxist theory and criticism, which had been founded at the University of Frankfurt in the 1920s and was the home of the Frankfurt school. In 1934, after the Nazis' rise to power, the institute moved to New York, where it remained active under the direction of Max Horkheimer. After the war it returned to Frankfurt, as did Horkheimer and Adorno. The latter invited Scholem to dinner at his home the following day, with several other friends. In addition to Scholem, the guests included half-Jewish philosopher Helmuth Plessner and his wife, Monika; and the German publisher Peter Suhrkamp and his wife, Annemarie Seidel. This meeting with Suhrkamp in Adorno's home took place a short time after Scholem had made an agreement in principle in Ascona with Brody, to publish his work with Rhein Verlag. Scholem's meeting with Suhrkamp at this point and its outcome indicate Scholem's interest in making his works available to the German public.

The Suhrkamp publishing house is usually said to have been founded in 1950, when it finally separated from the S. Fischer Verlag.[95] However, Suhrkamp's roots extend further back and are closely connected with the actions of Peter Suhrkamp under Nazi rule. In 1932 Suhrkamp began to work in the S. Fischer Verlag—which had been established in 1886 by Samuel Fischer, a Hungarian Jew—and he quickly became the editor of its magazine *Neue Rundschau*. In 1936 the owners of the publishing house, Fischer's heirs, were forced to flee from Nazi Germany, and they turned the firm over to Suhrkamp, who ran it in their absence. Beginning in 1942, he was forced to change the name of company to Suhrkamp Verlag vorm[als] S. Fischer (Suhrkamp Publisher, formerly S. Fischer). Under Nazi rule Suhrkamp helped many of S. Fischer's authors, including Berthold Brecht, escape from Germany, and he obtained permission to publish the writings of otherwise banned authors such as Hermann Hesse. In April 1944 Suhrkamp was arrested by the Gestapo and was imprisoned for nearly a year in various prisons in Berlin and the Sachsenhausen concentration camp. He was suddenly released in February 1945, on the verge of death from serious pneumonia. Although he recovered from that illness, he was never again entirely healthy, and he died in 1959 at the age of sixty-eight. After the war Suhrkamp became the first German publisher to receive the right to operate in Berlin from the American authorities. After the return of the owners of the S. Fischer Verlag, he decided, with Hesse's encouragement, to establish his own publishing house. Thirty-three of the forty-eight authors of the publisher who remained in Germany and worked with Suhrkamp during the Nazi years, including Hesse and Brecht, decided to leave S. Fischer and move to the new house, which soon settled in Frankfurt.[96] In 1952, Siegfried Unseld, a young and energetic editor, joined the publisher, and he built up the sales and public relations departments. Unseld had been born in 1924 and served in the German army during World War II. He was promoted to partnership in January 1958, due in large part to the influence of Scholem's friend Hanns Wilhelm Eppelsheimer, the director of the Frankfurt municipal library, who lived in the apartment above the publisher's offices in Frankfurt and was Suhrkamp's confidant.[97] After Suhrkamp's death, Unseld became the director of the publishing house and shaped its image over the following five decades.[98]

It may be assumed that Scholem met Suhrkamp—or at least his right-hand man, Friedrich Podszus—for the first time along with Adorno in 1950 in Frankfurt, during his visit to Germany after attending his second Eranos conference. The subjects of their meeting, to which the following section of this chapter is devoted, was the publication of a collection of Benjamin's work under Adorno's editorship, and the possibility of cooperation with Scholem and receiving some of Benjamin's letters in his possession for future volumes.[99] Scholem and Suhrkamp began to correspond directly in 1953, and their letters focused on the plan of publishing a complete edition of Benjamin's writing. The connection between Scholem and the publishing house grew closer after Suhrkamp's death and Unseld's assumption of the directorship. In 1959, a short time before the publication of a volume of Scholem's Eranos lectures,[100] Unseld expressed interest in the volume and indirectly proposed, through Adorno, to had Suhrkamp publish it. Scholem rejected the proposal because he had already signed a contract with the Rhein Verlag.[101] However, in the early 1960s Unseld suggested that Scholem might publish a small volume of his collected articles with Suhrkamp. This proposal led to the publication of the first volume of *Judaica* in 1963. This and subsequent volumes reprinted articles by Scholem intended for a wider audience. Three volumes in all were published during Scholem's lifetime, and three more were published posthumously; collectively, they played a major role in Scholem's reputation among readers in Germany.[102]

While the first volume was being prepared for publication, tension emerged between Scholem and the Rhein Verlag, where he had published three books by 1963. During the summer of 1962, Brody mistakenly thought that Unseld was trying to convince Scholem to transfer all his future work to his house and also to take over the Rhein Verlag by spreading a rumor that it was on the verge of collapse and then purchasing it, which aroused Brody's anger. After a short exchange of letters on the matter, Scholem and Brody resolved the misunderstanding. However, in that year Olga Fröbe-Kapteyn, the founder of the Eranos conferences and a close friend of Brody, died, and a short time later he decided to retire from publishing.[103] In 1966 Brody sold the literary rights in his possession—including rights to the works of James Joyce, Hermann Broch, Adolf Portmann, and Gershom Scholem—to the Südwest Verlag, which was located in Munich.

When Unseld informed Scholem about this, he wrote to the Südwest Verlag and protested the transfer of the rights to his work without his knowledge. He justified his unequivocal opposition to the transfer in the following way: "You must understand that for a Jewish author, who intentionally published his books with a Swiss publisher, it is not the same thing if the publisher of his books remains in Switzerland or [the rights are transferred] . . . to a book publisher in Germany."[104] He went on to explain his decision in detail: "I am not prepared to have the publishing of my work pass without my knowledge or clear agreement into the hands of a German publisher, and I wish to assume that you will honor this view. Were the rights to my work to pass into the hands of Suhrkamp Verlag, I would have no objection, considering the countenance and character of that publishing house. In any other instance I expect that the rights to my books will pass from the Rhein Verlag to myself."[105]

These words emphasize the importance that Scholem gave at that time to personal acquaintance with the people with whom he was in contact in Germany. However, the fact that this letter was written while Scholem was in Frankfurt leaves some room to assume that his desire to transfer his works to Suhrkamp was stronger than his objection to German publishing houses in general. Perhaps this letter is part of Unseld's effort to obtain the rights to the work of desirable authors who had been connected with the Rhein Verlag and the rights to whose works had been passed from Brody to the Südwest Verlag. In any case, a month later, to the joy of Scholem and Unseld, an agreement was signed between the publishers according to which the rights to the works of Scholem,

Portmann, Broch, and Joyce would be ceded to Suhrkamp, an agreement that received newspaper coverage.[106]

This official transition marked the beginning of close cooperation and warm friendly relations between Scholem and Unseld and the Suhrkamp publishing house. During the following decades, Scholem published all of his German books with Suhrkamp, including two more volumes in the Judaica series and his two autobiographical books.[107] It is impossible to exaggerate the importance of Unseld and his activities in the process of Scholem's entry into public consciousness in Germany and the presentation of his writings and figure in a manner that aroused interest among German readers. At the same time, it appears that the story of Scholem's acceptance in Germany is also related to the history of the reception of another important German Jewish intellectual, whose writings were also published by Suhrkamp. I refer to Benjamin, who had a great influence on Scholem in his youth, and in the publication of whose writings in Germany after the war Scholem played a large part.

The Story of a Friendship

In 1966 Suhrkamp published two volumes of the correspondence between Benjamin and his friends, edited by Scholem and Adorno.[108] The publication of these letters was an important milestone in the reception of Benjamin in postwar Germany and a turning point in Scholem's entry into the consciousness of the German reading public. Although from the end of the war until that year, six of Scholem's books had already been published in German, most of them were intended for a limited academic audience and had been published by small publishing houses. Scholem's work with Adorno on Benjamin's correspondence and the controversy that arose following the publication of these volumes were a breakthrough for Scholem into the awareness of German readers and the vibrant intellectual world in Germany in the late 1960s and early 1970s.

In 1940, soon after learning about Benjamin's suicide and its circumstances, Scholem wrote to Adorno about the need to publish the letters in Benajmin's literary estate, many of which were in Scholem's possession in Jerusalem.[109] In another letter to Adorno, Scholem emphasized the great importance of editing and publishing an edition of Benjamin's letters to his friends and colleagues.[110] The figure of Benjamin was central to the relationship between Scholem and Adorno over the years, and their correspondence revolved around their joint efforts to perpetuate the memory and thought of their late friend. They had met through Benjamin, and despite certain reservations that Scholem had about Adorno, which were connected to what Scholem had heard from Benjamin, their first meetings in 1938 in New York had made a very positive impression on Scholem:

"The good spirit that prevailed in the meetings between Adorno and me was due not so much to the cordiality of the reception as to my considerable surprise at Adorno's appreciation of the continuing theological element in Benjamin. I had expected a Marxist who would insist on liquidation of what were in my opinion the most valuable furnishings in Benjamin's intellectual household. Instead I encountered here a man who definitely had an open mind and even a positive attitude towards these traits, although he viewed them from his own dialectical perspective."[111]

In other words, Adorno's way of interpreting Benjamin did not negate what, for Scholem, was the basic condition for understanding his friend's theories, thus changing Scholem's earlier, negative opinion about Adorno and opening the way for dialogue with him. Indeed, Adorno was the person closest to Scholem during his visit to the IfS, which, as noted above, had moved from Frankfurt to the United States in 1934. Their complementary interpretation of Benjamin was always in the background of the deep intellectual differences between them—primarily about Adorno's Marxist thought and the activity of the IfS that was influenced by this worldview—but it was also the basis for their understanding and cooperation over the years.

No one had more influence on the first stage of Benjamin's reception in Germany than Adorno. Thanks to Adorno's persistence in collecting and arranging Benjamin's writings, Benjamin went from being a forgotten intellectual to being one of the most important thinkers of Germany and a beacon for various thinkers.[112] Starting in the early 1950s, Scholem helped and advised Theodor and Gretel Adorno in their editing of the two volumes of Benjamin's collected work, which Suhrkamp published in 1955. Among other things, Scholem sent them copies of Benjamin's writings that were in his possession.[113] In the fall of 1959 Adorno wrote to Scholem, informing him that the Suhrkamp publishing house, under the new leadership of Unseld, had decided to publish a 250–300-page volume of Benjamin's letters. Adorno added a proposal to this information: "I would like to ask you whether you would be willing to take upon yourself, along with me, the task of editing."[114] Scholem immediately answered in the affirmative, and the two began to search for letters among Benjamin's friends.[115]

The joint task of editing, which was the basis of the correspondence between the two at that time and for the purpose of which they met almost every year around the time of Scholem's stay in Ascona, brought the two men close personally as well. This closeness, based on their mutual friend, was always charged with tension deriving from the large differences in character and temperament between the two. A good example of this can be seen in the way Adorno introduced Scholem in the 1960s to Lotte Tobisch, a Viennese society matron who was his close friend, while they were at Sils-Maria, a Swiss resort. When Adorno presented his friend with all the honor due her, including her titles of nobility, as "Baronin Lotte Tobisch von Labotaýn," Scholem's immediate and spontaneous response, in Berlin slang was, "Mensch, det ooch noch!" (loosely translated: "Man, not this, too!"). This response, absolutely opposite to the way Tobisch had been introduced to him, made her laugh heartily, and from that moment on they were fast friends. Adorno, however, remained stunned by what Scholem had done till the end of his life, and every time he was reminded of the episode, he said seriously, "How Scholem behaved! Just dreadful!"[116] Adorno could not cope with Scholem's occasional bluntness and with his need to be in the center all the time.[117] In a later letter to Tobisch, Adorno described the way Scholem had behaved during Adorno's sixty-fifth birthday party:

> On my birthday, Unseld gave a little party for me with a small circle of friends. Scholem was there, and he behaved in an egocentric manner, without tact, and, I must say, repulsively. You need the patience of an angel to cope with him. He simply could not stand that the party was in my honor (and I didn't manage, you can believe me, to feel that way at all!) and not for him, and in fact he exploited the opportunity just to attack me facetiously. The others thought it was disgusting to the same degree. Two days later he was at our house, businesslike and entirely sober. But what's the meaning of it in the end, when you want to believe that he [Scholem] is so decent and at the same time his primary instinct is so base. I'm only complaining to you. Please don't speak to anyone about this, or immediately a dreadful scream will arise out of Israel.[118]

In his memoir about Scholem, Rolf Tiedemann, Adorno's student and the editor of the complete edition of Benjamin's work, described Adorno and Scholem as absolutely different from one another—opposite in their nature like "a sea creature and a land animal"—but at the same time as belonging to the same family and the same element: "Adorno's enthusiasm and Scholem's skepticism were two sides of the same coin."[119] According to Tiedemann, Scholem's fame preceded him at the IfS as a supreme authority, though it was not clear to the members of the institute just what that authority was.[120] His research in Kabbalah, his being the oldest and closest of Benjamin's living friends, and his authoritative appearance made a big impression on the members. Of course, Adorno—who was eight years younger than Scholem—shared this impression, and it certainly was an element in the complex relationship between the two.

Their work together on the correspondence lasted about seven years, and although during those years and even before them, various writings by Benjamin were published (some edited by Adorno and others by Scholem), one may see the publication of the two volumes of letters as a turning point in Benjamin's reception in Germany. These volumes were important both because of their content and because of the political circumstances in Germany in the years after their publication. With respect to their content, for the first time they showed not just Benjamin's ideas but the man himself in a comprehensive fashion in his social context. Hence they were a significant contribution to the formation of a biographical picture of Benjamin.[121] With respect to the circumstances in Germany, the controversy aroused by the printed correspondence is bound up with its content. Criticism of the way the correspondence had been edited was mainly leveled at Adorno, and it was connected to the ideological world of the student revolution of 1967–68 in Germany. On the intellectual level, ideologists of the student movement appropriated and enlisted Benjamin's Marxist thought as inspiration for their revolt, so that he became their philosopher of history (*Geschichtsphilosoph*).[122] This appropriation was bound up with the process of "patricide" with regard to Adorno, and it included harsh criticism of his interpretation and understanding of Benjamin.[123] At the beginning of the protest movement Adorno supported the students, and the IfS in Frankfurt was an intellectual hothouse for a worldview that nourished the revolt. However, when Adorno later expressed opposition to the extremism, violation of the law, and violence that began to characterize the actions of the students, the violence was also directed against him. Together with Horkheimer and the sociologist and philosopher Jürgen Habermas, Adorno became a representative of the establishment for the students and was seen as a conservative and even a reactionary, and as a man not brave enough to draw practical conclusions from his theories.[124] In this context, the criticism of the way Adorno had edited Benjamin's writings was part of the effort to locate him politically and socially with relation to the events of the day, to a large degree under the influence of the attitudes of the students who represented the new Marxist left and led the events in Germany.[125]

The main accusation against the editors of Benjamin's letters was the tendentiousness in their choice of what to include. The critics claimed that behind the editorial policy lay a conscious endeavor to blur Benjamin's affiliation with Marxism and with influential figures with a Marxist world view such as Brecht and Asja Lacis, his friend and lover. Adorno was accused of having systematically attempted to hide the Marxist side of Benjamin's thought in editing his writings, and of administering the Benjamin archive in a tendentious manner and as if it were his personal property.[126] Moreover, the critics claimed that Adorno and Horkheimer had removed the communist tendencies from Benjamin's articles since the 1930s—the ones he had sent at the time for publication in the *Zeitschrift für Sozialforschung*, the journal of the IfS—by means of extreme editing, which

Benjamin had been forced to accept because of his economic dependence on the institute.[127] Arendt argued in a three-part article in *Merkur* that the editing of the correspondence reflected Scholem's desire to make Benjamin closer to Judaism or Adorno's dialectical Marxism. Arendt accused both sides of exploiting Benjamin's economic distress to attach him and his thinking to their worldview.[128]

Adorno was deeply wounded by the attacks against him, and he expressed his indignation in a letter to Scholem. Adorno asked Scholem to defend him against his attackers and to speak on his behalf regarding his capacity to interpret Benjamin—a capacity that had been doubted by his critics.[129] In his long answer to Adorno, Scholem advised him not to take the criticism so seriously. He refused to write an answer justifying Adorno's legitimacy in interpreting Benjamin because he had no doubt of that legitimacy. To the same extent, Scholem had no doubt of the legitimacy of other interpretations of Benjamin that disagreed with his and Adorno's, even if he and Adorno thought them erroneous.[130] In his letter, Scholem analyzed the various criticisms at length, coming to the conclusion that most of the arguments were aimed at Adorno and were in the realm of legitimate controversy, although they came to the figure of Benjamin from an entirely different position from that of the editors and contained many errors and inaccuracies. Scholem explained this by the very character of Benjamin's writings: because of their complexity, he argued, they could not be given a single, authoritative interpretation that would negate other interpretations.[131] This was also the weak point of the criticisms of Adorno's position: "To tell the truth, the nature of Benjamin's writing in his last ten years was such that I am convinced that one cannot offer an apparently unequivocal interpretation of his thoughts, which are sometimes expressed in opaque terms."[132]

To help Adorno out of his difficulties, Scholem proposed initiating a public discussion with the critics of the published correspondence, in which the critics would be confronted with their arguments and be forced to provide precise answers. To take part in such a discussion, which Scholem suggested could even take the form of a radio program, he was willing to come to Frankfurt for a few days, if financing could be found for such a trip. In the margins of the letter, apparently while reading it, Adorno wrote down his doubts regarding the effectiveness of such a debate, and in fact, it was never held.[133] Nevertheless, Scholem's letter helped Adorno cope with the criticism.[134]

In his letter to Adorno Scholem also tried to shift the debate from the personal to the professional level, and thereby to deflect it from Adorno to the various interpretations of Benjamin and his theories—which he thought were more legitimate subjects for discussion. However, it did not escape Scholem that the background of the criticism was a personal attack anchored solidly in the ideology of the day. The criticism went beyond the area of research and was aimed directly at Adorno and what he represented for his critics: "These attacks are not directed primarily at me, because for clear reasons they have nothing against me, and they feel no resentment toward me. Rather, they are mainly attacks upon you. This is an expression of rage accumulated over a long time and deep resentment of your lack of Marxist activism, but maybe also against your position in German intellectual life in general."[135]

As a postscript to the letter, Scholem added a curious sentence that is consistent with what has been said here. He noted that the method used by Adorno's critics "remind me very much of Kurzweil's polemic against me."[136] His mention of the Israeli literary critic Baruch Kurzweil in this context was not coincidental. Kurzweil's critique of Scholem over the years had dealt less with his scholarship than with his person, and the attacks shifted away from Scholem's research to what Scholem represented for Kurzweil politically, socially, and religiously.[137] In 1967 Kurzweil wrote a series of critical articles about Scholem, some of the fiercest he ever wrote. In one of these articles, he referred to Benjamin's published correspondence and Scholem's interpretation of Benjamin: "Scholem's interpretation of W. Benjamin's attitude toward the Land of Israel and Judaism is *extremely subjective*, and his effort to 'judaize' Benjamin is derived from Scholem's efforts to interpret Benjamin as if he were G. Scholem."[138] Scholem attributed the character of the critiques of Adorno to current political trends in Germany and thus removed himself from the storm center by, among other things, making it parallel to the dispute about him in Israel. Interestingly, while Scholem chose not to respond publicly to Kurzweil's accusations in Israel, he was willing to come to Frankfurt especially to confront the criticism there alongside Adorno. The reason for this might have been the comprehensive character of Kurzweil's critique, or perhaps he made the offer because he had been merely a guest in Germany and had not experienced the criticism intensely. Moreover, the possibility of public exposure that attended the polemics might have interested him. In any event, Scholem differentiated his situation in Israel from that of Adorno in Germany, though he saw them as parallel.

As noted, the dispute about the significance of Benjamin and the manner of understanding his life and writing that arose after the publication of his letters was a turning point in the history of Benjamin's reception in Germany and contributed greatly to the increased interest in him, while attributing current meaning to his thought. The role of Adorno and Scholem in this process was decisive, and their critics did not deny their large part in raising Benjamin from oblivion and interpreting his writings.[139] However, while Adorno's contribution was mainly in editing and publishing Benjamin's work, Scholem's contribution was in tracing

FIGURE 10 Gershom Scholem in front of a picture of Walter Benjamin, 1978. From the collection of the National Library of Israel, Jerusalem.

the outline of Benjamin's biography. After Adorno's death from a heart attack in the summer of 1969, Scholem continued to devote a significant part of his intellectual powers to work connected to Benjamin, both assisting in the project of publishing all of his writings with Suhrkamp[140] and publishing essays on his life and thought. Actually, everything that Scholem published about Benjamin and all of Benjamin's work that he edited shed light on Benjamin's life and dealt with the connection between that life and his thought.[141] Tiedemann claimed that one of Scholem's aspirations was to write a comprehensive biography of Benjamin, but because of the paucity of sources, he gave up on the idea, though it preoccupied him all his life, and until his death he never ceased placing tesserae in the mosaic of his late friend's image.[142] Noteworthy among these were his memoir about Benjamin, which became Scholem's first autobiographical work; the late correspondence between Scholem and Benjamin, which was recovered from an archive in East Germany and was published in 1980; and the last article that Scholem wrote, dealing with the Benjamin family tree, which was published a short time after his death.[143]

While a deep analysis of Scholem's way of interpreting Benjamin is beyond the scope of this discussion, a short discussion of what Scholem believed to be the key to understanding Benjamin is certainly in order. As noted above, Scholem saw the common denominator for the collaboration and mutual understanding between Adorno and himself in their agreement that the metaphysical Jewish element was the basis of Benjamin's thought and life, though the two men drew different conclusions from the study of Benjamin's writings. The view that Benjamin was a Jewish thinker and that his thought had a hidden, esoteric aspect[144] was the essence of Scholem's understanding of Benjamin, and this view did not change during his lifetime. In his articles he often criticized the Marxist interpreters who, because of their secular outlook, neutralized the Jewish and metaphysical element in Benjamin's writing.[145] Scholem also criticized his friends and colleagues for not giving that aspect of Benjamin's thought sufficient weight, and of course he criticized those who regarded his interpretation as his own tendentious and political position. Along with Adorno, Scholem constructed the image of Benjamin as a central Jewish thinker and intellectual in Germany,[146] and Benjamin's acceptance as such by the Germans served as a catalyst for Scholem's own acceptance. In other words, the story of Scholem's successful acceptance in Germany during the 1960s and 1970s was bound up with his friendship with Benjamin and, to a large degree, thanks to that friendship. Because of his work on Benjamin's writings, increasing attention was paid to Scholem and his own work. In this process Scholem, known at first only to a handful of scholars and experts, became one of the most important intellectuals of his time in Germany.

An important point in this context is the fact that everything that Scholem wrote about Benjamin was in German and was published in Germany and, with a single exception, none of what Scholem wrote about Benjamin was translated into Hebrew during his lifetime. The question of why Scholem chose to revive the memory of his friend in Germany and not in Israel is an interesting one, and it is certainly impossible to answer it unequivocally. Did Scholem think that Benjamin's thought and nomadic character were irrelevant to or inappropriate for an Israeli audience? Or is the answer that Scholem attached Benjamin to the German side of his life, which he had officially given up when he moved to Palestine? Perhaps, paradoxically, only in Germany could Scholem present the tragic figure of Benjamin with its full poignancy and attractive power for him, as he understood and identified with it. Nostalgia and longing for the German empire, which permeated large parts of Benjamin's work, were alien in Israel and known only to those who had experienced that period in a primary or secondary manner and yearned for it in the time of the Federal Republic.[147] In this context, the feeling of not belonging, which characterized Scholem, is also important. In an interview with Jörg Drews, a German literary scholar, filmed in Scholem's home in Jerusalem in 1976 and broadcast on German television that year, Scholem described Benjamin with the following words: "I always believed that he had a decidedly Jewish consciousness—and at the same time the consciousness of a man alien in his society, in any society. He was, as I put it, an outsider, just as Freud and Kafka were outsiders in the societies in which they lived."[148]

CHAPTER 9

BERLIN, AGAIN
THE FINALE

So I notice: I love this old man. "Why? There's no knowing!" You, in any event, would also have felt that way!

HARTMUT VON HENTIG TO NINA FRITZSCHE, WINTER 1981[1]

A Public Figure

In 1965, at the age of sixty-eight, Gershom Scholem retired from the Hebrew University after forty years. During that time he had played an important role in setting the path of the university and Jewish studies in general at several crossroads. His involvement in the various activities of the university and the National Library left a deep impression on those institutions that is noticeable to this day. He had taken part in the activities of the Institute of Microfilmed Hebrew Manuscripts, the Institute for Hebrew Bibliography, and the Hebrew Codicology and Paleography Project and had helped train a generation of scholars and their students, who were until recently the backbone of the Department of Jewish Thought at the Hebrew University and similar departments at other universities. However, his greatest contribution, as was noted at the ceremony at the Hebrew University where he was awarded an honorary doctorate in the winter of 1968, was "that he made research into Kabbalah a truly scientific field of Jewish studies by building and raising it to its heights—he created the tools and he did most of the work, baking the bricks and building the entire building."[2] Of course, these words of praise are extravagant, and the many important innovations in the study of Kabbalah since Scholem's death, some of which conflict with his basic assumptions, show that the work of building this structure is far from finished, and indeed it may never be. Nonetheless, Scholem did establish the field as a scholarly discipline, and he did so in three countries and three different languages.

Scholem received recognition for his work in Israel before his retirement, but that recognition increased after he left the Hebrew University. He received the

Israel Prize in 1958, and the Rothschild Prize in 1961. A year after he received his honorary doctorate from the university, he was named Yekir Yerushalayim (distinguished citizen of Jerusalem) for his activity on behalf of the city an honorary member of the Weizmann Institute of Science. In 1957 he received the Harvey Prize from the Technion in Haifa.[3] He also received the Bialik Prize for Jewish Studies in 1977 and an honorary doctorate from the University of Tel Aviv in 1980. At the end of 1958 David Ben-Gurion had appointed Scholem a member of the committee that prepared for the establishment of the Israel Academy of Sciences and Humanities, and he served first as the academy's vice president and then as its president, in 1968–74.[4]

Scholem also enjoyed growing renown in the United States, both as a scholar of Kabbalah and as a Jewish intellectual. In recognition of his academic prowess he received honorary doctorates from Hebrew Union College in 1949 and Brandeis University in 1980. In 1970 he was made a member of the American Academy of Arts and Sciences. He devoted a significant part of his intellectual energy to teaching and scholarship in the United States, and he served as a visiting professor at many academic institutions such as Hebrew Union College, Brandeis University, the Jewish Theological Seminary in New York, Princeton University, and Yale University.[5] An interesting example of Scholem's influence as an intellectual is found in Chaim Potok's *Book of Lights*, published in 1981. There Scholem is represented by the character Jacob Keter, who became an influential figure in life of the main protagonist, a stand-in for Potok.[6]

From the end of the 1960s on, he began to reap the fruit of his work in Germany as well. In the fall of 1969, at the age of seventy-two, Scholem received the Reuchlin Prize from the city of Pforzheim, where Johannes Reuchlin, a Christian Hebraist, had been born in 1455. The prize was awarded every two years for outstanding scholarly work in the humanities, and the recipient was chosen by the Heidelberg Academy of Sciences. The head of the academy, Georg Gadamer, discreetly asked Scholem if he would be willing to accept the prize. After considering the matter, Scholem said he would, although the Nazi past of earlier recipients aroused certain doubts in him. His willingness to accept ultimately derived from his connection with Reuchlin, "for whom the Jewish people has preserved an honorable place in its memory, and he was, one might say, my first predecessor in Germany."[7]

On September 10, 1969, the prize was awarded to Scholem in the presence of the notables of the city, and in his short words of thanks at the beginning of his lecture—titled "Kabbalah Research from Reuchlin to the Present"—he drew a parallel between himself and the Reuchlin: "Were I to believe in reincarnation, perhaps I might sometimes be drawn into thinking, that under the new

FIGURE 11 A display window of a book shop in Pforzheim, Germany, 1969. Photographer: Eva Bischop. Courtesy of Stadtarchiv Pforzheim, Institut für Stadtgeschichte S1 17-1-1969-29.

conditions of scholarship in our day, the soul of the first scholar of the language and world Judaism, especially of Kabbalah, was reincarnated in me—Johannes Reuchlin, the man who, about five hundred years ago, founded Jewish studies in Europe."[8] This interesting and obscure sentence has been interpreted in various ways. Moshe Idel saw in it the great centrality that Scholem accorded to Reuchlin in research into central concepts of Kabbalah—which connected Reuchlin's period to that of Scholem.[9] Peter Schäfer saw a parallel only in the pioneering situation of the two figures in Scholem's eyes, a parallel that neither pointed to Scholem's connection to the Christian tradition of Reuchlin nor shed light on Scholem's attitude toward Christianity in general.[10] In my opinion, it is also possible that in his first public occasion on this scale in Germany, Scholem wished to shift the emphasis from the significance of the event for relations between Germans and Jews to a different dimension, slightly mystical, slightly humorous, and related to scholarship alone. By doing so he evaded an encounter with Germany to the full extent of its meanings but still connected the event to himself.[11] By taking this position, in contrast to those he took in his later speeches,

Scholem was able to restrict the lecture itself to the subject of his scholarship and not discuss his life.

The historical import that lay behind granting the Reuchlin Prize to Scholem is shown in Gadamer's explanation of the choice of recipient. In addition to mentioning Scholem's contribution to research in Kabbalah, which brought him close to Reuchlin's spirit, Gadamer spoke of the symbolism of the award: "However, on the other hand, the City of Pforzheim is honoring a clear and convincing representative of his people, who stands for the unity of human culture with scientific and ethical reason (*Vernunft*)—and this is in spite of the doubts that arise in the wake of the crime committed against the Jews by National-Socialist Germany."[12]

The award ceremony, which was Scholem's first occasion on this scale in Germany, received little publicity, and that only in local media. Nevertheless, it may be assumed that this initial public recognition influenced other bodies to give him subsequent awards. In 1970 three books by Scholem were published by Suhrkamp, including *Judaica 2*,[13] and in 1972 he was made a fellow of the Nordrhein-Westfälische Akademie der Wissenschaften (North Rhine–Westphalian Academy of Sciences, Humanities, and Art).[14] However, the turning point that symbolizes Scholem's entry into the consciousness of the German intellectual world took place in the summer of 1974.

At the end of 1973 Scholem received a letter from Friedheld Kemp, the director of the Literature Department of the Bayerische Akademie der schönen Künste Archiv (Bavarian Academy of Fine Arts), announcing that at the latest meeting of the department it had been decided to give Scholem the academy's literary prize for 1974. Scholem already knew Kemp, who had been present at his lecture on the Jews of Germany in March 1973 at the Institut für Zeitgeschichte in Munich. The letter shows that Kemp was slightly uncomfortable with awarding a literary prize to a man who regarded himself primarily as a scholar, and after the announcement of the decision, he immediately added: "Please don't be surprised: we decided long ago that for us, not only poets and novelists are regarded as literary."[15] Scholem immediately and unreservedly agreed to accept the honor offered to him, but in his reply he did not conceal his surprise and amusement at the irony of awarding such a prize to a scholar:

> Your letter of December 20 was a great surprise for me. How could I imagine, that after many decades of academic research and its expression in German, Hebrew, and English, I would receive a literary prize from a German academy! I call this signs and wonders. I am very curious to hear the reasons for giving the prize, which are doubtless connected to my writing in German and its style. I thank you very much for

this esteem, which I certainly owe to your deep acquaintance with my writing, and I will accept the prize that your academy has decided to give me—though I must ask in concern why I received it. But I remember a line from the poems of Karl Kraus: "We want to be surprised."[16]

The ceremony was held on July 15, and Scholem asked the organizers to send invitations to several of his close friends, including Jörg Drews (a journalist and specialist in German literature), Martin Broszat, Jürgen Habermas, and Siegfried Unseld.[17] The awarding of the prize in Munich naturally received more media attention than Scholem's receipt of the Reuchlin Prize five years earlier, especially in the pages of the *Süddeutsche Zeitung*, where Drews published an article about the awarding of the prize in which he called Scholem "a Jewish scholar and German author." In the article Drews pointed out the small number of Scholem's readers in Germany, in contrast to his English and French readers, and the opportunity for change created by the awarding of this prize: "This situation must change, and perhaps the literary prize will bring about a small alteration." On behalf of the German reading public, Drews reminded Scholem in his article that people hoped to read more books by him about Walter Benjamin and about prewar German Jewish intellectual life, which had been irretrievably lost.[18]

The lecture that Scholem gave was printed in entirety in the weekend edition of the *Süddeutsche Zeitung*, along with the judges' explanations for awarding the prize to him.[19] Scholem's speech concentrated on his personal situation, as someone standing "between German and Hebrew, [and between] German literature and Hebrew [literature]."[20] The speech was decidedly autobiographical, and it contained the outlines that Scholem would later flesh out in *From Berlin to Jerusalem*.[21] But in contrast to the book, toward the end of the lecture he included a retrospective look at the later years of his life, especially about his dealing with Germany and the German language after the Holocaust, in the light of his trip in 1946 and his regular participation in the Eranos conferences. Scholem had not presented such an accounting in public before this, nor did he do so afterward, either in Germany or in Israel.

Another thing that Scholem did for the first time during the award ceremony was publicly and consciously shake the hand of a former Schutzstaffel (SS) man: Hans Egon Holthusen, the head of the Bavarian Academy of Fine Arts, which was giving the prize to Scholem. Holthusen's membership in the Nazi party in his youth was known because of the refusal of the Jewish poet Mascha Kaléko to accept the Fontane Prize of the Berlin Akademie der Künste (Berlin Academy of the Arts) in 1959, since Holthusen was one of the judges,[22] and also because his memoirs as an SS member had been published in *Merkur* in 1966.[23] In Munich

FIGURE 12 Gershom Scholem delivering a speech on receiving the literature prize of the Bavarian Academy of Fine Arts, in Munich, on July 15, 1974. Photographer: Hans Piper. From the collection of the National Library of Israel, Jerusalem.

in the 1970s, the ambivalence that had characterized Scholem's attitude to the public realm in Germany after the Holocaust completely disappeared. As noted, the awarding of the prize in Munich can be said to symbolize the turning point in the reception of Scholem and his writing in Germany. This became evident as events unfolded in succeeding years. In the summer of 1975 he was appointed as an extraordinary member (Ausserordentliches Mitglied) of the Literature Department of the Berlin Academy of the Arts. In a letter to his brother Reinhold in Australia, Scholem complained that he had to go to give a speech the following year at the annual meeting of the academy. "Most likely I will be the only Berliner there," he wrote.[24]

In the fall of 1975 Scholem's autobiographical book about his friendship with Benjamin was published, and parts of it appeared on the front page of the weekend supplement of the *Süddeutsche Zeitung* shortly before its publication.[25] The book was widely reviewed in the literary supplements of most of the important newspapers of Germany. The book was received against the background of the disputes of the late 1960s about the way Theodor Adorno and Scholem had presented Benjamin and the influence of his thought on the extreme left circles of the students at that time. The importance of the book lay both in its providing another element for understanding the image of the philosopher, who had become a symbol, and in its biographical aspect. A review published in *Die Zeit* stated that the book presented Benjamin "as he was, not as he should have been" and argued that Scholem thus also drew a portrait of the history of the collapse of Jewish emancipation in Germany.[26] Indeed, Scholem's book was regarded as the first biography of Benjamin, or as the most important contribution until then toward such a biography. However, along with the interest it aroused by presenting the admired figure of Benjamin in a new light, the book also called attention to Scholem and his life for the first time on a large scale and with wide circulation, since his memory and the documents in his possession were decisive sources for presenting Benjamin and his life to the German reader.[27]

Less than a year later, on June 20, 1976, the German television channel ARD broadcast a forty-five-minute interview with Scholem by Drews. The interview was the third in a series titled "Life Stories as History" (Lebensgeschichte als Zeitgeschichte). The first had been devoted to the philosopher Manès Sperber and the second to the Austrian author Friedrich Torberg (a friend of Scholem), both of whom were Jews. Scholem's interview was filmed in his home at 28 Abarbanel Street in Jerusalem, partly in the living room, against the background of his library, and partly in his workroom, on both sides of his desk. The interview treated four topics: Kabbalah, Benjamin, Zionism and the Israel-Arab conflict, and Scholem's life during the years shortly before and after his emigration.[28] In editing the film, Drews interspersed the conversation with scenes of ancient and modern Jerusalem, the eastern and western parts of the city, the Judean Desert and the covers of Scholem's books that had already been published in German.

The interview was roundly criticized by the television critics of two of the important German newspapers. But the criticism was directed not at Scholem, but at Drews for the way he had directed and edited the interview. In addition, Scholem's Jewishness, or at least the external, stereotypical signs of it, preoccupied the critics. The *Frankfurter Allgemeine Zeitung* wrote that aesthetically the program was "on an amateur level (the camera mainly roamed from Scholem's elephantine ears to his enormous nose, like the Matterhorn)," and with respect to the content, Drews did not succeed in making the fragmentary conversation into a convincing portrait of Scholem. The fact that during the interview no question was asked about German-Jewish relations was, in the critic's opinion, a great failure on Drews's part: he had "missed the opportunity to examine the historical consciousness of the representative of a new generation versus a man who embodies the figure of Jewish history like few others."[29] *Die Zeit* also criticized both the agitated and scattered cinematography, which did not concentrate on Scholem, and the choice of displaying all the covers of the books published by Suhrkamp one after another during the interview. The program about Scholem was compared to the finals in the European soccer championship between Germany and Czechoslovakia, which was broadcast on another network at the same time: "The presentation of the figure of Gershom Scholem became, toward the end of the film, an advertisement for a publishing company. Thereby the viewer ultimately reached the level of a soccer game: advertisements in the Belgrade stadium, advertisements in the report on Scholem. Colorful pictures, random transition from picture to picture, absurd editing. The spectators are in the bleachers. The people in the Old City of Jerusalem. The victory cup. Scholem's collected writings."[30] The criticism did not disturb Scholem, and he was glad to have received the exposure. A short time after the interview was broadcast, he wrote to his brother Reinhold about his present condition in an amused but not dissatisfied tone: "In case this interests you, at the moment I am regarded in Germany, among the gentile scholars, 'the second best after Buber.'"[31] Indeed, Scholem's success in German intellectual circles was expressed in the observance of his eightieth birthday, on December 5, 1977.

About two months before that birthday, Scholem's autobiographical *Von Berlin nach Jerusalem* (later published in English as *From Berlin to Jerusalem*) was published in Germany.[32] The closeness in time of these two events led to their combination in the press, and the praise of Scholem in honor of his birthday was universally mingled with praise for his book. For example, Drews spoke of the book as a present that Scholem had given to Germany in honor of his birthday.[33] Scholem's importance for contemporary German culture at the beginning of his ninth decade was reinforced by publication of the book about his youth, which presented the readers with the story of German Jewry before the Holocaust. The central narrative of the book, expressed in its title, was on his personal, Zionist decision before the war to leave Germany and settle in Palestine, and this was understood as continuing pre-Holocaust German-Jewish culture. This narrative provided a key for understanding Scholem and his work as representing entire worlds that had been destroyed. Hellmut Becker, a friend of Scholem and director of the Max-Planck-Institut für Bildungsforschung (Max Planck Institute for the Study of Education) in Germany, explained this as follows: "Scholem already parted from us in his parents' home. However, he wrote works in the German language, which open a window onto Judaism for us, and in *From Berlin to Jerusalem* he gives us the key to those works."[34]

In Jerusalem, Scholem's birthday was celebrated by his students and admirers. All the daily newspapers dedicated their literary supplements to him, especially to his scholarship—without mentioning the volume of memoirs about his youth.[35] In honor of the event a conference was held on December 4–5 on the messianic idea in Judaism, and relatively young scholars from various fields of Jewish studies gave papers.[36] On December 12, the German embassy in Israel held an evening event in Scholem's honor in the Recanati Room of the Tel Aviv Museum. All the proceedings of the evening were in German, and three people came from Germany to congratulate the guest of honor at the party and make speeches: Unseld, Habermas, and Becker. The evening began with a reception at the home of the German ambassador to Israel, Klaus Schütz, who previously had been the mayor of Berlin for about a decade.[37] Afterward the public part of the evening began at the museum, to which five hundred invitations had been made available. According to Becker, all of them had been snatched up in less than a day.[38] This part of the evening was opened by Unseld, who congratulated Scholem and praised the importance of Scholem's autobiography as a contemporary historical document. Then Habermas gave the central lecture, in which he analyzed Scholem's scholarship and thought. Finally, Becker summed up the evening and mentioned the significance of Scholem's work for how Jews and Germans understood themselves in relation to each other.[39] After the congratulations and speeches, Scholem read the first sections of his autobiographical work in German. Years afterward Habermas recalled the reaction of the Israeli German (Yekke) crowd to Scholem's words and the way they were spoken, a scene that touched his heart: "In the concert hall a large audience was assembled, rather advanced in age. It turned out that this audience had no difficulty in following the precisely formulated sentence of this artist of German prose. As someone coming from the Rhine region, I noticed, that with every mention of a Berlin street name, a murmuring of identification and memory was heard in the hall."[40]

The publication of Scholem's autobiographical work in conjunction with his eightieth birthday created a connection in Germany between Scholem's image in the present and his youth in prewar Germany. The language in which he wrote contributed to this connection, for it was a Berlin German full of humor that had remained free of the deformations imposed by the Nazi regime. All of these elements were a factor in the success of Scholem and his book in reaching intellectual circles in Germany. Shortly after his return from Israel, Becker reported this in a letter to Scholem: "It is especially interesting to me to see how much your book, *From Berlin to Jerusalem*, is reaching members of the younger generation. It has already been given as a gift thirty times, and especially among young people we have received a very strong response. I hope that this is not a phenomenon limited to the circle of my acquaintance, and that the trend will characterize the success of the book in general."[41]

In November 1977 copies of the letters Scholem had written to Benjamin in 1933–1940 reached him from the archive in East Berlin where they had been held. Scholem had known about the existence of those letters for a long time, and in 1966 he had even gone to Potsdam, in East Germany, to see them. At that time he was promised that he would receive copies of the precious documents, but it took more than a decade for that promise to be fulfilled. Scholem was pleased by arrival of the unexpected package, which he called "the most precious and welcome present I could have received on my eightieth birthday."[42] In 1980, Scholem published these letters along with Benjamin's letters to him from those years, which had remained in his possession.[43] The book received attention in the German press, where Scholem was already a well-known figure —especially in connection with Benjamin. The later correspondence was treated in literary supplements as a kind of correction to the two volumes of Benjamin's letters published in 1966, which Scholem had edited with Adorno. A number of reviews pointed out that, unlike the earlier work, the later letters were published in full, and they corrected and balanced the distorted picture presented by the earlier work for they also presented Benjamin's ambivalent attitude toward the Institut für Sozialforschung (Institute for Social Research, IfS) in the 1930s.[44] Scholem also felt that the new volume of correspondence corrected a certain lack of understanding that had been expressed in the accusations leveled against him after publication of the first collection of letters that he had wanted to persuade Benjamin to move to Palestine.[45]

On May 8, 1980, Scholem gave a public lecture in the town of Wolfenbüttel, near Hanover, Germany. He spoke in the famous seventeenth-century Herzog-August Library, which had become the headquarters of the Lessing-Akademie, established in 1971 to study the life and work of Gotthold Ephraim Lessing and the Enlightenment period. Scholem's lecture was given as part of a symposium on the early stage of Spinoza's influence on religious thought, and it was titled "The Growing Dispute around Spinozism and Its Consequences."[46] The lecture was the finale of the entire symposium, and it—or, to be more precise, Scholem —received attention in the local press: "The words of the eighty-three-year-old scholar, who spoke full of temperament and with highly polished diction, in an absolutely clearly structured lecture, summing up the scholarly evidence with precision, were a masterpiece of philosophical and philological thought."[47] According to another article, "this was an opportunity, which has become quite rare in Germany, to hear a lecture characterized both by meticulous scholarly precision, a sense of investigation, and witty irony."[48] Scholem was pleased to have the opportunity to visit this famous library for the first time, and he even found a fragment of a kabbalistic work there, another part of which was in his possession in Jerusalem.[49] Half a year later, Scholem was named "a member of the scientific senate" of the academy, and he remained in this office until his death.[50]

On June 2, 1981, Scholem received almost the greatest honor he could receive from the German academic establishment: the membership committee of the *Orden Pour le Mérite für Wissenschaft und Künste* made him a foreign member (*ausländisches Mitglied*) of the order.[51] The military distinction of *Pour le Mérite* was established in 1740 by Frederick II of Prussia. In 1842 a later king of Prussia, Frederick William IV, under the influence of Alexander von Humboldt, established a humanities branch parallel to the military distinction, to be awarded in the areas of the sciences and humanities, medicine, and the arts. After the fall of the German Empire, the bearers of the distinction formed an independent association of outstanding intellectuals and artists who had been given the medal, without connection to the army. This organization was recognized by the Weimar Republic in 1924, and it began to accept new members, including the artists Max Liebermann and Kathe Kollwitz. With the rise of the Nazis, Hermann Göring removed all Jews and suspected communists from the organization's ranks. After the war the significance of the order and its independent administration were restored to their form under the republic, and in 1954 the president of Germany placed the order under his jurisdiction. Thus the version of the order as a free organization in the republic was combined with its original form as a distinction awarded by the Prussian Empire.

Both Germans and foreigners could belong to the order. When Scholem became a member, there were always thirty German members, and the number of foreign members was not allowed to exceed thirty. Among the foreign members when Scholem was accepted into the order were two of his acquaintances, the author Elias Canetti and the art historian Ernst Gombrich. Among the German members Scholem at least knew Gadamer, who had played an important role in awarding Scholem the Reuchlin Prize in 1969, and the historian and author Golo Mann. On the German side, Scholem was known by name to many members of the order, according to the historian and physicist Heinz Maier-Leibnitz when, about a year later, he described the special atmosphere of the meeting at which Scholem was chosen for membership. His words show the special, almost mystical, place that Scholem occupied among German intellectuals: "When, during the meeting Scholem's name was mentioned for the first time we had an extremely interesting experience. Some of us knew him, and everyone spoke in his favor with great conviction and eloquence. Everyone could also answer our questions, but it was as if they knew more than they could say. An almost celebratory atmosphere was created, and a special spirit suffused our assembly, which is usually sober. The original plan was to choose an artist, but this was almost completely set aside in response to the proposal to choose Scholem."[52]

Scholem met his new colleagues at the next meeting of order in the Hotel Bad Schachen, in Lindau, in southern Germany, on September 26–29, 1981. At the meeting he was given a diploma testifying to his membership in the order. "Among the twenty-seven foreign members, there are nine Jews, almost a minyan [prayer quorum], and we know half of them (most of them!)," Fania wrote from

FIGURE 13 Medal of the *Orden Pour le Mérite für Wissenschaft und Künste*. Photographer: axentis.de /Georg Lopata. Courtesy of Archiv des Orden Pour le Mérite.

Switzerland a short time afterward to Dalia and Malachi Beit-Arié. "Gershom is the only one from Israel, and he also emphasized that strongly, also saying that it had never occurred to him that he might be accepted in this exclusive order on the basis of his scholarship in the area of Judaism."[53]

The meeting in Lindau dealt with various subjects, including a possible meeting with the president of Germany, Karl Carstens, in the discussion of which Scholem took an active part. The discussion revolved around the way the members of the order could contribute to the president's work with such a meeting. The connection between the order and the institutions of government, which went back to the days of the empire, was maintained in activities of this kind. The connection between science and the government is also shown in the form of the badge of the order, which was to be given to Scholem in June 1982, at the time of the annual meeting of the members of the order in Bonn. The design of the badge remained exactly as it had been set by Fredrick William IV in 1842, with the emperor's initials arranged in a cross shape with crowns over them and the seal of the Prussian eagle, all in gold, surrounded by the words "Pour le Mérite" in a blue enamel ring.

Neither the seal of the Prussian emperor nor the form of the cross interfered with Scholem's great joy in having been chosen as a member of the order. The only thing he was sorry about, as he said to Habermas—facetiously, of course—was the paragraph in the regulations that stated that the medallion itself belonged to the German Republic, and he had to make certain that, after his death, the medallion would be sent back to Bonn as soon as possible.[54] In fact, Scholem would not actually receive the medallion. Instead, in June 1982 a speech would be made in his memory in the presence of his widow, Fania. Some time later a photograph of the medallion was sent to her as a momento. As was customary, Scholem's name was engraved on it, attesting that he was worthy of wearing it.[55]

As well as becoming a member of an order with a long tradition and deeply rooted in German culture, Scholem took part in an entirely new venture—the Wissenschaftskolleg zu Berlin. The institution's first year of activity was the academic year of 1981–82, but it time it created a tradition of its own, of which Scholem, who was a fellow during its first year and the last year of his life, was one of the founders and central pillars.

The First Fellow

The last chapter of Scholem's life was played out on the same stage as the first act, but the scenery had changed almost beyond recognition. Berlin in the early 1980s was a divided city, and West Berlin was in the heart of, and completely surrounded by, East Germany, which was part of the Soviet bloc. Culturally and scientifically, Berlin was far from being a vital center. Its isolated location and the climate in its two universities after the violent riots of the student revolt in 1968 gave the intellectual life there a negative public image in West Germany.[56] However, the city had great potential because of its past and because its geographical and political fate made it once again, after half a century—though in a different way—a symbol of the encounter between East and West. To change the negative image of the city and exploit its inherent potential, in 1980 the first institute for advanced study in Germany was founded there. The institute was named after Ernst Reuter, a communist activist of the Weimar period who had been persecuted and exiled under the Nazis and had served as the mayor of Berlin during the Soviet blockade between June 1948 and May 1949.[57] It was called the Wissenschaftskolleg zu Berlin (literally, the science college "to" or "for"—not in—Berlin), with the intention of creating a certain distance between it and its geographical location.[58] The goal of this distancing was to prevent absolute identification of the institute with the city, while also creating a connection between the two that would enhance the influence of the institute on academic life in Berlin. The main change needed, in the opinion of the founders of the institute, was the restoration of the ideals of excellence and academic elitism to the city, since they had been absent in Berlin since the violent events of the student revolt of 1968. With this goal, Peter Wapnewski was chosen as the first rector of the institute. A professor of medieval German literature, Wapnewski had previously taught at universities in Heidelberg, Berlin, and Karlsruhe. He left the Free University of Berlin following the violent actions of the students in 1967–68. Thus, with his support of intellectual elitism, he symbolized opposition to the principles of the student movement.[59] The institute was supposed to function according to the model of the Institute for Advanced Study in Princeton, New Jersey, at which prominent intellectuals and academics were invited to spend a year to work in an optimal atmosphere and make connections with one another and exchange ideas.

Another important goal was for the institute to renew the intellectual life and scientific tradition of Berlin, which had characterized the city before the Nazi regime, and to restore to Berlin, if only for a year, artists and intellectuals who —like Ernst Reuter—had been forced to leave the city or cut off connections with Germany during the Nazi period. Thus, it would be possible to create continuity and renew the splendid past of the city during the long years before it was divided and before the moral pollution that spread in it from the 1930s until the mid-1940s.

The institute was supposed to host forty fellows every year, but during the first year the number was limited to eighteen. Thanks to Becker, in the autumn of 1980 Scholem was officially invited to serve as a fellow during the institute's first year. To the great pleasure of the founders and director of the institute, he accepted the invitation, despite the apprehensions that naturally attended the thought of a journey and a year's absence from home at his advanced age.[60] The hope of the institute to reconnect the threads that had been severed under the Nazis and renew the tradition that had characterized the unified Berlin and its rich culture, which in large part had been Jewish, found its perfect embodiment in the figure of Scholem.[61] As a close friend of Benjamin and as someone who had experienced the end of the empire and the first Weimar years, and who had taken an active part in the flourishing culture that had characterized them but who had also emigrated in time to avoid personally experiencing the period over which the institute tried to skip, Scholem was its ideal standard bearer in its first year of activity. Moreover, Scholem had made a name for himself in West Germany as a scholar of Judaism and was a well-known and well-liked figure.

For that reason, in the summer of 1981, about three months before Scholem's planned arrival, Wapnewski made a request of Scholem that expressed the great honor and respect in which he was held by the director of the institute in Berlin and the director's view of him as the embodiment of its aims: "In preparatory discussions, we thought it would be worthy of this house if [at the opening ceremony] it were represented by itself, that is to say, by one of its fellows, or, to be precise, by the most prominent and important of them."[62] Wapnewski asked Scholem to give a lecture on the evening of the institute's inauguration. It could be about any subject Scholem might choose, but it would have to be limited to thirty minutes, "since we wish expressly to make it possible for high representatives of the state to speak, so as to affirm their responsibility for our house (they are: two government ministers, the current mayor, a senator, and perhaps also the President of the Republic)."[63] Scholem was pleased by the invitation and the honor it entailed, and he immediately accepted. In his answer one can sense the tone of mischievous irony and enthusiasm that were to characterize his future stay in the city of his youth:

> It goes without saying that I cannot refuse your request. Thus, as I have been asked, I will give, with a puffed-up chest—on condition that I do not suffer from bronchitis exactly then, something that is quite likely to happen in November—this ceremonial opening scholarly lecture, in which I will present myself properly before the honorable gentlemen who will speak before me, as a Jew, as an Israeli, as a Berliner, and as a scholar of Kabbalah. The restriction to thirty minutes is particularly justified, since after the five or six speakers who will precede me . . . , one must take into account, willy-nilly, that the audience, aside from the speakers, will already have fallen asleep in the meanwhile. Will I be able to maintain a good atmosphere in the audience? This is a complex question, since I do not wish to exaggerate especially my Berlin sense of humor (*meinen Berliner Mutterwitz*), considering the seriousness of the subject (which I still must choose) and the greatness of the hour. Thus I will have to count on openness on all parts, and on the possible free distribution of anti-sleeping pills. Perhaps it would be best not to write the subject of the lecture in the invitation, to preserve the necessary tension. Your honorable invitation came almost at the same time as the announcement that I was chosen to be a foreign member of the Orden Pour le Mérite für Wissenschaften und Künste, which I also was forced to accept with gratitude (*mit Dank annehme*). . . . So that I can appear in good form in the presence of the president of Germany (*Bundespresidänten*), the current mayor, and the rector of the institute.[64]

Fania and Gershom Scholem arrived in Berlin on October 6, after vacationing in Sils-Maria, in Switzerland. The elderly couple were housed in an apartment that had been prepared for them in the Dahlem neighborhood, not far from the institute—which was located in the Grunewald neighborhood, in a villa built in the early twentieth century. The other fellows for the first year of the institute, who came from Eastern and Western Europe, America, and Israel, had also gathered in Berlin.[65] On November 6 the ceremonial inauguration of the institute took place, and after all the speeches and congratulations, Scholem gave his half-hour lecture, titled "Die Stellung der Kabbala in der europäischen Geistesgeschichte" (The status of Kabbalah in European intellectual history).[66]

In addition to giving the ceremonial opening lecture, Scholem's activities during the weeks following his arrival were many and varied. He planned to write a monograph in German about Ephraim Joseph Hirschfeld—who was an enlightened intellectual, a mystic, a Jewish Freemason, and an adventurer—for which he had been gathering material for many years.[67] But he made time available for young colleagues and researchers to consult him and converse with him about their work. He devoted one evening to a lecture on his childhood and youth in Berlin, given to an audience that filled the auditorium of the Jewish community of the city. On the evening of October 11, Scholem took part in a public discussion about the Jews of Prussia that was held in the Hebbel-Theater, in honor of an exhibition on the subject that had opened in the national library in the city. The historians Saul Friedländer and Fritz Stern took part in that discussion, as did Schütz.[68]

Perhaps the most interesting activity that Scholem initiated during those weeks was the establishment of small circle to study the Zohar with him every week. On November 16, ten days after the official opening of the institute, six local academics met to read the commentary on the first chapters of Genesis (on the creation) in the Zohar, in the original Hebrew.[69] For the participants in this limited seminar, this first meeting was of special importance. In a text written the day after the meeting, Friedrich Niewöhner, a historian of philosophy at the Free University, connected the event to a seminar that Scholem had taught sixty years earlier in Franz Rosenzweig's Freies Jüdisches Lehrhaus in Frankfurt, just before emigrating to Palestine. In 1981, as he had done in 1923, Scholem taught kabbalistic texts to a limited group of people. In 1923, the subject included the hidden Midrash on the Book of Ruth from the Zohar.[70] Niewöhner saw the seminar in Berlin as the renewal of a tradition that had ceased, and the closing of a circle that had opened when Scholem left for Palestine. However, Niewöhner also emphasized the differences between the past and the present, mainly in the purpose of the studying:

> In his seminar on the Zohar in Berlin, 1981–82, Gershom Scholem, who was born in Berlin in 1897, connected with a tradition that had been severed two generations ago. Scholem is not interested here, as he was in 1923, in giving his students "access to the world of Judaism" (*From Berlin to Jerusalem* [Scholem 1982b] p. 182), and his students were both Jewish and non-Jewish. Scholem sought to read and clarify a

central source in the history of the spirit in an almost public manner, as "a kabbalist with the brain of a devil" (*Kabbalist mit dem Gehirn eines Teufels*), as he called himself in the context of the secrets of Kabbalah.[71]

One may assume that Scholem also regarded the seminar as a certain closing of a circle, for he sought to offer it in that format, although very few people could satisfy its requirements. This is also consistent with the great importance that Scholem attributed to his stay in Berlin. A little more than a year later, immediately after his death and the publication of his autobiographical work in Hebrew, Yoram Bronowski recalled "the rumor that reached my ears, according to which the old Gershom Scholem desired more than anything to live in Berlin and wander in the city of his youth, which no longer existed—thus Scholem spent some of the most emotional months of his last year in Berlin, which he had left more than fifty years earlier, in order never to return to it, slamming the door, one might say."[72]

The changes that had taken place in Berlin between the days of his youth and his final visit there—changes that Scholem had witnessed in the making during his repeated visits to the city—were enormous. For example, the vital residential quarter where he had spent his youth had been completely destroyed during World War II, and in 1981 it was a no man's land between East and West Berlin.[73] Despite this extreme change in scenery—perhaps because of it—one cannot discuss Scholem's sojourn in Berlin without connecting it to the earlier scenery of the city, especially that of his childhood and youth. Even in the presence of the changes, Scholem felt a deep and growing connection to the city, and this was certainly why he went there at least once in each of the last four years of his life.[74] In a letter to Dalia and Malachi Beit-Arié, which was mailed from Switzerland—two days before his arrival in Berlin—he summed up his stay in Switzerland and reported his plans for his next destination: "In these six weeks I didn't produce anything new, and I'll try to do something in Berlin, the city of my birth, and I'm considering being called to the Torah in December [1981], in memory of my first reading from the Torah in December 1911, in a synagogue that no longer exists."[75] Perhaps better than anything else, that sentence reflects Scholem's effort to tie together the ends of his life and create a biographical continuity in gestures toward his childhood, whose scenery had been lost.

In any event, Scholem felt at ease in Berlin and the Wissenschaftskolleg, and there is no sign of inner conflict or ambivalence connected to those places in the few remaining documents from this period in his life for firsthand testimony. In a letter to his older brother Reinhold, who was ninety, Scholem reported his impressions of the institute: "The atmosphere at the institute on the banks of

FIGURE 14 Gershom Scholem with Ivan Illich (*left*) Hartmut von Hentig (*right*) at the inauguration of the Wissenschaftskolleg zu Berlin, November 1981. From the collection of the National Library of Israel, Jerusalem.

the Halensee is sympathetic. There are a total of eighteen fellows, including some very smart people, and good connections are being made with most of them (nine foreigners!)."[76] The fact that Scholem did not count himself among the foreign fellows shows that his attachment to Berlin seemed natural and self-evident to him.

Another important factor in the good feelings that attended Scholem's stay in Berlin was the love and admiration that surrounded him from every side. Whether it was the Jewish community of the city, his older friends, or his new colleagues at the institute, it seems that Scholem had never been the center of attention as much as during those weeks. He had returned to Berlin as an academic authority and an admired figure, and he clearly enjoyed that status. A letter from the pedagogue Hartmut von Hentig, one of the fellows of the institute closest to Scholem at that time, to his niece in the United States, reflects the attitude of his colleagues at the institute and the attention he received. To demonstrate Scholem's place and the feelings toward him in the institute, von Hentig describes a photograph that was apparently taken on the evening of the inauguration. Here is his description of the moment that was perpetuated by the camera:

> There is a photograph from the first days of the institute, which I would gladly send to you, if I hadn't already given it away. It expresses something of the pleasure and honor that we feel toward the old scholar. Scholem is sitting in the middle, on a modern chair, in the form of a royal throne. To his right, on his knees, is Ivan Illich, and, to his left, your uncle. We look as if we were all talking at once. In any event, that's what our hands are doing. The three of us are deep in pure enjoyment! Scholem gives

that to us every day—mainly with dry humor (*trocken-keck*), sometimes melancholy, and always incidentally, and he is never arrogant.[77]

This moment of interaction among the three men reflects the status of the elderly scholar of Kabbalah from Jerusalem in the eyes of the younger generation of intellectuals in Berlin. However, that status received its full meaning only after Scholem's death, about three and a half months after the picture was taken.

In early December Scholem slipped and fell, receiving a blow to his hip. After being bedridden for some time, he flew back to Israel with his wife on December 17, a flight that had been planned in advance, to spend the time of the Christmas vacation in Israel. He was hospitalized in Hadassah Hospital in Jerusalem and forced to stay there even after his hip healed, because he was suffering from strong stomach aches whose cause was unclear to the doctors.[78] On February 21, 1982, at 3 o'clock in the morning, Scholem died at the age of eighty-four.

Concluding Remarks

The funeral took place the following day in Jerusalem. At 1 o'clock in the afternoon Scholem's body was placed on a stretcher in the area between the Israel Academy of Sciences and Humanities and the Van Leer Institute, wrapped in a prayer shawl and a blue cloth with the symbol of the Hebrew University and the Israeli flag. Habermas came from Germany and later reported his impressions of the official ceremony, at which many people were present—"especially older people, and of course immigrants from Germany, the Yekkes." At the ceremony, which, in Habermas's opinion, took place with a "lack of formality more characteristic of a quotidian action,"[79] Nathan Rotenstreich and Ephraim Urbach, president of the academy, spoke. The president of Israel, Yitzhak Navon, also attended the ceremony. At the request of its organizers, despite the presence of many German-speaking Israelis in the audience and despite the fact that he had prepared a eulogy the night before he traveled to Israel, Habermas was not invited to speak in memory of his friend. Thus the German language was completely missing from Scholem's funeral.[80] The procession took a long route via the campus on Mount Scopus to the cemetery in Sanhedria. The burial area where the interment took place still lacked trees and flowers, as the author Naomi Frankel described it: "The earth was still smooth and bare and strewn with stones. This barren earth is similar to the earth of the stony, old Jerusalem, to which the young scholar of Kabbalah came in 1923, and where he died in 1982."[81] On the fresh grave "two pompous wreaths with strident ribbons on them" stood out, both placed by the German ambassador—one in the name of the president of Germany, and the other on behalf of the mayor of Berlin.[82] In time Fania Scholem erected a gravestone, on which was written, beneath Scholem's name, the dates of his birth and death, the words "Founder of Research in Kabbalah," and a verse from the Book of Daniel, 1:17, with a slight change: "God give him [instead of "them"] knowledge and understanding of every book of wisdom."[83] Avraham Shapira pointed out that later on, when Fania replaced her husband's gravestone with a granite slab, she added another line, hinting at Scholem's connection with his country of origin: "A man of the Third Aliyah."[84]

Scholem's death was widely reported in the Israeli press, which expressed the great admiration felt for him and his work. The widespread effect of his death in Israel intensified with the publication of the expanded Hebrew version of his autobiographical *From Berlin to Jerusalem* a few weeks afterward.[85] While the publication of this book in Germany had been connected with Scholem's eightieth birthday, its publication in Israel was bound up with his death. On the thirtieth day after his funeral, a conference was held in Jerusalem at which six of his colleagues and close disciples spoke about various aspects of him and his scholarly work.[86] However, very slowly, an "almost oedipal" process of resistance to his dominance began.[87] This was doubtless necessary, since for decades Scholem had played a leading role in shaping the character of academic life in Israel, especially in Jerusalem.[88] Habermas was aware of the stirrings of this process on the evening after Scholem's funeral, in the home of Yehuda Elkana: "There I heard in silence what the other side had to say, with restrained aggressiveness, about Scholem and the control of German culture over the Israeli educational system (*Bildungssystem*), which aroused ambivalent feelings. I could taste the disputes with which Scholem lived."[89]

Scholem's death was reported in the press in Germany, too, especially in Berlin—where his friends and colleagues at the Wissenschaftskolleg had to cope with the surprising news. Of course, in Berlin there was neither the ambivalence nor the sense of an imminent conflict following the vacuum left by his death that colored the academic atmosphere in Jerusalem. In the corridors of the villa in Grunewald, the absence of the man who, shortly before, had filled them with his characteristic voice and temperament was felt, and Scholem's physical presence was replaced by memories. In a letter of condolence sent to Fania Scholem, Wapnewski reported this feeling: "Since the much admired Gershom Scholem left us—left us in two meanings of the word—he has been present among us in a special way. Please don't see this statement as a logical contradiction. No day passes without mention of his name in our house, there is no occasion when the suggestion is not made, that here he, Gershom Scholem, would certainly have told us something important, clarifying, removing doubt, or raising doubt. For all of us here he was not only a colleague and teacher, but also a model (*Vorbild*), with his meticulous intelligence and the goodness and purity that were inherent in his thinking, his actions, and his statements."[90]

In fact, immediately after the news of Scholem's death reached Berlin, Wapnewski began to organize a conference in Scholem's memory, which was also meant to be the concluding event of the first academic year of the institute. The conference was held on July 2, 1982. Fania attended, and speeches were given by Wapnewski; Ephraim Lahav, the representative of the Hebrew University in Europe; Maier-Leibnitz, chancellor of the order Pour le Mérite; and Schütz. Zvi Werblowsky arrived from Israel and gave a lecture on Scholem's academic work. In the name of Scholem's colleagues at the institute, von Hentig gave a speech. In the audience of 150 people were the Israeli ambassador to Germany; Scholem's two nieces, Edith Capon and Renee Goddard (the daughters of Werner Scholem); Becker, Unseld, and many other representatives of the press and public figures.[91] All the speeches given in Scholem's honor reflected the central and special place he had won among his acquaintances in Germany. But what was there about the figure of that eighty-four-year-old man that charmed his German colleagues? What gave him such great importance and meaning for them—meaning that far transcended the two months and ten days that he was at the institute, a period that was the peak of the three decades in which Scholem was active in postwar Germany?

To understand the way that Scholem was perceived and accepted in the country of his youth, which was fully expressed in the speeches in his memory at the ceremony at the institute in Berlin and in the memories of colleagues and friends after his death, one must consider two important and interconnected factors: who Scholem was for "the German side," and how this vision of him was represented in his connection with his surroundings, his way of speaking, and his conduct toward the people around him.

For his colleagues, Scholem was first of all a German Jew: "Scholem was a citizen of the world, but primarily he was a full and perfect representative of his people, of the form of its spiritual life, and of its tradition," said Maier-Leibnitz at the ceremony in Berlin.[92] Wapnewski described him in similar terms years later: "He was a representative of the fate of the German Jews (not of Jewish Germans)."[93] von Hentig saw Scholem's stay in Berlin as "the happy possibility of an exile's return home (*Heimkehr*)."[94] In addition, Scholem was what von Hentig called an "unmistakable Berliner (*unverkennbaren Berliner*)."[95] His German colleagues recognized this trait in every step he took and every word he wrote or spoke. His Berlin accent and manner of speaking, which were typical of the neighborhood where he had been born and which like the neighborhood had ceased to exist in the city, remained with him throughout his life, and his German colleagues enjoyed them.[96] Schütz also recalled this prominent characteristic of Scholem in his speech in Scholem's memory: "Scholem spoke and wrote in German in a way that many of us no longer even learned how. His use of the language remains . . . in a thought-provoking way, unblemished by the developments of the German language in the past fifty years; [Scholem's German] 'stands in proximity to the prose of the great German minds of the nineteenth century.'"[97] The way that Scholem spoke and the humor that accompanied what he said were engraved in the memories of those around him and often attributed to the intellectual world of prewar Berlin. "The words in his mouth were still 'clean,' to a certain extent they were unstained," Wapnewski wrote of him.[98] Thus, for example, Scholem ironically called his colleagues in the institute, who were living in the refurbished villa, "die Trockenmieter" (literally, dry renters),[99] a term used in early twentieth-century Berlin to describe a cheap housing solution found by poor families, who lived for half a year in new apartments whose walls had just been painted. When the paint on the walls dried, they would be replaced by wealthy tenants.[100] Aside from this, it must be pointed out that Scholem attributed great importance to his being a Berliner and saw it as a central element in his life. An example of this can be found in his relationship with Walter Pagel, a pathologist and historian of medicine who had been born in Berlin and moved to London in 1933. In a letter to Joseph Weiss, one of his closest students, Scholem states humorously that his fondness for Pagel and their closeness was derived from "the shared root of our soul, mine and Dr. Pagel's, is in the spark of the alien fire of the former community of Berlin, where our birth and origin are, and therefore we understand each other with hints."[101] I heard another anecdote that shows how Berlin German was rooted in Scholem from his niece, Renee Goddard, who was an actress. Her theater company in London put on the play *I Am a Camera*, which takes place in Berlin in the early 1930s. Goddard played the role of Natalia Landauer, the Jewish girl, and to portray her convincingly as a native of Berlin, on the stage she imitated the way her uncle spoke English. As fate would have it, Scholem came to see a performance, and at the end he approached her and commented in English, with a heavy accent, "yu ver zi onli von ai anderstut."[102] The former chief editor of the Suhrkamp publishing house, Walter Boehlich, reported on the dominance of the Berlin aspect of Scholem's appearance, in the words he composed in his honor: "Scholem, as mentioned, no longer wished to be German, but nevertheless he could not and did not wish to stop looking very German, in his own way. If anyone, then he was a typical German professor, of the good kind, of course, a Berliner in Jerusalem as well."[103]

The third factor in Scholem's essence that stood out in the eyes of his German colleagues was his being Israeli. In fact, he belonged to the generation of the founders of the State of Israel and was one of the people who shaped the nation's scientific and intellectual character. Scholem knew the leaders of the State of Israel, and for many years he was connected with the highest strata of Israeli society. For his German colleagues, he was a link to the young state, toward which their attitude was very complex. "For us he was the key to Israel," Habermas recalled years later. "Israel was the most difficult country for us."[104] The combination of these three factors—that Scholem was a German Jew, a Berliner, and an Israeli—was unique in the intellectual landscape of Germany. Consequently, the history of Scholem's reception in that country was a unique case. It may be said that no other Israeli intellectual or academic was received similarly or even close to the way that Scholem was. Being a German who had emigrated to Israel, taken part in the project of renewing the life of the Jewish people, established the field of academic research in Kabbalah, and returned to Germany gave him an authority in the eyes of his associates that went far beyond his field of knowledge. As early as the 1960s, when he was a regular guest of the IfS in Frankfurt, he was viewed by people like Adorno; Max Horkheimer; and even Herbert Marcuse, who lived in the United States, as an authority.[105] Habermas recalled that, when he was one of the younger members of the institute, he was often perplexed by the great respect that the members of Scholem's generation accorded him. In meetings in Unseld's home with Scholem, Adorno, and Ernst Bloch, when Habermas was present, he always detected "an invisible hierarchy" between Scholem and those around him, a hierarchy whose meaning he did not understand.[106] Even two or three decades later, members of the institute in Berlin thought of Scholem as a supreme authority, and although it is impossible to fully uncover the source of that authoritativeness, one can point to two likely parts of it. The first consists of his academic achievement, the enormous professional respect he received, and his great expertise in various fields. "Everything he says comes from a great treasury of knowledge and experience, from broad understanding of the world and human depth, sensitivity, and warmth,"[107] said Maier-Leibnitz at the ceremony in Scholem's memory.

The second source of Scholem's authority, in the view of his German colleagues, was in his belonging to a generation or group of Jewish intellectuals who emigrated from Germany before World War II and returned afterward, whether permanently (like Adorno, Karl Löwith, Helmuth Plessner, and others), or as frequent visitors, coming every year or two (like Marcuse). Habermas knew almost that entire generation of Jewish intellectuals in the field of sociology and philosophy, scholars who had emigrated to the West and returned to Germany in one way or another, and he identified an important role that they played for the

FIGURE 15 With Jürgen Habermas (*left*) and Siegfried Unseld (*center*), during Habermas's receipt of the Adorno Prize, Frankfurt 1980. From the collection of the National Library of Israel, Jerusalem.

younger generation in Germany: "They were the only ones who could tie us, the young people, back to our old tradition after the great breakdown." For this generation, whose members had been orphaned from their intellectual and spiritual predecessors because their teachers were stained with the moral blemish that accompanied everyone who took part in the Nazi state or the ideological world of Nazism, the exiled Jewish intellectuals offered a sort of salvation. Habermas called the meaning of their presence in Germany for the members of his generation the "Erlösung eines Problems" (the redemption of a problem). Thanks to their origin, which placed them at the heart of the German cultural tradition, and thanks to their blamelessness, the intellectuals who returned from exile could fill the vacuum that had been created by the culpability of their German teachers and provide an admirable example for the generation of intellectuals that emerged after the war. As Habermas put it, "they came as a moral authority, which possessed the means that could grant forgiveness to the generation that had become guilty."[108] Years later, in introducing a lecture by Elie Wiesel, the sociologist Wolf Lepenies—who succeeded Wapnewski as rector of the Wissenschaftskolleg—mentioned the role played by Scholem for the institute in the long term in similar fashion: "Scholem's acceptance was fortunate for the institute; whether the good fortune that was ours by chance has become today, fifteen years later, a good fortune that we have earned honorably, is for others to decide. It is a fact that Scholem's agreement to come to the institute as a fellow, his presence and his work in Berlin, in the new institution, gave scientific and ethical credit (*Wissenschaftsmoralischen Kredit*), by which it was nourished and upon which it could flourish. We were lucky with Gershom Scholem."[109]

Hence, Scholem's special place in Germany toward the end of his life derived from a unique combination of components of life. In addition, it is important to point out that Scholem was also seen as an indirect victim of the Nazi regime: his brother Werner had been murdered in the Buchenwald concentration camp; his family had been forced to emigrate to England and Australia; and his close friend Benjamin, who was identified with him perhaps more than anyone else, committed suicide while fleeing from the Nazis. As Unseld noted in a speech about Scholem's research, "just as we are amazed by every page of Jewish intelligence and can also smile at Jewish jokes, we also cannot forget with every page, that the Germans would have murdered the man who wrote that page, if he had fallen into their hands."[110]

One may also add the simple fact that Scholem was physically present in Germany during the years after the war, and he was available to his colleagues. This proximity, and of course his unique character, led many of his acquaintances to see him first of all as a good friend. As Becker wrote after Scholem's death, in him "we learned to recognize a genius of friendship."[111] But this closeness always existed alongside the estrangement derived from the double distance that Scholem represented for them. One aspect of the distance was temporal, since he belonged to the German past that had long since ceased to exist, and the other aspect was geographical, in that he was a citizen of Israel and a central figure in the academic and scientific system there—which placed him in the Levant. Of course, though this strangeness separated Scholem from his German colleagues, it was also one of his features that they found attractive. In his tribute to Scholem, von Hentig stated that those who had been with him during the first year at the institute in Berlin were not worthy to call themselves Scholem's fellows, because in this dialectic of closeness and distance, he was for them "an elder friend, like a father, and a young teacher, like a brother."[112]

As noted, the outer manifestations of Scholem's essence were a decisive factor in the way he was received in Germany. We have already mentioned his Berlin idiom as well as the sense of humor his displayed in communicating with those around him, which was anchored in the old German conceptional world. These outward manifestations were a larger part of something that cannot be precisely defined, but that appears in almost every testimony or document dealing with him, which can be called the Scholem experience. The paradox in the background of Scholem's understanding of the subject of his scholarly work, the contradiction inherent in the effort to report scientifically about phenomena underlaid by personal experience and in the effort to transmit what in fact exists beyond the realm of communication, is also found in the effort to analyze him on the basis of testimony about the way he was experienced. At the same time, the various sources show that to experience Scholem's presence and the temperament that characterized his speech and behavior was an integral part of acquaintance with him. Although his physical presence disappeared immediately after his death, his presence arose again with great vitality in all his friends' memories. The difficult of speaking about Scholem to understand him, without the possibility of experiencing him, also emerges in the words that Boehlich wrote in his memory. After speaking of Scholem's professional achievements and their meaning in Germany, Boehlich said that "perhaps it was necessary to experience him, how he used to say with enthusiasm and pleasure: 'He doesn't know! Scholem will explain it.' and then he would explain."[113] Drews also described this aspect as central for understanding Scholem. Several years before Scholem's death, Drews wrote:

> He said, "Berliners are a resilient kind of person (*resilienter Menschenschlag*)," using the adjective "resilient," what was apparently widespread in Prussia during his youth. He also knew himself to be so resilient, so unconquerable, and so rebellious, a Berliner, the sound of whose speech, even the Hebrew that he spoke, gave him away as such to his last day. At the same time, he would win over his listeners with his rough, dry charm (which he was capable of employing consciously and intentionally) and with his unique temperament.[114]

Although the Scholem experience characterized the relations of people in his German surroundings to him in general, it is still important to distinguish here between the way Scholem was viewed by those who knew him in the context of the IfS and the Suhrkamp publishing house—including Unseld, Habermas, Becker, Boehlich, and Rolf Tiedemann—and the way he was perceived in the last stage of his reception in Germany, at the Wissenschaftskolleg. The association of the members of the former group with Scholem mainly began in the 1960s, was built up slowly over years, and was characterized by professional collaboration along with friendship of a certain depth (one of the characteristics of which were the visits of these friends to the other side of Scholem's world, Israel). In contrast, Scholem's acquaintance with the other fellows of the Wissenschaftskolleg was relatively superficial and began only in the last two years of his life. The new period of Scholem's reception in Germany, added by his affiliation with the institute in Berlin, was his becoming a symbol for an entire generation, and the appropriation of that symbol for the academic and ideological needs of the institute. Of course, this appropriation was not a one-sided action, and its source —discussed below—was a reciprocal need, although the differences in the way it was understood in various circles are conspicuous.

Two additional points touching on Scholem's reception in Germany deserve mention. The first limits the extent of his reception, and the second enlarges the boundaries of its importance. Scholem's reception in Germany was never a mass phenomenon, and although his fame grew over the years, it always remained limited to relatively small intellectual circles. Scholem's writings and the recognition of their importance did not go beyond these circles during his life or afterward. Hence, Scholem was never an influential or iconic figure in Germany, as Benjamin and Habermas are today. The second point is that Scholem entered German public opinion to a large extent as an author, not as a scholar. This is shown by such events in his life as receiving the literary prize from the Bavarian Academy of Fine Arts in 1974, being appointed to the Literature Department of the Berlin Academy of the Arts in 1975, and being the subject of one episode of a television series dealing with Jewish writers. However, placing Scholem in the category of author gave him a broader role in German intellectual life after the war than he would have gained if he had had been regarded solely as a scholar. Unseld commented on this role after Scholem's death: "Scholem wrote his works, especially all of his important works in German, in spotless German prose, which, in addition to his erudition, gives him the name of one of the great academic writers of our time and assures him of continued influence on new generations."[115]

Scholem's role as an author—as someone who combined all the components discussed above, biographical as well as professional, and expressed them in his writing—was the foundation of his influence on new generations, or the future. Thus, one may see Scholem's role in Germany as bridging the gap between the past generation and the future one, while leaping over the abyss: the corrupt generation in between. This educational role was expressed to a great degree in his offering the coming generation a German language whose use did not suffer from the changes of time and events and that remained in its original context. In this way he could offer the younger generation continuity and thus retain intergenerational cohesion. For Germany, Scholem served as an important link in the chain of generations and the tradition of the German language, which was necessary in the efforts of the younger generation to overcome the moral and cultural degeneration that was an integral part of German culture in the 1930s and 1940s. Thus, surprisingly, Scholem, in the autumn of his life, became an author of the transitional generation that aspired to spiritual and moral renewal, an author who had the capacity to prepare this renewal and maintain it in himself. Thus, in much the way that he understood Shmuel Yosef Agnon's role for the generation of rebirth in Palestine and the State of Israel, almost half a century later, Scholem played the role of an author "who stands on the crossroads and looks in both directions."[116]

However, it would be an error to think that this role was projected on Scholem or given to him unilaterally. As noted earlier, Scholem made many efforts over the years to gain a place in the German intellectual world. His frequent trips, the books and articles that he published, the prizes he received, the lectures he gave, and the public symposia about the story of his family and his life—all of these reflect these efforts. In this context it is interesting to note that Scholem's last monograph in Hebrew was published in 1957, when he was sixty, with another twenty-four years of productive scholarly activity before him.[117] During that quarter-century Scholem published in German a monograph on medieval Kabbalah;[118] six collections of articles all originally written in that language;[119] three volumes of Walter Benjamin's letters, which he edited;[120] two new editions of *Major Trends in Jewish Mysticism*;[121] an interview with Drews that was published as a booklet; and two autobiographical books.[122] In English during those years Scholem published a monograph on ancient Hebrew mysticism, three volumes of articles, and two autobiographical books—all of them translated from German or Hebrew.[123] In Hebrew three volumes of articles and one autobiographical book were published.[124] This short list, which does not include articles, shows that the increasing honor Scholem received in Germany was a need that derived from both sides. Not only was there individuals in Germany interested in Scholem and his writing, but Scholem desired to attain recognition and honor in that country.

As noted, it is possible to view the stay of the Scholems in Berlin as symbolizing in extreme fashion the process of Scholem's return to the German world and to Jewish-German dialogue after World War II, which was central to this section of the book. However, this journey symbolizes both Scholem's return to a familiar world and his departure from Jerusalem and from the effort to realize the Zionist dream, which had disappointed him for so many years. In the Hebrew edition of his autobiography, Scholem mentions parenthetically his youthful hope that had gone unfulfilled over the years: "I no longer pinned any hope on the familiar combination known as 'Deutsch-Judentum,' whose full meaning is not conveyed by the rendering as 'German Jewry,' and I hoped for the renewal of Judaism only with its rebirth in the Land of Israel (and by rights my readers may ask whether I retain this hope to this day, after sixty years, and I have no answer, in the light of everything that has happened, except mere hope (*tochelet*), as a wise man has said: extended hope makes the heart sick)."[125]

Perhaps the search for a cure for this sickness of heart lay behind the great effort involved in shifting the center of Scholem's life from Jerusalem to Berlin at such an advanced age. Scholem's life in the Berlin winter of 1981 in the modest furnished apartment with the empty shelves, surrounded by much younger people, demonstrated the less brilliant aspect of his return to the city of his childhood and youth to the observant eyes of von Hentig, and gave the return a dimension of sadness: "I was able to understand how greatly this affected him and his wife by the influence of a picture by Anna Ticho,[126] the Israeli painter, which I helped them to hang in their apartment with a drill that I brought. The picture shows the stony landscape surrounding Jerusalem, and it nourished their souls greatly. No, it was not easy for them here!"[127]

Perhaps, hidden in the difficulty felt by the Scholems in their small, empty apartment on the periphery of cold, divided Berlin, was a deep longing for the period before all the alterations in their lives: the period when Berlin was the center; Jerusalem was a peripheral, rocky landscape; and the dream was still a dream.

AFTERWORD
FROM BERLIN TO JERUSALEM

Scholem's Jewish state was founded in Berlin. Although the emphasis is ostensibly on "Jerusalem," on the goal, what really lives in this book of memoirs is Berlin, as well as other European cities, the other arche-European cities where Scholem lived in his youth, such as Bern or Munich. But, above all, again and again, Berlin. As if by itself, a kind of hidden struggle between these two cities in Scholem's soul arises from the book. It is not conscious: consciously Scholem was entirely dedicated to Jerusalem from the time he adopted political Zionism as a youth. But as long as he dreamed about it, it was the Jerusalem one longs for from the depths of the north, it's the Berlin dream of Jerusalem, which is not, for example, similar to the Jerusalem dream about Jerusalem. . . . In the final analysis—indeed in the finality of the final analysis—Berlin won, and Jerusalem lost. It is difficult not to recall the rumor that reached my ears, according to which the old Gershom Scholem desired more than anything to live in Berlin and wander in the city of his youth, which no longer existed—thus Scholem spent some of the most emotional months of his last year in Berlin, which he had left more than fifty years earlier, in order never to return to it, slamming the door, one might say. And all of this was in order to realize that the true city of his dreams—his Jerusalem—was this rejected Berlin. And this, too, is Scholem's rebellion, which eventually rebelled against him.

YORAM BRONOWSKI, "MIBERLIN LIYERUSHALIYM UVERCHAZARAH"[1]

This book is centered on Scholem's attitude toward Germany during the six decades after he moved to Palestine. Although he usually presented himself outwardly as a Zionist who had turned his back on German culture, after World War II his increasing closeness to Germany is noticeable—closeness that at the same time symbolizes a distancing from Israel. His ambivalence regarding a connection with the German intellectual world in the first years after the war was succeeded in time by a desire to be a part of that world. This desire complemented that of German intellectuals to connect with the Jewish heritage of their country that had been characteristic of it during the years before the Holocaust. The peak of this process for Scholem can be seen in the publication of his autobiography in the autumn of his life, which was also the point of departure for the present study. The importance of *From Berlin to Jerusalem* for understanding Scholem's life is in the connection of its beginning to its end. Hence, the final section of this book will be devoted to this work.

The first edition of Scholem's autobiography was published in German in 1977, close to the time of his eightieth birthday. An expanded Hebrew edition was published in Israel immediately after his death in 1982.[2] The enormous importance of this book for understanding Scholem's life is of course inherent in its content, which is laden with information, impressions, and experiences and testifies to one of the most fertile periods in Jewish creativity. However, the reader cannot help feeling that, in spite of the abundant external details and descriptions of life, one learns very little about Scholem's inner life.[3] This feeling has been corroborated since the publication of his early diaries, through which it is possible to see more clearly that the feelings he reported at a distance in time were not always consistent with the way he experienced events when they occurred. The sense that behind the decidedly exoteric nature of the autobiography lies a complex and hidden side of his life that he sought to conceal accompanies the reader throughout the captivating plot of the book. This is evidently connected to the nature of autobiographical writing, which exists both in the present in which it is being written and in the past that is being recounted. Thus, one can also learn about the late Scholem from the autobiography—mainly from its form and from what it does not include, though this can be intuited between the lines. As noted, *From Berlin to Jerusalem* was the point of departure for my biographical discussion of Scholem, and it raises two key questions for understanding Scholem's life between the two poles that were central to this discussion and presented at the start of the book: Why did Scholem stop the story of his life when he reached the age of twenty-eight, at his arrival in the Land of Israel and his absorption there—a conscious decision that did not imply any intention to continue this story in the future?[4] And why did he write the book in German and publish it first in Germany?

When the book was published, Scholem had already decided he would not write a sequel. In a letter to the editor of the Germania Judaica series in Bonn, Jutta Bohnke-Kollwitz, he explained his decision: "While it's nice that my book gave you pleasure, I don't think it will be continued. Here the matter becomes too difficult. Indeed, it was much less difficult—though, in the light of the special circumstances of the memory of the Jews who were murdered it was certainly not easy—to write critically about matters from my youth, than about the difficult developments in the Land of Israel during the past fifty years. There is no lack of great episodes that I do not wish to present to a German readership. I will continue, but not in the direction that I plotted in this volume."[5]

The clear picture, easily presented to the German public, altered shortly after Scholem's arrival in the Land of Israel, and this prevented him from documenting his later life. These changes, discussed at length in the first two parts of this book, caused him to become disappointed with the path of Zionist and its manner of implementation. This disappointment was caused by the gap between the Zionist utopia in Scholem's imagination and the reality that developed over the years. Any effort to implement a utopian idea naturally contains the seeds of disappointment—for no reality, as ideal as it might appear, can compete with the manner in which it was dreamed. In this sense, disappointment was a necessary component of the process of all immigration motivated by the Zionist ideology, and it has been shared by many immigrants from the time of the First Aliyah to the present. In addition, there was Scholem's political and cultural worldview, which ran counter to the direction of the Yishuv and the State of Israel, causing a widening rift between him and them.

After the riots of 1929, which made it clear to Scholem that the Yishuv intended to establish a society very different in character from what he had imagined and hoped for, and after the immediate need created by the persecution of the Jews and the Holocaust finally set the path for territorial Zionism,[6] further moments of crisis ensued. The Six-Day War of 1967 was another decisive milestone on this path, for Scholem fiercely opposed the annexation of the conquered territories and soon afterward criticized the post-1967 settler movement Gush Emunim (Bloc of the faithful), arguing that they were dangerous because they were "like Sabbateans."[7] However, in contrast to earlier years, after the Holocaust Scholem gradually withdrew into the realm of scholarship and refrained from political activity and from publicly expressing his positions. An anecdote told by Fania shows how far he distanced himself from the leaders of the country. In the 1970s, Yitzhak Rabin, the prime minister of Israel, visited Helmut Schmidt, the chancellor of Germany, the latter "wanted to make an impression on him [Rabin] as a man of culture, and he displayed some of Scholem's books on the table and began to talk about them. Rabin didn't understand what he was talking about."[8] Rabin was the fifth prime minister of the State of Israel; Scholem had known the first four personally and had had some contact with them. A former general and a graduate of the Kadoori Agricultural School, Rabin was the first prime minister with a military background, as well as the last prime minister in Scholem's lifetime who belonged to the Labor Party. After the elections for the ninth Knesset in 1977, the year when Scholem's autobiography was published in German and he celebrated his eightieth birthday, Menachem Begin became prime minister, and the power of the right emerged. According to Rolf Tiedemann, Scholem did not vote for the Labor Party in those elections, though he had favored it in the past. Rather, he voted for Ratz, a small splinter party headed by Shulamit Aloni.[9] Tiedemann recalled visiting the hotel where the Scholems were staying in Frankfurt in the summer of 1972, on the evening when the massacre occurred at the Munich Olympics. While the television and radio in their room loudly reported the events, Scholem opened his heart to Tiedemann, who commented "I had never before heard Scholem speak so completely without inhibitions, about Zion, which had long since ceased to be a symbol for him."[10]

In the spring of 1981 Tiedemann met Scholem in Germany again. In the background was the crisis between Begin and Chancellor Helmut Schmidt following his statements in Riyadh.[11] Scholem bitterly remarked that the crisis would certainly guarantee another term for Begin after the coming Israeli elections, because of his bombast against Germany and the Germans. In the collision between his two worlds in the context of the Middle East conflict, Scholem distanced himself from the political winds blowing in Israel. In this context, the conversation between him and Tiedemann touched on the Israeli-Palestinian conflict. "I asked how, in his opinion, it would be possible to find a solution to the problem of the Palestinians," Tiedemann wrote. "His answer was spoken softly, in a tired tone: 'Today there is no solution.'"[12] This despair, which Scholem expressed a few months before being invited to become a fellow of the Wissenschaftskolleg in Berlin was characteristic of his attitude toward Israel in the final years of his life. That is how Tiedemann described him, and that is how Fania remembered him during those years: "In his last years he was almost in despair. I think he died in despair. He said that now we had only hope."[13] Evidently Scholem sought to avoid recounting the history of this despair by interrupting the story of his life for the German reader (and several years later for the Hebrew reader as well) a few years before the first great crisis, in 1929. Nevertheless, the question remains: Why did he try to avoid it? Here is the place to ask the second question again: Why did Scholem choose to write his book in German and publish it in Germany first?

In the light of Scholem's reception in Germany, we may assume that the great interest that the story of his life aroused in the rediscovery of a lost territory for German culture encouraged him to put his memories in writing. As early as

1964, at an evening in honor of Suhrkamp's publication of the first volume of *Judaica*, Scholem spoke not only about the book but also about himself, its author, and the story of his life.[14] In 1967 and 1969 Scholem spoke on the radio about his life and research, and in 1973 he gave a lecture in Munich that he later turned into an article combining his memories with a survey of the history of German Jewry before 1933.[15] In 1975 his book of memoirs about Walter Benjamin was published, and this was an important step in the process of his reception.[16] Scholem's significance for the Germans as a symbol of a lost period made the story of his life interesting to and relevant for them and thus prepared the soil for publication of his book of memoirs. Another aspect of this question is related to Scholem himself. Here we can connect the answer to the role of the German language in relation to Hebrew in Scholem's world, a constant theme in the present book: at various periods of his life, each language represented the world that stood behind it. In the Gershom Scholem Archive is a handwritten sheet of paper containing a comparison between the processes undergone by the two languages and his place in relation to them. This comparison was written during the 1960s, apparently while Scholem was preparing for an evening event hosted by the Suhrkamp publishing house in Frankfurt in 1964.[17] Here is what he wrote:

> In 1923 I went to Palestine, which we then referred to with the translation of the Hebrew term, "Eretz-Yisrael," the Land of Israel. Until 1930 I retained a connection with my mother tongue. In 1933 I lost that connection with it and did not experience or suffer the German language at that stage, which Hitler brought with him. And thus I remained. When I write German now and then, I am an *antiquated* writer. I still write the German of my youth and it happens that I am frightened when it turns out that words, images, and associations that had meaning, splendor, and unity, have become taboo, and they can no longer be used, at least for this generation, because in the language of the Third Reich, they were ground into death (like the word *Anliegen*).[18] But I had the same experience, though in the opposite direction, with *the Hebrew language*. The language we have developed in Israel is no longer the language we sought to learn fifty years ago, from the old books, when a certain splendor arose from them before us (I might even say: the splendor of revelation), marvelously seductive. And what happened in the meanwhile? Where does the process of the rebirth of the Hebrew language take place? In the transition of the ancient language —which, historically, is laden with eternal languages and the weight of religious associations—from the book to the debased language of children.[19]

In this fragment Scholem juxtaposes the two side of his life by examining the way in which he experienced the Hebrew and German languages in relation to one another. His experience of the languages is similar but moves in opposite directions. While the German he spoke remained static and frozen and was not part of the changes that took place in the language under the Nazis,[20] he witnessed the dynamic changes that took place in Hebrew and even took part in them. In German, words that were common in his youth had disappeared because their meaning had been distorted during the Nazi regime, when they became laden with tension and destructive force. In Hebrew, words with religious connotation, which had been preserved during thousands of years of religious use, shed the tension of their original meaning, were apparently neutralized, and became an ostensibly innocent daily language in the mouths of infants. The similarity in Scholem's experience of the languages is expressed in the fear that seized him when he observed the changes both had undergone. But even here there is a difference in his attitude toward the essence of the change. The archaism of his German added a dimension of innocence whose significance was solely symbolic, for the danger had passed. However, his knowledge of the deep religious meaning of words in Hebrew brought home to him the great danger in the cultural and political processes that Israel was undergoing.[21]

The contrasts between the languages was parallel to the contrasts within Scholem between Germany and Israel and between the years before the Holocaust and those after it. *From Berlin to Jerusalem* represents the connection between the two worlds he had lived in and demonstrates the way they stand opposite to one another in his life. In other words, through narrating the story of his leaving Germany years before the Nazi era, Scholem paved his way back to Germany after the Holocaust. Moreover, the history of the coming into being of *From Berlin to Jerusalem*—a literary project that took many years—is the history of his reception in Germany. Just as in his continued denial of the existence of any Jewish-German dialogue before World War II he became part of such a dialogue after it, the story of his turning his back on Germany in the 1920s became part of his welcome in it in the 1960s and 1970s. Moreover, the writing of his memoirs—during which he encountered Scholem the Zionist, the young man he had been—is what made it possible for him, morally speaking, to return to the locale of his childhood in the present. By telling the story of his departure from the cycle of assimilation of the Jews of Germany and describing in detail the path that led to his becoming Israeli, it became possible for him to open the door for a personal dialogue with Germans, which became more vital as he became more disappointed with Israel. The narrative directed at the German reader, describing how Scholem had left German culture for the sake of renewing Hebrew culture, paradoxically prepared his return to Germany.

The place of memory of the Holocaust in both of his worlds in the period around the publication of the book is also interesting. The Holocaust was probably the central event in Scholem's life, and it is also central to this book. In Germany, the Holocaust as a historical event began to seep into broad public consciousness in 1979, to no small degree following the broadcast of the popular American television series *Holocaust*—which, by telling the story of the Weiss family, humanized the victims of the Holocaust for the younger generation of Germans and increased awareness and the public feeling of responsibility for it. In contrast, Begin's rise to power in 1977 symbolized the instrumentalization of the Holocaust and its harnessing to the political needs of the Israeli right.[22] Although Scholem frequently defended Israel's official political stand in public, especially from attacks on the part of the German left, among his friends he did not conceal his negative attitude toward the winds blowing in Israel beginning in 1977—an attitude also visible in his actions. This attitude developed as he felt a growing closeness to Germany and Berlin, which began to take shape for him as the place of Jewish memory. Although he does not discuss this explicitly, his memoirs of his youth are permeated with events that were of current significance at the time of the book's publication, and in his words about the past one can sense his disappointment with the present. This feeling is well expressed in a passage from the book that has been quoted above: "I no longer pinned any hope on the familiar combination known as 'Deutsch-Judentum,' whose full meaning is not conveyed by the rendering as "German Jewry," and I hoped for the renewal of Judaism only with its rebirth in the Land of Israel (and by rights my readers may ask whether I retain this hope to this day, after sixty years, and I have no answer, in the light of everything that has happened, except mere hope (*tochelet*), as a wise man has said: extended hope makes the heart sick)."[23]

The writing of an autobiography not only takes place in the past and the present, but it also links the two levels: the older writer of the book, who is also its younger hero. This strange coexistence leads to a paradoxical encounter between the two on a stage that was invented particularly for that purpose. The paradox created by this encounter can be resolved only by donning a Janus mask that separates the present from the past but makes it possible for them to share that stage.[24] During such an encounter an effort is sometimes made to resolve the paradox or close a certain gap for the writer in the present, the source of which lies in the changes that have taken place since the time in the past with which the autobiography deals.[25] The young Scholem's desire to convert the periphery into a center of Jewish life by building a new center in Jerusalem did not succeed, and Berlin—the city he had abandoned—never relaxed its grip on his soul. The two worlds that constitute the stage of the autobiographer—that of the past and that of the present—in this case were not only far distant from one another temporally, geographically, culturally, and politically, but they were also separated by the historical events that Scholem and the Jewish people experienced. Perhaps the only way for him to resolve this inner conflict, which threatened to destroy his world, was to live dialectically between the poles, to be called at the same time Gershom and Gerhard, Shalom and Scholem, and to change the stage and the makeup permanently: to be a "metaphysical clown."[26]

NOTES

Introduction: The Metaphysical Clown

1. Ozick 1983, 148.

2. See the remarks of Betty Scholem in Scholem and Scholem 1989, 516.

3. Gershom Scholem to Harry Heymann, letter dated January 27, 1917, in Scholem 1994, 68.

4. Gershom Scholem to Aharon Heller, July 17, 1917, ibid., 83.

5. Strauss was the secretary of the Zionist leader and journalist Kurt Blumenfeld until his death in 1963, and she helped Scholem type the German version of *From Berlin to Jerusalem*, which he dictated to her. According to Strauss, she worked for Scholem until his death in 1982. See Strauss and Voss 2004, 88.

6. Scholem 2012a, 1.

7. A humorous example of Scholem's self-knowledge can be found in a letter to his mother from October 30, 1930. While on vacation in Meran, Italy, Betty Scholem was robbed, and in a letter to her son she reported the incident and her discontent with the local police officer, who wanted to know her mother's maiden name for the report. In his response Scholem wrote: "You should know: little superfluous scraps of information like this are likely to be of great use to scholars. If a scholar should ever wonder whether Scholem actually lived, or whether he was a legendary figure (the thunder god), then this entry in the police files of Meran could light his path through the thicket. Here he will find confirmation of the information that his mother's name was Betty, and of the information reported regarding his maternal grandparents" (Scholem and Scholem 1989, 226–27).

8. For Habermas's own description of his relationship with Scholem, see Habermas 2007.

9. The only previous biography (Biale 1979) was published in Scholem's lifetime.

10. An English translation was published in Scholem 1997a, 51–71.

Part 1: "Continuity of the Crisis"

This epigraph comes from Scholem 1990, 54.

1. Cultural Contexts

1. Bergmann 1927, 325.

2. Scholem 1982b, 193. This account presented here is based on ibid., 193–95. For a

parallel description see the English translation of the shorter German version of Scholem's autobiography (Scholem 2012a, 161–74).

3. Scholem 2012a, 163.

4. Ibid., 168–69.

5. Scholem 1982b, 201.

6. Up to this point in the letter, it appears in his autobiography (Scholem 1982b, 213).

7. *Gartenlaube* (garden arbor) was the title of a family newspaper published from 1853 to 1944. At its height, it was extremely popular and had a very large circulation.

8. Scholem to Kraft, December 17, 1924, in Scholem 1994, 222.

9. For more on this, see Aschheim 1982; M. Brenner 1998.

10. On the movement of these cultural centers, see Z. Shavit 1993.

11. Scholem 2012a, 43–44.

12. Ibid., 94.

13. Scholem 1990, 463.

14. Scholem 2012b, 118–19.

15. Agnon 1918.

16. Scholem 2000, 244.

17. Scholem 1982b, 134; Laor 1998, 126–27.

18. The published translations were of Agnon's "Ma'ase Rabbi Gadiel Hatinok"; "Ma'alot Umordot," "Ma'ase Azriel Moshe Shomer Hasfarim," and "Beit Hakenesset Hagadol."

19. Agnon 2000, 293.

20. M. Brenner 1998, 198–99.

21. Shaba 1990, 196.

22. Scholem 1982b, 187. See also Grosche and Rohde 1991, 38–43; Laor 1993, 80–81.

23. Scholem 1997a, 46.

24. Scholem 2012a, 157.

25. Scholem, "Tagebücher: Ende 1922, Juli 1934–Nov. 34; 1935–48," 19, file 265/22, Gershom Scholem Archive, National Library of Israel, Archives Department (SchA).

26. Scholem 1995c, 214.

27. Buber commissioned the translation, which was published in the fourth issue of *Der Jude*. See Scholem 1981c, 82, and 2000, 430.

28. Scholem 2000, 375–76. In this matter Scholem was influenced by Ahad Haam's essay "Etza tova" (Good advice).

29. Scholem, "Tagebücher: Ende 1922, Juli 1934–Nov. 34; 1935–48," 19, file 265/22, SchA.

30. Ibid., 95–97.

31. Ibid., 202 (my emphasis).

32. The letter was reprinted in Mosès 1994. For an English translation, see Scholem 1997a, 27–29.

33. Morag 1993, 216–17.

34. Scholem 1997a, 27.

35. Ibid.

36. Ibid., 28 (my emphasis).
37. Scholem 2012b, 95.
38. Scholem 1997a, 28–29.
39. Scholem 1995b, 59.
40. Scholem 2012b, 96.
41. See Scholem 1974d, 273–75.
42. Morag 1993, 211.
43. Katz 2008, 146; Myers 1995, 40.
44. Scholem 1982b, 222.
45. Katz 2001, 439.
46. See ibid., 221–22; Katz 20080, 150–51.
47. Myers 1995, 37–40; Katz 2014, 131–32.
48. Scholem 1937, 8.
49. Ahad Haam 1950, 106.
50. Bialik 1968, 35. See also Rubin 2004, 249–61.
51. Bialik 1968, 37.
52. Ibid., 36.
53. Ibid., 40.
54. Meir 2004, 120–24. See also Bartal 1997, 78–79.
55. Bartal 1997, 79–81.
56. Bartal 2000, 318–22.
57. Scholem's letter to Bialik was published in Scholem 1975b, 63.
58. Bialik to Scholem, July 20, 1925, in Bialik 1937–39, 48–49.
59. See, for example, Scholem 1938b and 1944a.
60. "Redemption through Sin," in Scholem 1971, 78–141; Scholem 1957c. On the background of these works in the idea of kinus see N. Zadoff 2007, 301–13.
61. His encyclopedia entries were collected and reprinted in Scholem 1974a.
62. Quoted in Mekitz Nirdamim 1861.
63. Quoted in Mekitzei Nirdamim 1964, 23.
64. The complex relations between Scholem and Buber are beyond the scope of the present discussion. For our purposes here, most important are Scholem's remarks about Buber in his memoirs, because "although our views diverged on many topics, to the degree that I got deeper into primary sources, I always respected and also admired Buber's personality, in which there was not a bit of dogmatism, and his heart was open to other opinions. In the years before my immigration we met many times, and he followed my path with attention and sympathy. His weaknesses did not escape me, but memories of the many conversations between us about Hasidism and Kabbalah . . . and the hopes he pinned on me, balanced Walter Benjamin's opinion [on Buber], which was mostly negative." (Scholem 1982b, 75).
65. Buber 1911.
66. Scholem 1975b, 457.
67. Buber 1906 and 1908. See also Scholem 2012a, 44; Mendes-Flohr 1991a, 96–109.
68. Gries 1990, 51; Laor 2002, 61–62.

69. For more on this meeting, see Scholem 1995c, 201–3.

70. Buber 1916.

71. Mendes-Flohr 1986, 121.

72. Some of the correspondence has been published in Buber 1990 and Scholem 1994.

73. Scholem 1917.

74. Scholem to Buber, July 2, 1925, Buber correspondence file, SchA.

75. Scholem 2012b, 127.

76. Quoted in M. Brenner 1998, 115.

77. See Meir 2004, 130–31.

78. [Klatzkin] 1929, 10. See also Ahad Haam 1950, 104–5.

79. Klatzkin to Scholem, May 3, 1924, and May 27, 1925, Klatzkin correspondence file, SchA. This project was not implemented.

80. Klatzkin to Scholem, May 27, 1925, ibid.

81. This refers to the *Jewish Encyclopedia*, which was published in twelve volumes in the United States in the period 1901–6.

82. Klatzkin to Scholem, August 25, 1925, Klatzkin correspondence file, SchA.

83. Simhoni to Scholem, February 12, 1926, ibid.

84. Simhoni to Scholem, March 10, 1926, ibid. A copy of this letter and Scholem's reply was written by hand on Simhoni's letter of February 12, 1926 (ibid.).

85. Scholem to Klatzkin, May 3, 1928, ibid.

86. Ibid.

87. Klatzkin to Scholem, September 20, 1928, ibid.

88. Scholem to Klatzkin, November 15, 1928, ibid.

89. Klatzkin to Scholem, December 13, 1928, ibid.

90. Klatzkin to Scholem, January 19, 1932, ibid.

91. Scholem to Klatzkin, January 7, 1932, ibid.

92. Scholem to Klatzkin, December 22, 1932, ibid.

93. M. Brenner 1998, 118.

94. Engelhardt 2006, 305.

95. See Abrams 2000; Katz 2008, 154–59.

96. On this turning point in Shocken's life, see Schocken 1989.

97. David 2003, 112–15.

98. Schocken 1989. See also Poppel 1973, 23.

99. Scholem to Schocken, January 18, 1918, in Scholem 1994, 138–40.

100. Scholem 1982b 115.

101. Laor 1995, 103, and 1998, 197; Hirschfeld 1994.

102. See David 2003, 181–83.

103. See Dahm 1993, 291–96; Schneider 1965, 37–44.

104. Scholem 1933a and 1933b.

105. Schneider to Scholem, January 26, 1933, in Scholem 1994, 414.

106. Scholem to Schneider, April 6, 1933, in ibid., 250–51.

107. Spitzer to Scholem, June 6, 1933, Salman Schocken correspondence file, SchA.

108. Scholem 1933–34; Kalisker 1933–34.

109. Ben Nachman 1935–36; Scholem 1936–37 and 1937–38.

110. Spitzer to Scholem, September 28, 1933, Salman Schocken correspondence file, SchA.

111. For more on this series, see Dahm 1993, 326–29; David 2003, 221–22.

112. Scholem to Spitzer, October 9, 1933, Salman Schocken correspondence file, SchA; Spitzer to Scholem, October 19, 1933, ibid.

113. Scholem 1935 and 1938b.

114. Scholem 1936.

115. Spitzer to Schocken, November 20, 1934, in Scholem and Weiss 2012, 335.

116. Spitzer to Scholem, November 29, 1934, and Scholem to Spitzer, December 13, 1934, Schocken correspondence file, SchA.

117. Scholem to Spitzer, December 17, 1934, in Scholem 1994, 257.

118. Poppel 1973, 33.

119. In 1941 Scholem's planned monograph on Kabbalah was finally published neither in German nor in Hebrew, but in English, and it became a cornerstone in Kabbalah scholarship (Scholem 1941). Scholem wrote the book in German, and it was translated into English by his friend, Georg Lichtheim.

120. See U. Cohen 2007, 84–87.

121. Scholem and Weiss 2012, 182–83.

122. David 2003, 401.

123. Scholem, "Tagebücher: Ende 1922, Juli 1934–Nov. 34; 1935–48," 114–15, file 265/22, SchA.

124. Scholem to Reinhold Scholem, March 25, 1974, in Scholem 1999, 97.

125. Scholem 1957b.

126. Scholem 1938a, 13.

127. According to the agreement between Scholem and the National and University Library, which was signed in Jerusalem on May 24, 1965, the university agreed to pay Scholem $45,000 in payments of $200 a month (file 22, SchA). According to the agreement, Scholem's books were to remain in his home until his death, after which they would be transferred to the library, where they would be given a separate room.

128. Scholem 1995c, 381.

129. Benjamin 1968, 60.

130. Dan 2010, 20.

131. Beit-Arié 1994, 125.

2. A Political Circle: Brit Shalom

1. Bergmann 1927, 132–33.

2. Scholem, Bergmann, Kohn, Magnes, Radler-Feldman, and Schapiro 1926a and 1926b.

3. Ibid. See also Kedar 1976 266.

4. Kedar 1976, 232–34.

5. Quoted in ibid., 248–49.

6. File 253, SchA. The list of members in 1930 contains thirty-eight names.

7. Kedar 1976, 234.

8. Ibid., 234–36. See also Ratzabi 2002.

9. See Lavsky 1996, 162–80. On the idea of Bildung, see Aschheim 2007, 14; Mosse 1985 and 1990, 126–28.

10. Ahad Haam 1997, 267.

11. See, for example, Scholem 1995c, 80–81, and 2000, 29. On Ahad Haam's idea of a spiritual center, see Zipperstein 1993, 67–104.

12. Scholem 1995c, 82 and 111.

13. Scholem's diary entry dated August 18, 1916 (Scholem 1995c, 387–88).

14. Scholem 2012a, 56.

15. Ratzabi 2009, 260–66. This teaching of Buber's was also a source of disappointment for his disciples and of criticism that Buber did not take the path that he himself had laid out.

16. Buber 1911. See also Mendes-Flohr 1986 and 1991a, 85.

17. See Anidjar 1996; Biale 2001, 107–10; Huss 2005, 145–47, and 2007; Raz-Krakotzkin 1999, 48–52, and 2002, 100–5.

18. Here Anidjar and, following him, Raz-Krakotzkin (2002, 100), base themselves on one sentence from Scholem (1941, 365), in which he describes the feeling of the reader of kabbalistic texts.

19. Raz-Krakotzkin 2002, 100.

20. See, for example, the entries dated November 26, 1914, and January 23, 1915 (Scholem 1995c, 61 and 83).

21. Ibid., 195–96.

22. Scholem's diary entry dated January 4, 1916 (ibid., 226).

23. Scholem's diary entry dated March 8, 1916 (ibid., 281).

24. On this view of the school of Ahad Haam, see Ratzabi 2009, 259–60; Anita Shapira 1992, 18–19; Zipperstein 1993, 77–79.

25. On Scholem's study of Arabic, see, for example, the diary entry for September 10, 1916 (Scholem 1995c, 396). The list of books he brought to Palestine when he immigrated includes at least ten Arabic grammar books. There were also over thirty books in his private library on Arabic and Islamic literature in German. See Scholem, "Verzeichnis der Bücher des Dr. Gerhard Scholem (1923)," 5–6, SchA.

26. *Hashiloach* was the Hebrew newspaper established by Ahad Haam in Odessa in 1896. In 1920 it was transferred to Jerusalem, and Joseph Klausner became its editor until it ceased publication in 1927. During its Jerusalem years it became identified with the Revisionist camp.

27. Scholem, "Der Zionismus wird seine Katastrophe überleben (Ende 1924)," folder 52, SchA.

28. Avraham Shapira called these passages "Zionist esoterica," based on what he heard from Scholem himself (Shapira 1998, 10). Shapira edited some of these passages in a Hebrew translation (Scholem 1990). Many other passages written between 1924 and 1932 are in file I-II/277 and other folders, SchA.

29. Weidner 2003, 105. Weidner discusses this period in Scholem's life at length on pages 104–29.

30. See Y. Shavit 1991, 113.

31. Scholem 1982b 195.

32. Scholem 1997a, 27–29.

33. See Herzog 2009, 232.

34. See Halkin 2014, 195–97; Anita Shapira 1992, 154–56; Y. Shavit 1988, 28–57.

35. Jabotinsky 2011, 261–62.

36. Lavsky 1996, 162–67.

37. Anita Shapira 1992, 163–64.

38. Scholem, "Die Verzweiflung des Siegenden," April 12, 1926, 1, file 277 I/57, SchA.

39. See Anita Shapira 1992, 83–85. The declarations in support of Jewish immigration and settlement in Palestine were the Balfour Declaration of 1917 and the British mandate, which was declared at San Remo in April 1920 and went into effect in September 1923.

40. Scholem 1928b, 644.

41. Scholem 1928c, 139.

42. In a diary entry dated May 22, 1915, Scholem even identifies himself with the figure of the messiah, but after a few months he changed his opinion (1995c 120–21 and 158).

43. See Scholem 1957c. See also Scholem 1971, 35–36.

44. Ratzabi 2002, 176. This was Scholem's view after Hitler's rise to power and the Holocaust. On the complex attitude of Zionism toward the messianic idea, see Kolat 1998; Y. Shavit 1991.

45. Morris 2001, 111–16.

46. Anita Shapira 1992, 174.

47. Sela 1994, 61. See also H. Cohen 2015.

48. Anita Shapira 1992, 177.

49. These articles were published in Scholem 1990, 68–89.

50. Ibid., 74–82.

51. Ibid., 75.

52. Ibid., 76.

53. Ibid., 79.

54. Scholem 1981c, 173–74.

55. Scholem 1990, 81–82.

56. Anita Shapira 1992, 186–94; Y. Shavit 1988, 60; Shimoni 1995, 247.

57. Quoted in Anita Shapira 1992, 395–96, note 74; see also 192–93.

58. Scholem 1990, 69.

59. Ibid., 70.

60. "Lesha'aruriyat hasifriyah hamikhlalanit" 1931. The international commission here refers to the arrival of Sir John Hope Simpson in Palestine in 1930 to examine the subject of Jewish immigration and settlement. On these events in Palestine, see Morris 2001, 116–17.

61. Chaim Ariav to Scholem, February 24, 1930, quoted in "Lesha'aruriyat hasifriyah hamikhlalanit" 1931.

62. Babakov 1931.

63. Scholem 1931. See also Biale 1979, 179.

64. Scholem 2003, 88.

65. Scholem to Buber, May 25, 1930, in Buber 1990, 343.

66. On the history of this association, see Heller 2004.

67. Dan 2007, 294.

68. Gershom Scholem, "Brit Shalom: Re'aiyon im professor Gershom Shalom," interview by Yehuda Kaveh, May 1972, Interview Number (91) 6, 6, Hebrew University of Jerusalem Oral History Division (OHD).

69. Ibid.

70. Scholem 1990, 88.

71. Scholem 1975b, 49–51; and 1995b, 56–57.

72. Scholem, 1995b, 121.

73. Scholem, "Brit Shalom," 12–13, OHD.

74. Scholem 1980b, 22.

75. Ibid.

76. For example, the Pilegesh circle. See N. Zadoff 2008.

3. Religious Contexts

1. Scholem 1958, 215. For a Hebrew translation, see Scholem 1990, 37.

2. Scholem 1995b, 116. See also B. Schäfer 2003, 135–41; Scholem 2012a, 78–79.

3. Scholem to Buber, June 2, 1925, Buber correspondence file, SchA.

4. Scholem 1975b, 63.

5. Z. Shavit 1999, 91.

6. Scholem to Kraft, December 17, 1924, in Scholem 1994, 222. The passage is quoted in full in chapter 1.

7. See Huss 2005 and 2007; Meir 2011.

8. Scholem 1937, 9.

9. Huss 2005, 142–44.

10. Ibid., 145.

11. Scholem 1997a, 4–5. For the German original, see Scholem 1994, 471–72.

12. Scholem 1938a, 13. The English version lacks the tendentious tone of the Hebrew: "we shall succeed in reconstructing the origins of Jewish mysticism and in determining its various manifestations and mutations" (Scholem 1937, 12).

13. Huss 2005, 145–46.

14. Scholem 1941, 350. My interpretation here is in the direction of the words of Shaul Magid on cultural secularization in Scholem (see Magid 2011, 515).

15. Mendes-Flohr 1991a, 344, and 1991b, 234. Mendes-Flohr also placed Scholem among the members of the circle, but, as I show below, there is good reason to assume that he was not a regular participant. On the background of the formation of the circle, see Mendes-Flohr 1991b, 233–37.

16. For the minutes of this meeting, see Mendes-Flohr 1991a, 344–46, and 1991b, 237–39.

17. I base the following remarks mainly on Scholem's diary entry of July 13, 1939, in Scholem, "Tagebücher: Ende 1922, Juli 1934–Nov. 34; 1935–48," 51, file 265/22, SchA. This entry contains the only evidence that suggests Scholem was a guest of the circle and not a central figure in it, and this evidence emerges at the beginning of the entry in his German diary: "I agreed to give an introductory lecture in Magnes's home for *his* circle, the Yoke, about the meaning of what we can still connect to the word 'Torah' today" (my emphasis). As noted, this finding complements and sharpens Mendes-Flohr's observations and reconciles the contradiction in the choice of the circle's name to which he refers: "In the light of the religious anarchism which Scholem believed characterized his colleagues, it is seemingly paradoxical that they chose to call the group Ha'Ol (the Yoke)—a name expressly taken from a Rabbinic Midrash" (Mendes-Flohr 1991b, 239–40). If Scholem did not belong to this circle, his anarchistic position does not apply to the entire group. This is also consistent with the criticism that Scholem received from the members of the circle, as discussed at length below.

18. Scholem, "Tagebücher: Ende 1922, Juli 1934–Nov. 34; 1935–48," 51 file 265/22, SchA.

19. Ibid.

20. Quoted in Mendes-Flohr 1991a, 345.

21. Quoted in ibid.

22. Quoted in ibid., 345–46.

23. Quoted in ibid., 346.

24. See, for example, Scholem 1997a, 16–17 and 86, and 2012b, 32–33.

25. See, for example, the diary entry in which he discusses Herzl's *The Jewish State* (Scholem (1995c, 81). See also the diary entry of December 25, 1918, in Scholem 2000, 423–24. On Werner and Gershom Scholem see: M. Zadoff 2018.

26. Scholem 2012a, 53–54. See also Scholem 1981c, 6–7.

27. Mendes-Flohr 1991a, 347.

28. On this organization, see Heller 2004. In an interview with Meir Lemed in 1964, Scholem claimed that he still advocated anarchism as a political doctrine, but with the knowledge that it could not be implemented in reality (Scholem 1995b, 122).

29. Scholem, "Tagebücher: Ende 1922, Juli 1934–Nov. 34; 1935–48," 52, file 265/22, SchA.

30. See Dan 2007, 293–98; Shedletzky 2007.

31. Scholem 2012b, 33–34 and 275.

32. Scholem returned to this paradox several times in his thought and research, including in his ten aphorisms on Kabbalah. For the original German with commentary, see Biale 1985, 73–76 and 86–88.

33. Scholem 1997a, 271.

34. See Scholem 2012a, 80.

35. See Talmon 1970, 157.

36. Scholem 1990, 149.

Part 2: The Unparalleled Catastrophe

This epigraph comes from Scholem 1997a, 162.

4. Responses to the Holocaust

1. Quoted in N. Zadoff and Meir 2005, 1:382.

2. Porat 1990, 34–40; Weitz 1994, 31 and 35.

3. Weitz 1994, 27–28.

4. Porat 1990, 40.

5. Ibid., 78.

6. See Ofer 1996, 473–74; Weitz 1994, 49–53.

7. Porat 1984, 100.

8. Ibid., 120–24; Porat 1986, 120–30.

9. Zameret 2009, 280.

10. The pamphlet was published as Dinur 1943. The quotes here are from the reprinted version in Dinur 1948, 14–34. Identification of the participants is based on Porat 1984, 123–24, note 67, and 1986, 119.

11. Dinur 1948, 18.

12. Ibid., 20.

13. Ibid., 22.

14. Ibid., 23.

15. Ibid. See also Zameret 2009, 281–82, and note 77.

16. Dinaburg was Dinur's original name.

17. Scholem to Dinaburg [Dinur], April 1, 1943, file 69/6, Dinur collection, Central Archives for the History of the Jewish People (CAHJP).

18. Zameret 2009, 282–87.

19. See Talmon 1970, 160–61.

20. Weitz 1996, 377. See also Ofer 1996, 487.

21. Porat 1986, 106–7; Ofer 1996, 483.

22. Scholem, "Tagebücher: Ende 1922, Juli 1934–Nov. 34; 1935–48," 66, file 265/22, SchA.

23. Nordau 1909, 153.

24. Ahad Haam 1997, 267.

25. Scholem 1957c and 1973b.

26. Scholem, "Tagebücher: Ende 1922, Juli 1934–Nov. 34; 1935–48," 65, file 265/22, SchA.

27. For the Hebrew original of the article, see Scholem 1944b. In the following I will quote from the English translation, which appeared in: Scholem 1997a, 51–71.

28. Scholem 1997a, 51.

29. Ibid., 53–55.

30. Ibid., 55.

31. Ibid., 56.

32. Ibid., 56–57.

33. Ibid.

34. Ibid., 57.

35. Ibid., 59.

36. Ibid., 61.

37. Ibid., 66.

38. Ibid., 67.

39. Ibid., 66.

40. Ibid., 67.

41. Ibid., 69.

42. Ibid., 70.

43. Ibid., 70–71.

44. M. Brenner 2010, 166.

45. Bergmann 1985, 640.

46. Scholem to Benjamin, June 30 1939, in Benjamin and Scholem 1989, 255–56.

47. See Morris 2001, 121–60; Anita Shapira 1992, 219–76.

48. Anita Shapira 1992, 235.

49. Ibid., 246.

50. Ibid., 247–49.

51. See Reichman 2008, 3:250–270; Anita Shapira 1992, 253–54.

52. Anita Shapira 1992, 288.

53. Ibid., 286–88.

54. See Gelber 1982, 388.

55. Ibid., 386–88.

56. Scholem 1975b, 61.

57. Scholem 1997a, 69.

58. Ibid., 68 and 70.

59. Scholem to Spiegel, May 8, 1945, in Scholem 1994, 442.

60. Scholem 1997a, 56.

61. Scholem 1980a, 4.

62. Scholem 1981c, 109.

63. This lecture was published in the bulletin of the Leo Baeck Institute. For an English translation, see Scholem 1971, 304–13.

64. Scholem 1981c, 109.

65. Scholem 1971, 311.

66. Ibid., 312.

67. Scholem, "Tagebücher: Ende 1922, Juli 1934–Nov. 34; 1935–48," 74, file 265/22, SchA.

68. Ibid., 79–80.

5. The Journey to Salvage Looted Books and Manuscripts

1. Beit-Arié 1994, 120–21.

2. Honigmann 2002, 112.

3. Poste 1958, 334.

4. See Gallas 2013; Herman 2008, 149–88; Pomrenze 1997 and 2002.

5. Kurtz 2006, 154; Schidorsky 2006, 198.

6. Roth 1944.

7. Ibid., 257.

8. See Herman 2008, 45–47.

9. Baron 1945, 6–7; Cohen Grossman 2002, 149–50; Kurtz 2006, 154–55.

10. Commission on European Jewish Cultural Reconstruction 1946.

11. Peiss 1946; Waite 2002, 216–18.

12. Magnes to Weizmann, May 4, 1945, file 2056, Magnes Collection, CAHJP.

13. Hava'adah Lehatzalat Otzrot Hagolah, minutes of meeting May 6, 1945, file 2057, Magnes Collection, CAHJP.

14. Ibid.

15. Weltsch 1946.

16. Ibid.

17. Ibid.

18. Senator to Fekete, January 6, 1946, file 2056, Magnes Collection, CAHJP.

19. Ibid.

20. Hava'adah Lehatzalat Otzrot Hagolah, minutes of meeting on January 24, 1946, file 23, SchA.

21. Hava'adah Lehatzalat Otzrot Hagolah, va'adat mishne lekvi'at yachasim im mosdot acherim," minutes of meeting on March 31, 1946, file 2057, Magnes Collection, CAHJP.

22. Letter of appointment of the members of the legal committee, January 25, 1946, file 2056, Magnes Collection, CAHJP. On this committee, see also Schidorsky 2008, 240–43.

23. "Tazkir hava'adah hamishpatit she'al yad hava'ad lehatzalat otzrot hagolah," file 212/1–2, Otzrot Hagolah files 793, National Library of Israel Archive (NLIA). On the report of the legal committee and its work, see Schidorsky 2006, 198–203, and 2008.

24. "Tazkir hava'adah hamishpatit she'al yad hava'ad lehatzalat otzrot hagolah," 2, file 212/1–2, Otzrot Hagolah files 793, NLIA.

25. On this point the report is based on a pre-Nazi German law, which states that "a person who kills an heir maliciously is not worthy of inheriting, and the estate does not pass to him. It is also based on the words of Elijah to Ahab in the story of the vineyard of Naboth (1 Kings 21:19): "Hast thou killed, and also taken possession?" And it is based on precedents from the slaughter of the Armenians in Turkey, where it had been determined that property with no heirs would be transferred to the community to which the owner had belonged, as well as on the new Greek law for the restoration of stolen property to the Jewish community ("Tazkir hava'adah hamishpatit she'al yad hava'ad lehatzalat otzrot hagolah," file 212/1–2, Otzrot Hagolah files 793, NLIA).

26. Ibid., 3–4.

27. Ibid., 5.

28. Ibid., 6.

29. Ibid., 8.

30. "Zikhron dvarim shel hava'adah levchirat chaverim lamishlachat shetetze le'eropa bekesher lehatzalat otzrot hagolah," January 28, 1946, file 2056, Magnes Collection, CAHJP.

31. Schidorsky 2008, 386.

32. Scholem to Fekete, February 16, 1946, quoted in ibid., 346–48.

33. Magnes to Scholem, March 1, 1946, quoted in ibid., 349.

34. Scholem to Magnes, March 3, 1946, quoted in ibid., 349–50.

35. Fekete to Scholem and Yaari, March 14, 1946, quoted in ibid., 350.

36. The Hebrew University to Scholem and Yaari, March 21, 1946, file 212/1–2, Otzrot Hagolah files 793, NLIA.

37. Ibid.

38. Greenleigh to Magnes, April 2, 1946, file 23, SchA.

39. Bentwich to Magnes, April 12–14, 1946, file 2056, Magnes Collection, CAHJP.

40. Auslander 2005, 243–45.

41. Mandel 2002, 53–55.

42. Scholem and Yaari to the Hebrew University, April 19, 1946, file 23, SchA. See also Schidorsky 2008, 385–89.

43. Scholem and Yaari to the Hebrew University, April 30, 1946, file 23, SchA.

44. Ibid.

45. Scholem to Senator, April 24, 1946, file 23, SchA.

46. Ibid. See also Schidorsky 2008, 386.

47. Scholem to the Hebrew University, telegram, May 8, 1946, file 23, SchA.

48. Schidorsky 2008, 388.

49. Scholem to the Hebrew University, May 8, 1946, file 23, SchA. At that time Magnes had gone to the United States to, among other things, meet people in Washington about the Jewish books.

50. According to Yaari's report to the Hebrew University, quoted in Schidorsky 2008, 388.

51. Scholem, "Minesi'otai bishlihut be'eropa 1946. April 10–August 26," 9, file 265/24, SchA.

52. Scholem to the Hebrew University, May 11 and 22, 1946, file 23, SchA.

53. See Schidorsky 2008, 351.

54. Scholem to the Hebrew University, May 22, 1946, quoted in Schidorsky 2008, 353.

55. "Memorandum Submitted by the Commission on European Jewish Cultural Reconstruction to Rabbi Philip S. Bernstein," file 212/1–2, Otzrot Hagolah files 793, NLIA. According to this memorandum, the recommendation was based on the many letters that Pinson and Pomrenze had sent to the commission from Germany.

56. Ibid., 4.

57. Scholem to the Hebrew University, May 22, 1946, file 23, SchA.

58. Scholem to Magnes, May 22, 1946, file 2060, Magnes Collection, CAHJP.

59. Scholem to Senator, April 24, 1946, file 23, SchA.

60. Scholem to Magnes, May 22, 1946, file 2060, Magnes Collection, CAHJP.

61. See Scholem and Scholem 1989.

62. Heinz Pflaum (later Hiram Peri) was a professor of Romance philology at the Hebrew University and a friend of Scholem's family.

63. Scholem, "Minesi'otai bishlihut be'eropa 1946. April 10–August 26," 15, file 265/24, SchA.

64. Ibid., 14.

65. Scholem's report to the Hebrew University on his journey to Europe, quoted in Schidorsky 2008, 390.

66. Scholem, "Minesi'otai bishlichut be'eropa 1946. April 10–August 26," 17, file 265/24, SchA.

67. Scholem had lived in Bern for about a year and a half, beginning in 1918, in the company of Walter Benjamin. See Scholem 1981c, 52–85, and 2012a, 106–15.

68. Scholem, "Minesi'otai bishlichut be'eropa 1946. April 10–August 26," 18, file 265/24, SchA.

69. Ibid.

70. Ibid., 19.

71. Ibid., 20.

72. Ibid., 21.

73. Scholem to Hurwitz, June 8, 1949, in Scholem 1994, 318.

74. Bergmann to Senator, April 12, 1946, file 212/1, Otzrot Hagolah files 793, NLIA.

75. Senator to Scholem, April 18, 1946, ibid.

76. Scholem's report to the Hebrew University on his journey to Europe, quoted in Schidorsky 2008, 359–62. See also D. Shavit 1997, 132.

77. Rupnow 2002, 25–26.

78. Braunová 2000, 163.

79. Scholem, "Minesi'otai bishlichut be'eropa 1946. April 10–August 26," 27, file 265/24, SchA.

80. Scholem, "Yoman al sichotai beprag," 2, file 212/1–2, Otzrot Hagolah files 793, NLIA.

81. Ibid.

82. See Schidorsky 2008, 381.

83. Scholem, "Yoman al sichotai beprag," 3, file 212/1–2, Otzrot Hagolah files 793, NLIA.

84. Ibid.

85. Scholem to the Hebrew University, July 2, 1946, HUA, Scholem file, 1946. See also Scholem's report to the Hebrew University on his journey to Europe, quoted in Schidorsky 2008, 357.

86. Schidorsky 2008, 359–61. For a list of collections that were transferred to Niemes, see ibid.

87. Scholem to the Hebrew University, July 2, 1946, Gershom Scholem files, Hebrew University of Jerusalem Archive (HUA).

88. Scholem's report to the Hebrew University on his journey to Europe, quoted in Schidorsky 2008, 396–97. After Scholem's return, it was decided to focus the effort on recovering the books from the collections in Czechoslovakia. Indeed, many books were shipped to the National Library in Jerusalem in the following years, including parts of the great collection in the castle of Niemes and other castles. See Schidorsky 2006, 204–12; Weiss 2015.

89. Scholem to the Hebrew University, June 23, 1946, Gershom Scholem files, HUA.

90. Scholem to Magnes, June 30, 1946, file 2060, Magnes collection, CAHJP.

91. Scholem, "Minesi'otai bishlihut be'eropa 1946. April 10–August 26," 31, file 265/24, SchA.

92. Ibid.

93. Weltsch 1946.

94. Poste 1958, 340.

95. Pomrenze 2002, 2.

96. Pomrenze 1997, 15–16; Poste 1958, 351–53.

97. Poste 1958, 342.

98. Dawidowicz 1989, 315.

99. Lewinsky 2008, 54–58.

100. "Offenbach Archival Depot (OAD) Monthly Report," April 30, 1946, 5, National Archives and Record Administration (NARA).

101. Ibid.

102. "Offenbach Archival Depot (OAD) Monthly Report," June 31, 1946, 8 and 11, NARA; Poste 1958, 361.

103. Scholem's report to the Hebrew University on his journey to Europe, quoted in Schidorsky 2008, 367.

104. Scholem, "Minesi'otai bishlihut be'eropa 1946. April 10–August 26," 33, file 265/24, SchA.

105. Ibid.

106. Ibid., 34

107. Ibid., 34–35.

108. Scholem, "Resúmé der Besprechungen mit Capt. Benkowitz, Direktor des Archival Depot in Offenbach und Prof. Pinson, vom 4.–7.7.1946, 9.7.1946," 1, file 2060, Magnes Collection, CAHJP.

109. Ibid., 3.

110. Scholem's report to the Hebrew University on his journey to Europe, quoted in Schidorsky 2008, 365.

111. Scholem, "Resúmé der Besprechungen mit Capt. Benkowitz, Direktor des Archival Depot in Offenbach und Prof. Pinson, vom 4.–7.7.1946, 9.7.1946," 3, file 2060, Magnes Collection, CAHJP.

112. Scholem to Magnes, July 9, 1946, file 23, SchA.

113. Scholem to Wise, August 23, 1946, file 2060, Magnes Collection, CAHJP.

114. Scholem to Magnes, July 14, 1946, file 2060, Magnes Collection, CAHJP.

115. Scholem, "Minesi'otai bishlihut be'eropa 1946. April 10–August 26," 36, file 265/24, SchA.

116. Ibid., 40.

117. Magnes to Scholem, July 17, 1946, file 2060, Magnes Collection, CAHJP.

118. See Jaspers 1947.

119. Scholem to Simon, July 19, 1946, Simon correspondence file, SchA.

120. See Dahm 1993, 291–99. On Schneider and his publishing house, see also Schneider [1965].

121. On Loewenthal and his relations with Schneider, see Dahm 1993, 422–23.

122. Schneider [1965], 80–91; Waldmüller 1988.

123. Jaspers 1945, 3 (my emphasis). See also Schneider [1965], 82.

124. Jaspers 1945, 4–5.

125. For a survey of the central publications that were part of this phenomenon, see Laurien 2002.

126. Scholem to Simon, July 19, 1946, Simon correspondence file, SchA. Despite these words, the journal became one of the most influential philosophical and cultural publications in postwar Germany (see Laurien 2002, 64).

127. See Benzenhöfer 2007, 152–60.

128. The magazine, which was founded by Buber and Franz Rosenzweig, was intended to be a forum for Jewish-Christian dialogue, and it was edited by a Jew (Buber), a Catholic (Wittig), and a Protestant (Weizsäcker).

129. Scholem to Simon, July 19, 1946, Simon correspondence file, SchA.

130. Ibid.

131. Schneider to Scholem, August 12, 1965, Schneider correspondence file, SchA.

132. Scholem to Magnes, July 22, 1946, file 2060, Magnes collection, CAHJP.

133. Scholem, "Minesi'otai bishlihut be'eropa 1946," 37, file 265/24, SchA.

134. Scholem 1946a.

135. Ibid.

136. Ibid.

137. Scholem to Magnes, July 22, 1946, file 2060, Magnes collection, CAHJP.

138. Scholem 1946a.

139. Keynan 1997, 155–60.

140. Ibid., 159.

141. See Baumel 1997, 2–25.

142. Scholem 1946a.

143. Ibid.

144. Avni 1981, 28.

145. Scholem to Magnes, July 22, 1946, file 2060, Magnes collection, CAHJP.

146. On this collection and its history, see Heuberger 1996; Loewy 1965.

147. Scholem to the Hebrew University, July 29, 1946, in Scholem 1994, 320.

148. Allony 1993, 82.

149. Scholem's report to the Hebrew University on his journey to Europe, quoted in Schidorsky 2008, 373.

150. "Tazkir hava'adah hamishpatit she'al yad hava'ad lehatzalat otzrot hagolah," 9, file 212/1–2, Otzrot Hagolah files 793, NLIA.

151. Scholem to the Hebrew University, July 29, 1946, in Scholem 1994, 320.

152. Scholem to Horowitz, August 19, 1946, quoted in Schidorsky 1994, 383–84.

153. This tourist guidebook was edited by the librarian Hans Ludwig Held. The guidebook describes the central tourist attractions of the city and their history, ignoring the Nazi period.

154. Scharnagl 1946, 5.

155. Avni 1981, 35. See also Mankowitz 2002, 21.

156. Scholem's report to the Hebrew University on his journey to Europe, quoted in Schidorsky 2008, 369.

157. Scholem, "Minesi'otai bishlichut be'eropa 1946," 43, file 265/24, SchA.

158. Ibid.

159. Scholem's report to the Hebrew University on his journey to Europe, quoted in Schidorsky 2008, 372.

160. Ibid.

161. Allony 1993, 42.

162. Held 1912 and 1927.

163. Scholem 1925; Steinschneider (1895.

164. Steinschneider 1895, 60.

165. Scholem to the Hebrew University, July 29, 1946, in Scholem 1994, 320 (my emphasis).

166. Scholem's report to the Hebrew University on his journey to Europe, quoted in Schidorsky 2008, 373.

167. Scholem to the Hebrew University, July 29, 1946, in Scholem 1994, 321 (my emphasis).

168. Ibid.

169. Scholem, "Minesi'otai bishlichut be'eropa 1946," 44, file 265/24, SchA.

170. Ibid., 47.

171. Ibid., 48.

172. Ibid., 49.

173. Ibid., 52.

174. Ibid.

175. Ibid., 53.

176. See Schidorsky 1998.

177. Scholem, "Minesi'otai bishlichut be'eropa 1946," 53, file 265/24, SchA.

178. Ibid., 57.

179. Ibid., 53.

180. Ibid. See also Abramowitz to the author, August 21, 2007, Zadoff archive.

181. Grobman 1992, 158–60.

182. Kotler 1946, 15.

183. Ibid.

184. Ibid. In a diary entry dated August 8, Scholem briefly recorded his impressions of that evening: "In the evening from nine till one o'clock, with the teachers of the camps in the surroundings here in the chaplain's club: a friendly party. Many impressions. Two German Jews approached me and poured out their hearts about the attitude toward them in the camps. I was asked to speak, and I spoke for a quarter of an hour" (Scholem, "Minesi'otai bishlichut be'eropa 1946," 61, file 265/24, SchA). Many years later Abramowitz also remembered Scholem's participation with great warmth: "I remember his incredible

participation in the meeting of Hever Hamorim. He spoke about education to the teachers. But, he sang and danced with us throughout the night" (Abramovitz to the author, August 21, 2007, Zadoff archive).

185. Scholem, "Minesi'otai bishlichut be'eropa 1946," 60, file 265/24, SchA.

186. Ibid.

187. Scholem's report to the Hebrew University on his journey to Europe, quoted in Schidorsky 2008, 370.

188. Ibid.

189. Schidorsky 2008, 382–83.

190. Scholem, "Minesi'otai bishlichut be'eropa 1946," 61, file 265/24, SchA.

191. Ibid., 62.

192. Ibid. (my emphasis).

193. Ibid., 65.

194. Ibid., 66.

195. The account here is based on Friedman's memoirs and testimony. See H. Friedman 1990, 106–12 and 1992 interview by Joan Ringelheim, transcript, RG-50.030*0074, 29–35, US Holocaust Memorial Museum (USHMM).

196. See Herman 2008, 176.

197. Ibid., note 84.

198. H. Friedman 1990, 109.

199. H. Friedman, 1992 interview by Joan Ringelheim, transcript, RG-50.030*0074, 33, USHMM.

200. Ibid.

201. Otzrot Hagolah files, 046, 1947, HUA.

202. Scholem to Senator, March 9, 1947, ibid.

203. See Dawidowicz to Weinreich, February 16, 1947, call-P-675, box 55, folder 3, American Jewish Historical Society (AJHS).

204. Friedman to Scholem, March 21, 1947, Otzrot Hagolah files, 046/1947, HUA.

205. Bernstein to Scholem, March 25, 1947; Scholem to Friedman, March 25, 1947; Scholem to Bernstein, March 30, 1947, all ibid.

206. Scholem to the JDC office in Paris, April 10, 1947; the JDC office in Paris to the Hebrew University, April 14, 1947, both ibid.

207. See Scholem to the JDC office in Paris, April 27, 1947; memorandum of a telephone conversation between Senator and Porter, May 2, 1947, both ibid.

208. Receipt dated May 7, 1947, ibid.

209. Senator to Baron, May 11, 1947, ibid.

210. "Reshimat kitvei hayad me 'Otzrot Hagolah,'" June 22, 1947, file 212/1–2, Otzrot Hagolah files 793, NLIA.

211. Ibid., 11.

212. Mayer Abramowitz, "The Role of American Chaplains in Rescuing Holocaust Survivors in Europe, 1944–1948: Interview with Rabbi Mayer Abramowitz," interview by Alex Grobman, July 10, 1975, Interview Number (199) 92, 31–32, OHD.

213. Haeger and Long 1947.

214. Ibid.

215. Magnes to Scholem, February 16, 1948, Magnes correspondence file, SchA.

216. Scholem to Magnes, February 21, 1948, file 23, SchA.

217. Dawidowicz commented on the problems of this way of estimating the number of books in the crates in the warehouse: "Each case was estimated to hold 200 books, but that was an arbitrary figure. Cases with volumes of the Talmud held only about 100 books; cases with unbound periodicals, paperbound books, and pamphlets held about 500 items" (Dawidowicz 1989, 317).

218. Scholem to Baron, June 16, 1947, Gershom Scholem files, HUA.

219. H. Friedman 1990, 111, and 1992 interview by Joan Ringelheim, transcript, RG-50.030*0074, 34–35, USHMM.

220. Allony 1993, 11–38.

221. Scholem, "Tagebücher: Ende 1922, Juli 1934–Nov. 34; 1935–48," 107, file 265/22, SchA.

6. The Heart of Odysseus

1. Arendt and Scholem 2010, 140.

2. This is the fourth stanza of the poem, which he sent to Walter Benjamin in 1921. It was published in Scholem 2003, 145.

3. Schidorsky 2006, 204. See also Weiss 2015.

4. Diaspora Treasures Committee, minutes of a meeting on September 9, 1946, 3–6, file 212/1–2, Otzrot Hagolah files 793, NLIA. In similar spirit, at the end of his report to the Hebrew University, Scholem wrote: "I cannot free myself of the impression that despite the assurances these books were in danger as long as they were in Germany, and especially when changes took place in the method and composition of the administration. The main step was to remove what could be removed, and the question of secondary importance was to where" (quoted in Schidorsky 2008, 374).

5. Schidorsky 2006, 211.

6. Ibid., 226–37.

7. See ibid., 254–63; Braunová 2000, 166–68.

8. Senator to Scholem, September 1, 1946, Otzrot Hagolah files, 046/1946, HUA.

9. Scholem's report to the Hebrew University on his journey to Europe, quoted in Schidorsky 2008, 357.

10. Scholem 1947.

11. Scholem 1946a.

12. Senator to Scholem, September 1, 1946, Otzrot Hagolah files, HUA.

13. F. Scholem 1988, 28.

14. Keynan 1997, 110.

15. Ibid., 159; see also 158–60.

16. Ibid., 112–14 and 166–67.

17. Ibid., 104–5; Ofer 2007, 481.

18. See, for example, Roth 1944, 257, which linked the rescue of the books with the commandment to redeem prisoners in Jewish tradition.

19. Dawidowicz 1989, 316.

20. Beit-Arié 1983, 64. For a shortened translation of this passage, see Beit-Arié 1994, 121.

21. Scholem, "Minesi'otai bishlichut be'eropa 1946. April 10–August 26," 62 (my emphasis), file 265/24, SchA.

22. Morinis 1992, 4; see also 20.

23. Ibid., 4.

24. Dawidowicz 1989, 326.

25. Aschheim 2001b, 33–34.

26. Werner's wife, Emmy, and his two daughters, Edith and Renee, fled to England and lived in London after the war (M. Zadoff 2014. Scholem dedicated his autobiographical work, *From Berlin to Jerusalem* (2012a), to Werner.

27. Idel 1998, 71. See also Idel 1999, 107–8.

28. Arendt and Scholem 2010, 133.

29. Scholem to Bergmann, December 15, 1947, in Scholem 1994, 457.

30. Scholem, "Tagebücher: Ende 1922, Juli 1934–Nov. 34; 1935–48," 91–107, file 265/22," SchA.

31. Scholem to Bergmann, December 15, 1947, in Scholem 1994, 457.

32. Scholem, "Tagebücher: Ende 1922, Juli 1934–Nov. 34; 1935–48," 100, file 265/22, SchA.

33. F. Scholem 1983, 2.

34. Scholem 1971, 259 and 281.

35. N. Zadoff 2010. For an extended analysis of this essay by Scholem, see Hasan-Rokem 2016.

Part 3: Ein tiefes Heimweh

This epigraph comes from Burckhardt and Rychner 1970, 242.

7. Eranos

1. Mühsam 1979, 82.

2. Scholem 1981c, 171.

3. The top of the hill is 350 meters above sea level and 150 meters above the lake.

4. On this and the history of Monte Verità, see Green 1986; Landmann 2000.

5. Ries 2004, 21.

6. Reibnitz 2000, 426–29; Schabert 2009, 183.

7. Kerényi 1955.

8. Schabert 2009, 181–83.

9. Bremer 2004, 79.

10. On the change that took place in 1988 and the continued existence of the conferences, see Schabert 2011. I wish to thank Tilo Schabert discussing various aspects of the Eranos conferences to me in writing and in conversation. These explanations were vital for the discussions in this chapter.

11. Portmann 1955, 9.

12. Eliade 1955, 60.

13. Mirjam Zadoff describes the popular Czech spas of Karlsbad, Marienbad, and Franzensbad as a kind of stage (2012, 17–22). On the combination of recreation and formality at Eranos, see Schabert 2004, 10–11.

14. Corbin 1957, xix.

15. Scholem 1946b.

16. Hurwitz to Scholem, April 28, 1945, Hurwitz correspondence file, SchA.

17. Fröbe-Kapteyn to Scholem, May 2, 1946, Fröbe-Kapteyn correspondence file, SchA.

18. Scholem to Fröbe-Kapteyn, May 22, 1947, ibid.

19. Fröbe-Kapteyn to Scholem, September 10, 1947, ibid.

20. Scholem to Hurwitz, October 24, 1947, in Scholem 1994, 330.

21. Scholem to Fröbe-Kapteyn, October 7, 1948, Fröbe-Kapteyn correspondence file, SchA.

22. This lecture was published in German in the *Eranos Jahrbuch*, and later in English translation in Scholem 1965b, 87–117.

23. Jaffé 1968, 103–04. The letter was published in full in Scholem 1995a, 94–95.

24. Portmann 1962, 8; Schabert 2011, 133–34.

25. See Hakl 2013, 193; McGuire 1989, 147.

26. Scholem was not present at the conference in 1951. To date I have found evidence that Jung heard Scholem lecture only once, in 1950 (see Eliade 1990, 113).

27. McGuire 1989, 153. The fact that there is only one letter in the Jung file in the Gershom Scholem Archive reinforces the assumption that the connection between the two men was rather weak.

28. Dan 2007, 265. Elsewhere Dan goes so far as to call the conferences "the sanctum sanctorum of Jungianism" (ibid., 283).

29. Eliade 1977, xiii.

30. The list in the text is a rather random selection of intellectuals who took part more than once in the Eranos conferences in the 1950s and 1960s. Many participants lectured only once at Eranos and of course contributed thereby to the heterogeneous character of the group. From 1933 to 1989, 149 different lecturers participated in Eranos. For a full list of participants in the Eranos conferences over the generations, see Barone, Riedl, and Tischel 2004, 255–57.

31. Scholem 1960c. As shown by his eulogy for Neumann, Scholem greatly admired him and was close to him. However, he disagreed with Neumann's Jungian views (see Scholem 2012b, 29–30).

32. Portmann to Scholem and others, December 29, 1960, Portmann correspondence file, SchA.

33. Wasserstrom 1999, 186–87.

34. Scholem to Altmann, November 16, 1949, Altmann correspondence file, SchA.

35. Hakl 2013, 188–95.

36. This lecture was published in English in Scholem 1991, 140–96.

37. Scholem to Karl Kerényi, March 31, 1952, Kerényi correspondence file, SchA.

38. Magda Kerényi to Scholem, May 30, 1952, ibid.

39. His role with this organization is discussed at length in chapter 5.

40. Scholem, "Tagebücher 1952," 50, file 265/26, SchA.

41. Ibid.

42. Ibid., 48–49.

43. Ibid., 46.

44. Ibid., 45.

45. Ibid., 44.

46. On Brody and the Rhein Verlag, see Hack 1971 and 1979, 1153–78.

47. Scholem, "Tagebücher 1952," 40, file 265/26, SchA.

48. Scholem 1957a, 1960d, and 1962c.

49. Scholem, "Tagebücher 1952," 41, file 265/26, SchA.

50. Ibid., 39.

51. Scholem 1981a, 465–66.

52. See N. Zadoff 2007, 301, and the references in the note there.

53. As the title of his *Religion after Religion* (Wasserstrom 1999) suggests, Wasserstrom regards Scholem's scholarship as a new secular religion. The central weakness of Wasserstrom's argument, in my view, is the effort to place three intellectuals with such rich worlds of thought in the same category, for they differed too greatly in their lives, scholarship, and thought to have a single pattern imposed on them. Wasserstrom was also criticized sharply for the way he presented Corbin as ostensibly having fascist leanings. See, for example, Subtelny 2003; Versluis 2001.

54. Scholem to Stella Corbin, October 26, 1978, in Scholem 1999, 193.

55. Scholem 1981a, 466.

56. Corbin 1981, 4.

57. On Scholem's religious anarchism, see chapter 3.

58. Scholem 1958.

59. Scholem to Weiss, March 31, 1969, in Scholem and Weiss 2012, 214.

60. Scholem 1958, 209. This was reprinted in Scholem 1973a. For a Hebrew translation, see Scholem 1990, 32. This motive appears in other places in the ten aphorisms—for example, in the third and ninth. However, only the first aphorism, which is quoted here, contains a detailed discussion of this issue. Since their publication, these aphorisms have received a number of important interpretations, to which I have referred (see Biale 1985; Dan 2010, 106–25; P. Schäfer 1998).

61. For a discussion of this letter, see chapter 3.

62. See, for example, Corbin 1998, 3–4.

63. Idel 1988, 11.

64. Scholem 1955, 66. Most of the quoted passage, except the last sentence, was published in the introduction to Scholem 1965b, 3.

65. Barone, Riedl and Tischel 2004, 215.

66. Jung 1952.

67. Scholem, "Tagebücher: December 8, 1949–December 31, 1949; January 6, 1950–January 21, 1950; January 6, 1951; December 20, 1951; May 28, 1952–June 22, 1952; June 4,

1955," 44, file 265/25, SchA. See also Dan 2007, 273–74. On Jung's antisemitic tendencies in the context of his psychological theories, see Gilman 1994.

68. On the Scholem-Kurzweil debate, see Myers 1986; N. Zadoff 2007.

69. Kurzweil 1970, 233–34. See also N. Zadoff 2007, 335–36.

70. On Scholem's indirect responses Kurzweil, see N. Zadoff 2007, 340–60.

71. Scholem 2012b, 29.

72. See N. Zadoff 2007, 333, note 157.

73. See Idel 2005, 226.

74. Among the critics of Scholem was George Steiner, who published at that time a review in the *New Yorker* of the publication of the English version of Scholem's book on Shabtai Tzvi (Steiner 1973, 158).

75. Scholem to Kirsch, November 8, 1973, in Scholem 1999, 87.

76. Eliade 1990, 111.

77. Eliade 1988, 146–47. Scholem's lecture was published in an English translation in Scholem 1965b, 118–57.

78. Scholem 1969.

79. Lavi 1972, 13.

80. Ibid.

81. Since then the diary has been published in its entirety in many languages. For an English version, see Sebastian 2003.

82. So far I have been unable to find the Hebrew version of this letter, dated June 6, 1972, in Scholem's archive. For a German translation, see Scholem 1999, 278, note 2.

83. Scholem to Eliade, June 6, 1972, in Scholem 1999, 30.

84. Eliade to Scholem, June 25, 1972, in ibid.

85. The notes, which take up two pages, are dated July 18, 1972 (Eliade correspondence file, SchA).

86. Eliade to Scholem, March 10, 1973, in Scholem 1999, 316–17.

87. Scholem to Eliade, March 29, 1973, in Scholem 1999, 63.

88. Ibid.

89. Ibid.

90. Eliade to Scholem, April 28, 1973, Eliade correspondence file, SchA.

91. Sebastian to Scholem, March 1973, Sebastian correspondence file, SchA.

92. Scholem to Sebastian, June 3, 1973, ibid.

93. Rudolf to Werblowsky, February 20, 1978, Eliade correspondence file, SchA.

94. Cain to Scholem, August 29, 1979, Cain correspondence file, SchA.

95. Scholem to Cain, October 8, 1979, ibid.

96. These letters are in ibid. For Cain's conclusions, based on the information that he managed to gather over about a decade, see Cain 1989.

97. On the various opinions about and disputes regarding Eliade's past, see Müller 2004, 65–103; Rennie 1996, 143–77.

98. On the mutual intellectual influences of Eliade and Scholem and on the background of their participation in Eranos, see Idel 2005, 223–28.

99. Dan 2007, 1:278–79 and 283.

100. Indeed, Scholem devoted some of his intellectual energy to teaching in the United States, and he was a visitor at many academic institutions such as Hebrew Union College, Brandeis University, the Jewish Theological Seminary in New York, and Princeton University.

101. Wilson 2005, 21–37.

102. Davis 1979, 34–35.

103. Ibid., 35.

104. Wilson 2005, 37.

105. For a foundational work on the changes undergone by the German language during the Third Reich, see Klemperer 2006.

106. Scholem 1997a, 24.

8. Between Israel and Germany

1. Oz 1998, 213.

2. Arendt 1964.

3. R. Cohen 1993, 30 and 41. See also R. Cohen 2001, 256.

4. The letters were first published in the weekly magazine of the Organization of Immigrants from Central Europe (Scholem and Arendt 1963). Arendt agreed to publish them on condition that the two letters appear side by side. Half a year afterward the letters were published in an English translation in the British magazine *Encounter* (Scholem and Arendt 1964). The correspondence was published in Arendt and Scholem 2010, 428–65. Scholem's letter to Arendt also appeared in Scholem 2012b, 300–306, and Arendt's reply was reprinted in Arendt 2007, 465–71.

5. Arendt 1964, 117.

6. Scholem 2012b, 301.

7. Ibid., 302.

8. Arendt 2007, 466–67.

9. Mosès 2000a, 81–82.

10. Aschheim 2001b, 65–67; Suchoff 1997, 57–59.

11. Suchoff 1997, 58.

12. On Arendt's rude rejection of Oriental Jews, see Arendt to Jaspers, April 13, 1961, in Arendt and Jaspers 1992, 434–35.

13. Diner 1996, 155–56.

14. Aschheim 2001b, 66.

15. Arendt 2007, 343–74. The article was written in 1944 and published a year later in the *Menorah Journal*. In rejecting the article, the editor of *Commentary* wrote that it contained "too many anti-Semitic implications" (quoted in Bernstein 1996, 104–5).

16. Scholem to Arendt, January 28, 1946, in Arendt and Scholem 2010, 91–105.

17. Arendt 2007, 358–59.

18. Ibid., 361.

19. Ibid., 363.

20. Ibid., 362. These arguments are repeated in Arendt 1964, 61.

21. Arendt 2007, 364. Bernstein (1996, 112) writes that nowhere in her work does Arendt specify who those "revolutionary forces" were. Perhaps in part because of this fuzziness, Scholem concluded that Arendt's arguments were communist propaganda, which she categorically denied.

22. Arendt 2007, 367.

23. Scholem to Arendt, January. 28, 1946, in Arendt and Scholem 2010, 96.

24. Ibid., 95.

25. Scholem to Spiegel, July 14, 1941, in Scholem 1994, 435.

26. Scholem to Arendt, January 28, 1946, in Arendt and Scholem 2010, 96. See also Aschheim 2001a, 9.

27. Arendt to Scholem, April 21, 1946, in Arendt and Scholem 2010, 107–8.

28. See Monteanu Eddon 2003.

29. Arendt to Scholem, April 21, 1946, in Arendt and Scholem 2010, 108. However, according to Richard Bernstein, even when Arendt did identify with Zionism, "it was not because of any deep spiritual or emotional attachment to Zionism" (2001, 198).

30. On Scholem's attitude toward Magnes and the Ihud Association, see Heller 2004, 389–91.

31. Scholem to Arendt, January 28, 1946, in Arendt and Scholem 2010, 99.

32. Scholem 1997a, 51–71. This article is discussed at length in chapter 4.

33. Both Scholem and Arendt criticized Zionism for not changing anything in Diaspora patterns of thinking. As Scholem put it, "we came as rebels and found ourselves to be heirs" (ibid., 69).

34. Some of these moments of closeness are discussed in chapters 5 and 6.

35. Arendt to Blumenfeld, November 28, 1955, in Arendt and Blumenfeld 1995, 135.

36. Scholem, "Tagebücher: August 3, 1963–August 19, 1963," 1, file 265/27, SchA.

37. Scholem, "Tagebücher: August 3, 1963–August 19, 1963," 2–3, file 265/27, SchA.

38. See Arendt to Scholem, September 14, 1963, in Arendt and Scholem 2010, 457–58; Arendt to Jaspers, October 20, 1963, in Arendt and Jaspers 2001, 559.

39. Arendt to Blumenfeld, January 9, 1957, in Arendt and Blumenfeld 1995, 174–75.

40. Wasserstein 2009, 13.

41. See Scholem 2012b, 302.

42. Scholem's mission is discussed extensively in chapter 5. His notes about it were printed in *Haaretz* (Scholem 1946a). Arendt made her trip in 1949, and her impressions were published in *Commentary* (Arendt 1950).

43. Young-Bruehl 1982, 244.

44. The one Jew mentioned as such in her report was Arendt herself—to be precise, she referred to the reaction of Germans in Germany to the fact that she was Jewish (see Arendt 1950, 342).

45. Diner 1997, 182.

46. R. Cohen 2001, 260. Cohen discusses this group extensively, along with other groups. See also R. Cohen 1993, 46–55.

47. R. Cohen 2001, 261.

48. Young-Bruehl 1982, 328.

49. For an English translation, see Scholem 2012b, 298–300. It should be pointed out that, unlike Scholem, Arendt was in favor of executing Eichmann for juridical and personal reasons. See Arendt and Scholem 2010, 443–44.

50. Scholem 2012b, 299.

51. Ibid., 300.

52. Scholem stated many times that his criticism was mainly of Arendt's tone. He raised this point in his initial letter of response to her, as well as in his letter to the sociologist Kurt Wolff, more than a decade later. See Scholem to Wolff, December 30, 1975, in Scholem 1999, 124.

53. Rotenstreich 1994, 118.

54. Schlösser to Scholem, September 25, 1962, Schlösser correspondence file. SchA.

55. For her autobiography, see Susman 1964. Susman wrote about her meeting with Scholem with great warmth (see ibid., 70–71).

56. Susman 1946. Susman thought about being baptized as a Christian at the time of her engagement, because of pressure from her groom's parents. Her statements in her autobiography were identical to Scholem's account in his diary (see Susman 1964, 70–71).

57. Scholem to Susman, November 6, 1946, Deutsches Literaturarchiv Marbach, Margarete Susman files. In her autobiography Susman quoted this sentence in a milder formulation (see Susman 1964, 162).

58. See P. Schäfer 2007.

59. Scholem 1964. For an English translation, see Scholem 2012b, 61–64.

60. Scholem 2012b, 61.

61. Ibid., 63.

62. Reprinted in Scholem 1970a, 16–17. For an English translation, see Scholem 2012b, 68.

63. Arendt 1964 and 2007, 343–74. A similar argument can be seen between the lines of Scholem's article on Jewish studies of 1944 discussed in chapter 4.

64. Scholem 2012b, 64.

65. For an English translation, see Scholem 2012b 71–92.

66. Scholem 1979.

67. Scholem 2012b, 89.

68. Ibid., 91.

69. For Scholem's impressions of German Jewry at the time of his visit, see Scholem 1946a.

70. See chapter 5.

71. Scholem to the Hebrew University, July 29, 1946, in Scholem 1994, 320.

72. On this episode in the history of the State of Israel, see, for example, Segev 2010, 189–252. As far is known, Scholem did not express an opinion on the polemics regarding reparations either publicly or privately.

73. Barzel 1998, 205–8.

74. M. Friedman 1991, 324–25; Segev 2000, 197.

75. Reprinted in Scholem 1975b, 121.

76. Ibid., 122.

77. Scholem 1952. For the original letter of Scholem to Hans-Gert Falkenberg, on which only the year 1952 is written, see Scholem 1995a, 28–29.

78. An example of this from 1952 is Scholem's cancellation of his planned visit to the Protestant theologian Ernst Benz, one of the regular participants in Eranos, during Scholem's visit to Ascona in that year. Scholem cancelled the visit after he learned from Karl Löwith that Benz had been a member of the Nazi Party and served as a priest with the military in Ukraine during World War II. See Scholem, "Tagebücher 1952," 36, file 265/26, SchA.

79. Scholem 1957a, vii.

80. Scholem 1959.

81. Scholem 1960d. This was published in an English translation in Scholem 1965b.

82. For the lecture, see Scholem 1960a. For an English translation, see Scholem 1971, 142–66.

83. Scholem 1962b. For an English translation, see Scholem 1987.

84. Scholem 1962c. For an English translation, see Scholem 1991.

85. See Scholem to Conze, August 6, 1963, in Scholem 1995a, 105. Scholem was not aware at the time of Werner Conze's own Nazi and antisemitic past, which came to light only in the 1990s.

86. Scholem 1963.

87. Scholem 2012b, 67.

88. Scholem 1970a.

89. Broszat to Scholem, November 29, 1972, in Broszat correspondence file, SchA.

90. According to the official invitation to give a lecture, dated February 19, 1973, in file ID 502, Institut für Zeitgeschichte München Archiv.

91. Among the sixty-seven members of the audience were Hellmut Becker, the director of the Max Planck Institute; Emanuel Birnbaum, the chief editor of the newspaper *Süddeutsche Zeitung*; Friedhelm Kemp, the chief literary editor of the Bavarian Radio and the director of the Literature Department of the Bavarian Academy of Fine Arts; Nikolaos Loebkowitz, the rector of the University of Munich; Hans Paschke, the chief editor of the magazine *Merkur*; and Siegfried Unseld, the director of the Suhrkamp publishing house. For a full list of participants, see ibid.

92. Broszat, "Einführung zum Vortrag Gershom Scholem am 15.3.1973," 2, ibid.; B[irnbaum] 1973.

93. Scholem 1978 and 1979.

94. Scholem 1978. The article was reprinted posthumously in Scholem 1984a, 229–61.

95. See *Die Geschichte des Suhrkamp Verlages* 2000, 25.

96. This account of Suhrkamp's life is based on Michalzik 2003, 69–75; Unseld 1991, 16–21.

97. On Scholem's meeting with Eppelsheimer in 1946, see chapter 5.

98. See *Die Geschichte des Suhrkamp Verlages* 2000, 37 and 40; Michalzik 2003, 75–104; Weissberg 2012, 19.

99. Friedrich Podszus to Gretel Adorno, November 14, 1950, in Adorno, Suhrkamp, and Unseld 2003, 88.

100. Scholem 1960d.

101. See Adorno to Scholem, September 25, 1959, in Scholem and Adorno 2015, 176–77; Scholem to Adorno, November 16, 1949, ibid., 178–79.

102. See Scholem 1963, 1970a, 1973a, 1984a, 1992b, and 1997b.

103. Hack 1979, 1173.

104. Scholem to the Süddeutsche Verlag, September 13, 1966, Süddeutsche Verlag correspondence file, SchA.

105. Ibid.

106. See Unseld to Scholem, October 19, 1966, in Unseld 2004, 51; Scholem to Unseld, October 24, 1966, in Scholem 1995a, 150. For an example of the coverage of the deal in the German press, see Michalzik 2003, 134.

107. Scholem 1975c, 1977, 1992b, and 1997b.

108. Benjamin 1966.

109. Scholem to Adorno, November 11, 1940 in Scholem and Adorno 2015, 28–29. For a description of Benjamin's correspondence in Scholem's possession, see ibid., 45–49.

110. Scholem to Adorno, March 27, 1942, ibid., 47.

111. Scholem 1975c, 215.

112. See Garber 1987, 124–34; Küpper and Skrandies 2006, 23.

113. Benjamin 1955. On the history of the formation of these volumes and Scholem's part in preparing them, see Adorno, Suhrkamp, and Unseld 2003, 85–93. See also the correspondence between Scholem and Adorno in those years, which was published in Scholem and Adorno 2015.

114. Adorno to Scholem, September 25, 1959, in Scholem and Adorno 2015, 176.

115. Scholem to Adorno, November 16, 1959, ibid. Many of the letters in this volume deal with preparing Benjamin's correspondence for publication.

116. The anecdote appears in Meysels 2002, 113.

117. According to various accounts, this characteristic was central in Scholem's character, and he was aware of it. Renee Goddard, Scholem's niece, told me that he used to say of his behavior at social events, "Scholem schweigt, nur wenn er selber redet [Scholem is only quiet when he himself is speaking]."

118. Adorno to Tobisch, September 19, 1968, in Adorno and Tobisch 2003, 242.

119. Tiedemann 1998, 197–98. Tiedemann describes how the two quarreled for a long time over a true Sachertorte should be served with or without whipped cream.

120. Ibid., 197. See also Habermas 2007, 9.

121. Schöttker 1999, 115.

122. Bohrer 1998, 293.

123. Müller-Doohm 2003, 692.

124. Demm 2001, 162 and 246–47. Demm quotes Adorno's famous remark of February 1969: "I built a theoretical model of thought. How could I have imagined that people would want to implement it by means of Molotov cocktails?" (ibid., 247).

125. On the image of Benjamin in the student movement of the late 1960s, see Garber 1987, 152–61.

126. The prominent critics included Hamm 1967b, 361; Heissenbüttel 1967, 240. The magazine *Alternative* devoted an entire issue in the fall of 1967 to criticism of Adorno's editing of Benjamin's writing. For a summary of the criticism in its historical context, see Behrmann 1999, 349–67. For a summary of the criticism in the context of Benjamin's reception in Germany, see Garber 1987, 152–61; Küpper and Skrandies 2006, 22–25. See also the editor's comment in Scholem 1995a, 309–10.

127. H. Brenner 1969, 160–61.

128. Arendt 1968, 56 and 215.

129. Adorno to Scholem, January 31, 1968, in Scholem and Adorno 2015, 444–45.

130. Scholem to Adorno, February 8, 1968, in ibid., 447–54.

131. Ibid. See also Müller-Doohm 2003, 695.

132. Scholem to Adorno, February 8, 1968, in Scholem and Adorno 2015, 451.

133. Ibid. Adorno's remark in the margins of the letter is quoted in Scholem 1995a, 312, note 12.

134. Müller-Doohm 2003, 695–96.

135. Scholem to Adorno, February 8, 1968, in Scholem and Adorno 2015, 451.

136. Ibid., 454.

137. Kurzweil's critiques of Scholem were published in the 1950s and 1960s in the literary supplement of *Haaretz* and collected in Kurzweil 1970, 99–240.

138. Kurzweil 1970, 201–202.

139. On Adorno, see H. Brenner 1969, 158. On the history of Benjamin's reception, see Garber 1987, 135.

140. The complete edition of Benjamin's writings was published after Scholem's death (Benjamin 1989).

141. Scholem's articles about Benjamin were edited by Tiedemann (Scholem 1983b). See also Garber 1987, 140.

142. Tiedemann 1983, 216.

143. Benjamin and Scholem 1980 and 1989; Scholem 1981c and 1982a. To these must be added Scholem's editing of Benjamin's autobiographical work, which was found in his literary remains, and preparing it for publication by Suhrkamp (Benjamin 1970).

144. Scholem 2012b, 177.

145. For example, see ibid., 231, and Scholem 1981c.

146. A lecture in Scholem's memory attributed to Unseld was given in Frankfurt at a colloquium in honor of Benjamin's ninetieth birthday on July 1, 1982. The lecture begins: "Without Gershom Scholem—and I am personally convinced of this—without the encounter and constant communication over a quarter of century, Benjamin would not have become what he eventually became" ([Unseld], "Zum Gedanken an Gershom Scholem: Rede, gehalten beim Kolloquium zum 90. Geburtstag Walter Benjamins, Universität Frankfurt, 1. Juli 1982," file 34, SchA).

147. See M. Zadoff and N. Zadoff 2014.

148. Scholem 1980c, 24.

9. Berlin, Again: The Finale

1. Quoted in Hentig 2007, 573.

2. Eilat and Rotenstreich, "Hasenat shel ha'universita ha'ivrit biyerushaliym, biyeshivato beyom 6 be'adar 1968," 1, file 26, SchA.

3. See Cohn and Plesser 1988, 41–43.

4. Ibid., 41.

5. See ibid., 44–46.

6. Potok 1981. Another expression of Scholem's influence in the United States can be found in Weiner 1967, 57–89.

7. Scholem to Gadamer, July 7, 1969, in Scholem 1995a, 220.

8. The lecture was published by the city of Pforzheim as a special booklet and was reprinted in Scholem 1973a and 1990. The quote is from Scholem 1990, 309.

9. Idel 1998, 48. See also Idel 2010, 87.

10. P. Schäfer 2007, 2:562.

11. See Campanini 2005, 367.

12. A copy of the official explanation for granting the prize, which was read by Gadamer at the ceremony, is found with no heading in file 26, SchA. The quotation is from that document, 24.

13. Scholem 1970a. The other books are Scholem 1970b, and Benjamin 1970, which Scholem edited and prepared for publication. In October of that year Scholem and Unseld also began to discuss the possibility of translating into German the English version of Scholem's book about Shabtai Tzvi (which had been translated by Zwi Werblowsky and was published in the United States three years later [Scholem 1973]). See Unseld 2010, 307–8. The German version was finally published (by the Jüdischer Verlag, a subsidiary of Suhrkamp) in 1992, as a commemoration of the tenth anniversary of Scholem's death (Scholem 1992a). See Müller-Doohm 2014, 327.

14. The certificate of appointment to this academy is in folder 25, SchA.

15. Kemp to Scholem, December 20, 1973, Kemp correspondence file, SchA.

16. Scholem to Kemp, January 1, 1974, ibid.

17. Scholem to Clement Graf Podewils, May 8, 1974, Bayerische Akademie der schönen Künste Archiv.

18. Drews 1974. Articles about the prize were also published on July 17 in *Die Welt* and the Austrian *Die Presse*, and on the following day in the *Allgemeine Zeitung*.

19. Scholem 1974c. For an English translation, see Scholem 1997a, 20–24.

20. This is how Scholem described his planned lecture in a letter to Hans Egon Holthusen, the president of the Bavarian Academy, June 27, 1974, Bayerische Akademie der schönen Künste Archiv.

21. Scholem 2012a.

22. For Kaléko's letter and other correspondence connected to this incident, see Fischer-Defoy, 1997, 229–32. See also Rosenkranz 2007, 172–76.

23. Holthusen 1966. This article provoked a response from the Jewish author Jean Améry (1967). It also provoked a severe response from the literary critic Peter Hamm (1967a). Hamm showed that Holthusen's joining the SS was not a sin of his youth, as he

tried to present it, but that he retained Nazi positions as late as 1940. Itta Shedletzky told me in a conversation on November 2, 2010, that Walter Boehlich, Scholem's friend and the chief editor of Suhrkamp, had told her that Scholem agreed to receive the prize from Holthusen's hands, despite knowledge of his past.

24. Scholem to Reinhold Scholem, April 22, 1976, in Scholem 1999, 131.

25. Scholem 1975a (the full work is Scholem 1975c).

26. Dahlhaus 1975.

27. See Puttnies 1975.

28. Scholem, "Lebensgeschichte als Zeitgeschichte," Saarländischer Rundfunk Archiv. The interview was published in Scholem 1980c.

29. Puttnies 1976.

30. Momos [Jens] 1976.

31. Scholem to Reinhold Scholem, July 13, 1976, in Scholem 1999, 140.

32. Scholem 1977. For the English version, see Scholem 2012a.

33. Drews 1977, 1210.

34. Becker 1978, 131.

35. For example, one Israeli newspaper, *Yedioth Aharonot*, had as the main headline of its supplement on December 2, 1977: "Gershom Scholem—the Work and the Man." It included items by Joseph Dan, Nathan Rotenstreich, Gezel Kressel, and Moshe Halamish. The literary supplement of *Haaretz* for that day contained a survey of Scholem's work and its influence, to which Zwi Werblowsky, Yosef ben Shlomo, and David Flusser contributed.

36. The speakers included Yair Zakovitch, Shalom Rosenberg, Yehuda Liebes, and Mendel Pikarz.

37. See Habermas 2007, 16. According to Habermas, Scholem truly enjoyed the reception.

38. Becker 1978, 130.

39. Unseld's speech was not published, and I have not yet succeeded in locating a copy of it. For Habermas's lecture, see Habermas 1987. Becker published his speech on that evening shortly afterward (see Becker 1978, 128–30).

40. Habermas 2007, 16.

41. Becker to Scholem, January 9, 1978, in Becker correspondence file, SchA.

42. Benjamin and Scholem 1989, 5.

43. Benjamin and Scholem 1980.

44. The many reactions in the press can be found in the Zeitungsausschnitte Sammlung der Stadt Dortmund, Gershom Scholem files, Deutsches Literaturarchiv Marbach.

45. See Benjamin and Scholem 1989, 6–7. Also see Habermas's remarks several years later, with the publication of the Benjamin and Adorno correspondence (Habermas 1994).

46. The lecture was published after Scholem's death as Scholem 1984b.

47. Ke 1980.

48. B. H. 1980.

49. Gründer 1984, 11.

50. Scholem was appointed as a member at a meeting of the senate on September 26,

1980. The minutes of the meeting and lists of the members of the senate in 1980 and 1981 are in the archive of the Lessing-Akademie in Wolfenbüttel.

51. Maier-Leibnitz to Scholem, June 16, 1981, file 25, SchA.

52. Maier-Leibnitz, "Zur Scholem-Gedenkfeier," 3, Scholem files, Wissenschaftskolleg zu Berlin Archive.

53. Fania and Gershom Scholem to Dalia and Malachi Beit-Arié, October 4, 1981, Beit-Arié correspondence file, SchA.

54. Habermas to the author, August 15, 2010, Zadoff archive.

55. Rudolf König to Fania Scholem, August 18, 1982, file 25, SchA. A speech in memory of Scholem given by Carl-Friedrich von Weizsäcker was published in Weizsäcker 1985, 180–84.

56. Glotz et al. 2006, 34. The two universities are the Freie Universität Berlin and the Technische Universität Berlin.

57. Frühwald 2006, 13–16.

58. According to Wapnewski (see Glotz et al. 2006, 39).

59. See Glotz 2005, 170; Wapnewski 2007, 283–311.

60. Scholem made his acceptance conditional on the finding of suitable accommodations for him and his wife and payment equal to the salary of a German professor, as he was unable to rent out his own house in Jerusalem because of his valuable library, which he estimated then contained more than 15,000 volumes. See Scholem to Wapnewski, November 19, 1989, file 24, SchA.

61. Glotz et al. 2006, 34. See also Glotz 2005, 174.

62. Wapnewski to Scholem, July 6, 1981, Wapnewski correspondence file, SchA.

63. Ibid.

64. Scholem to Wapnewski, July 12, 1981 in Scholem files, Wissenschaftskolleg zu Berlin Archive. A shorter version of the passage from this letter is published in Wapnewski 2007, 390–91.

65. There were seven fellows from Germany, four from Poland, four from the United States (including the philosopher Ivan Illich, who had been born in Austria and was active in Mexico at that time), two from Israel (Scholem and Yehezkel Dror, a political scientist form the Hebrew University who had been born in Vienna), and one from Italy.

66. Scholem's lecture was published posthumously in the institute's yearbook (Scholem 1983a.

67. Scholem had already published an article on Hirschfeld (1962a).

68. See Awerbuch 1982.

69. See ibid.; Niewöhner, "An einem denkwürdigen Tag," 1, Scholem files, Wissenschaftskolleg zu Berlin Archive. Both Niewöhner and Awerbuch were part of this circle. The portion from the Zohar that Scholem designated for the seminar's participants was one he had edited almost fifty years earlier (Scholem 1936).

70. Niewöhner, "An einem denkwürdien Tag," November 20, 1981, 2–3, Scholem files, Wissenschaftskolleg zu Berlin Archive. On Scholem's activity at Rosenzweig's Freie Jüdische Lehrhaus, see Scholem 1982b, 185–86.

71. Niewöhner, "An einem denkwürdien Tag," November 20, 1981, 4 Scholem files, Wissenschaftskolleg zu Berlin Archive. See also Awerbuch 1982.

72. Bronowski 1982.

73. See Rebiger 2005, 92.

74. For a list of the years when Scholem visited the city, see Rebiger 2005, 91.

75. Fania and Gershom Scholem to Dalia and Malachi Beit-Arié, December 4, 1981, SchA, Beit-Arié correspondence file. Scholem was called to the Torah on December 2, 1911, in the Reform synagogue at Lindenstrasse 48–50. On that synagogue, see Rebiger 2005, 86.

76. Scholem to Reinhold Scholem, December 15, 1981, in Scholem 1999, 246.

77. von Hentig 2007, 571.

78. Scholem to Wapnewski, January 31, 1982, in Scholem 1999, 252–54. See also Wapnewski 2007, 391–92.

79. Habermas 1982, 438. The description of Scholem's funeral is based on this article and the notes of Becker 1982. Habermas and Becker had come to Israel specifically to attend the funeral, which Unseld also attended. See Habermas 2007, 16, and Habermas to the author, August 15, 2010, Zadoff archive.

80. Müller Doohm 2014, 301; [Unseld], "Zum Gedanken an Gershom Scholem: Rede, gehalten beim Kolloquium zum 90. Geburtstag Walter Benjamins, Universität Frankfurt, 1. Juli 1982," 3, file 34, SchA.

81. Frankel 1982, 6.

82. Habermas 1982, 440.

83. Frankel 1982, 6.

84. Avraham Shapira 2005, 19. The wave of immigration to Israel following World War I is generally called the Third Aliyah.

85. Scholem 1982b.

86. The six scholars were Ephraim Elimelech Urbach, Yosef ben Shlomo, Isaiah Tishby, Rivka Schatz, Malachi Beit-Arié, and Nathan Rotenstreich particpiated in the conference. See *Gershom shalom* 1983. An expanded version of this book was published in English (Mendes-Flohr 1994).

87. Harpaz 1990, 49.

88. The first harbinger of the oedipal process was a book published soon after Scholem's death, Schweid 1985. This process grew stronger about five years after Scholem's death, in response to the publication of Moshe Idel's book on Kabbalah (Idel 1988). See also N. Zadoff 2012.

89. Habermas 2007, 16.

90. Wapnewski to Fania Scholem, March 2, 1982, Scholem files, Wissenschaftskolleg zu Berlin Archive.

91. For a list of the participants, see "Gedenkstunde für Gershom Scholem," July 2, 1982. Scholem files, Wissenschaftskolleg zu Berlin Archive.

92. Maier-Leibnitz, "Zur Scholem-Gedenkfeier Berlin."

93. Wapnewski 2007, 385.

94. von Hentig to the author, June 20, 2008, Zadoff archive.

95. Ibid.

96. Scholem described the Berlin dialect as a "rough, flippant manner" of speaking (1981c, 14, and 2012a, 13).

97. Schütz, "Gershom Scholem: Unter dem Davidschild," July 2, 1982, 12, Scholem files, Wissenschaftskolleg zu Berlin Archive. Schütz was quoting from Drews 1982.

98. Wapnewski 2007, 396.

99. Frühwald 2006, 3.

100. See Fritzsche 1996, 191.

101. Scholem to Weiss, January 1, 1962, in Scholem and Weiss 2012, 291. See also Rebiger 2005, 98.

102. Conversation with Renee Goddard, January 10, 2008.

103. Scholem 1999, 464.

104. Habermas, interview by the author, July 3, 2006, Zadoff archive. See also Habermas 2007, 9.

105. Tiedemann 1983, 212.

106. Habermas, interview by the author, July 3, 2006, Zadoff archive. See also Habermas 2007, 9.

107. Maier-Leibnitz, "Zur Scholem-Gedenkfeier Berlin," 3.

108. In the original German: "Sie kamen als eine moralische Autorität, die die Gnadenmittel besaßen um eine schuldig-gewordene Generation zu entschuldigen." All the quotes from Habermas in this discussion are taken from Habermas, interview by the author, July 3, 2006, Zadoff archive.

109. Lepenies 1997, 3.

110. [Unseld], "Zum Gedanken an Gershom Scholem: Rede, gehalten beim Kolloquium zum 90. Geburtstag Walter Benjamins, Universität Frankfurt, 1. Juli 1982," 4, file 34, SchA. On Werner Scholem, see M. Zadoff 2018.

111. Becker 1982, 65.

112. von Hentig 1983.

113. Boehlich 1999, 464.

114. Drews 1986, 161. For additional reports about the Scholem experience, see Hentig 1983 and 2007, 570–73. Perhaps this tendency is what made Scholem the subject of many anecdotes told happily by his friends, students, and acquaintances in Germany, the United States, and Israel.

115. [Unseld], "Zum Gedanken an Gershom Scholem: Rede, gehalten beim Kolloquium zum 90. Geburtstag Walter Benjamins, Universität Frankfurt, 1. Juli 1982," 7, file 34, SchA.

116. Scholem 2012b, 96. For a lengthy discussion of Scholem's understanding of Agnon's role in Hebrew culture, see chapter 1.

117. The last Hebrew monograph was his book on Shabtai Tzvi (Scholem 1957c).

118. Scholem 1962b. This volume has yet to be translated into Hebrew. The aforementioned monograph on Hirschfeld, which Scholem intended to write at the institute in Berlin, was also going to be in German.

119. This refers to the three collections of Scholem's Eranos lectures (Scholem 1960d, 1962c, and 1970b), and three volumes of *Judaica* (Scholem 1963, 1970a, 1973a).

120. Benjamin 1966 and 1970; Benjamin and Scholem 1980.

121. Scholem 1957a. Another edition was published in 1980.

122. Scholem 1980c; Scholem 1975c, (1977).

123. Scholem 1960b, 1971, 1974a, and 2012b. Scholem's autobiographical works were translated by Harry Zohn (Scholem 2012a and 1981c.

124. The three volumes of articles are Scholem (1974b), 1975b, and 1981b. The autobiographical work is Scholem 1982b.

125. Scholem 1982b, 164. In citing the wise man, Scholem was referring to Proverbs 13: 12.

126. Anna Ticho, a Jerusalem artist, was married to Abraham Ticho, a famous ophthalmologist. The Tichos had been close friends of Scholem since shortly after his arrival in Palestine (Scholem 1982b, 207). Anna Ticho died in March 1980, several months before the Scholems' stay in Berlin.

127. von Hentig 1983.

Afterword: From Berlin to Jerusalem

1. Bronowski 1982.

2. Scholem 1977 and 1982b.

3. See Dan 1988, 4–5.

4. See Campanini 2005, 369.

5. Scholem to Bohnke-Kollwitz, December 27, 1977, in Scholem 1999, 166.

6. See the Hebrew version of his autobiography (Scholem 1982b, 58–59).

7. Scholem 1980b. For his opposition to the annexation of the territories conquered in 1967, see ibid. See also Scholem et al., *Bitachon veshalom* 1967.

8. F. Scholem 1990.

9. Tiedemann 1983, 215.

10. Ibid.

11. During a visit to Saudi Arabia, Schmidt publicly emphasized Germany's responsibility to various nations in the wake of the Holocaust, including the Palestinian nation, without mentioning Israel. Begin, who was conducting a political campaign at the time, responded vehemently and accused Schmidt personally and the German nation in general of Nazism. On this episode in the context of Israeli-German relations, see Segev 2000, 403–4.

12. Tiedemann 1983, 216.

13. F. Scholem 1990.

14. E. M. D. 1964.

15. Scholem 1978 and 2006.

16. Scholem 1975c.

17. This is confirmed by an article in the *Frankfurter Allgemeine Zeitung*, which repeats the main points of the passage (see E. M. D. 1964). Scholem spoke similarly in Munich in 1974 on receiving the literary prize of the Bavarian Academy of Fine Arts (see Scholem 1997a, 20–24).

18. On this word, whose basic meaning is "request," and its metamorphoses during the Third Reich, see Sternberger, Storz, and Süskind 1970, 13–17.

19. Untitled manuscript in file 277–1/74, SchA.

20. See Momigliano 1987, 256.

21. See Scholem to Rosenzweig, December 12, 1926, in Scholem 1997a, 27–29 (discussed in chapter 1). See also Scholem 1982b, 86–87.

22. Segev 2000, 396–404.

23. Scholem 1982b, 164.

24. See Moseley 2006, 10–11.

25. Mosès 2000b, 4.

26. Ozick 1983, 148.

REFERENCES

Archival Material

American Jewish Historical Society (AJHS), New York
Lucy Dawidowicz papers.
Bayerische Akademie der schönen Künste Archiv, Munich
Central Archives for the History of the Jewish People (CAHJP), Jerusalem
Ben-Zion Dinur Collection, P28, file 69/6.
Jehuda Magnes Collection, P3, files 2056, 2057, 2060.
Deutsches Literaturarchiv Marbach
Gershom Scholem files.
Margarete Susman files.
Hebrew University of Jerusalem Archive (HUA)
Gershom Scholem files.
Otzrot Hagolah files 046/1946-47.
Hebrew University of Jerusalem Oral History Division (OHD)
Abramowitz, Mayer. "The Role of American Chaplains in Rescuing Holocaust Survivors in Europe, 1944–1948: Interview with Rabbi Mayer Abramowitz." Interview by Alex Grobman. July 10, 1975. Interview Number (199) 92.
Scholem, Gershom. "Brit Shalom: Re'aiyon im professor Gershom Shalom." Interview by Yehuda Kaveh. May 1972. Interview Number (91) 6.
Institut für Zeitgeschichte München Archiv
File ID 502.
Lessing-Akademie Archiv, Wolfenbüttel
National Archives and Record Administration (NARA), Washington
"Offenbach Archival Depot (OAD) Monthly Reports: March–October, 1946." NARA II RG 260 390/45/22/06, boxes 259–60.
National Library of Israel, Archives Department, Jerusalem
"Reshimat kitvei hayad me'Otzrot Hagolah', June 22, 1947.
Gershom Scholem Archive (SchA), Collection 1599.
National Library of Israel Archive (NLIA), Jerusalem
Otzrot Hagolah files 793, file 212/1–2.
Saarländischer Rundfunk Archiv, Saarbrücken, Germany
Scholem, Gershom. *Lebensgeschichte als Zeitgeschichte: Gershom Scholem*. Interview by Jörg Drews. June 20, 1976. DVD.

US Holocaust Memorial Museum (USHMM), Washington
Friedman, Herbert. 1992. Interview by Joan Ringelheim, June 12, transcript, RG-50.030*0074. Accessed November 18, 2016. http://collections.ushmm.org/artifact/image/h00/00/h0000245.pdf.
Wissenschaftskolleg zu Berlin Archive
Scholem files.
Zadoff Archive (author's collection)
Abramowitz, Mayer, to Zadoff, August 21, 2007.
Habermas, Jürgen. Interview by the author, Munich, July 3, 2006.
——— to Zadoff, August 15, 2010.
Hentig, Hartmut von, to Zadoff, June 20, 2008.

Published Works by Gershom Scholem

1917. "Jüdische Jugendbewegung." *Der Jude*, March, 822–25.
1925. "He'arot vetikunim lirshimat kitvei hayad shebeminchen (kitvei yad bekabalah)." *Kiryat Sefer* 1, 4: 284–93.
1928a. "Das hebräische Buch: Eine Rundfrage." *Jüdische Rundschau*, April 4, 201–2.
1928b. "Ist die Verständigung mit den Arabern gescheitert?" *Jüdische Rundschau*, November 20, 644.
1928c. "Über die Theologie des Sabbatianismus im Lichte Abraham Cardozos." In *Der Jude: Sonderheft zu Martin Bubers fünfzigstem Gerburtstag*, 123–39.
1931. "Dr. Shalom 'oneh: mikhtav lama'arekhet." *Doar Hayom*, February 24.
1933a. *Bibliographia Kabbalistica: Die jüdische Mystik behandelnde Bücher und Aufsätze von Reuchlin bis zur Gegenwart*. Berlin: Schocken.
1933b. *Das Buch Bahir: Ein Schriftdenkmal aus der Frühzeit der Kabbala*. Berlin: Schocken.
1933–34. "Nach der Vertreibung aus Spanien: Zur Geschichte der Kabbala." *Almanach des Schocken Verlags* 5694:55–70.
1935. *Die Geheimnisse der Schöpfung: Ein Kapitel aus dem Sohar*. Berlin: Schocken.
1936. *Die Geheimnisse der Tora: Ein Kapitel aus dem Sohar*. Berlin: Schocken.
1936–37. "Zum Verständnis des Sabbatianismus: Zugleich ein Beitrag zur Geschichte der 'Aufklärung.'" *Almanach des Schocken Verlags* 5697:30–42.
1937. "Kabbala at the Hebrew University." *Reconstructionist* 3 (10): 8–12.
1937–38. "Die Frommen Deutschlands: Ein Kapitel jüdischer Religionsgeschichte." *Almanach des Schocken Verlags* 5698:53–64.
1938a. "Chakirat hakabalah ba'universitah ha'ivrit." *Yediot hauniversitah ha'ivrit* 4:7–13.
1938b. *Chalomotav shel hashabtai R. Mordechai Ashkenazi: Al dvar pinqas hahalomot shel R. Mordechai Ashkenazi talmido shel R. Avraham Revigo*. Leipzig: Schocken.
1941. *Major Trends in Jewish Mysticism*. Translated by George Lichtheim. New York: Schocken.
1944a. *Be'ikvot mashiach: Osef mekorot mereshit hitpatchut ha'emunah hashabta'it, melukatim mitoch ktavav shel R. Avraham Binyamin Natan ben Elisha Chaim Ashkenazi hamechuneh Natan Ha'azati, yotz'im la'or mitoch kitvei hayad al yedei Gershom Shalom*. Jerusalem: Tarshish.

1944b. "Mitokh hirhurim al hokhmat yisrael: hakdamah lehartza'at yovel shelo titkaiyem." In *Luach Haaretz lishnat tashad*, 94–112. Tel Aviv: Schocken.
1946a. "Hayehudim begermania kayom." *Haaretz*, October 4.
1946b. *Major Trends in Jewish Mysticism*. Translated by George Lichtheim. 2nd ed. New York: Schocken.
1947. "Leshe'elat hasifriyot hayehudiyot hashdudot." *Haaretz*, October 5.
1952. "Ein Brief aus Israel." *Deutsche Universitätszeitung* 7 (23–24): 11.
1955. "Betrachtungen eines Kabbala–Forschers." *Du* 4 (April): 64–65.
1957a. *Die jüdische Mystik in ihren Hauptströmungen*. Zurich: Rhein Verlag.
1957b. "LeSalman Schocken ben hashmonim." *Haaretz*, Ocober 29.
1957c. *Shabtai Tzvi vehatnu'ah hashabta'it beiyemei chaiyav*. Tel Aviv: Am Oved.
1958. "Zehn unhistorische Sätze über Kabbala." In *Geist und Werk: Aus der Werkstatt unserer Autoren zum 75. Geburtstag von Dr. Daniel Brody*, 209–15. Zurich: Rhein Verlag.
1959. "Einleitung von Gershom Scholem." In Georg Langer, *Neun Tore: Das Geheimnis der Chassidim*, 9–10. Munich: Planegg.
1960a. "Die Krypto-jüdische Sekte der Dönme (Sabbatianer) in der Türkei." *Numen* 7 (1): 93–122.
1960b. *Jewish Gnosticism, Merkabah Mysticism and Talmudic Tradition*. New York: Jewish Theological Seminary of America.
1960c. "Nachruf auf Erich Neumann." *Das neue Israel* 13 (6): 13.
1960d. *Zur Kabbala und ihrer Symbolik*. Zurich: Rhein Verlag.
1962a. "Ein verschollener jüdischer Mystiker der Aufklärungszeit: E. J. Hirschfeld." *Year Book of the Leo Baeck Institute* 7:247–78.
1962b. *Ursprung und Anfänge der Kabbala*. Berlin: De Gruyter.
1962c. *Von dem mystischen Gestalt der Gottheit: Studien zu Grundbegriffen der Kabbala*. Zurich: Rhein Verlag.
1963. *Judaica*. Frankfurt: Suhrkamp.
1964. "Wider den Mythos vom deutsch–jüdischen Gespräch." In *Auf gespaltenem Pfad: Für Margarete Susman*, edited by Manfred Schlösser, 228–32. Darmstadt, Germany: Erato–Presse.
1965a. "Noch ein Mal: Das deutsch-jüdische 'Gespräch.'" *Bulletin des Leo Baeck Instituts* 30: 167–72.
1965b. *On the Kabbalah and Its Symbolism*. New York: Schocken.
1969. "On Sin and Punishment: Some Remarks Concerning Biblical and Rabbinical Ethics." In *Myths and Symbols: Studies in Honor of Mircea Eliade*, edited by Joseph M. Kitagawa and Charles H. Long, 163–77. Chicago: Chicago University Press.
1970a. *Judaica 2*. Frankfurt: Suhrkamp.
1970b. *Über einige Grundbegriffe des Judentums*. Frankfurt: Suhrkamp.
1971. *The Messianic Idea in Judaism: And Other Essays on Jewish Spirituality*. New York: Schocken.
1973a. *Judaica 3: Studien zur jüdischen Mystik*. Frankfurt: Suhrkamp.
1973b. *Sabbatai Sevi: The Mystical Messiah*. Translated by Zwi Werblowsky. Princeton, NJ: Princeton University Press.

1974a. *Kabbalah*. Jerusalem: Keter.
1974b. *Mechkarim umekorot letoldot hashabta'ut vegilgileiah*. Jerusalem: Mosad Bialik.
1974c. "Mein Weg zur Kabbala: Ein Credo, vorgetragen vor der Bayerischen Akademie der Schönen Künste." *Süddeutsche Zeitung*, July 20–21.
1974d. "Zionism—Dialectic of Continuity and Rebellion." In *Unease in Zion*, edited by Ehud Ben Ezer, 263–96. New York: Quadrangle.
1975a. "Aus der Geschichte einer Freundschaft: Münchener Erinnerungen an Walter Benjamin." *Süddeutsche Zeitung*, August 16–17.
1975b. *Dvarim bego: Pirkei morashah utchiyah*. Edited by Avraham Shapira. Tel Aviv: Am Oved.
1975c. *Walter Benjamin: Die Geschichte einer Freundschaft*. Frankfurt: Suhrkamp.
1977. *Von Berlin nach Jerusalem: Jugenderinnerungen*. Frankfurt: Suhrkamp.
1978. "Zur Sozialpsychologie der Juden in Deutschland 1900–1933." *Die Krise des Liberalismus zwischen den Weltkriegen*, edited by Rudolf von Thadden, 256–77. Göttingen, Germany: Vandenhoeck & Ruprecht.
1979. "On the Social Psychology of the Jews in Germany: 1900–1933." In *Jews and Germans from 1860 to 1933: The Problematic Symbiosis*, edited by David Bronsen, 9–32. Heidelberg, Germany: Winter.
1980a. "L'identité juive: Entretiens avec Gershom Scholem." By Jean Bollack and Pierre Bourdieu, *Actes de la recherche en sciences sociales* 35 (1): 3–19.
1980b. "The Threat of Messianism: An Interview with Gershom Scholem." By David Biale, *New York Review of Books*, April 14, 22.
1980c. "*. . . und alles ist Kabbala": Gershom Scholem im Gespräch mit Jörg Drews*. Munich: Edition Text + Kritik.
1981a. "Identifizierung und Distanz: Ein Rückblick." In *Denken und Mythische Bildwelt*, edited by Adolf Portmann and Rudolf Ritsema, 463–67. Frankfurt: Insel.
1981b. *Pirkei yesod behavanat hakabalah usmaleah*. Translated by Joseph Ben-Shlomo. Jerusalem: Mosad Bialik.
1981c. *Walter Benjamin: The Story of a Friendship*. Translated by Harry Zohn. London: Faber and Faber.
1982a. "Ahnen und Verwandten Walter Benjamins." *Bulletin des Leo Baeck Instituts*, 61:29–55.
1982b. *Miberlin liyerushalayim: zichronot ne'urim*. Tel Aviv: Am Oved.
1983a. "Die Stellung der Kabbala in der europäischen Geistesgeschichte." In *Wissenschaftskolleg zu Berlin Jahrbuch 1981/82*, edited by Peter Wapnewski, 281–89. Berlin: Quadriga.
1983b. *Walter Benjamin und sein Engel: Vierzehn Aufsätze und kleine Beiträge*, edited by Rolf Tiedemann. Frankfurt: Suhrkamp.
1984a. *Judaica 4*. Frankfurt: Suhrkamp.
1984b. "Die wachsende Kontroverse über den Spinozismus und ihre Folgen." In *Spinoza in der Frühzeit seiner religiösen Wirkung*, edited by Karlfried Gründer and Wilhelm Schmidt-Biggemann, 15–25. Heidelberg, Germany: L. Schneider.
1987. *Origins of the Kabbalah*. Edited by Zwi Werblowsky. Translated by Allan Arkush. Princeton, NJ: Princeton University Press.

1990. *Od davar: Pirkei morashah utchiyah*. Vol. 2. Edited by Avraham Shapira. Tel Aviv: Am Oved.
1991. *On the Mystical Shape of the Godhead: Basic Chapters in the Kabbalah*. New York: Schocken.
1992a. *Sabbatai Zwi: Der mystische Messias*. Frankfurt: Jüdischer Verlag.
1992b. *Judaica 5: Erlösung durch Sünde*. Frankfurt: Suhrkamp.
1994. *Briefe I: 1914–1947*, edited by Itta Shedletzky. Munich: Beck.
1995a. *Briefe II: 1948–1970*, edited by Thomas Sparr. Munich: Beck.
1995b. *Retzifut umered: Gershom Shalom be'omer uvesiach*. Edited by Avraham Shapira. Tel Aviv: Am Oved.
1995c. *Tagebücher: 1. Halbband 1913–1917*. Edited by Karlfried Gründer, Friedrich Niewöhner, and Herbert Kopp-Oberstebrink. Frankfurt: Jüdischer Verlag.
1997a. *On the Possibility of Jewish Mysticism in Our Time and Other Essays*. Edited by Avraham Shapira. Philadelphia: Jewish Publication Society.
1997b. *Judaica 6: Die Wissenschaft vom Judentum*. Edited by Peter Schäfer, Frankfurt: Suhrkamp.
1999. *Briefe III: 1971–1982*. Edited by Itta Shedletzky. Munich: Beck.
2000. *Tagebücher: 2. Halbband 1917–1923*, edited by Karlfried Gründer, Herbert Hopp-Oberstebrink, Friedrich Niewöhner, and Karl E. Grözinger. Frankfurt: Jüdischer Verlag.
2003. *The Fullness of Time: Poems*. Translated by Richard Sieburth. Jerusalem: Ibis.
2006. *Die Erforschung der Kabbala*, edited by Thomas Knofel and Klaus Sander. 2 CDs. Cologne: Supposé.
2012a. *From Berlin to Jerusalem: Memories of My Youth*. Translated by Harry Zohn. Philadelphia: Paul Dry.
2012b. *On Jews and Judaism in Crisis: Selected Essays*. Edited by Werner Dannhauser. Philadelphia: Paul Dry.

Published Works by Gershom Scholem and Coauthors

Arendt, Hannah, and Gerhard Scholem. 2010. *Der Briefwechsel, 1939–1964*, edited by Marie Luise Knott and David Heredia. Berlin: Suhrkamp.
Benjamin, Walter, and Gerhard Scholem. 1980. *Briefwechsel 1933–1940*. Edited by Gershom Scholem. Frankfurt: Suhrkamp.
———. 1989. *The Correspondence, 1932–1940*. Edited by Gershom Scholem.Translated by Gary Smith and Andre LeFevere. New York: Schocken.
Scholem, Betty, and Gershom Scholem. 1989. *Mutter und Sohn im Briefwechsel 1917–1946*. Edited by Itta Shedletzky and Thomas Sparr. Munich: Beck.
Scholem, Gershom, et al. 1967. "Bitachon veshalom—ken, sipuach—lo." *Haaretz*, December 15.
Scholem, Gershom, and Theodor W. Adorno. 2015. *"Der liebe Gott wohnt im Detail": Briefwechsel 1939–1969*. Edited by Asaf Angermann. Berlin: Suhrkamp.
Scholem, Gershom, and Hannah Arendt. 1963. "Ein Briefwechsel über Hannah Arendts Buch zwischen Prof. Gershom Gerhard Scholem und Hannah Arendt." MB, August 16, 2–4.

———. 1964. "'Eichmann in Jerusalem': An Exchange of Letters between Gershom Scholem and Hannah Arendt." *Encounter*, January, 51–56.

Scholem, Gershom, [Shmuel] Hugo Bergmann, Hans Kohn, Judah Leib Magnes, Yehoshua Radler-Feldman, and Jesajah Schapiro. 1926a. "Erklärung." *Jüdische Rundschau*, April 23, 231.

———. 1926b. "Giluy da'at." *Doar Hayom*, April 11.

Scholem, Gershom, and Joseph Weiss. 2012. *Halifat mikhtavim 1948–1964*. Edited by Noam Zadoff. Jerusalem: Carmel.

Other References

Abrams, Daniel. 2000. "Defining Modern Academic Scholarship: Gershom Scholem and the Establishment of a New (?) Discipline." *Journal of Jewish Thought and Philosophy* 9 (2): 267–302.

Adorno, Theodor W., Peter Suhrkamp, and Siegfried Unseld. 2003. *"So müsste ich ein Engel und kein Autor sein": Adorno und seine Frankfurter Verleger*. Edited by Wolfgang Schopf. Frankfurt: Suhrkamp.

Adorno, Theodor W., and Lotte Tobisch. 2003. *Der private Briefwechsel*. Edited by Bernhard Kraller and Heinz Steinert.Vienna: Droschl.

Agnon, S. Y. 1918. "Die Erzählung vom Toraschreiber." *Der Jude*, no. 4, 253–64.

———. 2000. *Me'atzmi el atzmi*. Tel Aviv: Schocken.

Ahad Haam. 1950. "Al dvar otzar hayahadut balashon ha'ivrit." In Ahad Haam, *Kol kitvei Ahad Haam*, 104–14. Tel Aviv: Dvir.

———. 1997. "The Jewish State and the Jewish Problem." In *The Zionist Idea: A Historical Analysis and Reader*, edited by Arthur Herzberg, 262–69. Philadelphia: Jewish Publication Society.

Allony, Nehemya. 1993. *"Ktav-yad shel Moshe Rabenu": Yomanei masa legilui kitvei–yad ivriym*. Jerusalem: Reuven Mas.

Améry, Jean. 1967. "Fragen an Hans Egon Holthusen—und seine Antwort." *Merkur*, April, 393–400.

Anidjar, Gil. 1996. "Jewish Mysticism Alterable and Unalterable: On Orienting Kabbalah Studies and the Zohar of Christian Spain." *Jewish Social Studies* 3 (1): 89–157.

Arendt, Hannah. 1950. "The Aftermath of Nazi Rule: Report from Germany." *Commentary*, October, 342–53.

———. 1964. *Eichmann in Jerusalem: A Report on the Banality of Evil*. New York: Penguin.

———. 1968. "Walter Benjamin." *Merkur*, January, 50–65; March, 209–24; and April, 305–15.

———. 2007. *The Jewish Writings*. Edited by Jerome Kohn and Ron H. Feldman. New York: Schocken.

——— and Kurt Blumenfeld. 1995. *". . . in keinem Besitz verwurzelt": Die Korrespondenz*, edited by Ingeborg Nordmann and Iris Pilling. Hamburg, Germany: Rotbuch.

——— and Karl Jaspers. 1992. *Correspondence 1926–1969*. Edited by Lotte Köhler und Hans Saner. New York: Harcourt Brace Jovanovich.

Aschheim, Steven. 1982. *Brothers and Strangers: The East European Jew in German and German Jewish Consciousness 1800–1923*. Madison: University of Wisconsin Press.

———. 2001a. "Hannah Arendt in Jerusalem." In *Hannah Arendt in Jerusalem*, edited by Steven Aschheim, 1–15. Berkeley: University of California Press.

———. 2001b. *Scholem, Arendt, Klemperer: Intimate Chronicles in Turbulent Times*. Bloomington: Indiana University Press.

———. 2007. *Beyond the Border: The German Jewish Legacy Abroad*. Princeton, NJ: Princeton University Press.

Auslander, Leora. 2005. "Coming home? Jews in Postwar Paris." *Journal of Contemporary History* 40 (2): 237–59.

Avni, Haim. 1981. *Im yehudim bemachanot ha'akurim: Rishmei shlichut, 1945–1947*. Sdeh Nachum, Israel: Chaverim.

Awerbuch, Marianne. 1982. "Scholem zum Gedenken: 'Brücken von reinen Willen. Zum Tode des Judaisten und Religionswissenschaftlers Gershom Scholem.'" *Der Tagesspiegel*, February 23.

B. H. 1980. "Historische Schlagzeilen: Gershom Scholem sprach in Wolfenbüttel." *Hannoversche Allgemeine*, May 13.

B[irnbaum], I[mmanuel]. 1973. "Juden in Deutschland vor 1933: Gershom Scholem sprach im Münchner Institut für Zeitgeschichte." *Süddeutsche Zeitung*, March 17–18.

Babakov, A. 1931. "Mikhtav galui lach. David Yalin uVen Zvi." *Doar Hayom*, February 21.

Baron, Salo. 1945. "The Spiritual Reconstruction of European Jewry." *Commentary*, November 1, 4–12.

Barone, Elisabetta, Matthias Riedl, and Alexandra Tischel, eds. 2004. *Pioniere, Poeten, Professoren: Eranos und der Monte Verità in der Zivilisationsgeschichte des 20. Jahrhunderts*. Würzburg, Germany: Königshausen und Neumann.

Bartal, Israel. 1997. "The Ingathering of Traditions: Zionism's Anthology Projects." *Prooftexts* 17 (1): 77–93.

———. 2000. "The Kinnus Project: Wissenschaft des Judentums and the Fashioning of a 'National Culture' in Palestine." In *Transmitting Jewish Traditions: Orality, Textuality and Cultural Diffusion*, edited by Yaakov Elman and Israel Gershoni, 310–23. New Haven, CT: Yale University Press.

Barzel, Neima. 1998. "Hakavod, hasin'ah vehazikaron badiyunim beshe'elat hapitzuiym vehashilumim migeramniah bishnot hachamishim." *Yad Vashem* 24:203–25.

Baumel, Judith Tydor. 1997. *Kibbutz Buchanwald: Survivors and Pioneers*. New Brunswick, NJ: Rutgers University Press.

Becker, Hellmut. 1978. "Gershom Scholem 80 Jahre: Eine Ansprache und ein Buchbericht." *Neue Sammlung* 18 (2): 128–31.

———. 1982. "'Wenn ein Weiser stirbt, kann niemand ihn ersetzen': Zum Tode Gershom Scholem." *Orientierung* 46 (6): 63–65.

Behrmann, Günter C. 1999. "Kulturrevolution: Zwei Monate im Sommer 1967." In *Die intellektuelle Gründung der Bundesrepublik: Eine Wirkungsgeschichte der Frankfurter Schule*, edited by Clemens Albrecht, Günter C. Behrman, Michael Bock, Harald Homan, and Friedrich H. Tenbruck, 312–86. Frankfurt: Campus.

Beit-Arié, Malachi. 1983. "Yachaso shel Shalom lasefer velasifriyah." In *Gershom Shalom: Al ha'ish ufoalo—dvarim shene'emru beyom hashloshim lehistalkuto*, 63–70. Jerusalem: Magnes and Mosad Bialik.

———. 1994. "Gershom Scholem as Bibliophile." In *Gershom Scholem: The Man and His Work*, edited by Paul Mendes-Flohr, 120–27. Albany: State University of New York Press.

Ben Nachman, Mosche. 1935–36). "Hymnus vom Schicksal der Seele." Translated by Gershom Scholem. *Almanach des Schocken Verlags* 5696:86–89.

Benjamin, Walter. 1955. *Schriften*. 2 vols. Edited by Theodor W. Adorno and Gretel Adorno. Frankfurt: Suhrkamp.

———. 1966. *Briefe*. Edited by Gershom Scholem and Theodor W. Adorno. 2 vols. Frankfurt: Suhrkamp.

———. 1968. "On Unpacking My Library." In Walter Benjamin, *Illuminations*, edited by Hannah Arendt and translated by Harry Zohn, 59–67. New York: Harcourt Brace.

———. 1970. *Berliner Chronik*. Edited by Gershom Scholem. Frankfurt: Suhrkamp.

———. 1989. *Gesammelte Schriften, unter Mitwirkung von Theodor W. Adorno und Gershom Scholem*. 7 vols. Edited by Rolf Tiedemann and Hermann Schweppenhäuser. Frankfurt: Suhrkamp.

Benzenhöfer, Udo. 2007. *Der Arztphilosoph Viktor von Weizsäcker: Leben und Welt im Überblick*. Göttingen, Germany: Vandenhoeck & Ruprecht.

Bergmann, Shmuel Hugo. 1927. "Geistiges Leben." *Palästina* 10 (3): 132–34 and (6): 323–25.

———. 1985. *Tagebücher und Briefe*. Vol. 1: 1901–1948. Edited by Mirjam Sambursky. Königstein, Germany: Jüdischer Verlag bei Athenäum.

Bernstein, Richard J. 1996. *Hannah Arendt and the Jewish Question*. Cambridge, MA: MIT Press.

———. 2001. "Hannah Arendt's Zionism?" In *Hannah Arendt in Jerusalem*, edited by Steven Aschheim, 194–202 Berkeley: University of California Press.

Biale, David. 1979. *Gershom Scholem: Kabbalah and Counter-History*. Cambridge, MA: Harvard University Press.

———. 1985. "Gershom Scholem's Ten Unhistorical Aphorisms on Kabbalah: Text and Commentary." *Modern Judaism* 5 (1): 67–93.

———. 2001. "Shabbtai Zvi and the Seductions of Jewish Orientalism." In *The Sabbatian Movement and Its Aftermath: Messianism, Sabbatianism and Frankism*, edited by Rachel Elior, 85–110. Jerusalem: Mandel Institute.

Bialik, Hayim Nahman. 1937–39. *Igrot Haim Nahman Bialik*. Edited by Fischel Lachover. Vol. 3. Tel Aviv: Dvir.

———. 1968. "Hasefer ha'ivri." In Hayim Nahman Bialik, *Divrei Sifrut*, 32–56. Tel Aviv: Dvir.

Boehlich, Walter. 1999. "Ein Jude aus Deutschland: Nach Gershom Scholems Tod." In Gershom Scholem, *Briefe III: 1971–1982*, edited by Itta Shedletzky, 463–64. Munich: Beck.

Bohrer, Karl Heinz. 1998. "1968: Die Phantasie an die Macht? Studentenbewegung

—Walter Benjamin—Surrealismus." In *1968: Vom Ereignis zum Gegenstand der Geschichtswissenschaft*, edited by Ingrid Gilcher-Holtey, 288–300. Göttingen, Germany: Vandenhoeck & Ruprecht.

Boswell, James. 2008. *The Life of Samuel Johnson*. Edited by David Womersley. London: Penguin.

Braunová, Andrea. 2000. "Origin of the Book Collection of the Library of the Jewish Museum in Prague." *Judaica Bohemiae* 36:160–72.

Bremer, Thomas S. 2004. "The *Genius Loci Ignotus* of Eranos and the Making of a Sacred Place." In *Pioniere, Poeten, Professoren: Eranos und der Monte Verità in der Zivilisationsgeschichte des 20. Jahrhunderts*, edited by Elisabetta Barone, Matthias Riedl, and Alexandra Tischel, 79–82. Würzburg, Germany: Königshausen und Neumann.

Brenner, Hildegard. 1969. "Theodor W. Adorno als Sachwalter des Benjaminschen Werkes." In *Die neue Linke nach Adorno*, edited by Wilfried F. Schoeller, 158–75. Munich: Kindler.

Brenner, Michael. 1998. *The Jewish Renaissance in Weimar Germany*. New Haven, CT: Yale University Press.

———. 2010. *Prophets of the Past: Interpreters of Jewish History*. Princeton, NJ: Princeton University Press.

Bronowski, Yoram. 1982. "Miberlin liyerushaliym uverchazarah." *Haaretz*, April 30.

Buber, Martin. 1906. *Die Geschichte des Rabbi Nachman*. Frankfurt: Rütten und Loening.

———. 1908. *Die Legende des Baalschem*. Frankfurt: Rütten und Loening.

———. 1911. *Drei Reden über das Judentum*. Frankfurt: Rütten und Loening.

———. 1916. "Die Losung." *Der Jude*, April, 1–3.

———. 1990. *Chilufei iga rot: Kerekh rishon 1918–1938*. Edited by Grete Schaeder. Jerusalem: Mosad Bialik.

Burckhardt, Carl J., and Max Rychner. 1970. *Briefe 1926–1965*. Edited by Claudia Mertz-Rychner. Frankfurt: S. Fischer Verlag.

Cain, Seymour. 1989. "Mircea Eliade, the Iron Guards, and Romanian Antisemitism." *Midstream*, November, 27–31.

Campanini, Saverio. 2005. "A Case for Sainte-Beuve: Some Remarks on Gershom Scholem's Autobiography." In *Creation and Re-Creation in Jewish Thought: Festschrift in Honor of Joseph Dan on the Occasion of His Seventieth Birthday*, edited by Rachel Elior and Peter Schäfer, 363–400. Tübingen, Germany: Mohr Siebeck.

Cohen, Hillel. 2015. *Year Zero of the Arab-Israeli Conflict: 1929*. Waltham, MA: Brandeis University Press.

Cohen, Richard I. 1993. "Breaking the Code: Hannah Arendt's *Eichmann in Jerusalem* and the Public Polemic—Myth, Memory and Historical Imagination." *Michael* 13:29–85.

———. 2001. "A Generation's Response to *Eichmann in Jerusalem*." In *Hannah Arendt in Jerusalem*, edited by Steven Aschheim, 253–77. Berkeley: University of California Press.

Cohen, Uri. 2007. *Hahar vehagiv'ah: Ha'universitah ha'ivrit beyerushalayim bitkufat trom ha'atzma'ut vereshit hamedina*. Tel Aviv: Am Oved.

Cohen Grossman, Grace. 2002. "Scholar as Political Activist: Salo W. Baron and the Founding of the Jewish Cultural Reconstruction." In *For Every Thing a Season: Proceedings of the Symposium on Jewish Ritual Art*, edited by Joseph Gutmann, 146–57. Cleveland, OH: Cleveland State University Press.

Cohn, Margot, and Rivka Plesser. 1988. *Gershom Scholem (1897–1982): Commemorative Exhibition*. Jerusalem: Jewish National and University Library.

Commission on European Jewish Cultural Reconstruction. 1946. "Tentative List of Jewish Cultural Treasures in Axis–Occupied Countries." Supplement to *Jewish Social Studies* 8 (1).

Corbin, Henry. 1957. "The Time of Eranos." In *Man and Time: Papers from the Eranos Yearbooks*, edited by Joseph Campbell, xiii–xx. New York: Pantheon.

———. 1981. "A Letter by Henry Corbin." In *The New Polytheism: Rebirth of the Gods and Goddesses*, edited by David L. Miller, 1–6. Dallas, TX: Spring.

———. 1998. *Alone with the Alone: Creative Imagination in the Sūfism of Ibn 'Arabī*. Princeton, NJ: Princeton University Press.

Dahlhaus, Carl. 1975. "Geschichte einer Freundschaft: Gershom Scholem über Walter Benjamin." *Die Zeit*, November 28.

Dahm, Volker. 1993. *Das jüdische Buch im Dritten Reich*. Munich: Beck.

Dan, Joseph. 1988. *Gershom Scholem and the Mystical Dimension of Jewish History*. New York: New York University Press.

———. 2007. "Gershom shalom, chavurat 'eranos,' vedat shele'ahar hadat'." In *Sefer zikaron leGershom Shalom bimlot 'esrim vechamesh leftirato*, edited by Joseph Dan, 1:265–304. Jerusalem: Mandel Institute.

———. 2010. *Al Gershom Shalom: Treisar ma'amarim*. Jerusalem: Shazar.

David, Anthony. 2003. *The Patron: A Life of Salman Schocken, 1877–1959*. New York: Metropolitan.

Davis, Fred. 1979. *Yearning for Yesterday: A Sociology of Nostalgia*. New York: Free Press.

Dawidowicz, Lucy S. 1989. *From That Place and Time: A Memoir, 1938–1947*. New York: W. W. Norton.

Demm, Sabine. 2001. "Die Studentenbewegung von 1968 in Frankfurt am Main: Eine Chronologie." *Archiv für Frankfurts Geschichte und Kunst* 67:161–247.

Die Geschichte des Suhrkamp Verlages: 1. Juli 1950 bis 30. Juni 2000. 2000. Frankfurt: Suhrkamp.

Diner, Dan. 1996. "Hannah Arendt: Jüdisches Selbstverständnis im Schatten der Eichmann–Kontroverse." In *Hannah Arendt und die Berliner Republik: Fragen an das vereinigte Deutschland*, edited by Bernward Baule, 151–65. Berlin: Aufbau.

———. 1997. "Hannah Arendt Reconsidered: On the Banal and the Evil in Her Holocaust Narrative." *New German Critique* 71 (spring–summer): 177–90.

Dinur, Ben–Zion. 1943. *Goralenu umilchamtenu: Chamesh ptichot miyom ha'evel vehaze'akah*. Tel Aviv: Merkaz mifleget po'alei eretz yisrael.

———. 1948. *Zakhor: Dvarim al hashoah ve'al likchah*. Jerusalem: Yad Vashem.

Drews, Jörg. 1974. "Dank an Gershom Scholem: Der Literaturpreis der Bayerischen Akademie der Schönen Künste wurde dem jüdischen Gelehrten und deutschen Schriftsteller verliehen." *Süddeutsche Zeitung*, July 16.

———. 1977. "Arbeit an der jüdischen Identität: Zum 80. Geburtstag von Gershom Scholem ([5].XII.1977)." *Merkur*, December, 1207–11.

———. 1982. "'Die Kabbalisten wußten etwas, das wir nicht wissen': Zum Gedanken an Gershom Scholem." *Süddeutsche Zeitung*, April 3–4.

———. (1986). "Nachwort." In Gershom Scholem, *Briefe an Werner Kraft*, edited by Werner Kraft, 147–61. Frankfurt: Suhrkamp.

E. M. D. 1964. "Unter dem David-Schild: Gershom Scholem sprach in Frankfurt über Judaica." *Frankfurter Allgemeine Zeitung*, October 9.

Eliade, Mircea. 1955. "Les danseurs passent, la danse reste." *DU* 4 (April): 60–62.

———. 1977. *No Souvenirs: Journal 1957–1969*. Translated by Fred H. Johnson. New York: Harper and Row.

———. 1988. *Autobiography*. Volume 2: *1937–1960, Exile's Odyssey*. Translated by Mac Linscott Ricketts. Chicago: University of Chicago Press.

———. 1990. *Journal I: 1945–1955*. Translated by Mac Linscott Ricketts. Chicago: University of Chicago Press.

Engelhardt, Arndt. 2006. "Palimpsests and Questions of Canonisation: The German-Jewish Encyclopedias in the Weimar Era." *Journal of Modern Jewish Studies* 5 (3): 301–21.

Fischer-Defoy, Christine, ed. 1997. *". . . und die Vergangenheit sitzt immer mit am Tisch": Dokumente zur Geschichte der Akademie der Künste (West) 1945/1954–1993*. Berlin: Akademie der Künste.

Frankel, Naomi. 1982. "Gershom Shalom shebalev." *Moznaim* 55, nos. 1–2: 6–10.

Friedman, Herbert A. 1990. *Roots of the Future*. Jerusalem: Gefen.

Friedman, Maurice. 1991. *Encounter on the Narrow Ridge: A Life of Martin Buber*. New York: Paragon House.

Fritzsche, Peter. 1996. *Reading Berlin 1900*. Cambridge, MA: Harvard University Press.

Frühwald, Wolfgang. 2006. "Wirkungen der Freiheit." In *25 Jahre Wissenschaftskolleg zu Berlin: 1981–2006*, edited by Dieter Grimm and Reinhart Meyer-Kalkus, 1–27. Berlin: Akademie.

Gallas, Elisabeth. 2013. *"Das Leichenhaus der Bücher": Kulturrestitution und jüdisches Geschichtsdenken nach 1945*. Göttingen, Germany: Vandenhoeck & Ruprecht.

Garber, Klaus. 1987. *Rezeption und Rettung: Drei Studien zu Walter Benjamin*. Tübingen, Germany: Niemeyer.

Gelber, Yoav. 1982. "Hamediniyut habritit vehatzionit be'eretz Israel betzel hachashash mehitkomemut yehudit 1942–1944." *Hatzionut* 7:342–96.

Gershom Shalom: Al ha'ish ufoalo—dvarim shene'emru beyom hashloshim lehistalkuto. 1983. Jerusalem: Magnes and Mosad Bialik.

Die Geschichte des Suhrkamp Verlages: 1. Juli 1950 bis 30. Juni 2000. 2000. Frankfurt Suhrkamp.

Gilman, Sander L. 1994. "Psychoanalysis and Anti-Semitism: Tainted Greatness in a Professional Context." In *Tainted Greatness: Antisemitism and Cultural Heroes*, edited by Nancy A. Harrowitz, 93–107. Philadelphia: Temple University Press.

Glotz, Peter 2005. *Von Heimat zu Heimat: Erinnerungen eines Grenzgängers*. Munich: Econ.

———et al. 2006. "Dieses Haus hatte Fortune . . .: Peter Glotz, Otto Häfner, Joachim Nettelbeck, Christoph Schneider, Joachim Stoehr, Peter Wapnewski im Gespräch." In *25 Jahre Wissenschaftskolleg zu Berlin: 1981–2006*, edited by Dieter Grimm and Reinhart Meyer-Kalkus, 33–56. Berlin: Akademie.

Green, Martin. 1986. *Mountain of Truth: The Counterculture Begins, Ascona, 1900–1920.* Hanover, NH: University Press of New England.

Gries, Zeev. 1990. "Hareka hayehudi lefo'alo shel Buber be'itzuv hasipur hachasidi." *Mechkarei yerushalayim befolklor yehudi*, 11–12:46–56.

Grobman, Alex. 1992. *Rekindling the Flame: American Jewish Chaplains and the Survivors of European Jewry, 1944–1948*. Detroit, MI: Wayne State University Press.

Grosche, Heinz, and Klaus Rohde. 1991. *Geschichte der Juden in Bad Homburg vor der Höhe 1866 bis 1945*. Frankfurt: W. Kramer.

Gründer, Karlfried. 1984. "Vorbemerkung." In *Spinoza in der Frühzeit seiner religiösen Wirkung*, edited by Karlfried Gründer and Wilhelm Schmidt-Biggemann, 9–11. Heidelberg, Germany: L. Schneider.

Habermas, Jürgen. 1982. "Tod in Jerusalem: Am Grabe von Gershom Scholem—am Ende einer Ära." *Merkur*, April, 438–40.

———. 1987. "Die verkleidete Tora (1978)." In Jürgen Habermas, *Philosophisch–politische Profile*, 377–91. Frankfurt: Suhrkamp.

———. 1994. "Das Falsche im Eigenen." *Die Zeit*, September 23.

———. 2007. "Begegnungen mit Gershom Scholem." *Münchner Beiträge zur jüdische Geschichte und Kultur* 1 (2): 9–18.

Hack, Bertold. 1971. "Der Verleger Daniel Brody und seine Familie." In Hermann Broch and Daniel Brody, *Briefwechsel 1930–1951*, edited by Bertold Hack and Marietta Kleiss, 1175–90. Frankfurt: Buchhändler-Vereinigung.

———. 1979. "Verlagsbibliographie des Rhein-Verlages 1920–1972." In *Archiv für Geschichte des Buchwesens*, edited by Bertold Hack and Marietta Kleiss, 1153–216. Frankfurt: Buchhändler-Vereinigung.

Haeger, Robert, and Bill Long. 1947. "Lost EC Treasure Found in Palestine." *Stars and Stripes*, European ed., December 9.

Hakl, Thomas Hans. 2013. *Eranos: An Alternative Intellectual History of the Twentieth Century*. Montreal: McGill University Press.

Halkin, Hillel. 2014. *Jabotinsky: A Life*. New Haven, CT: Yale University Press.

Hamm, Peter. 1967a. "Bemerkungen zu einem Geständnis." *Frankfurter Hefte* 22:137–38.

———. 1967b. "Unter den Neuerern der Wichtigste." *Frankfurter Hefte* 22:359–64.

Harpaz, Yoram. 1990. "Metil tzel anak." *Kol Ha'ir*, January 19.

Hasan-Rokem, Galit. 2016. "The Star of David and the Stars Outside: The Poetics and Semiotics of Jewish Folklore and of Zionism." Images: *Journal of Jewish Art and Visual Culture* 9 (1): 78–99.

Heissenbüttel, Helmut. 1967. "Vom Zeugnis des Fortlebens in Briefen." *Merkur*, March, 232–44.

Held, Hans Ludwig. 1912. *Talmud Legenden: Dem Talmud nacherzählt und eingeleitet*. Munich: Sachs Verlag.

———. 1927. *Das Gespenst des Golem: Eine Studie aus der hebräischen Mystik mit einem Exkurs über das Wesen des Doppelgängers*. Munich: Allgemeine Verlagsanstalt.

Heller, Joseph. 2004. *MiBrit Shalom leIhud: Yehudah Leib Magnes vehama'avak al medinah du le'umit*. Jerusalem: Magnes.

Hentig, Hartmut von. 1983. "Die Welt aus den Angeln zu heben: Letzte erste Begegnung mit Gershom Scholem." *Frankfurter Allgemeine Zeitung*, February 26.

———. 2007. *Mein Leben—bedacht und bejaht: Schule, Polis, Gartenhaus*. Munich: Hanser.

Herman, Dana. 2008. "Hashavat Avedah: A History of Jewish Cultural Reconstruction, Inc." PhD diss., McGill University.

Herzog, Annabel. 2009. "'Monolingualism' or the Language of God: Scholem and Derrida on Hebrew and Politics." *Modern Judaism* 29 (2): 226–38.

Heuberger, Rachel. 1996. *Bibliothek des Judentums: Die Hebraica- und Judaica-Sammlung der Stadt- und Universitätsbibliothek Frankfurt am Main—Entstehung, Geschichte und heutige Aufgaben*. Frankfurt: Klostermann.

Hirschfeld, Ariel. 1994. "Schocken und Agnon: Münz und Masal." In *Der Schocken Verlag / Berlin: Jüdische Selbstbehauptung in Deutschland 1931–1938*, edited by Saskia Schreuder and Claude Weber, 191–200. Berlin: Akademie Verlag.

Holthusen, Hans Egon. 1966. "Freiwillig zur SS." *Merkur*, October, 921–39; and November, 1037–49.

Honigmann, Barbara. 2002. "Double Burial." In *Contemporary Jewish Writing in Germany: An Anthology*, edited by Leslie Morris and Karen Remmler, 109–14. Lincoln: Nebraska University Press.

Huss, Boaz. 2005. "Ask No Questions: Gershom Scholem and the Study of Contemporary Jewish Mysticism." *Modern Judaism* 25 (2): 141–58.

———. 2007. "'Authorized Guardians': The Polemics of Academic Scholars of Jewish Mysticism against Kabbalah Practitioners." In *Polemical Encounters: Esoteric Discourse and Its Others*, edited by Kocku von Stuckrad and Olav Hammer, 81–104. Leiden, the Netherlands: Brill.

Idel, Moshe. 1988. *Kabbalah: New Perspectives*. New Haven, CT: Yale University Press.

———. 1998. "Mekomo shel hasemel behaguto shel gershom shalom." *Mada'ei Hayahadut* 38:43–72.

———. 1999. "Academic Studies of Kabbalah in Israel: 1923–1998. A Short Survey." *Studia Judaica* 8:91–114.

———. 2005. *Ascensions on High in Jewish Mysticism: Pillars, Lines, Ladders*. Budapest: Central European University Press.

———. 2010. *Old Worlds, New Mirrors: On Jewish Mysticism and Twentieth-Century Thought*. Philadelphia: University of Pennsylvania Press.

Jabotinsky, Vladimir. 2011. "On the Iron Wall (1923)." In *The Origins of Israel 1882–1948: A Documentary History*, edited by Eran Kaplan and Derek J. Penslar, 257–63. Madison: University of Wisconsin Press.

Jaffé, Aniela. 1968. *Aus Leben und Werkstatt von C. G. Jung: Parapsychologie—Alchemie—Nationalsozialismus. Erinnerungen an den letzten Jahren*. Zurich: Rascher.

Jaspers, Karl (1945). "Gleitwort." *Die Wandlung*, November, 3–6.

———. 1947. *The Question of German Guilt*. Translated by E. B. Ashton. New York: Dial.

Jung, Carl Gustav. 1952. *Antwort auf Hiob*. Zurich: Rascher.

Kalisker, Abraham. 1933–34. "Hachschara." *Almanach des Schocken Verlags* 5694:97–98.

Katz, Shaul. 2001. "'Mada tahor' be'universita le'umit: makhon einstein lematematikah umekhonim aherim bauniversitah haivrit bizman hithavutah." In *Toldot vehatchalot, ha'universita ha'ivrit: shorashim*, edited by Shaul Katz and Michael Heyd, 397–456. Jerusalem: Magnes.

———. 2008. "Gershom Shalom utchilat darko ba'universita ha'ivrit." *Catharsis* 3:144–63.

———. 2014. "The Scion and the Tree: The Hebrew University of Jerusalem and Its German Epistemological and Organizational Origins." In *The Institution of Science and the Science of Institutions: The Legacy of Joseph Ben David*, edited by Marcel Herbst, 103–44. Dordrecht, the Netherlands: Springer Science and Business Media.

Ke, Dr. 1980. "Mystischen Kern der Philosophie Spinozas beleuchtet: Professor Gershom Scholem (Jerusalem) sprach in der Augustenhalle über Spinozas Wirken." *Wolfenbütteler Zeitung*, May 12.

Kedar, Aharon. 1976. "Letoldoteiah shel Brit Shalom bashanim 1925–1928." In *Pirkei mehkar betoldot hatzionut mugashim leIsrael Goldstein behagi'o ligvurot al yiedei talmidei hamakhon leyahadut zmanenu umoraiv*, edited by Yahuda Bauer, Moshe Davis, and Israel Kolat, 224–85. Jerusalem: Hasifriyah Hatzionit.

Kerényi, Karl. 1955. "Was bedeutet der Name Eranos?" *DU* 4 (April): 39–40.

Keynan, Irit. 1997. *Lo nirga hara'av: Nitzolei hasho'ah ushlichei eretz yisrael—Germaniah 1946–1948*. Jerusalem: Am Oved.

[Klatzkin, Jakob]. 1929. "Ptihah." In *Eshkol: Entziklopedia Israelit*, 1:10–13. Berlin: Eshkol.

Klemperer, Viktor. 2006. *The Language of the Third Reich: LTI Lingua Tercii Imperii: A Philologist's Notebook*. London: Continuum.

Kolat, Israel. 1998. "Tzionut umeshchiut." In *Meshichiut ve'eskhatologia: Kovetz ma'amarim*, edited by Zvi Baras, 47–59. Jerusalem: Shazar.

Kotler, Leib. 1946. "A mesibas morim baym chaplain Abramowitz." *Undzer Lebn*, August 25, 15.

Küpper, Thomas, and Timo Skrandies. 2006. "Rezeptionsgeschichte." In *Benjamin —Handbuch: Leben, Werk, Wirkung*, edited by Burkhardt Linder, Thomas Küpper, and Timo Skrandies, 17–56. Stuttgart, Germany: J. B. Meltzer.

Kurtz, Michael J. 2006. *America and the Return of Nazi Contraband: The Recovery of Europe's Cultural Treasures*. Cambridge: Cambridge University Press.

Kurzweil, Baruch. 1970. *Bema'avak al erkei hayahadut*. Jerusalem: Schocken.

Landmann, Robert. 2000. *Ascona—Monte Verità: Auf der Suche nach dem Paradies*. Frauenfeld, Switzerland: Huber.

Laor, Dan. 1993. "Agnon in Germany, 1912–1924: A Chapter of a Biography." *AJS Review* 18 (1): 75–93.

———. 1995. *Shai Agnon: Hebetim chadashim*. Tel Aviv: Sifryiat Po'alim.

———. 1998. *Chaiyei Agnon: Biografiah*. Jerusalem: Schocken.

———. 2002. "Agnon and Buber: The Story of a Friendship or, the Rise and Fall of the 'Corpus Hasidicum.'" In *Martin Buber: Contemporary Perspectives*, edited by Paul Mendes-Flohr, 48–86. Syracuse: Syracuse University Press.

Laurien, Ingrid. 2002. "Zeitschriftlandschaft Nachkriegszeit: Zu Struktur und Funktion politisch-kultureller Zeitschriften 1945–1949." *Publizistik* 47 (1): 57–82.

Lavi, Theodore. 1972. "Tik Mircea Eliade." *Toladot* 1:13–18.

Lavsky, Hagit 1996. *Before Catastrophe: The Distinctive Path of German Zionism*. Detroit, MI: Wayne State University Press.

Lepenies, Wolf. 1997. "Einleitung." In Elie Wiesel, *Ethik und Erinnerung*, 1–10. Berlin: de Gruyter.

"Lesha'aruriyat hasifriyah hamikhlalanit: Tshuvah lemar A. Babakov lemikhtavo hagalui bedoar hayom miyom 3 adar leshana zo." 1931. *Doar Hayom*, March 1.

Lewinsky, Tamar. 2008. *Displaced Poets: Jiddische Schriftsteller im Nachkriegsdeutschland, 1945–1951*. Göttingen, Germany: Vandenhoeck & Ruprecht.

Loewy, Ernst. 1965. "Die Judaica-Sammlung der Frankfurter Stadt- und Universitätsbibliothek." *Bulletin des Leo Baeck Instituts* 8 (29): 55–64.

Magid, Shaul. 2011. "Mysticism, History, and the 'New' Kabbalah: Gershom Scholem and the Contemporary Scene." *Jewish Quarterly Review* 101 (4): 511–25.

Mandel, Maud S. 2002. "Philanthropy or Cultural Imperialism? The Impact of American Jewish Aid in Post-Holocaust France." *Jewish Social Studies* 9 (1): 53–94.

Manea, Norman. 2008. "Nomadic Language." In *The Writer Uprooted: Contemporary Jewish Exile Literature*, edited by Alvin Rosenfeld, 1–26. Bloomington: Indiana University Press.

Mankowitz, Zeev W. 2002. *Life between Memory and Hope: The Survivors of the Holocaust in Occupied Germany*. Cambridge: Cambridge University Press.

McGuire, William. 1989. *Bollingen: An Adventure in Collecting the Past*. Princeton, NJ: Princeton University Press.

Meir, Jonatan. 2004. "Hithavuto vegilgulav shel mif'al tirgum uvi'ur sefer hazohar lehillel zeitlin." *Kabbalah* 10:119–57.

———. 2011. *Rechovot Hanahar: Kabbalah ve'exoteriut biyerushalaiym*. Jerusalem: Yad Ben Zvi.

Mendes-Flohr, Paul. 1986. "Martin Buber's Reception among Jews." *Modern Judaism* 6 (2): 111–26.

———. 1991a. *Divided Passions: Jewish Intellectuals and the Experience of Modernity*. Detroit, MI: Wayne State University Press.

———. 1991b. "The Yoke of the Kingdom in Jerusalem." In *The Jewish Legacy and the German Conscience: Essays in Memory of Rabbi Joseph Asher*, edited by Moses Rischin and Raphael Asher, 233–45. Berkeley, CA: Judah L. Magnes Museum.

———, ed. 1994. *Gershom Scholem: The Man and His Work*. Albany: State University of New York Press.

Mekitz Nirdamim 1861. "Mekitz Nirdamim." *Hamagid*, September 12.

Mekitzei Nirdamim. 1964. *Mekitzei Nirdamim (1864–1964): Dvarim shene'emru bechagigah bimlot me'ah shanah lachevra beyom revi'i, 4 bekhislev 1964 beveit hasfarim hale'umi biyerushalayim bekiriyat ha'universitah biyerushalyim*. Jerusalem: Mekitzei Nirdamim.

Meysels, Lucian O. 2002. *Die Welt der Lotte Tobisch*. Vienna: Edition Va Vene.

Michalzik, Peter. 2003. *Unseld: Eine Biographie*. Munich: Karl Blessing.

Momigliano, Arnaldo, 1987. *On Pagans, Jews and Christians*, 254–63. Middletown, CT: Wesleyan University Press.

Momos [Walter Jens]. 1976. “Meditationen über Gott im Husch–Husch–Stil: *ARD*, Sonntag, 20. Juni—‘Gershom Scholem.’” *Die Zeit*, June 25.

Monteanu Eddon, Raluca. 2003. “Gershom Scholem, Hannah Arendt and the Paradox of ‘Non-Nationalist’ Nationalism.” *Journal of Jewish Thought and Philosophy* 12 (1): 55–68.

Morag, Shelomo. 1993. “The Emergence of Modern Hebrew: Some Sociolinguistic Perspectives.” In *Hebrew in Ashkenaz: A Language in Exile*, edited by Lewis Glinert, 208–21. New York: Oxford University Press.

Morinis, Alan. 1992. “Introduction: The Territory of the Anthropology of Pilgrimage.” In *Sacred Journeys: The Anthropology of Pilgrimage*, edited by Alan Morinis, 1–28. London: Praeger.

Morris, Benny. 2001. *Righteous Victims: A History of the Zionist-Arab Conflict, 1881–2001*. New York: Vintage.

Moseley, Marcus, 2006. *Being for Myself Alone: Origins of Jewish Autobiography*. Stanford, CA: Stanford University Press.

Mosès, Stéphane. 1994. *Der Engel der Geschichte: Franz Rosenzweig, Walter Benjamin, Gershom Scholem*. Frankfurt: Jüdischer Verlag.

———. 2000a. “Das Recht zu Urteilen: Hannah Arendt, Gershom Scholem und der Eichmann–Prozess.” In *Hannah Arendt Revisited: “Eichmann in Jerusalem” und die Folgen*, edited by Gary Smith, 78–92. Frankfurt: Suhrkamp.

———. 2000b. “Gershom Scholems Autobiographie.” In *Gershom Scholem: Literatur und Rhetorik*, edited by Stéphane Mosès and Sigrid Weigel, 3–15. Cologne: Bühlau.

Mosse, George L. 1985. *German Jews beyond Judaism*. Bloomington: Indiana University Press.

———. 1990. “Gerschom [*sic*] Scholem as a German Jew.” *Modern Judaism* 10 (2): 117–33.

Mühsam, Erich. 1979. “Ascona (1905).” In Erich Mühsam, *Ascona, vereinigte Texte aus den Jahren 1905, 1930 und 1931*, 7–83, Zurich: Sanssouci Verlag.

Müller, Hannelore. 2004. *Der Frühe Mircea Eliade: Sein rumänischer Hintergrund und die Anfänge seiner universalistischen Religionsphilosophie*. Münster, Germany: LIT.

Müller-Doohm, Stefan. 2003. *Adorno: Eine Biographie*. Frankfurt: Suhrkamp.

———. 2014. *Jürgen Habermas: Eine Biographie*. Berlin: Suhrkamp.

Myers, David. 1986. “The Scholem-Kurzweil Debate and Modern Jewish Historiography.” *Modern Judaism* 6 (3): 261–86.

———. 1995. *Re-Inventing the Jewish Past: European Jewish Intellectuals and the Zionist Return to History*. New York: Oxford University Press.

Nordau, Max. 1909. *Zionistische Schriften*. Cologne: Jüdischer Verlag.

Ofer, Dalia. 1996. “Fifty Years After: The Yishuv, Zionism, and the Holocaust, 1933–1948.” In *Major Changes within the Jewish People in the Wake of the Holocaust*, edited by Israel Gutman, 463–95. Jerusalem: Yad Vashem.

———. 2007. “She’erit hapletah bahistoriografia hayisraelit.” *Iunim bitkumat yisrael* 17:465–511.

Oz, Amos. 1998. *Kol hatikvot: Machshavot al zehut israelit*. Tel Aviv: Keter.

Ozick, Cynthia. 1983. “The Fourth Sparrow: The Magisterial Reach of Gershom Scholem.” In Cynthia Ozick, *Art and Ardor*, 138–50. New York: Knopf.

Peiss, Reuben. 1946. "European Wartime Acquisitions and the Library of Congress Mission." *Library Journal* 12 (15.6): 863–76 and 911.

Pomrenze, Seymour J. 1997. "Offenbach Reminiscences and the Restitutions to the Netherlands." In *The Return of Looted Collections (1946–1996): An Unfinished Chapter: Proceedings of an International Symposium to Mark the 50th Anniversary of the Return of Dutch Book Collections from Germany in 1946. Amsterdam, 15 and 16 April 1996*, 11–18. Amsterdam: Stichting beheer IISG.

———. 2002. "The Restitution of Jewish Cultural Treasures after the Holocaust: The Offenbach Archival Depot's Role in the Fulfillment of U.S. International and Moral Obligations (A First Hand Account)." In *Proceedings of the 37th Annual Convention of the Association of Jewish Libraries (Denver, CO—June 23–26, 2002)*. Accessed August 29, 2016. http://databases.jewishlibraries.org/sites/default/files/proceedings/proceedings2002/pomrenze.pdf.

Poppel, Stephen M. 1973. "Salman Schocken and the Schocken Verlag: A Jewish Publisher in Weimar and Nazi Germany." *Harvard Library Bulletin* 21, 1: 20–49.

Porat, Dina. 1984. "Al Domi: Palestinian Intellectuals and the Holocaust, 1943–1945." *Studies in Zionism* 5, 1: 97–124.

———. 1986. "Martin Buber in Eretz–Israel during the Holocaust Years, 1942–1944." *Yad Vashem Studies* 17:93–143.

———. 1990. *The Blue and the Yellow Stars of David: The Zionist Leadership in Palestine and the Holocaust, 1939–1945*. Cambridge, MA: Harvard University Press.

Portmann, Adolf. 1955. "Eranos." DU 4 (April): 8–10.

———. 1962. "Vom Sinn und Auftrag der Eranos–Tagungen." In *Der Mensch im Spannungsfeld der Ordnungen*, edited by Olga Fröbe-Kapteyn, 7–28. Zurich: Rhein Verlag.

Poste, Leslie Irlyn. 1958. "The Development of U.S. Protection of Libraries and Archives in Europe During World War II." PhD diss., University of Chicago.

Potok, Chaim. 1981. *The Book of Lights*. New York: Knopf.

Puttnies, Hans Georg. 1975. "Das dritte Gesicht Walter Benjamins: Gershom Scholem schrieb die erste Biographie des Philosophen und Literaten." *Frankfurter Allgemeine Zeitung*, October 7.

———. 1976. "Ein Gespräch über Bäume: Scholems Portrait im Fernsehen." *Frankfurter Allgemeine Zeitung*, June 22.

Ratzabi, Shalom. 2002. *Between Zionism and Judaism: The Radical Circle in Brith Shalom, 1925–1933*. Leiden, the Netherlands: Brill.

———. 2009. "Ha'ideah hapolitit shel hayahadut: 'Ishei merkaz eropah be'Brit Shalom' vezikotehem leAhad Ha'am uleBuber." In *"Brit Shalom" vehatzionut hadu le'umit: hashe'elah ha'aravit keshe'elah yehudit*, edited by Adi Gordon, 251–85. Jerusalem: Carmel.

Raz-Krakotzkin, Amnon. 1999. "Orientalism, mada'ei hayahadut vehachevrah hayisraelit: mispar he'arot." *Jama'a* 3:34–61.

———. 2002. "Bein 'Brit Shalom' levein beit hamikdash: Hadialektika shel ge'ulah umeshichiut lefi Gershom Shalom." *Teoriyah Uvikoret* 20:87–112.

Rebiger, Bill. 2005 "'Das Wesentliche spielt sich nicht auf der Leipziger Strasse ab, sondern . . . im Geheimen': Gershom Scholem und Berlin." *EAJS Newsletter* 16:81–99.

Reibnitz, Barbara von. 2000. "Der Eranos–Kreis: Religionswissenschaft und Weltanschauung oder der Gelehrte als Laien–Proester." In *Kreise—Gruppen—Bünde: Zur Soziologie moderner Intellektuellenassoziation*, edited by Richard Faber and Christine Holste, 425–40. Würzburg, Germany: Königshausen und Neumann.

Reichman, Shalom. 2008. "Hithavut mapat hayishuv biymei hamandat." In *Toldot hayishuv hayehudi be'eretz yisrael me'az ha'aliyah harishonah: Tkufat hamandat habriti*, edited by Moshe Lissak, 3:173–299. Jerusalem: Mosad Bialik.

Rennie, Bryan S. 1996. *Reconstructing Eliade: Making Sense of Religion*. Albany: State University of New York Press.

Ries, Elisabeth. 2004. "Monte Verità, Ascona: Oberfläche und Unterströmungen am Berg der Wahrheit." In *Pioniere, Poeten, Professoren: Eranos und der Monte Verità in der Zivilisationsgeschichte des 20. Jahrhunderts*, edited by Elisabetta Barone, Matthias Riedl, and Alexandra Tischel, 21–32. Würzburg, Germany: Königshausen und Neumann.

Rosenkranz, Jutta. 2007. *Mascha Kaléko: Biographie*. Munich: DTV.

Rotenstreich, Nathan. 1994. "Gershom Scholem's Conception of Jewish Nationalism." In *Gershom Scholem: The Man and His Work*, edited by Paul Mendes-Flohr, 104–19. Albany: State University of New York Press.

Roth, Cecil. 1944. "The Restitution of Jewish Libraries, Archives and Museums." *Contemporary Jewish Record* 7, no 3: 253–57.

Rubin, Adam. 2004. "Jewish Nationalism and the Encyclopaedic Imagination: The Failure (and Success) of Ahad Haam's *Otsar Hyahadut*." *Journal of Modern Jewish Studies* 3 (3): 247–67.

Rupnow, Dirk. 2002. "'Ihr müsst sein, auch wenn ihr nicht mehr seid': The Jewish Central Museum in Prague and Historical Memory in the Third Reich." *Holocaust and Genocide Studies* 16 (1): 23–53.

Schabert, Tilo. 2004. "Introduction: The Eranos Experience." In *Pioniere, Poeten, Professoren: Eranos und der Monte Verità in der Zivilisationsgeschichte des 20. Jahrhunderts*, edited by Elisabetta Barone, Matthias Riedl, and Alexandra Tischel, 9–20. Würzburg, Germany: Königshausen und Neumann.

———. 2009. "In the Fading of Divine Voices: The Song of Eranos." In *Gott oder Götter? God or Gods?*, edited by Tilo Schabert and Matthias Riedl, 181–88. Würzburg, Germany: Königshausen undNeumann.

———. 2011. "From Olga Froebe-Kapteyn to the Amici di Eranos: On the History of the Eranos–Tagungen at Ascona." In *Die Stadt—Zentrum und Achse der Welt: The City—Centre and Axis of the World*, edited by Matthias Riedl and Tilo Schabert, 133–42. Würzburg, Germany: Königshausen und Neumann.

Schäfer, Barbara. 2003. *Berliner Zionistenkreise: Eine vereinsgeschichtliche Studie*. Berlin: Metropol.

Schäfer, Peter. 1998. "'Die Philologie der Kabbalah ist nur eine Projektion auf eine Fläche': Gershom Scholem über die Wahren Absichten seines Kabbalastudiums." *Jewish Studies Quarterly* 5 (1): 1–25.

———. 2007. "Gershom shalom vehanatzrut." In *Sefer zikaron leGershom Shalom bimlot 'esrim vechamesh leftirato*, edited by Joseph Dan, 2:561–84. Jerusalem: Mandel Institute.

Scharnagl, Karl. 1946. "Introductory." In *Munich: A Guide*, edited by Hans Ludwig Held, 5–6. Munich: Pflaum.

Schidorsky, Dov. 1998. "Confiscation of Libraries and Assignments to Forced Labor: Two Documents of the Holocaust." *Libraries and Culture* 33 (4): 347–88.

———. 2006. "The Salvaging of Jewish Books in Europe after the Holocaust: The Efforts of the Hebrew University and of the Jewish National and University Library—Success and Failure." In *Jüdischer Buchbesitz als Raubgut: Zweites hannoverisches Symposium*, edited by Regine Dehnel, 197–212. Frankfurt: Klostermann.

———. 2008. *Gvilim nisrafim ve'otiot porchot: Toldoteihem shel osfei sfarim vesifriot be'eretz yisrael unisionot lehatzalat srideihem le'achar hasho'ah*. Jerusalem: Magnes.

Schneider, Lambert. [1965]. *Rechenschaft über vierzig Jahre Verlagsarbeit 1925–1965: Ein Almanach*. Heidelberg, Germany: Lambert Schneider.

Schocken, Gershom. 1989. "Darko shel Salman Schocke el hayahadut uvetochah." *Haaretz*, October 20.

Scholem, Fania. 1983. "Fania Shalom mesaperet al Gershom Shalom: Bimlot shanah leftirato," By Naomi Frankel, *Yediot Acharonot*, literary supplement, February 11.

———. 1988. "Beshulei ha'hakdamah' ha'avudah shenitgaltah." In Gershom Scholem, *Shabtai Tzvi vehatnu'ah hashabta'it beiyemei chaiyav*, 27–29. 2nd ed. Tel Aviv: Am Oved.

———. 1990. "Ani katavti, hu chatam." *Kol Ha'ir*, January 19.

Schöttker, Detlev. 1999. *Konstruktiver Fragmentarismus: Form und Rezeption der Schriften Walter Benjamins*. Frankfurt: Suhrkamp.

Schweid, Eliezer. 1985. *Judaism and Mysticism According to Gershom Scholem*. Atlanta, GA: Scholars.

Sebastian, Mihail. 2003. *Journal 1935–1944: The Fascist Years*. Translated by Patrick Camiller. London: Pimlico.

Segev, Tom. 2000. *The Seventh Million: The Israelis and the Holocaust*. New York: Henry Holt.

Sela, Avraham. 1994. "The 'Wailing Wall Riots' (1929) as a Watershed in the Palestine Conflict." *Muslim World* 84, nos. 1–2: 60–94.

Shaba, Shlomo. 1990. *Hozeh Brach: Sipur chaiyav shel Haim Nachman Bialik*. Tel Aviv: Dvir.

Shapira, Anita. 1992. *Land and Power: The Zionist Resort to Force 1881–1948*. Oxford: Oxford University Press.

Shapira, Avraham. 1998. "Hakiyumi vehahistori be'aspeklaria biografit shel Gershom Shalom." In Gershom Scholem, *Retzifut umered: Gershom Shalom be'omer uvesiah*, edited by Avraham Shapira, 7–24. Tel Aviv: Am Oved.

———. 2005. "Im moreshet torat chaiyav umif'alei chaiyav shel Meir Ayali." In *Hayashan yitchadesh vehachadash yitkadesh: Al zehut, tarbut veyahadut—Asufah lezikhro shel Meir Ayali*, edited by Yehuda Friedlander, Uzi Shavit, and Avi Sagi, 18–24. Tel Aviv: Hakibbutz Hame'uchad.

Shavit, David. 1997. *Hunger for the Printed Word: Books and Libraries in the Jewish Ghettos of Nazi-Occupied Europe*. Jefferson, NC: McFarland and Company.

Shavit, Yaacov. 1988. *Jabotinsky and the Revisionist Movement, 1925–1948*. London: Routledge.

———. 1991. "Realism and Messianism in Zionism and the Yishuv." In *Jews and*

Messianism in the Modern Era: Metaphor and Meaning, edited by Jonathan Frankel, 100–27. New York: Oxford University Press.

Shavit, Zohar. 1993. "On the Hebrew Cultural Center in Berlin in the Twenties: Hebrew Culture in Europe—the Last Attempt." *Gutenberg-Jahrbuch* 68:371–80.

———. 1999. "Hashlavim ha'ikariyim behitpatchuto shel hamerkaz be'eretz Israel vehafikhato lemerkaz hegemoni." *Bniyatah shel tarbut ivrit be'eretz Israel*, edited by Moshe Lissak and Zohar Shavit, 1:87–92. Jerusalem: Mosad Bialik.

Shedletzky, Itta. 2007. "Auf der Suche nach dem verlorenen Judentum: Zur 'historischen Gestalt.'" *Münchner Beiträge zur jüdischen Geschichte und Kultur* 1 (2): 30–47.

Shimoni, Gideon. 1995 *The Zionist Ideology*. Waltham, NH: Brandeis University Press.

Steiner, George. 1973. "Inner Lights." *New Yorker*, October 22, 152–74.

Steinschneider, Moritz. 1895. *Die hebraeischen Handschriften der K. Hof- und Staatbibliothek in Muenchen*. Munich: Palm'schen Hofbuchhandlung.

Sternberger, Dolf, Gerhard Storz, and Wilhelm E. Süskind. 1970. *Aus dem Wörterbuch des Unmenschen*. Munich: DTV.

Strauss, Hedi, and Johanna Voss. 2004. *Mein immergrünes Dorf: Vom Schicksal der Juden aus Stammheim in der Wetterau*. Frankfurt: Vario.

Subtelny, Maria E. 2003. "History and Religion: The Fallacy of Metaphysical Questions (a Review Article)." *Iranian Studies* 36 (1): 91–101.

Suchoff, David. 1997. "Gershom Scholem, Hannah Arendt, and the Scandal of Jewish Particularity." *Germanic Review* 72 (1): 57–76.

Susman, Margarete. 1946. *Das Buch Hiob und das Schicksal des jüdischen Volkes*. Zurich: Steinberg.

———. 1964. *Ich habe viele Leben gelebt: Erinnerungen*. Stuttgart, Germany: Deutsche Verlags-Anstallt.

Talmon, Jacob L. 1970. *Israel among the Nations*. London: Macmillan.

Tiedemann, Rolf. 1983. "Erinnerung an Scholem." In Gershom Scholem, *Walter Benjamin und sein Engel: Vierzehn Aufsätze und kleine Beiträge*, edited by Rolf Tiedemann, 211–21. Frankfurt: Suhrkamp.

———. 1998. "Erinnerung an Scholem." In *Frankfurter Adorno Blätter*, edited by Rolf Tiedemann, 5:196–206. Munich: Edition Text + Kritik.

Unseld, Siegfried. 1991. "Vorwort." In *Peter Suhrkamp: Zur Biographie eines Verlegers in Daten, Dokumenten und Bildern*, edited by Siegfried Unseld, 7–24. Frankfurt: Suhrkamp.

———. 2004. *Briefe an die Autoren*, edited by Rainer Weiss Frankfurt: Suhrkamp.

———. 2010. *Chronik 1970: Mit den Chroniken Buchmesse 1967, Buchmesse 1968 und der Chronik eines Konfliktes 1968*. Berlin: Suhrkamp

Versluis, Arthur. 2001. "*Religion after Religion: Gershom Scholem, Mircea Eliade and Henry Corbin at Eranos*, Steven Wasserstrom [Book Review]." *Esoterica* 3:289–92.

Waite, Robert G. 2002. "Returning Jewish Cultural Property: The Handling of Books Looted by the Nazis in the American Zone of Occupation, 1945 to 1952." *Libraries and Culture* 37 (3): 213–28.

Waldmüller, Monika. 1988. *Die Wandlung: Eine Monatsschrift Herausgegeben von Dolf*

Sternberger mit Mitwirkung von Karl Jaspers, Werner Krauss und Alfred Weber, 1945–1949. Marbach, Germany: Deutsche Schillergesellschaft.

Wapnewski, Peter. 2007. *Mit dem anderen Auge: Erinnerungen, 1959–2000.* Berlin: Berlin Verlag.

Wasserstein, Bernard. 2009. "Blame the Victim: Hannah Arendt among the Nazis—The Historian and Her Sources." *Times Literary Supplement*, October 9, 13–15.

Wasserstrom, Steven M. 1999. *Religion after Religion: Gershom Scholem, Mircea Eliade and Henry Corbin at Eranos.* Princeton, NJ: Princeton University Press.

Weidner, Daniel. 2003. *Gershom Scholem: Politisches, esoterisches und historiographisches Schreiben.* Munich: Wilhelm Fink.

Weiner, Herbert. 1967. *9½ Mystics: The Kabbalah Today.* New York: Holt, Rinehart and Winston.

Weiss, Yfaat. 2015. "Von Prag nach Jerusalem: Jüdische Kulturgüter und israelische Staatsgründung." *Vierteljahrhefte für Zeitgeschichte* 63 (4): 513–38.

Weissberg, Liliane. 2012. *Über Haschisch und Kabbala: Gershom Scholem, Siegfried Unseld und das Werk von Walter Benjamin.* Marbach, Germany: Deutsche Schillergesellschaft.

Weitz, Yechiam. 1994. *Muda'ut vechoser onim: Mapai lenokhach hashoa.* Jerusalem: Yad Ben Zvi.

———. 1996. "Yishuv, Diaspora, and Holocaust: Myth and Reality." *Yivo Annual* 23:365–90.

Weizsäcker, Carl Friedrich von. 1985. *Wahrnehmung der Neuzeit.* Munich: Hanser.

Weltsch, Robert. 1946. "Hasifriyah hayehudit hagdolah ba'olam: bikur befrankfurt a.n main—metropolin amerika'i." *Haaretz*, January 4.

Wilson, Janelle L. 2005. *Nostalgia: Sanctuary of a Meaning.* Lewisburg, PA: Bucknell University Press.

Young-Bruehl, Elisabeth. 1982. *Hannah Arendt: For the Love of the World.* New Haven, CT: Yale University Press.

Zadoff, Mirjam. 2012. *Next Year in Marienbad: The Lost World of Jewish Spa Culture.* Translated by William Templer. Philadelphia: University of Pennsylvania Press.

———. 2018. *Werner Scholem: A German Life.* Philadelphia: University of Pennsylvania Press.

——— and Zadoff, Noam. 2014. "From Mission to Memory: Walter Benjamin and Werner Scholem in the Life and Work of Gershom Scholem." *Journal of Modern Jewish Studies* 13 (1): 58–74.

Zadoff, Noam. 2007. "Be'arugut Hanihilism: hapulmus bein Baruch Kurzweil leGershom Shalom al cheker hashabta'ut." *Kabbala* 16:299–360.

———. 2008. "'Portretim bilti dimioniyim': Chug pilegesh, chaverut vesatira ba'universitah ha'ivrit." *Cathedra* 126:67–82.

———. 2010. "*Gershom Scholem, The Star of David: History of a Symbol.* Expanded Version Including Supplements by the Author, Edited and Revised by Galit Hasan-Rokem, Footnotes Reconstructed by Shlomo Zucker, Museum of Art Ein–Charod 2008 (Hebrew)." In *Tel Aviver Jahrbuch für Deutsche Geschichte*, edited by José Brunner, 38:289–95. Göttingen, Germany: Wallstein.

———. 2012. “Al Joseph Weiss veGershom Shalom: Divrei hakdamah.” In Gershom Scholem and Joseph Weiss, *Chalifat Mikhtavim 1948–1964*, edited by Noam Zadoff, 10–32. Jerusalem: Carmel.

——— and Jonatan Meir. 2007. “‘Divrei shalom’ ‘o ‘haiyei Moharash’: chibur satiri meginzei Joseph Weiss.” In *Sefer zikaron leGershom Shalom bimlot ‘esrim vechamesh leftirato*, edited by Joseph Dan, 1:365–84. Jerusalem: Mandel Institute.

Zameret, Zvi. 2009. “Bein palestinotzentriuot leyudotzentriut: Ben Zion Dinaburg (Dinur) vesho’at yehudei eropa.” In *Shoah mimerchak tavo: Ishim bayishuv ha’eretz–yisraeli veyachasam lasho’ah, 1933–1948*, edited by Dina Porat, 263–96. Jerusalem: Yad Ben Zvi.

Zipperstein, Steven J. 1993. *Elusive Prophet: Ahad Haam and the Origins of Zionism*. Berkeley, CA: University of California Press.

INDEX OF NAMES